Seraph of the End

―VAMPIRE REIGN―

16

STORY BY **Takaya Kagami**

ART BY **Yamato Yamamoto**

STORYBOARDS BY **Daisuke Furuya**

CHARACTERS

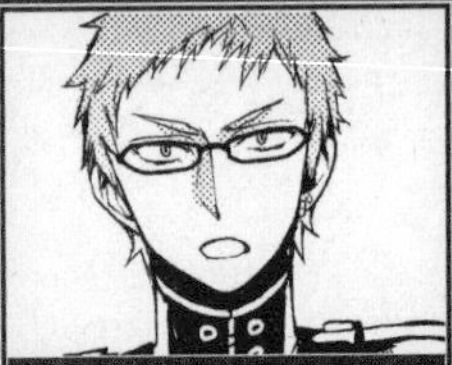

SHIHO KIMIZUKI

Yuichiro's friend. Smart but abrasive. His Cursed Gear is Kiseki-o, twin blades.

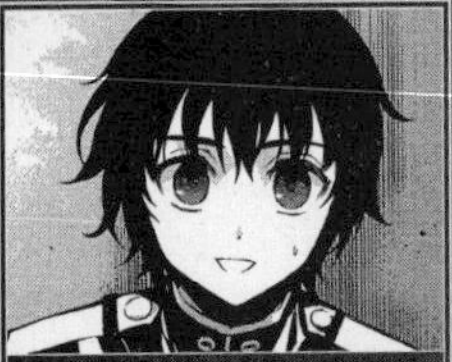

YOICHI SAOTOME

Yuichiro's friend. His sister was killed by a vampire. His Cursed Gear is Gekkouin, a bow.

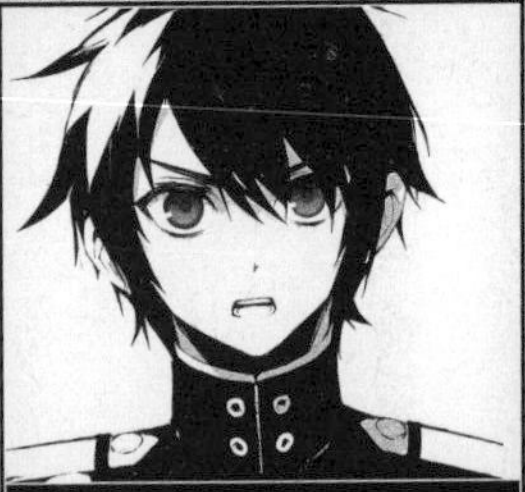

YUICHIRO HYAKUYA

A boy who escaped from the vampire capital, he has both great kindness and a great desire for revenge. Lone wolf. His Cursed Gear is Asuramaru, a katana.

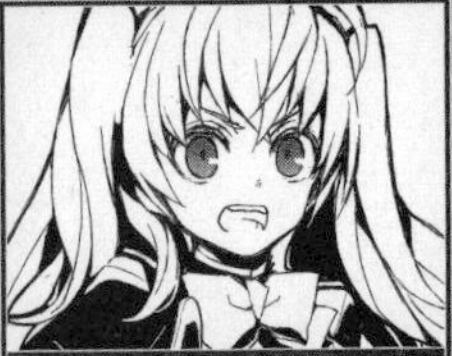

MITSUBA SANGU

An elite soldier who has been part of the Moon Demon Company since age 13. Bossy. Her Cursed Gear is Tenjiryu, a giant axe.

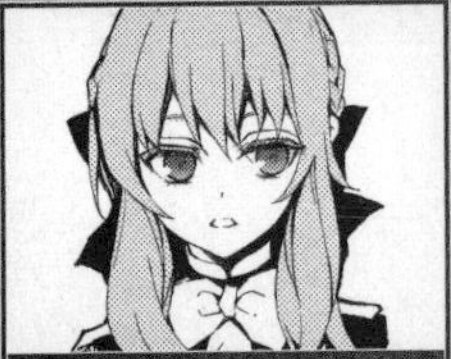

SHINOA HIRAGI

Guren's subordinate and Yuichiro's surveillance officer. Member of the illustrious Hiragi family. Her Cursed Gear is Shikama Doji, a scythe.

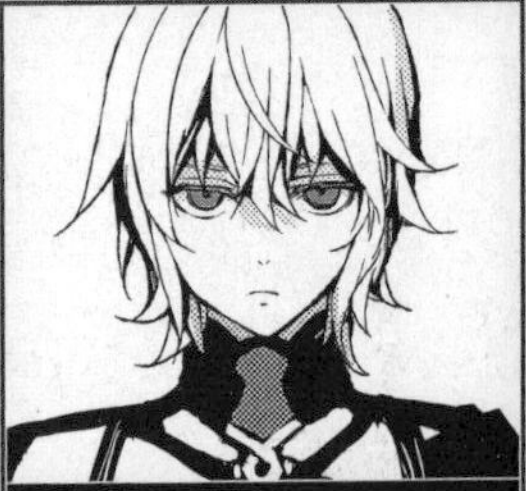

MIKAELA HYAKUYA

Yuichiro's best friend. He was supposedly killed but has come back to life as a vampire. Currently working with Shinoa Squad.

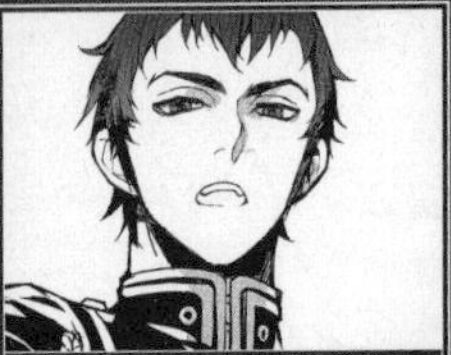

KURETO HIRAGI

A Lieutenant General in the Demon Army. Heir apparent to the Hiragi family, he is cold, cruel and ruthless.

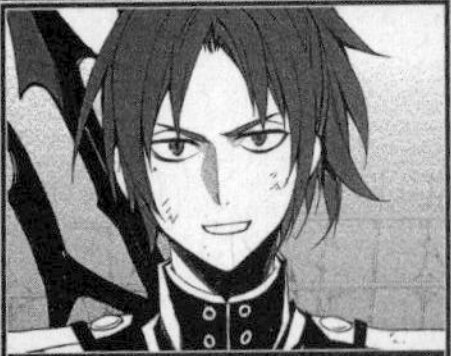

MAKOTO NARUMI

Former leader of Narumi Squad. After his entire squad died during the battle of Nagoya, he deserted the Demon Army with Shinoa Squad.

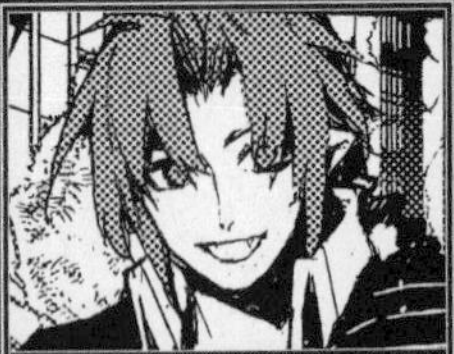

CROWLEY EUSFORD

A Thirteenth Progenitor vampire. Part of Ferid's faction.

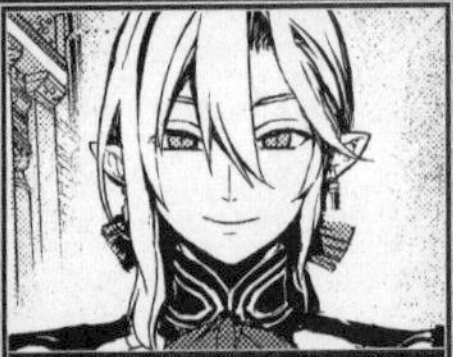

FERID BATHORY

A Seventh Progenitor vampire, he killed Mikaela.

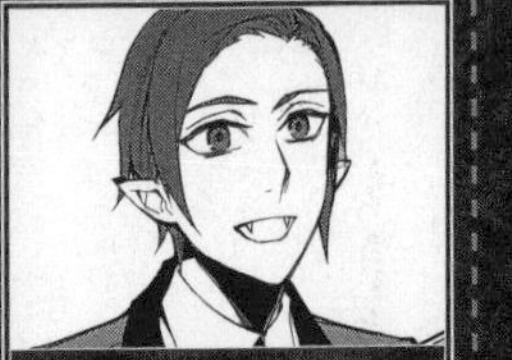

KY LUC

A Fifth Progenitor vampire under Second Progenitor Urd Geales. Currently guarding the two vampires undergoing exposure torture.

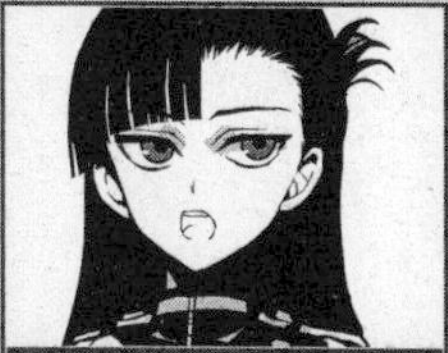

SHIGURE YUKIMI

A 2nd Lieutenant and Guren's subordinate along with Sayuri. Very calm and collected.

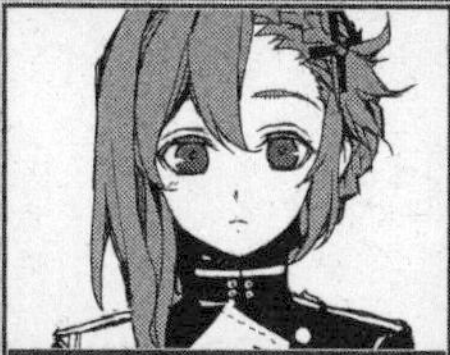

SAYURI HANAYORI

A 2nd Lieutenant and Guren's subordinate. She's devoted to Guren.

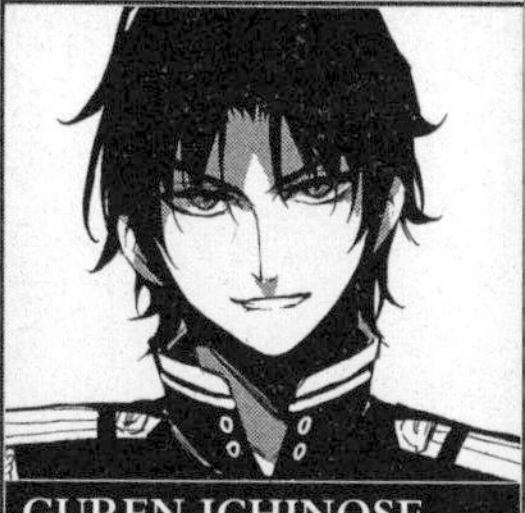

GUREN ICHINOSE

Lieutenant Colonel of the Moon Demon Company, a Vampire Extermination Unit. He recruited Yuichiro into the Japanese Imperial Demon Army. He's been acting strange ever since the battle in Nagoya... His Cursed Gear is Mahiru-no-yo, a katana.

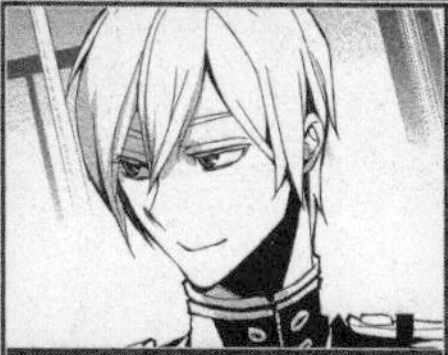

SHINYA HIRAGI

A Major General and an adopted member of the Hiragi Family. He was Mahiru Hiragi's fiancé.

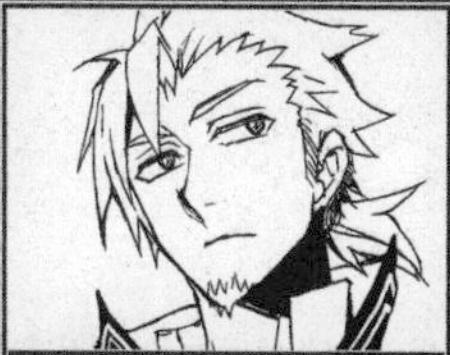

NORITO GOSHI

A Colonel and a member of the Goshi family. He has been friends with Guren since high school.

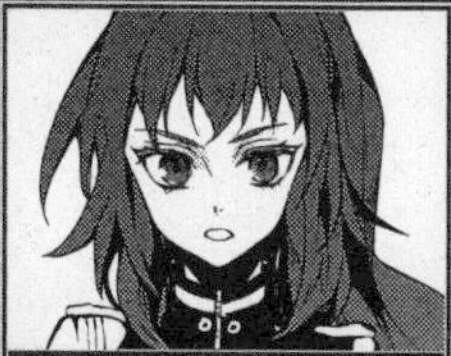

MITO JUJO

A Colonel and a member of the Jujo family. She has been friends with Guren since high school.

STORY

A mysterious virus decimates the human population, and vampires claim dominion over the world. Yuichiro and his adopted family of orphans are kept as vampire fodder in an underground city until the day Mikaela, Yuichiro's best friend, plots an ill-fated escape for the orphans. Only Yuichiro survives and reaches the surface.

Four years later, Yuichiro enters into the Moon Demon Company, a Vampire Extermination Unit in the Japanese Imperial Demon Army, to enact his revenge. There he gains Asuramaru, a demon-possessed weapon capable of killing vampires. Along with his squad mates Yoichi, Shinoa, Kimizuki and Mitsuba, Yuichiro deploys to Shinjuku with orders to thwart a vampire attack.

In a battle against the vampires, Yuichiro discovers that not only is his friend Mikaela alive, but he also has been turned into a vampire. After misunderstandings and near-misses, Yuichiro and Mikaela finally meet each other in Nagoya.

Kureto Hiragi begins an experiment on the Seraph of the End at Nagoya Airport. Caught up in the cruel procedure, the Moon Demon Company suffers extreme losses. Even worse, Guren appears to betray his friends, participating in the experiment and gravely wounding Yuichiro. To further complicate things, vampires appear to stop the experiment and Ferid stages a coup, capturing the Vampire Queen and throwing everything into chaos.

Declaring enough is enough, Shinoa Squad deserts the Demon Army and escapes Nagoya to hide away in a small seaside town. Ferid tracks them down and tells them that Guren was the one who caused the Catastrophe eight years ago, and that all the answers are in Osaka. The group arrives just in time to meet up with Second Progenitor Urd Geales and a horde of vampire nobles. They're all captured, and Ferid and Krul are sentenced to torture by exposure by Urd Geales.

Meanwhile, Kureto carries out a successful coup d'état in Shibuya, taking control of the Demon Army from his father, Tenri. However, the godlike being, Shikama Doji, which had been possessing Tenri, now possesses him. Back in Osaka, Yuichiro and friends finish their training and begin their battle with Ky Luc to rescue Ferid and Krul...

Seraph of the End
—VAMPIRE REIGN—

16

CONTENTS

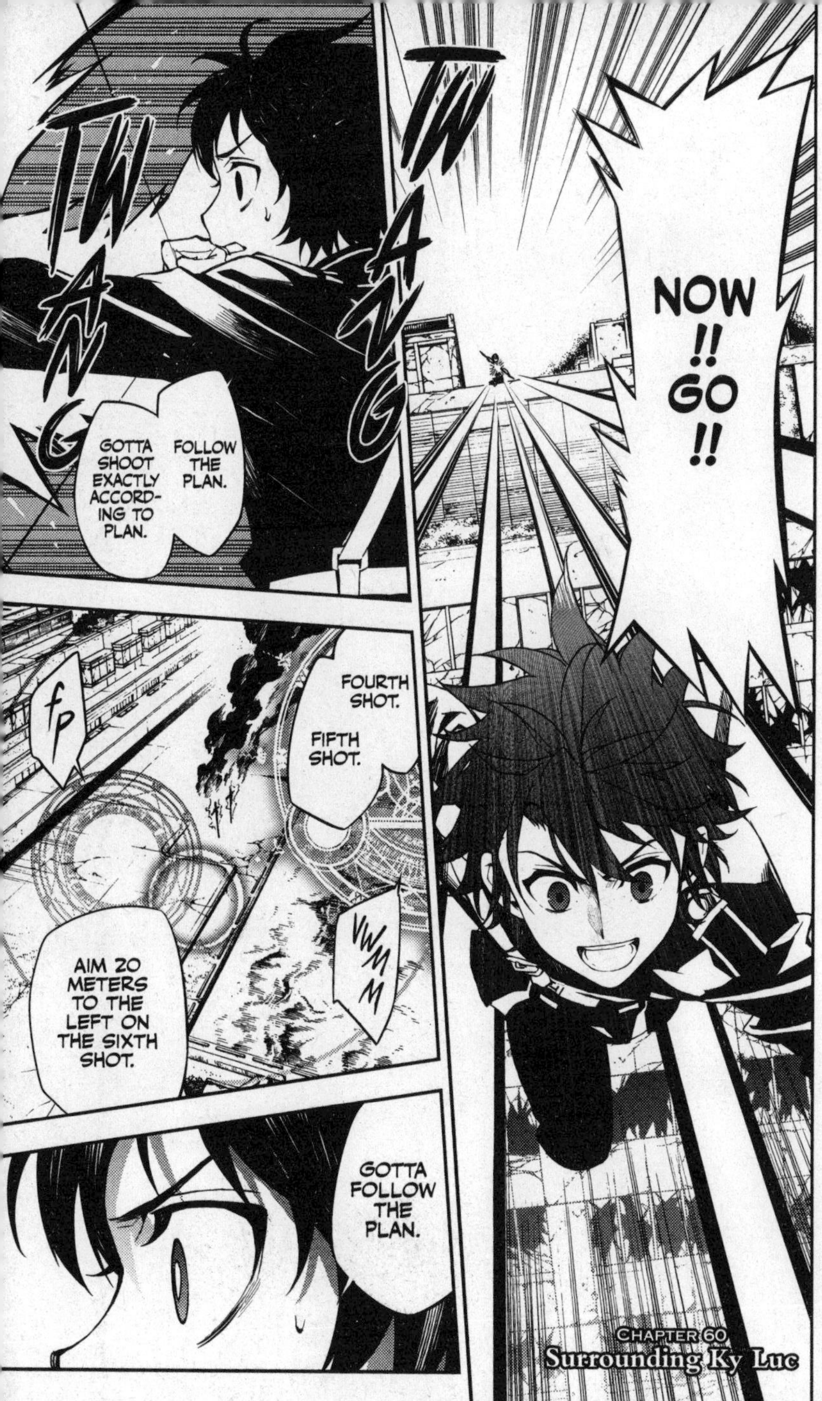
NOW!! GO!!
CHAPTER 60
Surrounding Ky Luc
TWANG
FOLLOW THE PLAN.
GOTTA SHOOT EXACTLY ACCORDING TO PLAN.
TWANG
FOURTH SHOT.
FIFTH SHOT.
fp
VWMM
AIM 20 METERS TO THE LEFT ON THE SIXTH SHOT.
GOTTA FOLLOW THE PLAN.

CHAPTER 60
Surrounding Ky Luc

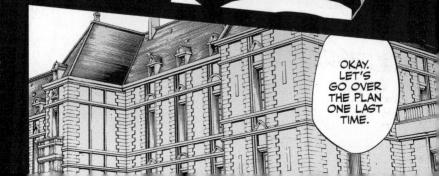

OKAY.
LET'S
GO OVER
THE PLAN
ONE LAST
TIME.

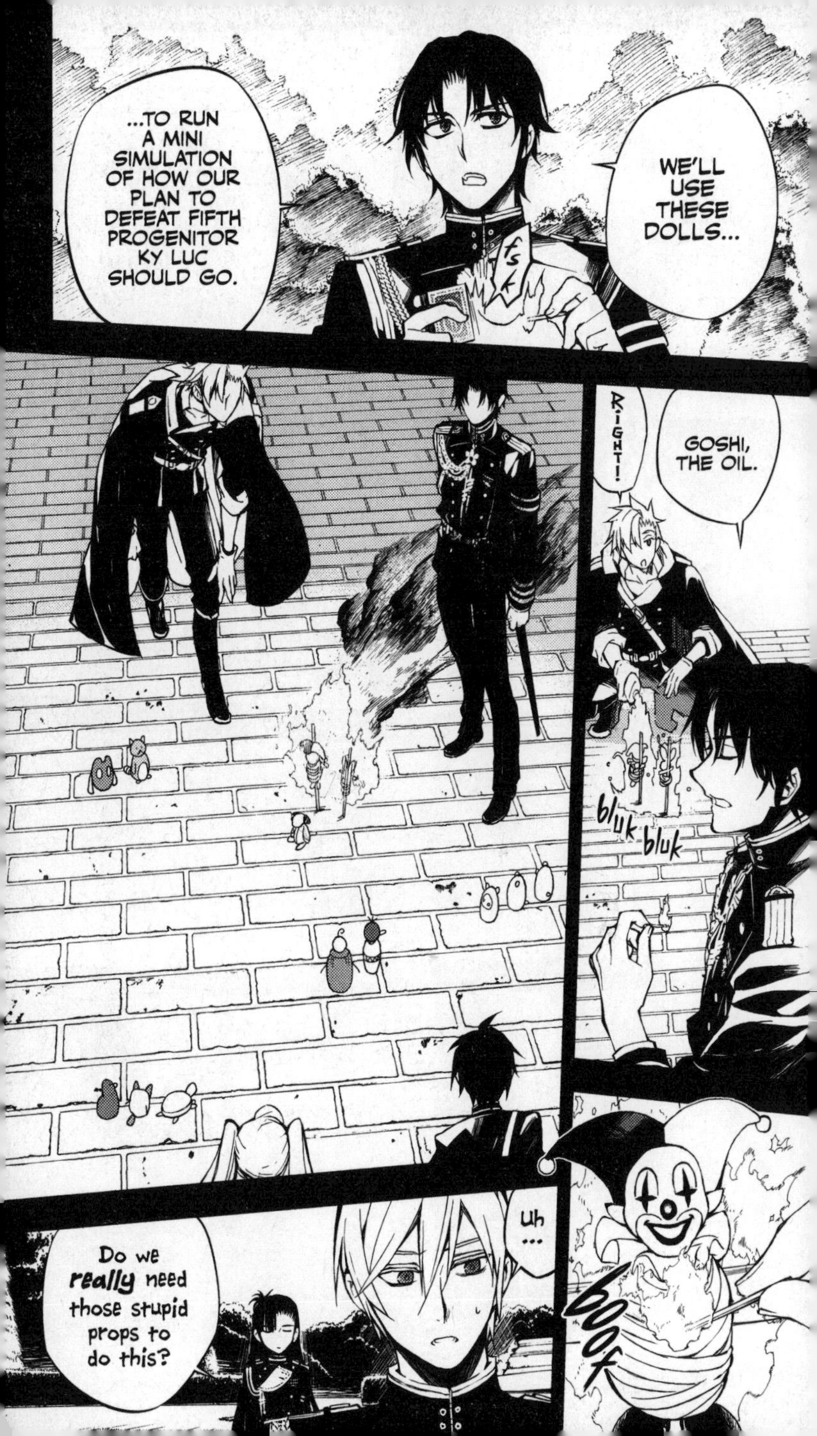
WE'LL USE THESE DOLLS...
...TO RUN A MINI SIMULATION OF HOW OUR PLAN TO DEFEAT FIFTH PROGENITOR KY LUC SHOULD GO.
tsk
GOSHI, THE OIL.
RIGHT!
bluk bluk
boof
Uh...
Do we **really** need those stupid props to do this?

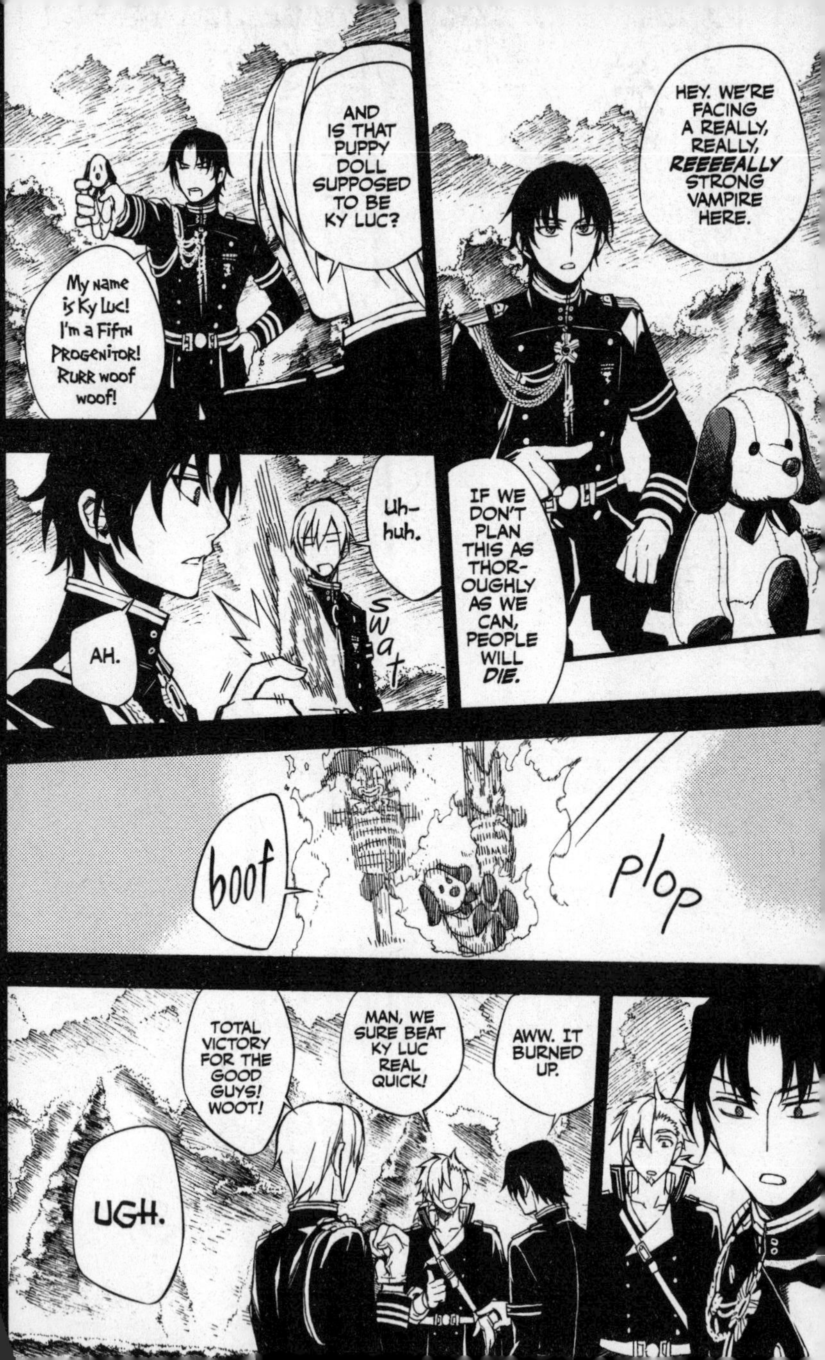
HEY. WE'RE FACING A REALLY, REALLY, REEEEALLY STRONG VAMPIRE HERE.
AND IS THAT PUPPY DOLL SUPPOSED TO BE KY LUC?
My name is Ky Luc! I'm a Fifth Progenitor! Rurr woof woof!
IF WE DON'T PLAN THIS AS THOROUGHLY AS WE CAN, PEOPLE WILL DIE.
Uh-huh.
SWAT
AH.
plop
boof
AWW. IT BURNED UP.
MAN, WE SURE BEAT KY LUC REAL QUICK!
TOTAL VICTORY FOR THE GOOD GUYS! WOOT!
UGH.

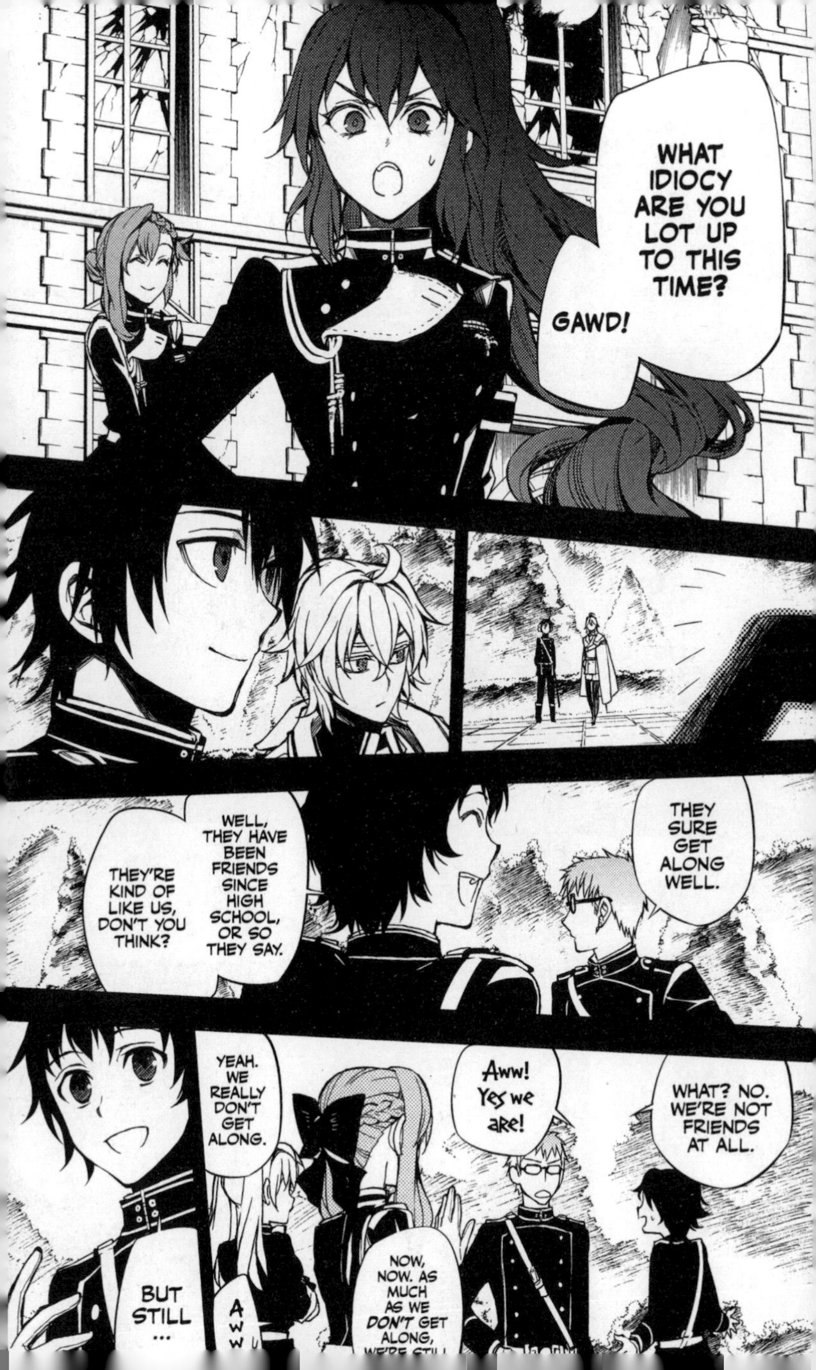
WHAT IDIOCY ARE YOU LOT UP TO THIS TIME?
GAWD!
THEY SURE GET ALONG WELL.
WELL, THEY HAVE BEEN FRIENDS SINCE HIGH SCHOOL, OR SO THEY SAY.
THEY'RE KIND OF LIKE US, DON'T YOU THINK?
WHAT? NO. WE'RE NOT FRIENDS AT ALL.
Aww! Yes we are!
YEAH. WE REALLY DON'T GET ALONG.
NOW, NOW. AS MUCH AS WE *DON'T* GET ALONG,
AWW
BUT STILL ...

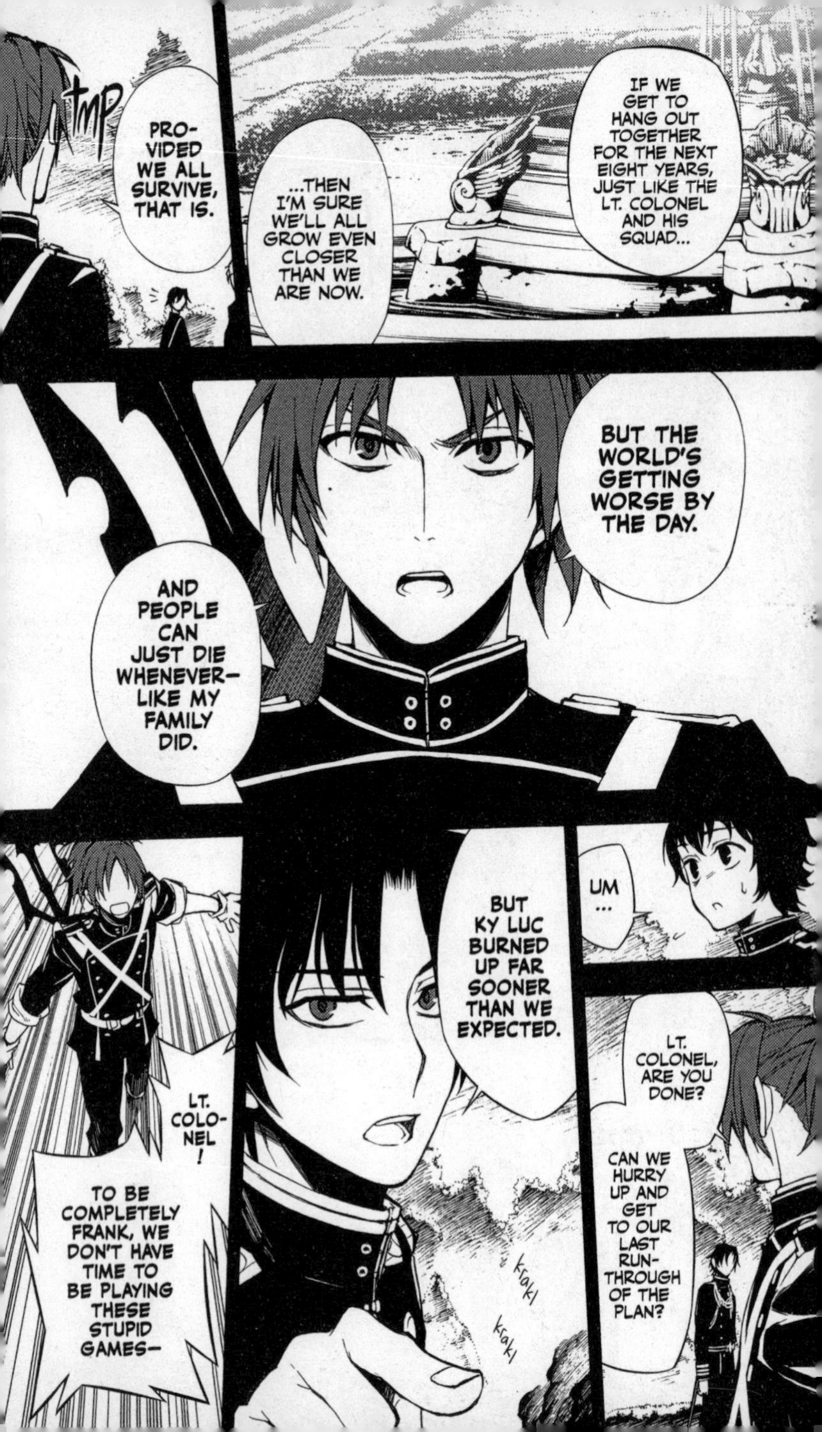

IF WE GET TO HANG OUT TOGETHER FOR THE NEXT EIGHT YEARS, JUST LIKE THE LT. COLONEL AND HIS SQUAD...
...THEN I'M SURE WE'LL ALL GROW EVEN CLOSER THAN WE ARE NOW.
TMP
PRO-VIDED WE ALL SURVIVE, THAT IS.
BUT THE WORLD'S GETTING WORSE BY THE DAY.
AND PEOPLE CAN JUST DIE WHENEVER—LIKE MY FAMILY DID.
UM ...
LT. COLONEL, ARE YOU DONE?
CAN WE HURRY UP AND GET TO OUR LAST RUN-THROUGH OF THE PLAN?
BUT KY LUC BURNED UP FAR SOONER THAN WE EXPECTED.
kraki
kraki
LT. COLO-NEL!
TO BE COMPLETELY FRANK, WE DON'T HAVE TIME TO BE PLAYING THESE STUPID GAMES—

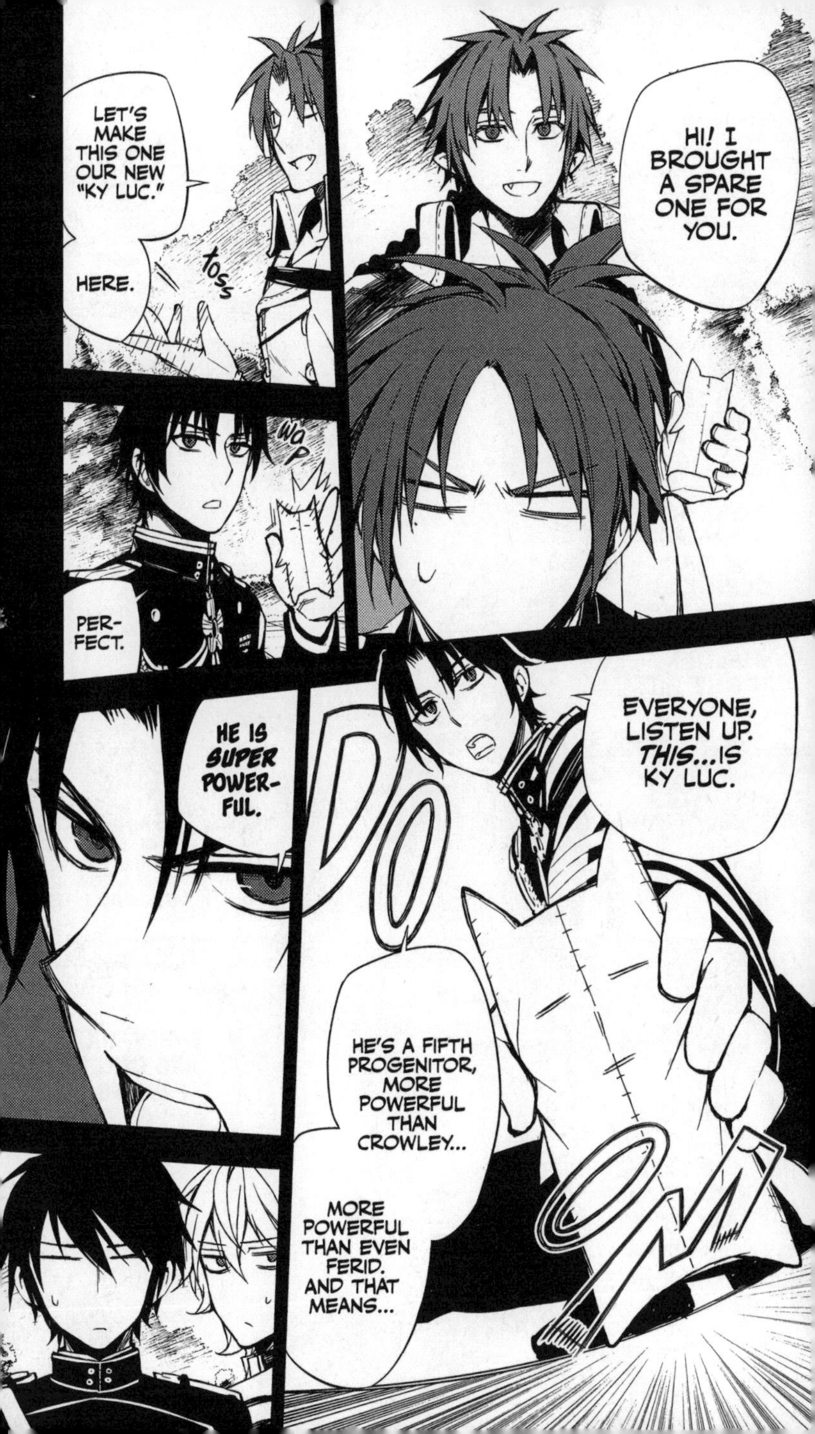
HI! I BROUGHT A SPARE ONE FOR YOU.
LET'S MAKE THIS ONE OUR NEW "KY LUC."
HERE.
TOSS
WAP
PER-FECT.
EVERYONE, LISTEN UP. *THIS*...IS KY LUC.
DOON
HE'S A FIFTH PROGENITOR, MORE POWERFUL THAN CROWLEY...
MORE POWERFUL THAN EVEN FERID. AND THAT MEANS...
HE IS **SUPER** POWER-FUL.

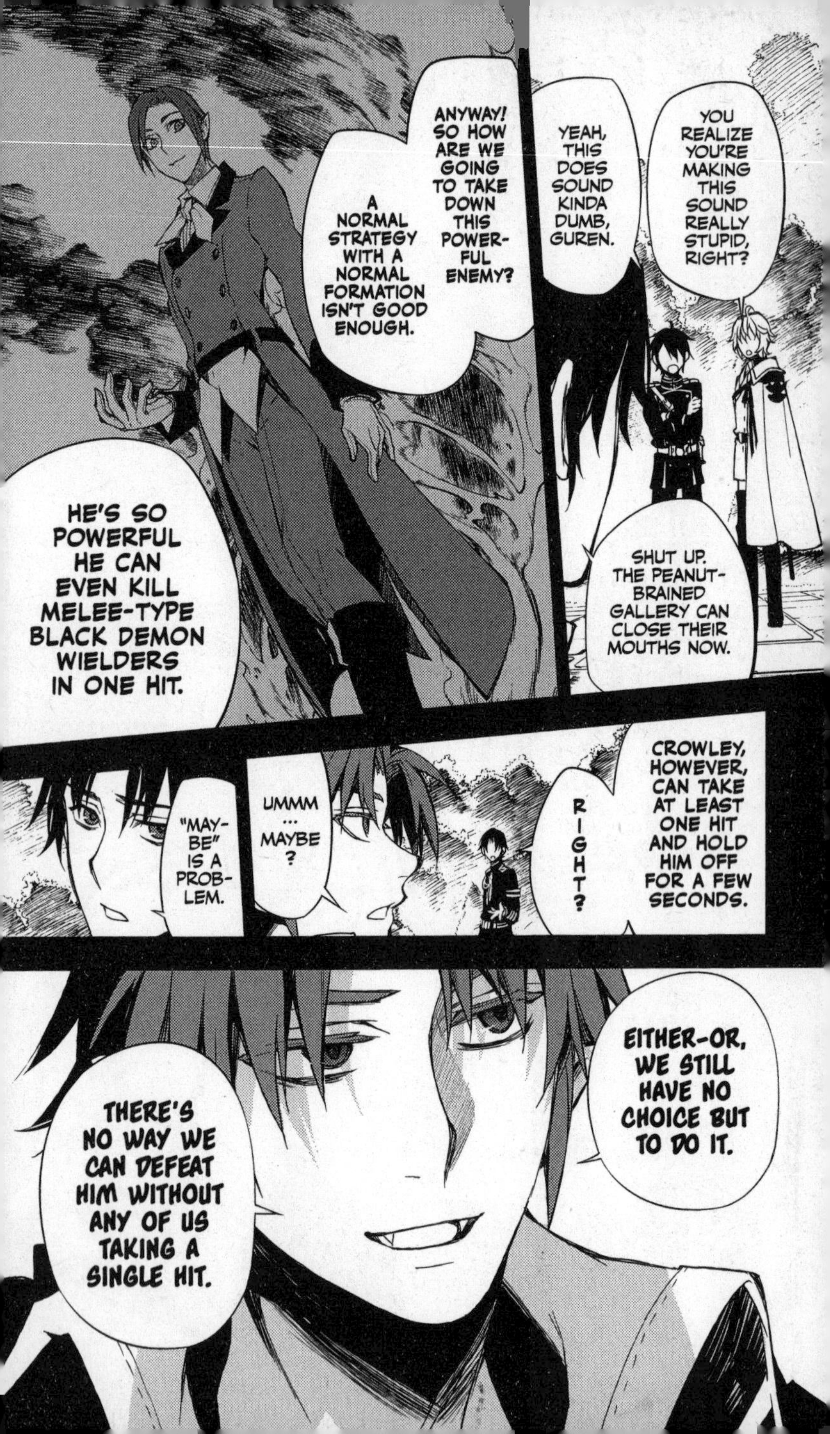
YOU REALIZE YOU'RE MAKING THIS SOUND REALLY STUPID, RIGHT?
YEAH, THIS DOES SOUND KINDA DUMB, GUREN.
SHUT UP. THE PEANUT-BRAINED GALLERY CAN CLOSE THEIR MOUTHS NOW.
ANYWAY! SO HOW ARE WE GOING TO TAKE DOWN THIS POWERFUL ENEMY?
A NORMAL STRATEGY WITH A NORMAL FORMATION ISN'T GOOD ENOUGH.
HE'S SO POWERFUL HE CAN EVEN KILL MELEE-TYPE BLACK DEMON WIELDERS IN ONE HIT.
CROWLEY, HOWEVER, CAN TAKE AT LEAST ONE HIT AND HOLD HIM OFF FOR A FEW SECONDS.
RIGHT?
UMMM ... MAYBE?
"MAYBE" IS A PROBLEM.
EITHER-OR, WE STILL HAVE NO CHOICE BUT TO DO IT.
THERE'S NO WAY WE CAN DEFEAT HIM WITHOUT ANY OF US TAKING A SINGLE HIT.

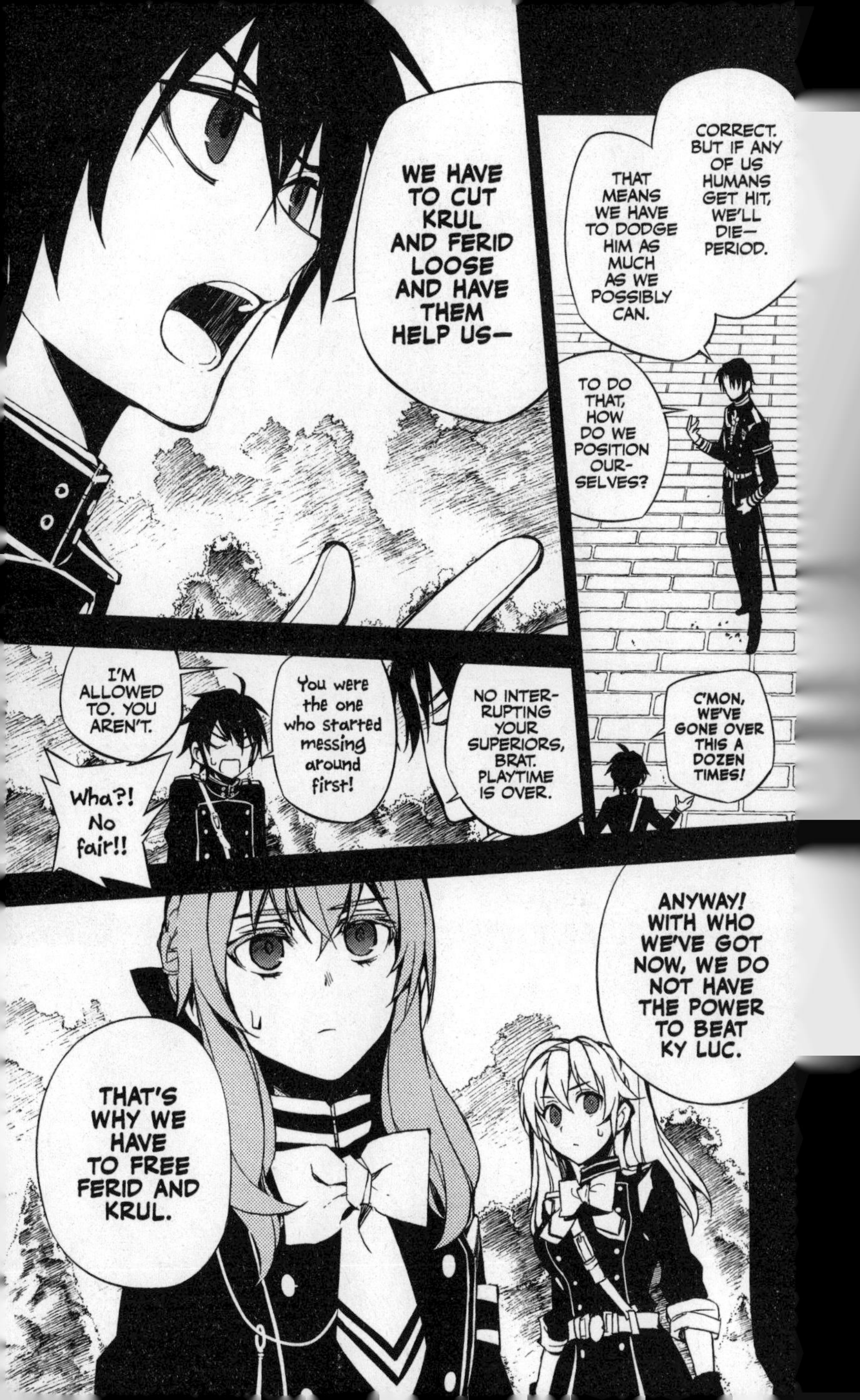

CORRECT. BUT IF ANY OF US HUMANS GET HIT, WE'LL DIE—PERIOD.
THAT MEANS WE HAVE TO DODGE HIM AS MUCH AS WE POSSIBLY CAN.
TO DO THAT, HOW DO WE POSITION OUR-SELVES?
WE HAVE TO CUT KRUL AND FERID LOOSE AND HAVE THEM HELP US—
C'MON, WE'VE GONE OVER THIS A DOZEN TIMES!
NO INTER-RUPTING YOUR SUPERIORS, BRAT. PLAYTIME IS OVER.
You were the one who started messing around first!
I'M ALLOWED TO. YOU AREN'T.
Wha?! No fair!!
ANYWAY! WITH WHO WE'VE GOT NOW, WE DO NOT HAVE THE POWER TO BEAT KY LUC.
THAT'S WHY WE HAVE TO FREE FERID AND KRUL.

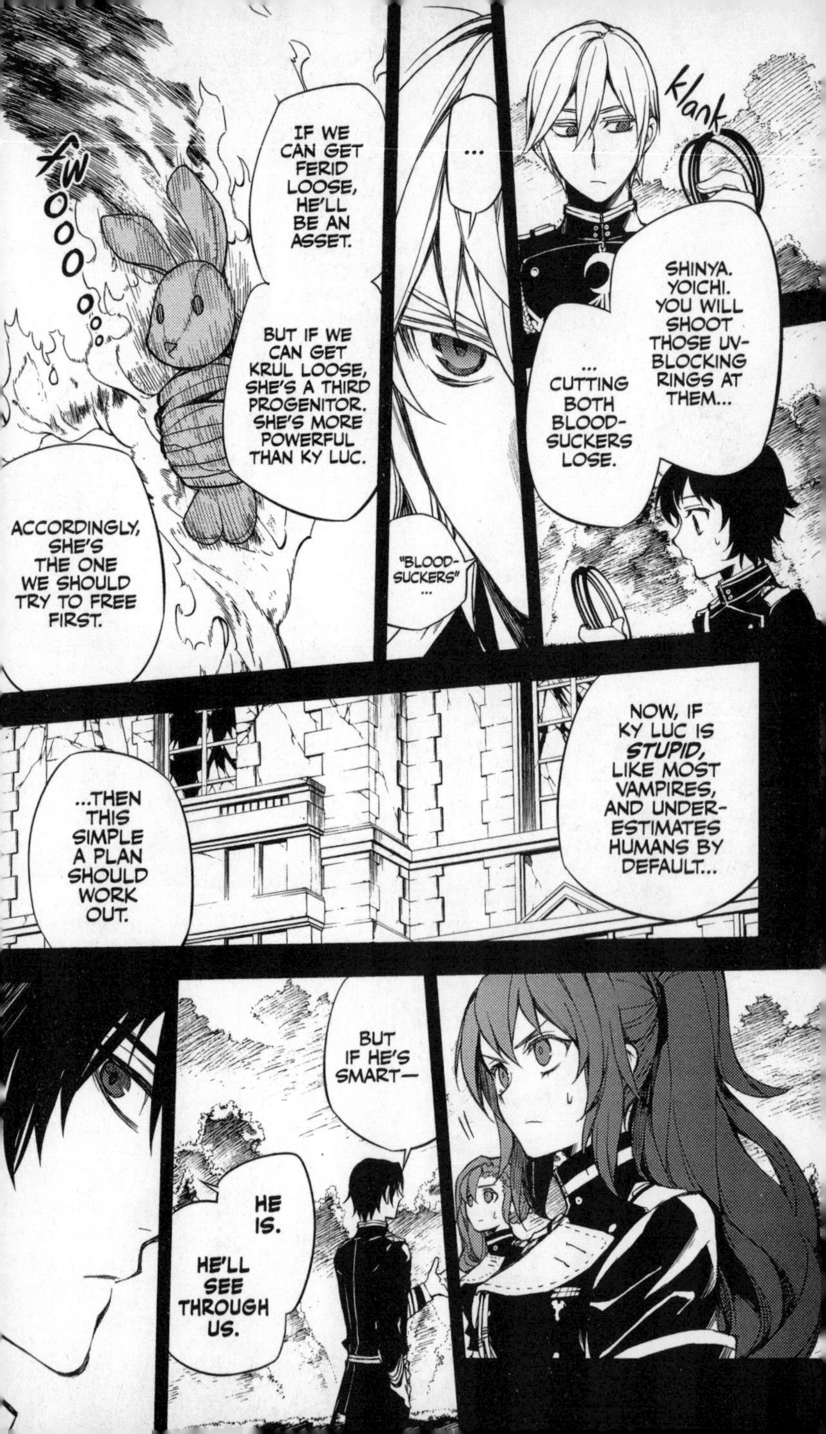
klank
SHINYA. YOICHI. YOU WILL SHOOT THOSE UV-BLOCKING RINGS AT THEM...
... CUTTING BOTH BLOOD-SUCKERS LOSE.
...
"BLOOD-SUCKERS"...
IF WE CAN GET FERID LOOSE, HE'LL BE AN ASSET.
BUT IF WE CAN GET KRUL LOOSE, SHE'S A THIRD PROGENITOR. SHE'S MORE POWERFUL THAN KY LUC.
FWOOOOooo
ACCORDINGLY, SHE'S THE ONE WE SHOULD TRY TO FREE FIRST.
NOW, IF KY LUC IS STUPID, LIKE MOST VAMPIRES, AND UNDER-ESTIMATES HUMANS BY DEFAULT...
...THEN THIS SIMPLE A PLAN SHOULD WORK OUT.
BUT IF HE'S SMART—
HE IS.
HE'LL SEE THROUGH US.

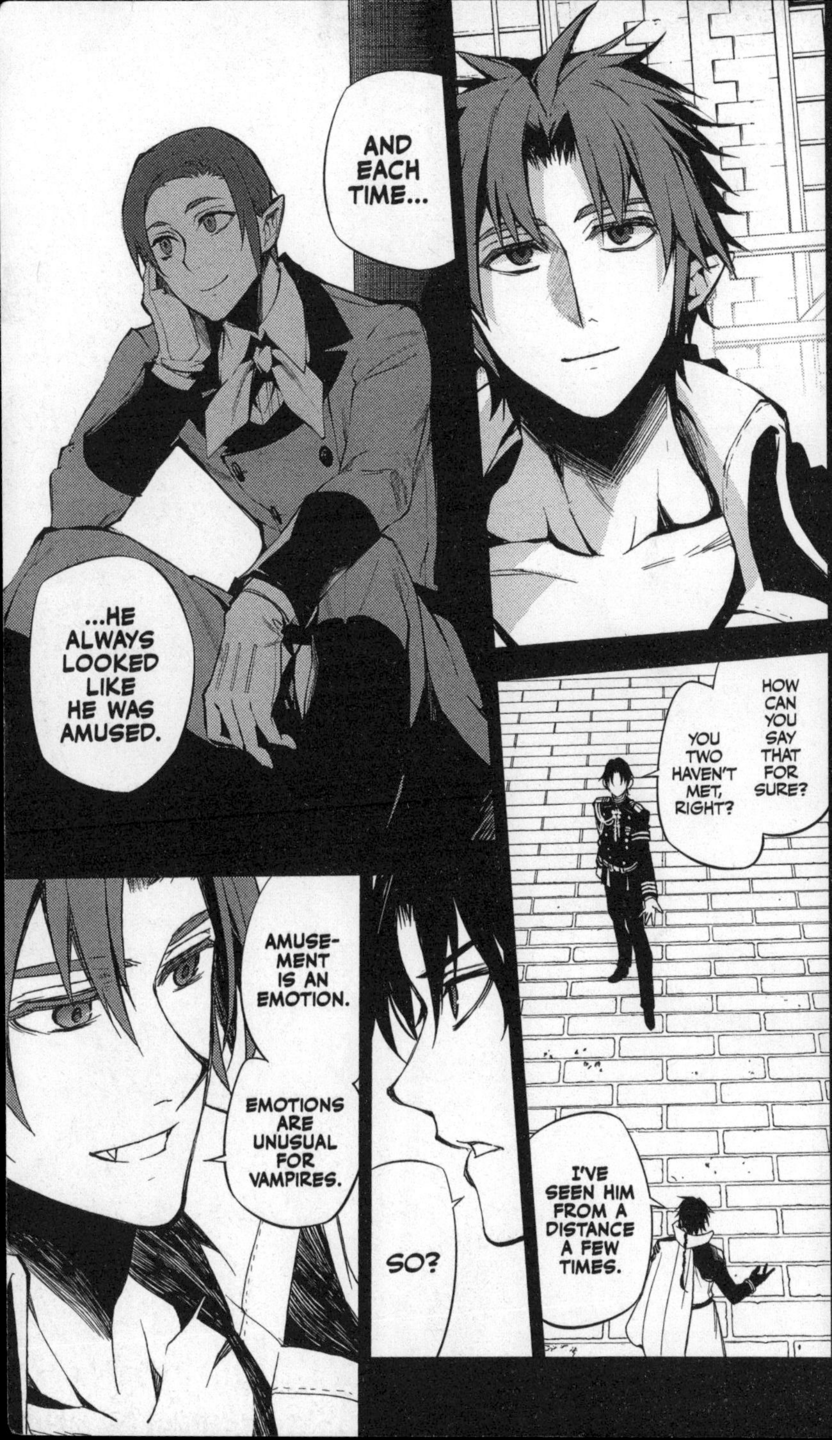
AND EACH TIME...
...HE ALWAYS LOOKED LIKE HE WAS AMUSED.
HOW CAN YOU SAY THAT FOR SURE?
YOU TWO HAVEN'T MET, RIGHT?
I'VE SEEN HIM FROM A DISTANCE A FEW TIMES.
SO?
AMUSEMENT IS AN EMOTION.
EMOTIONS ARE UNUSUAL FOR VAMPIRES.

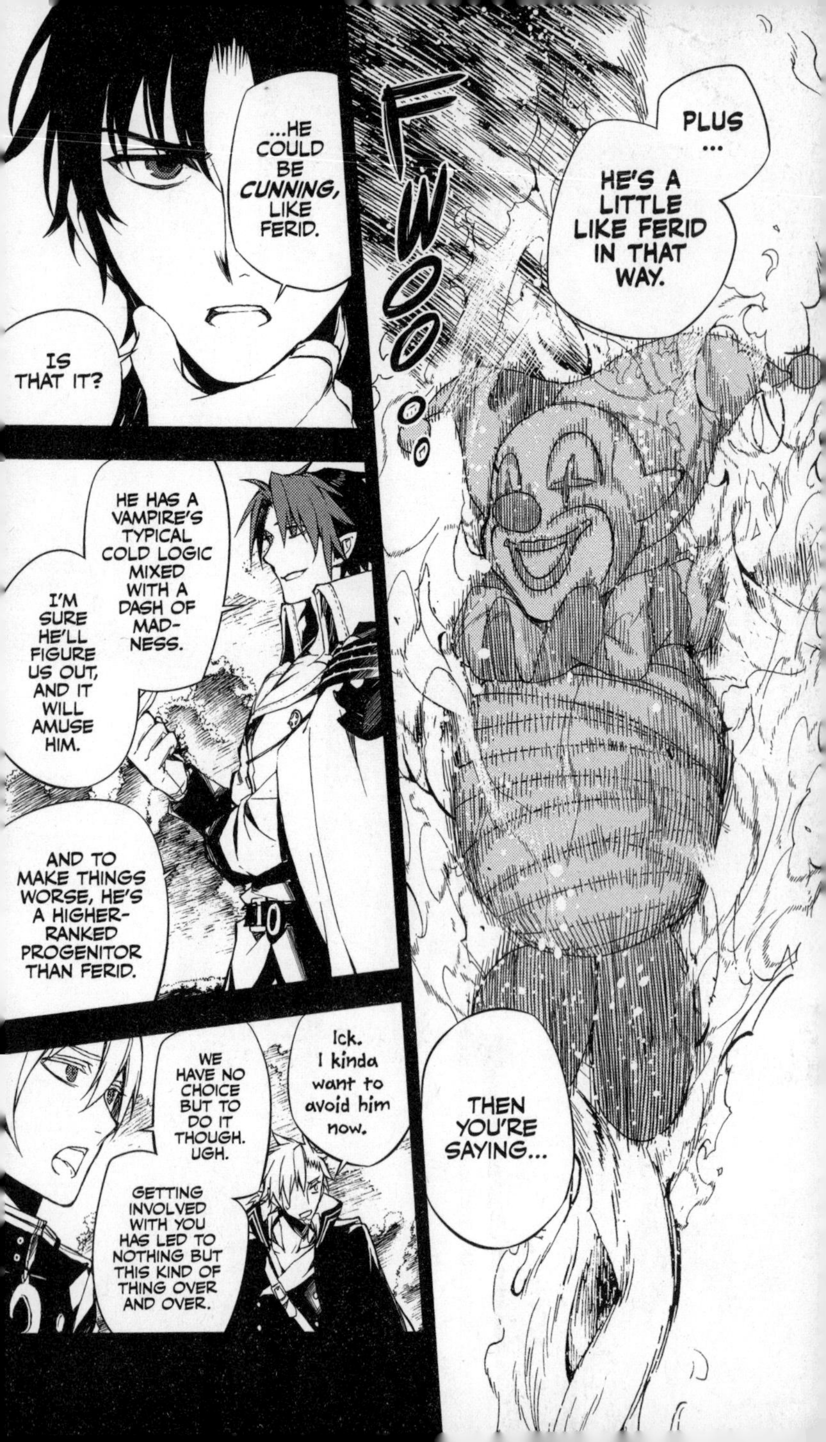
PLUS ...
HE'S A LITTLE LIKE FERID IN THAT WAY.
FWOOOO
THEN YOU'RE SAYING...
...HE COULD BE *CUNNING,* LIKE FERID.
IS THAT IT?
HE HAS A VAMPIRE'S TYPICAL COLD LOGIC MIXED WITH A DASH OF MAD-NESS.
I'M SURE HE'LL FIGURE US OUT, AND IT WILL AMUSE HIM.
AND TO MAKE THINGS WORSE, HE'S A HIGHER-RANKED PROGENITOR THAN FERID.
10
Ick. I kinda want to avoid him now.
WE HAVE NO CHOICE BUT TO DO IT THOUGH. UGH.
GETTING INVOLVED WITH YOU HAS LED TO NOTHING BUT THIS KIND OF THING OVER AND OVER.

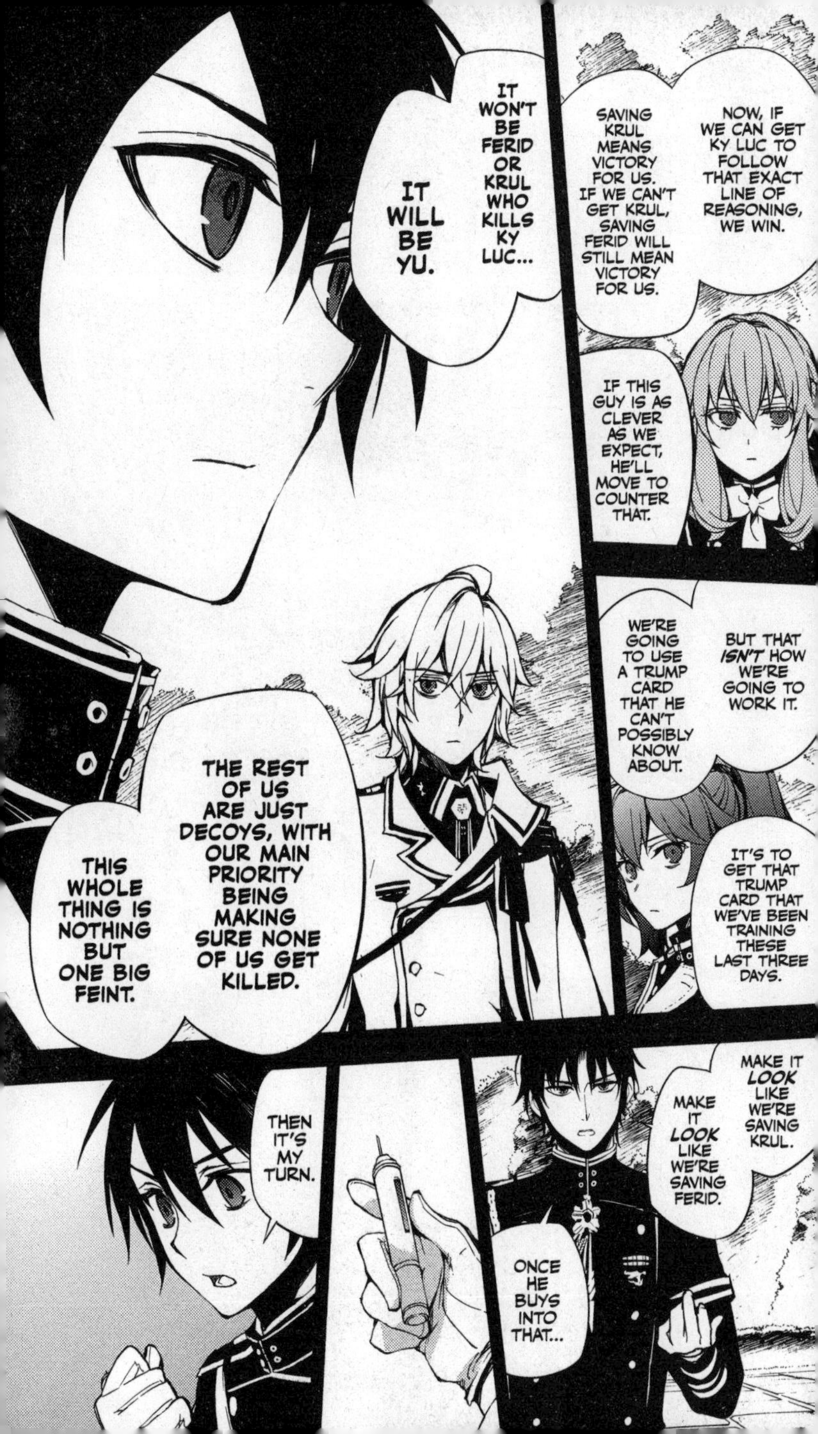

NOW, IF WE CAN GET KY LUC TO FOLLOW THAT EXACT LINE OF REASONING, WE WIN.
SAVING KRUL MEANS VICTORY FOR US. IF WE CAN'T GET KRUL, SAVING FERID WILL STILL MEAN VICTORY FOR US.
IF THIS GUY IS AS CLEVER AS WE EXPECT, HE'LL MOVE TO COUNTER THAT.
BUT THAT *ISN'T* HOW WE'RE GOING TO WORK IT.
WE'RE GOING TO USE A TRUMP CARD THAT HE CAN'T POSSIBLY KNOW ABOUT.
IT'S TO GET THAT TRUMP CARD THAT WE'VE BEEN TRAINING THESE LAST THREE DAYS.
IT WON'T BE FERID OR KRUL WHO KILLS KY LUC...
IT WILL BE YU.
THE REST OF US ARE JUST DECOYS, WITH OUR MAIN PRIORITY BEING MAKING SURE NONE OF US GET KILLED.
THIS WHOLE THING IS NOTHING BUT ONE BIG FEINT.
MAKE IT *LOOK* LIKE WE'RE SAVING KRUL.
MAKE IT *LOOK* LIKE WE'RE SAVING FERID.
ONCE HE BUYS INTO THAT...
THEN IT'S MY TURN.

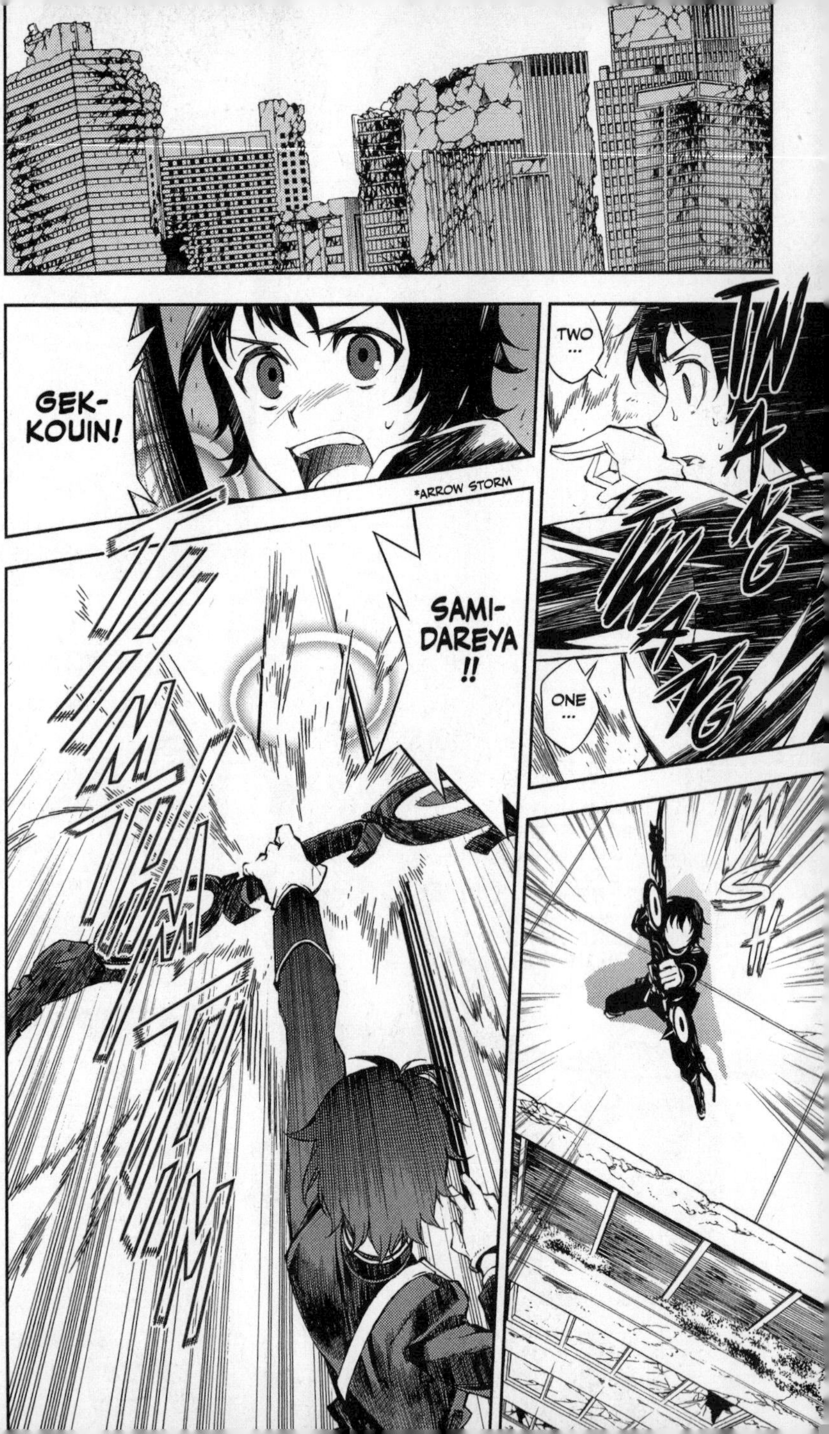
TWO...
TWANG
TWANG
ONE...
GEK-KOUIN!
SAMI-DAREYA!!
*ARROW STORM
WHSH

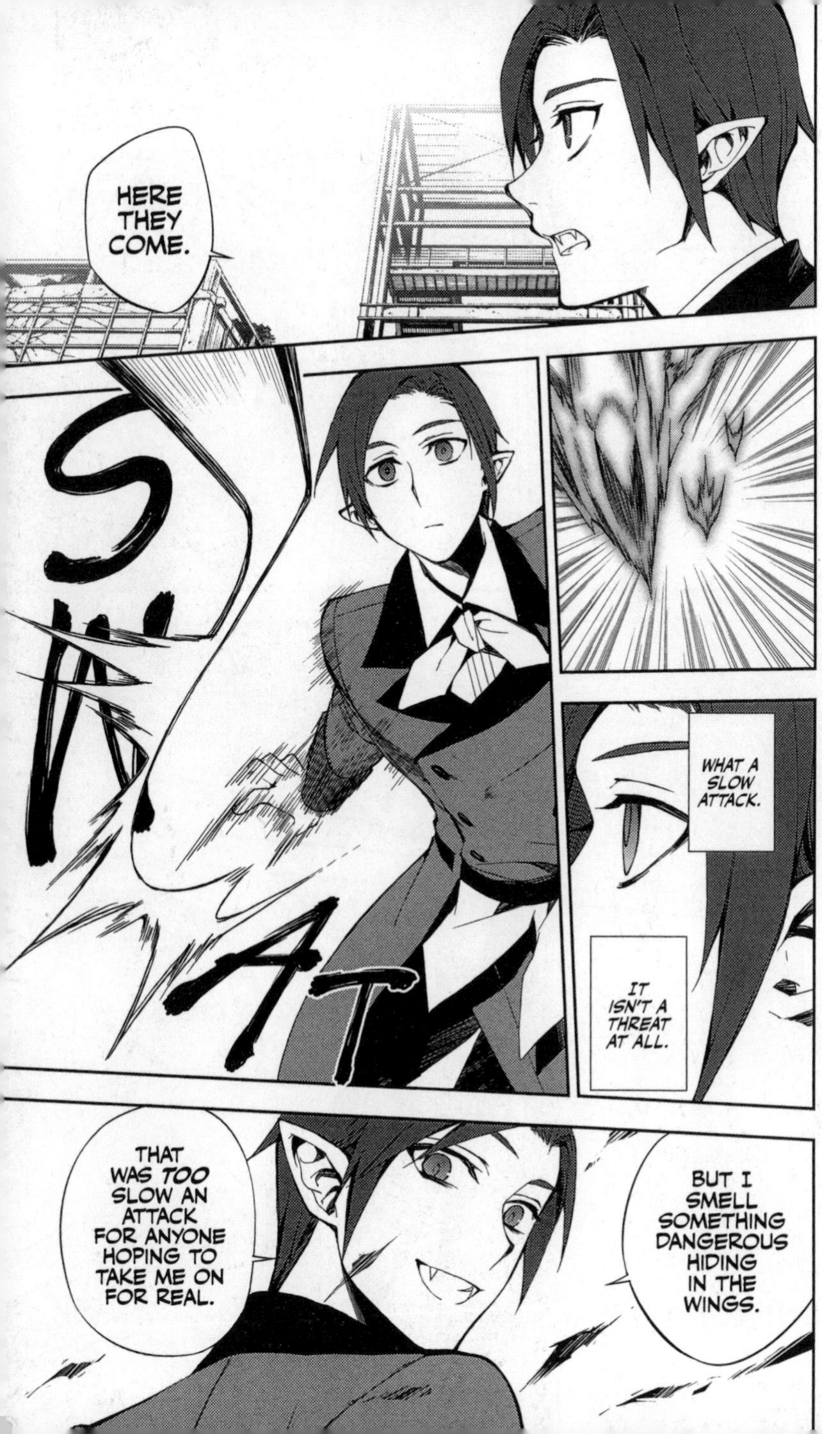
HERE THEY COME.
WHAT A SLOW ATTACK.
IT ISN'T A THREAT AT ALL.
SWAT
BUT I SMELL SOMETHING DANGEROUS HIDING IN THE WINGS.
THAT WAS *TOO* SLOW AN ATTACK FOR ANYONE HOPING TO TAKE ME ON FOR REAL.

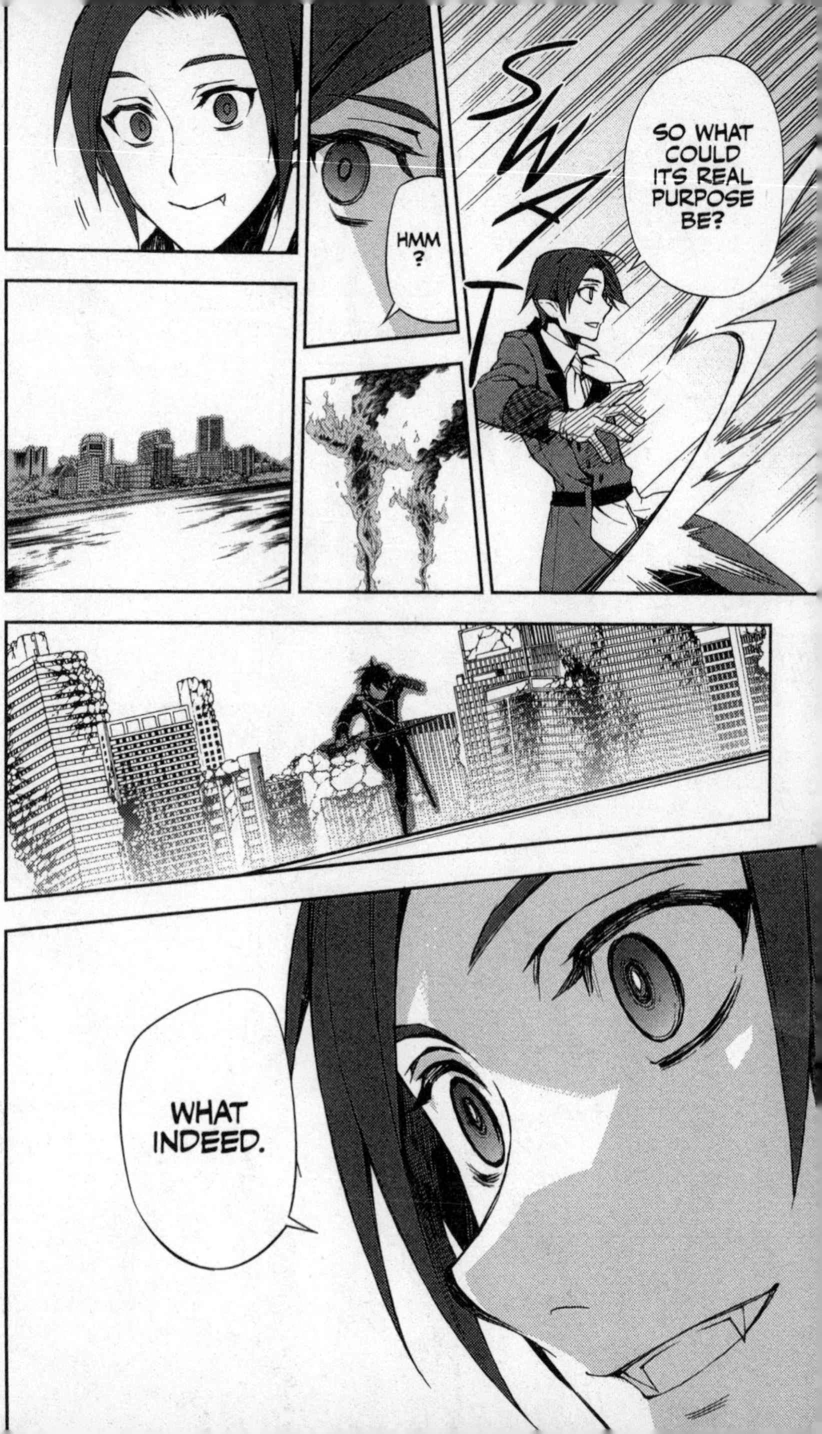
SO WHAT COULD ITS REAL PURPOSE BE?
SWAT
HMM ?
WHAT INDEED.

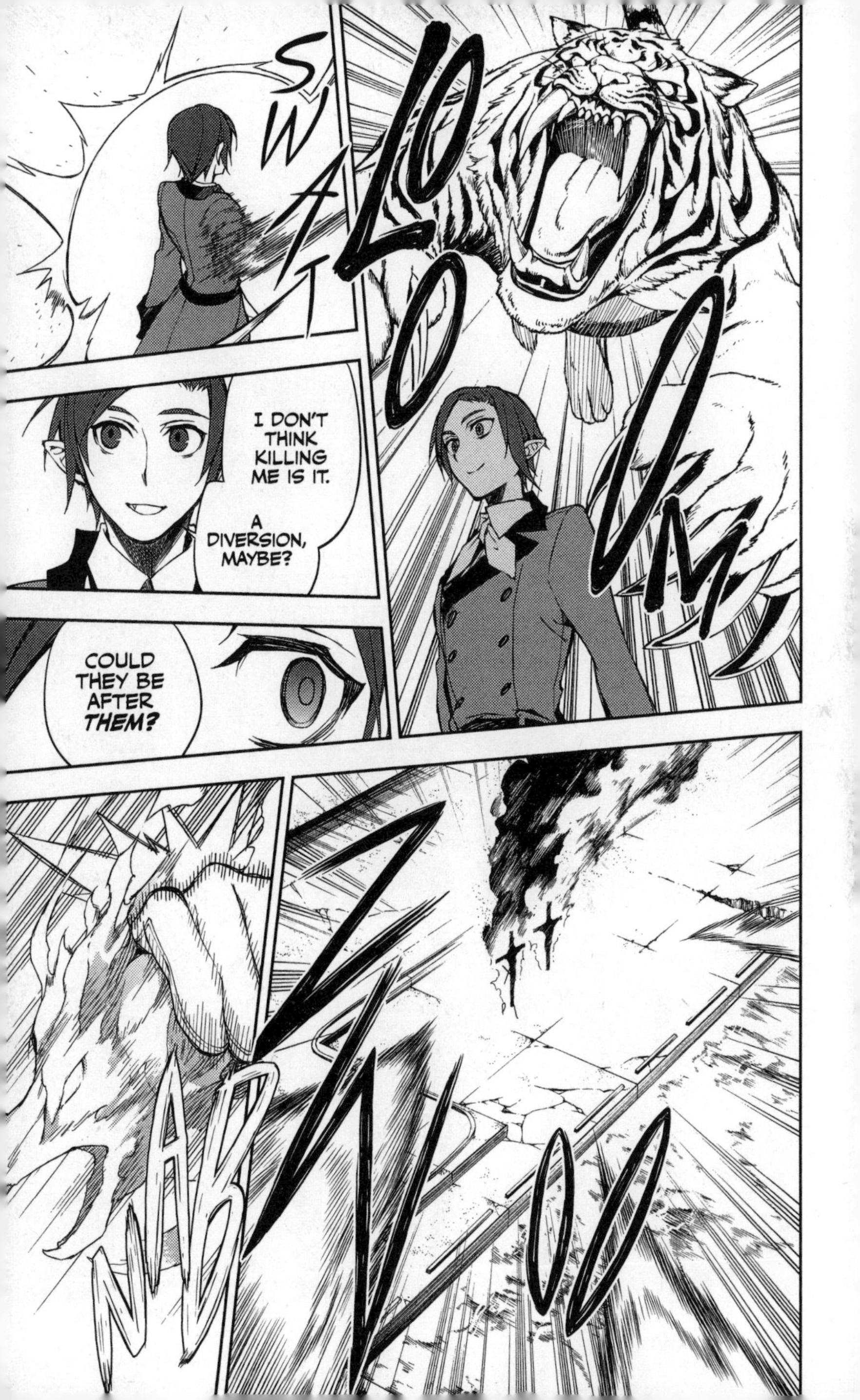
SWAT
I DON'T THINK KILLING ME IS IT.
A DIVERSION, MAYBE?
COULD THEY BE AFTER *THEM?*

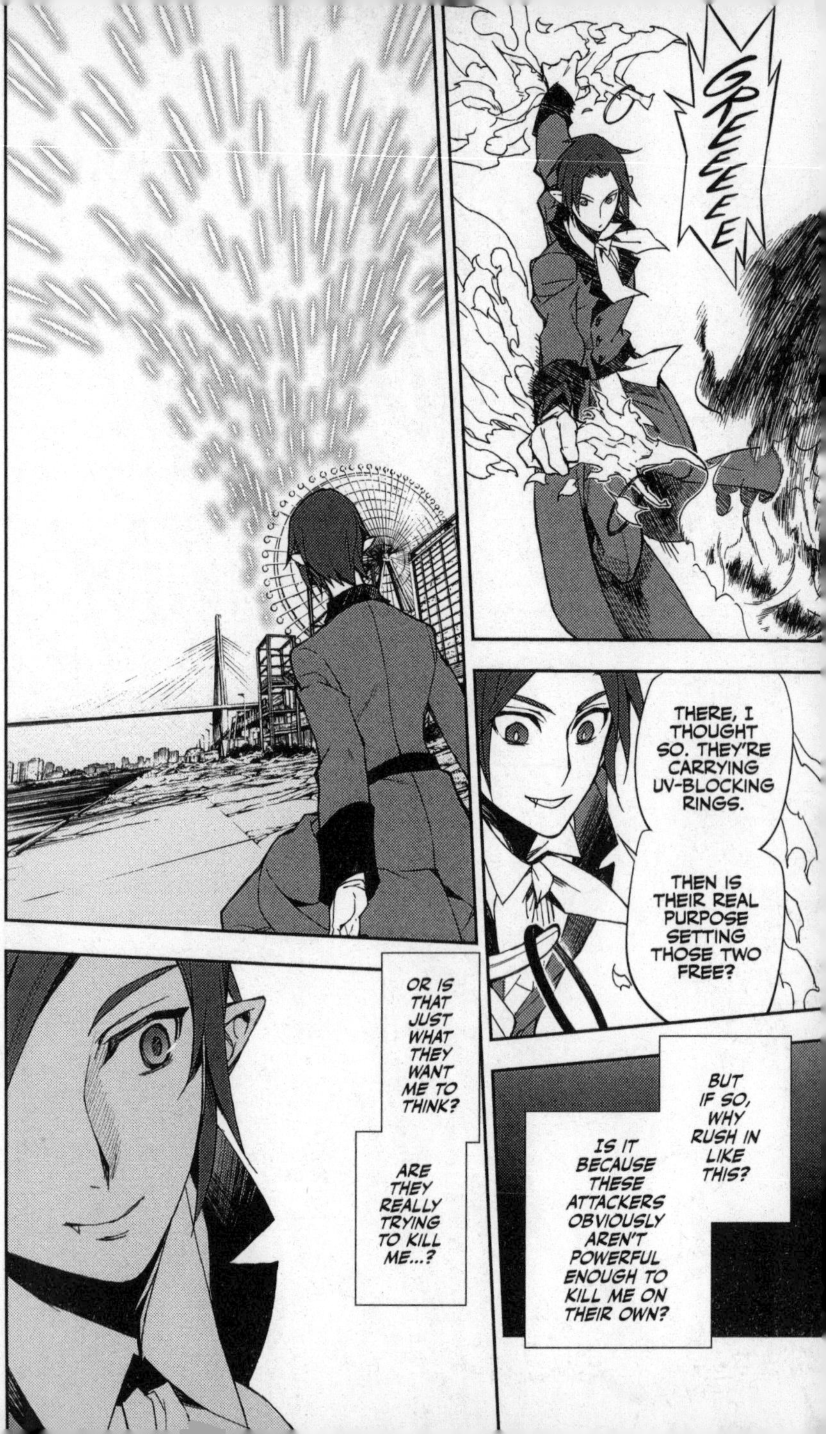
GREEEEE
THERE, I THOUGHT SO. THEY'RE CARRYING UV-BLOCKING RINGS.
THEN IS THEIR REAL PURPOSE SETTING THOSE TWO FREE?
OR IS THAT JUST WHAT THEY WANT ME TO THINK?
ARE THEY REALLY TRYING TO KILL ME...?
BUT IF SO, WHY RUSH IN LIKE THIS?
IS IT BECAUSE THESE ATTACKERS OBVIOUSLY AREN'T POWERFUL ENOUGH TO KILL ME ON THEIR OWN?

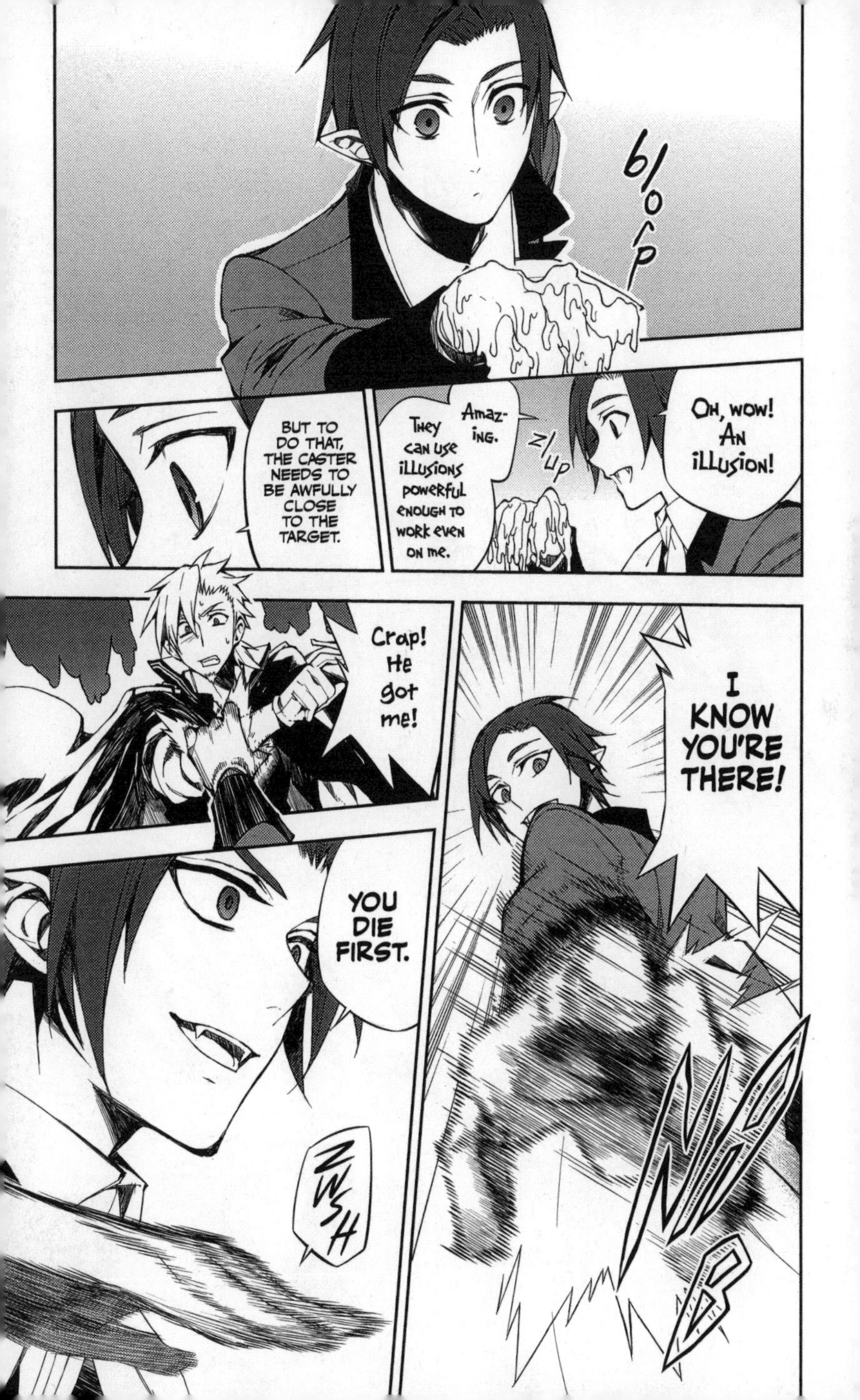
blorp
OH, WOW! AN illusion!
zlup
Amazing.
They can use illusions powerful enough to work even on me.
BUT TO DO THAT, THE CASTER NEEDS TO BE AWFULLY CLOSE TO THE TARGET.
I KNOW YOU'RE THERE!
Crap! He got me!
YOU DIE FIRST.
ZWSH

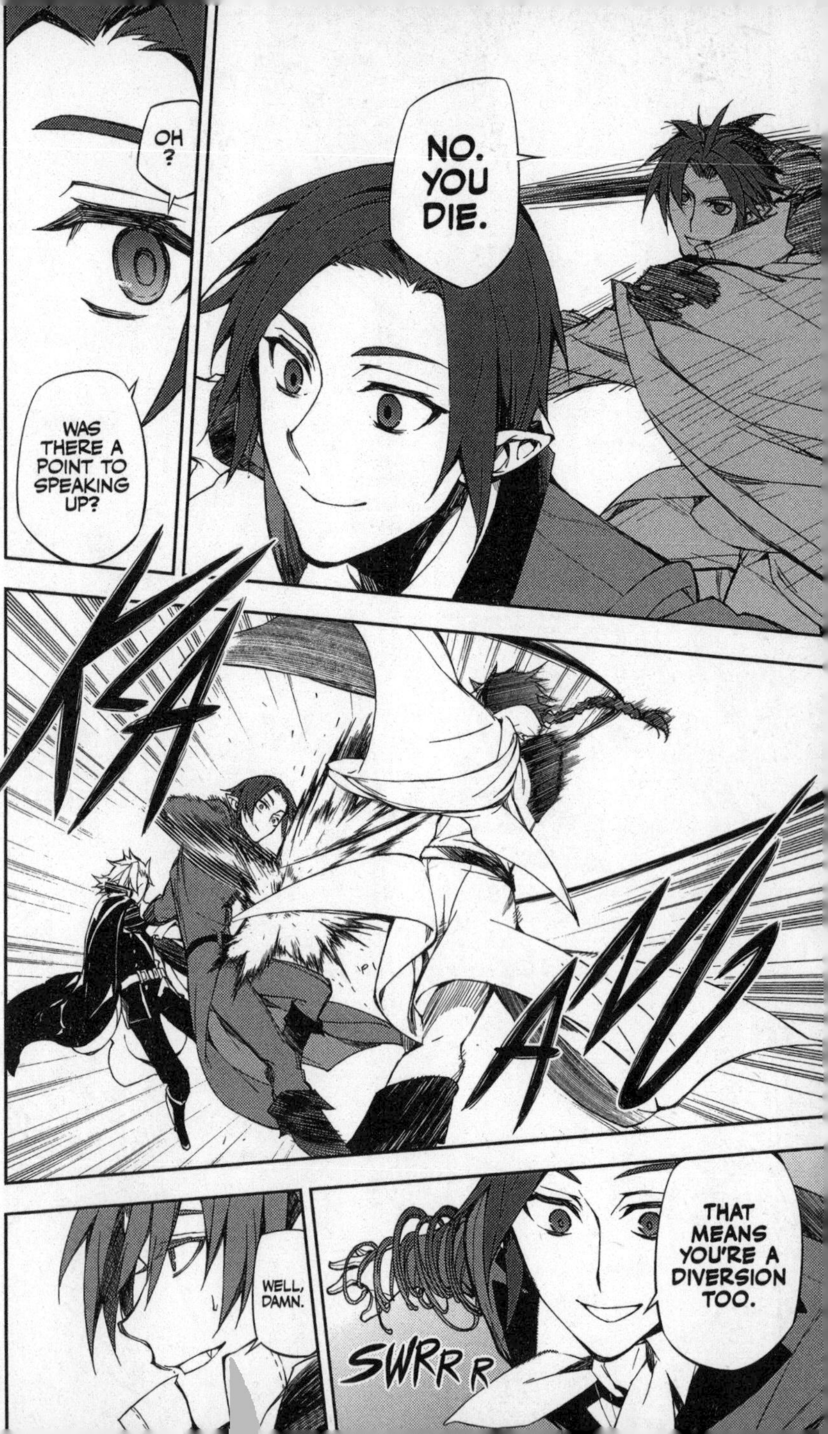
NO. YOU DIE.
OH?
WAS THERE A POINT TO SPEAKING UP?
KA
ANG
THAT MEANS YOU'RE A DIVERSION TOO.
SWRRR
WELL, DAMN.

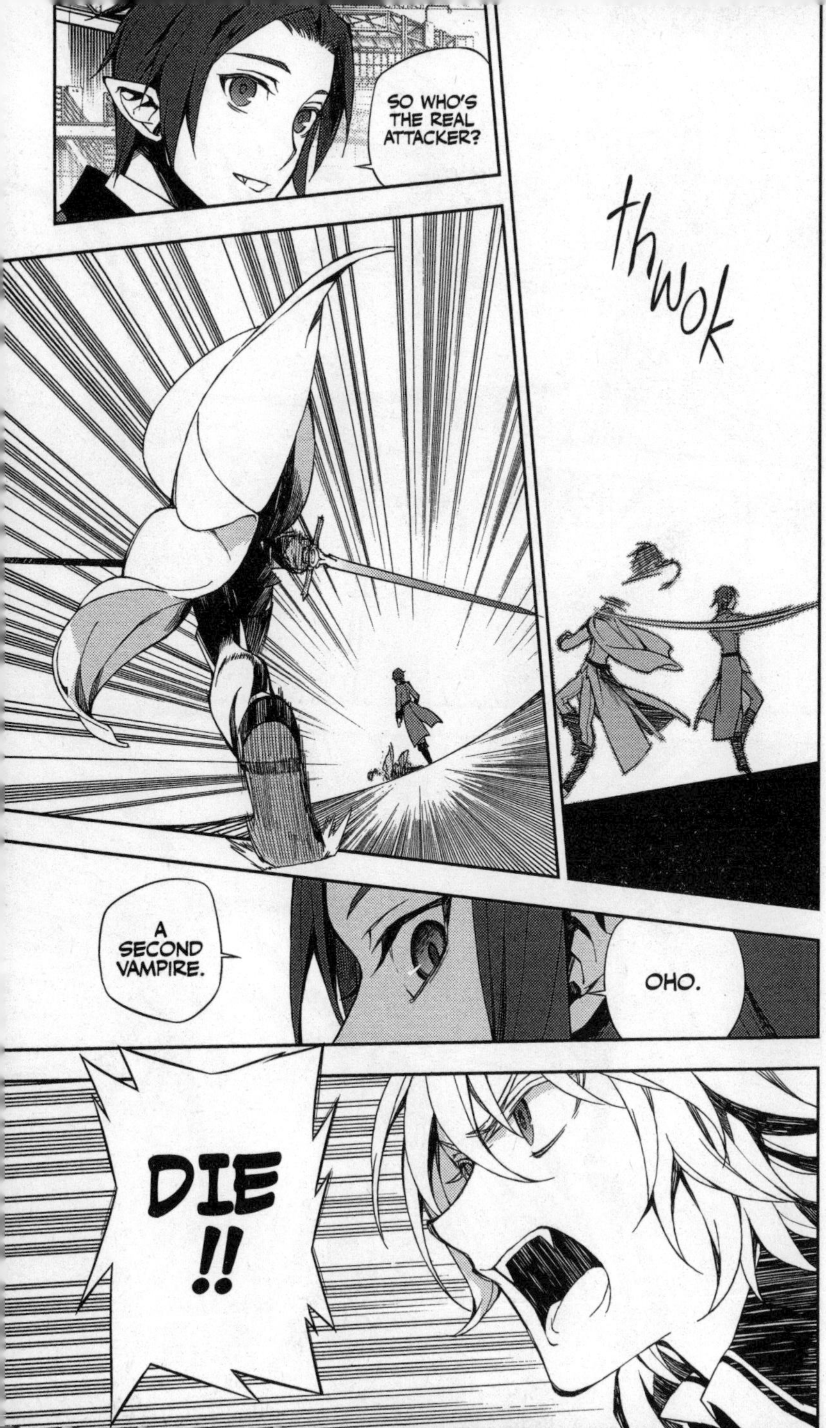
SO WHO'S THE REAL ATTACKER?
thwok
OHO.
A SECOND VAMPIRE.
DIE!!

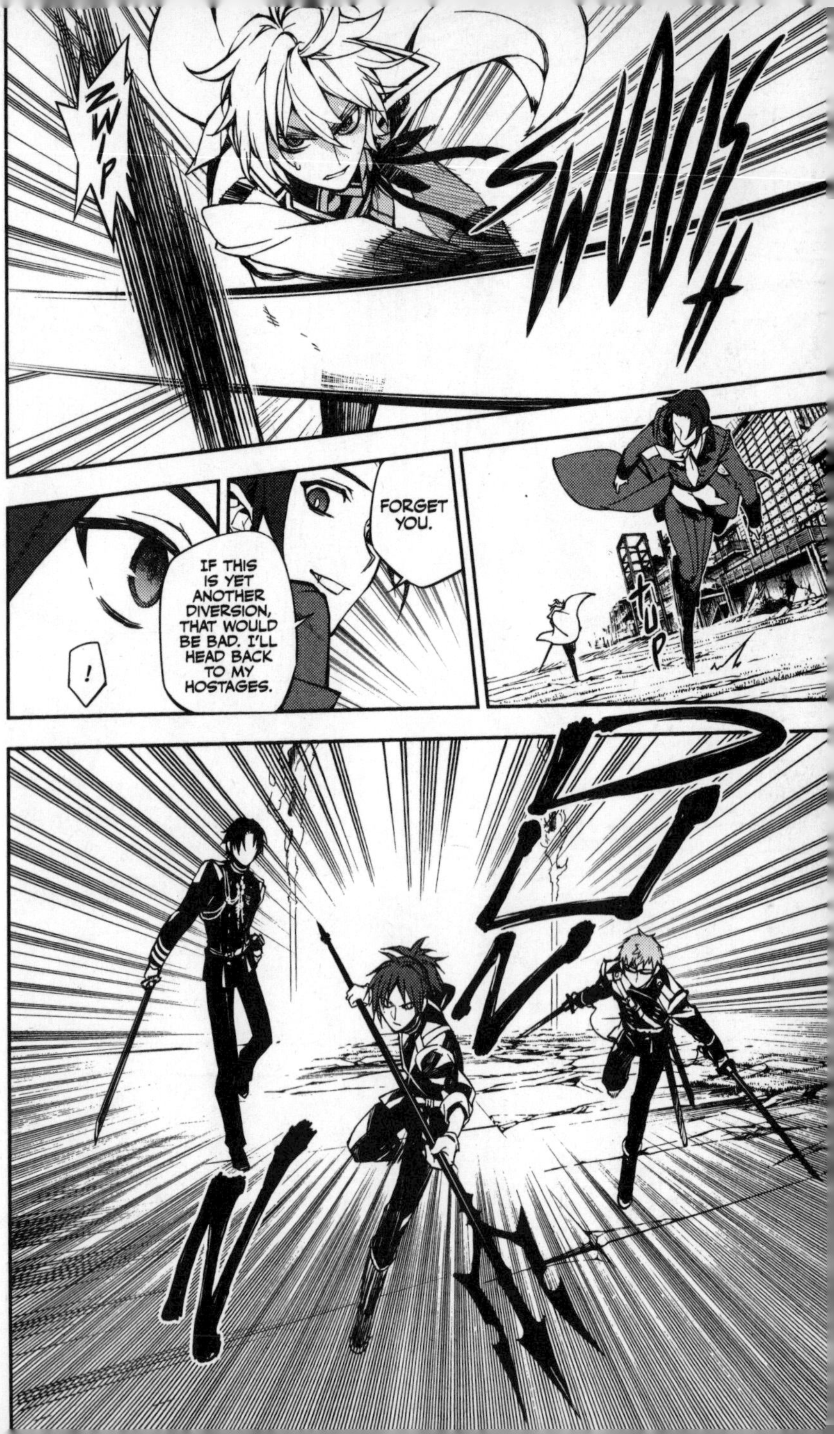
SWOOSH
ZWIP
THUP
FORGET YOU.
IF THIS IS YET ANOTHER DIVERSION, THAT WOULD BE BAD. I'LL HEAD BACK TO MY HOSTAGES.
!

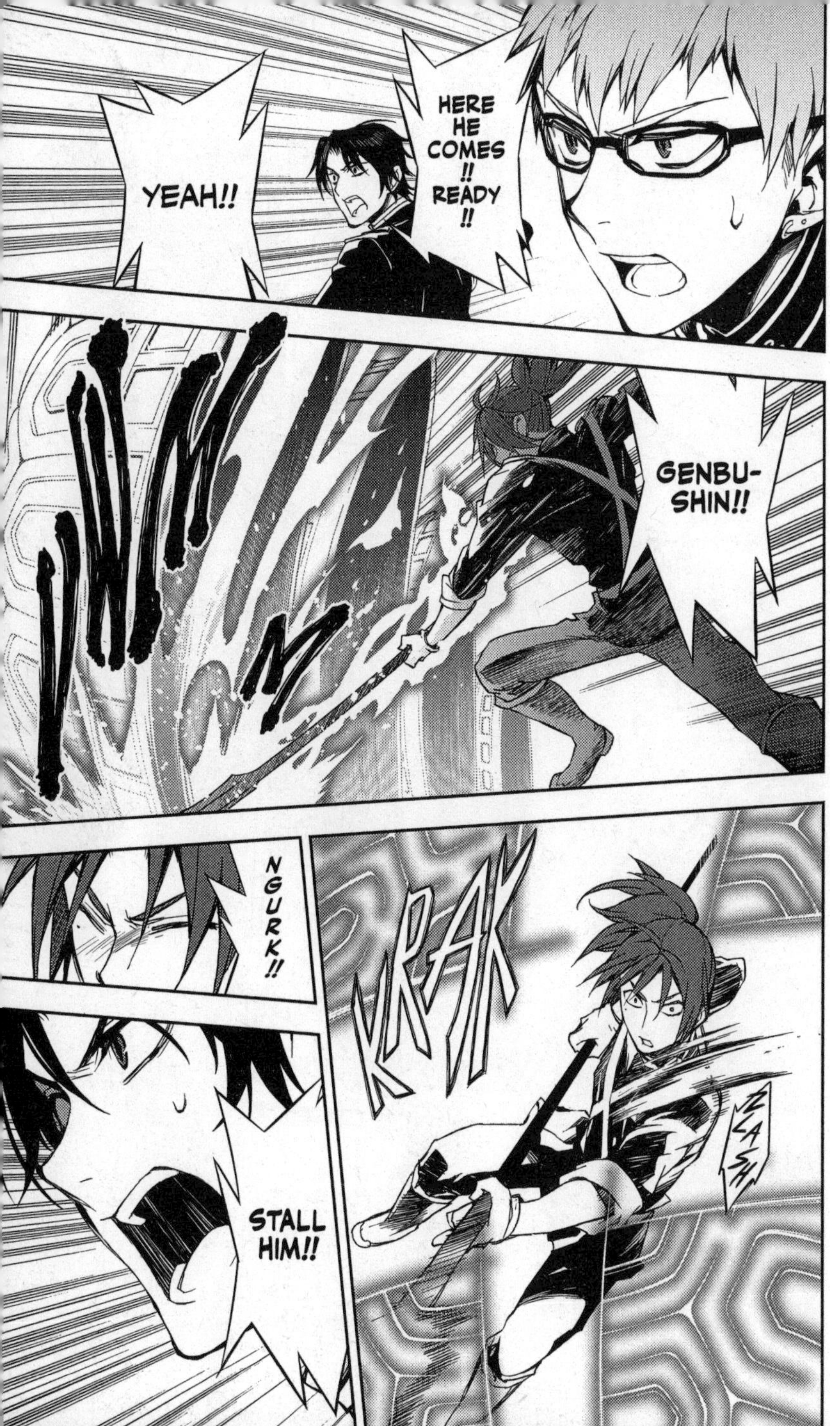
HERE HE COMES!! READY!!
YEAH!!
GENBU-SHIN!!
KRAK
ZLASH
NGURK!!
STALL HIM!!

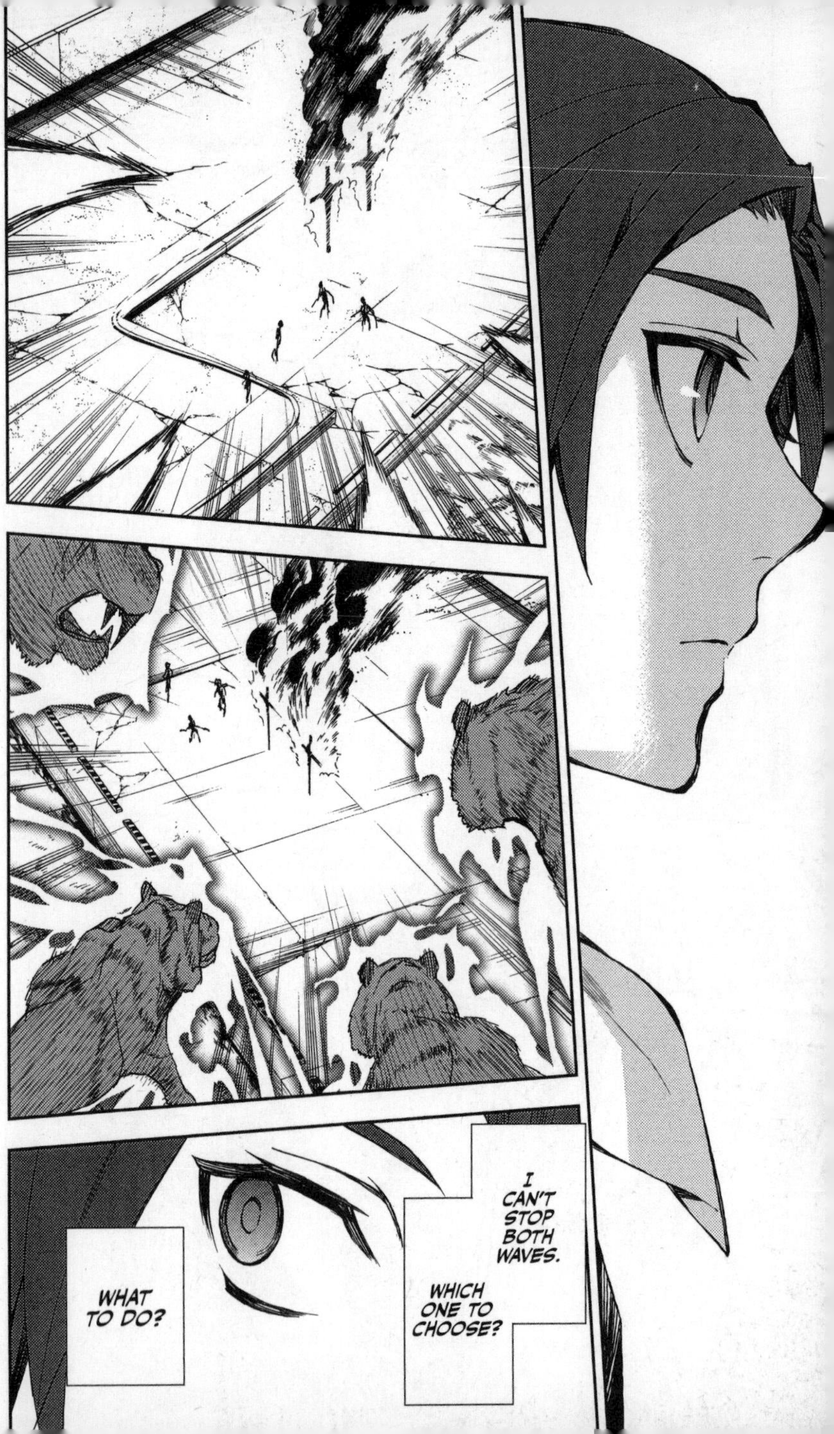
I CAN'T STOP BOTH WAVES.
WHICH ONE TO CHOOSE?
WHAT TO DO?

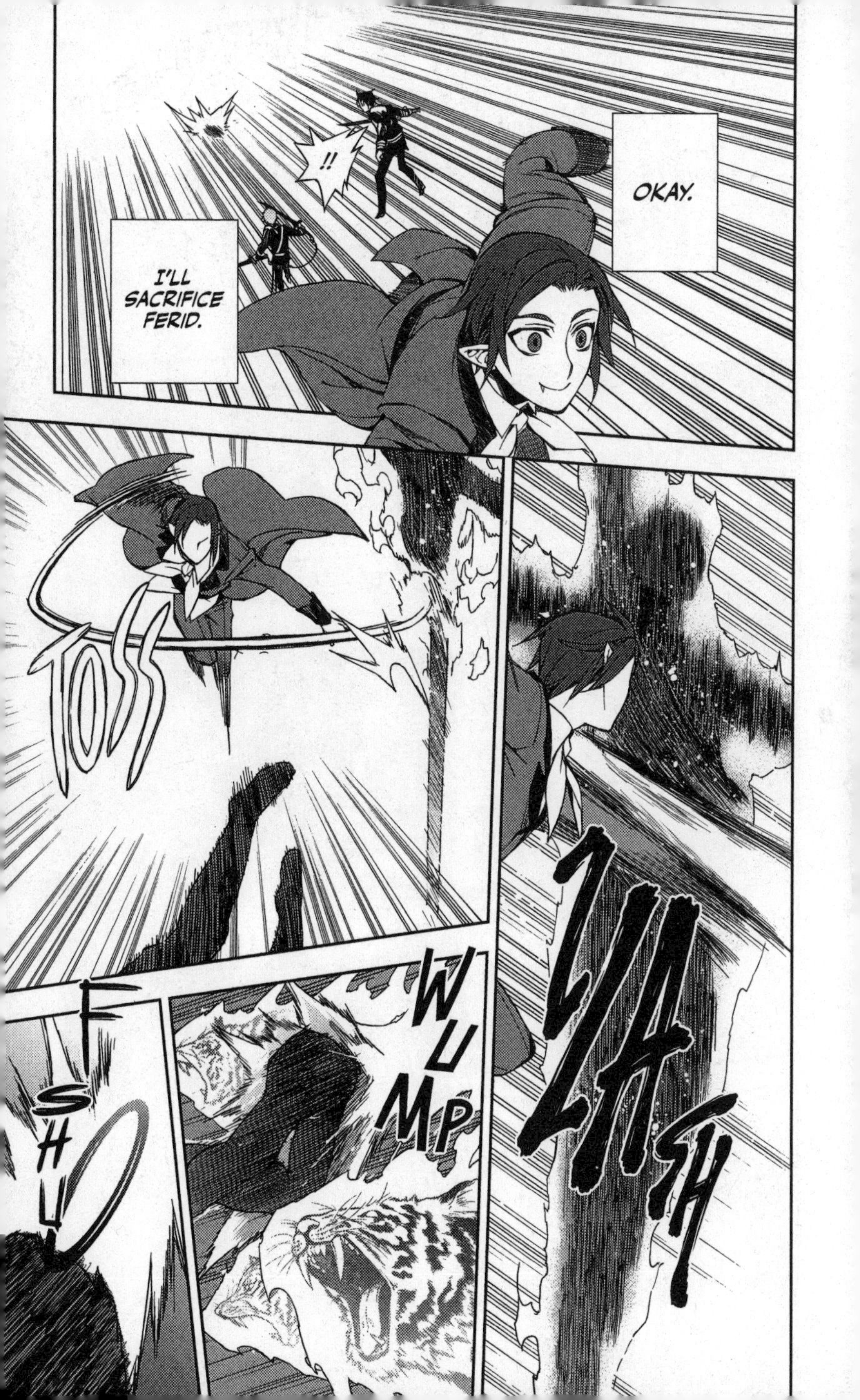

OKAY.
!!
I'LL SACRIFICE FERID.
SLASH
TOSS
WUMP
FSHU

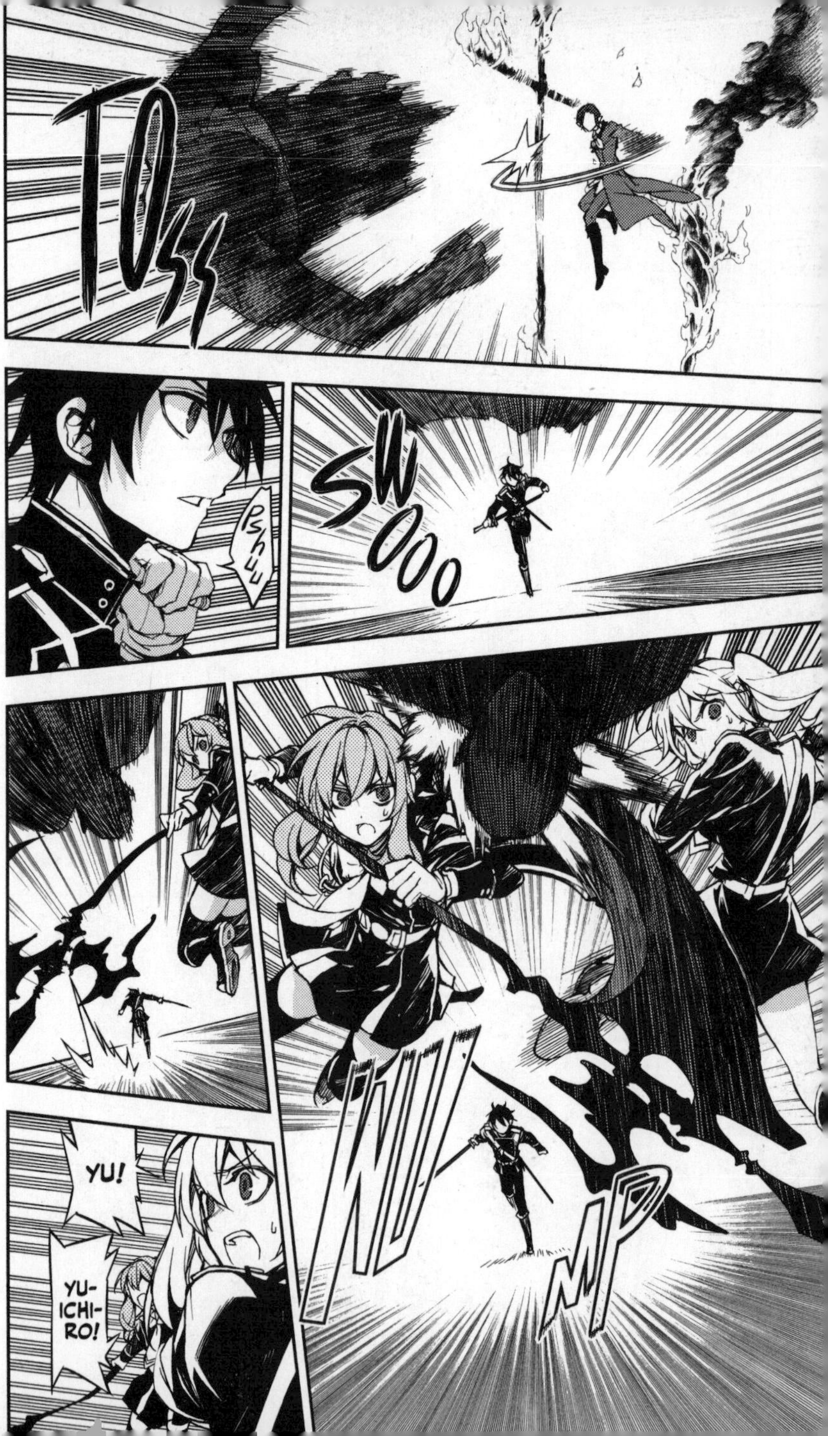
TOSS
SWOOO
PSHUU
WUMP
YU!
YU-ICHIRO!

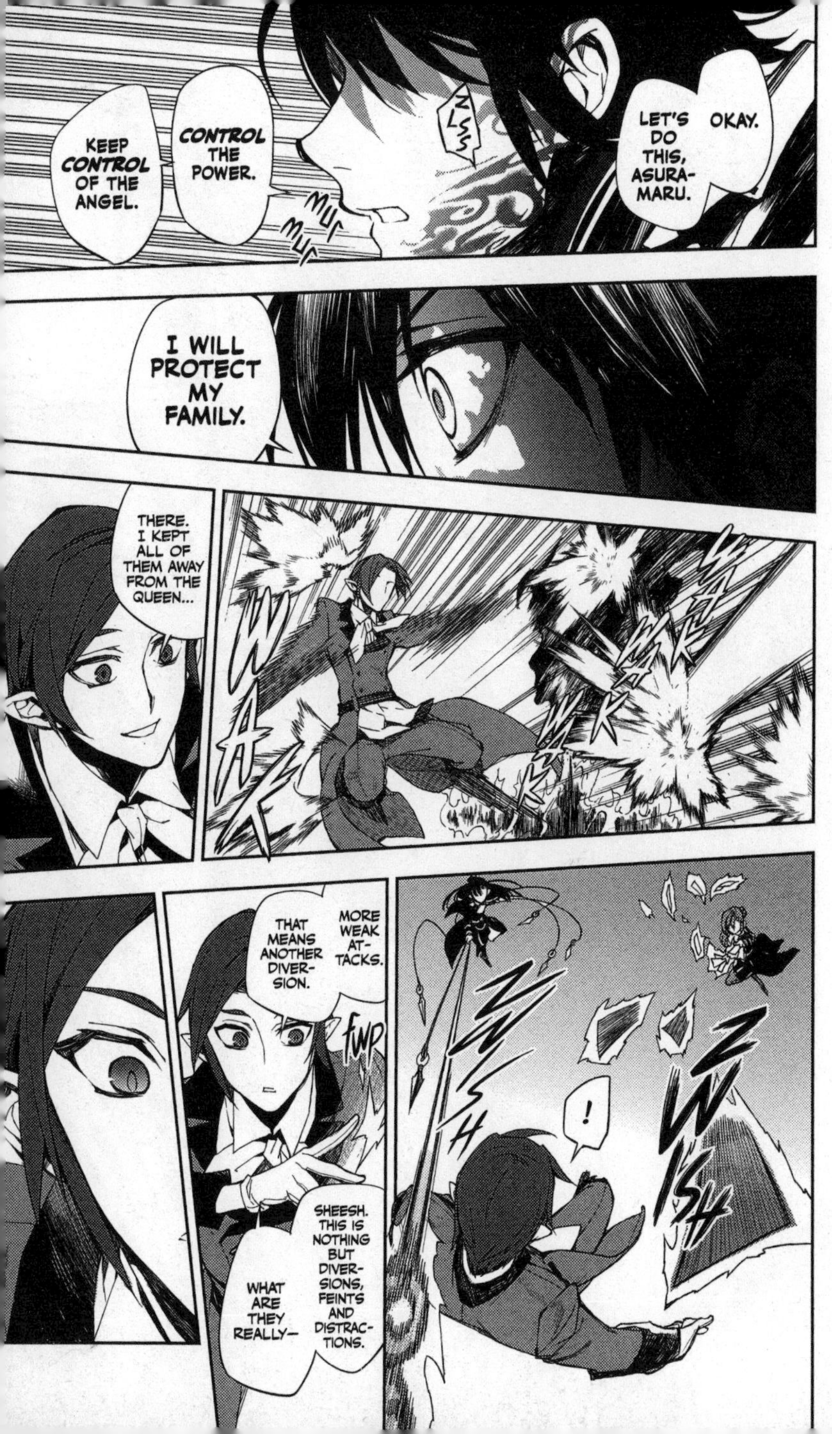

OKAY.
LET'S DO THIS, ASURA-MARU.
CONTROL THE POWER.
KEEP CONTROL OF THE ANGEL.
MUF MUF
I WILL PROTECT MY FAMILY.
WAKK WAKK
WHAK
THERE. I KEPT ALL OF THEM AWAY FROM THE QUEEN...
ZWISH
!
ZWISH
MORE WEAK AT-TACKS.
THAT MEANS ANOTHER DIVER-SION.
FWP
SHEESH. THIS IS NOTHING BUT DIVER-SIONS, FEINTS AND DISTRAC-TIONS.
WHAT ARE THEY REALLY—

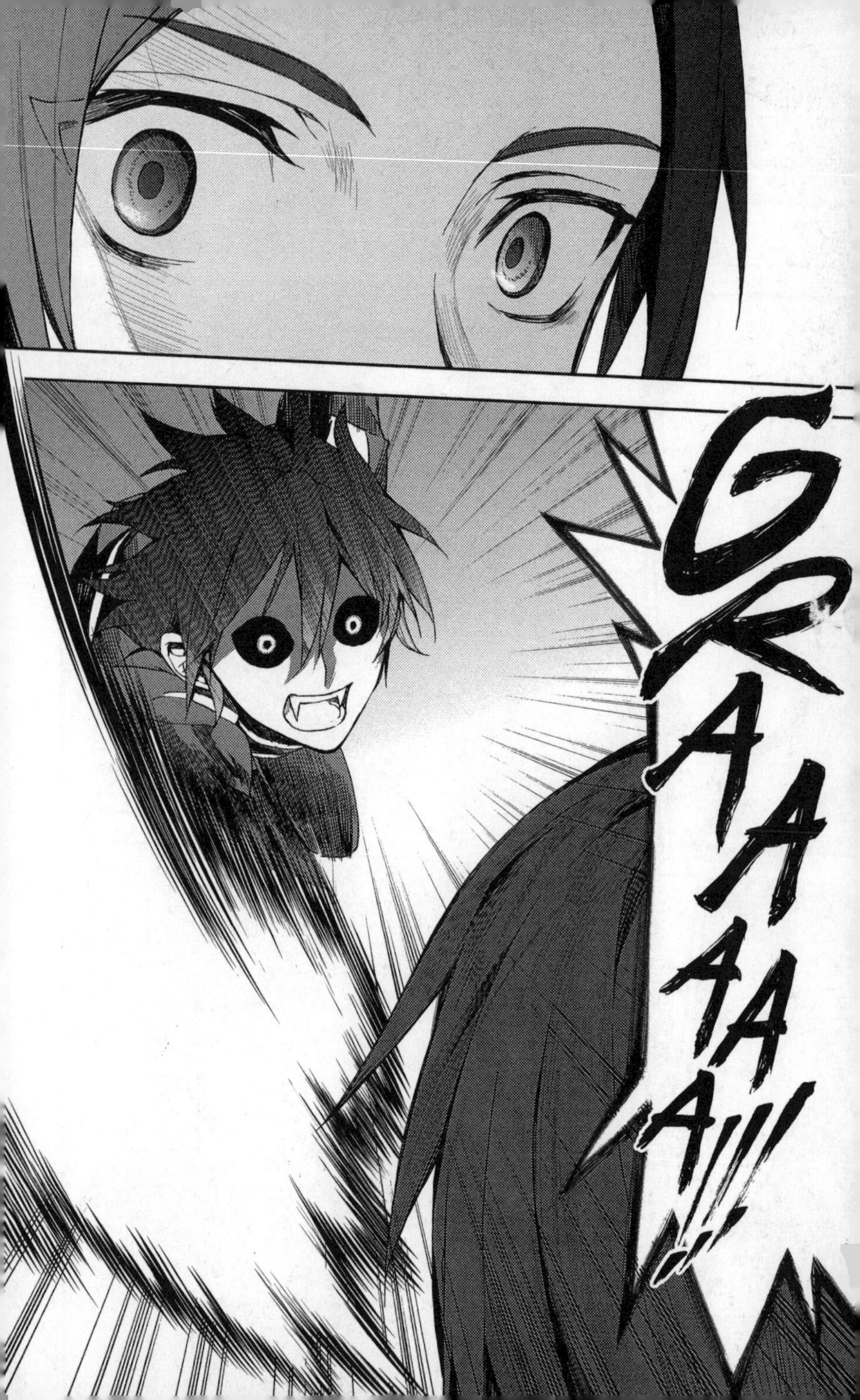
GRAAAAA!!

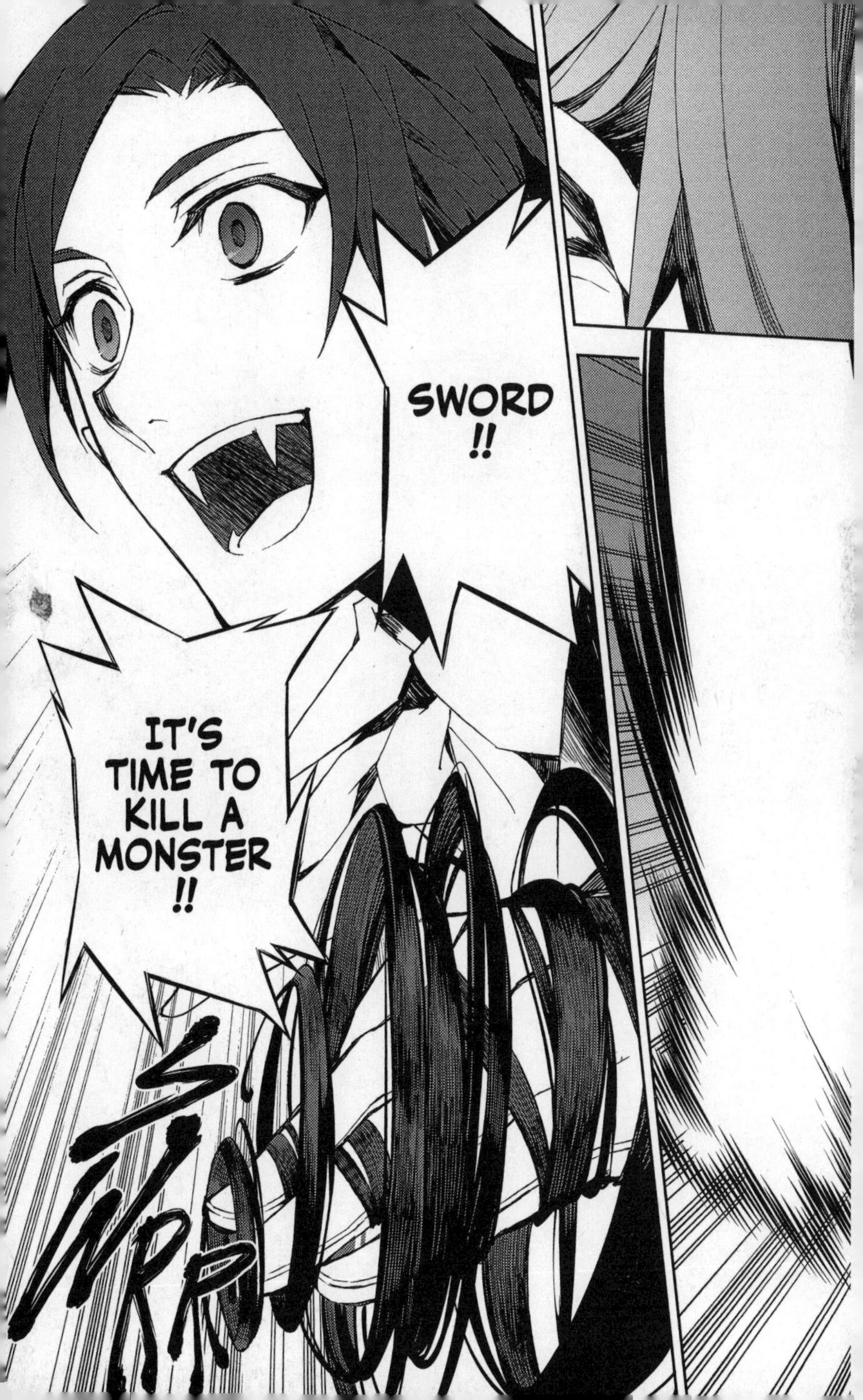
SWORD !!
IT'S TIME TO KILL A MONSTER !!
SWRR

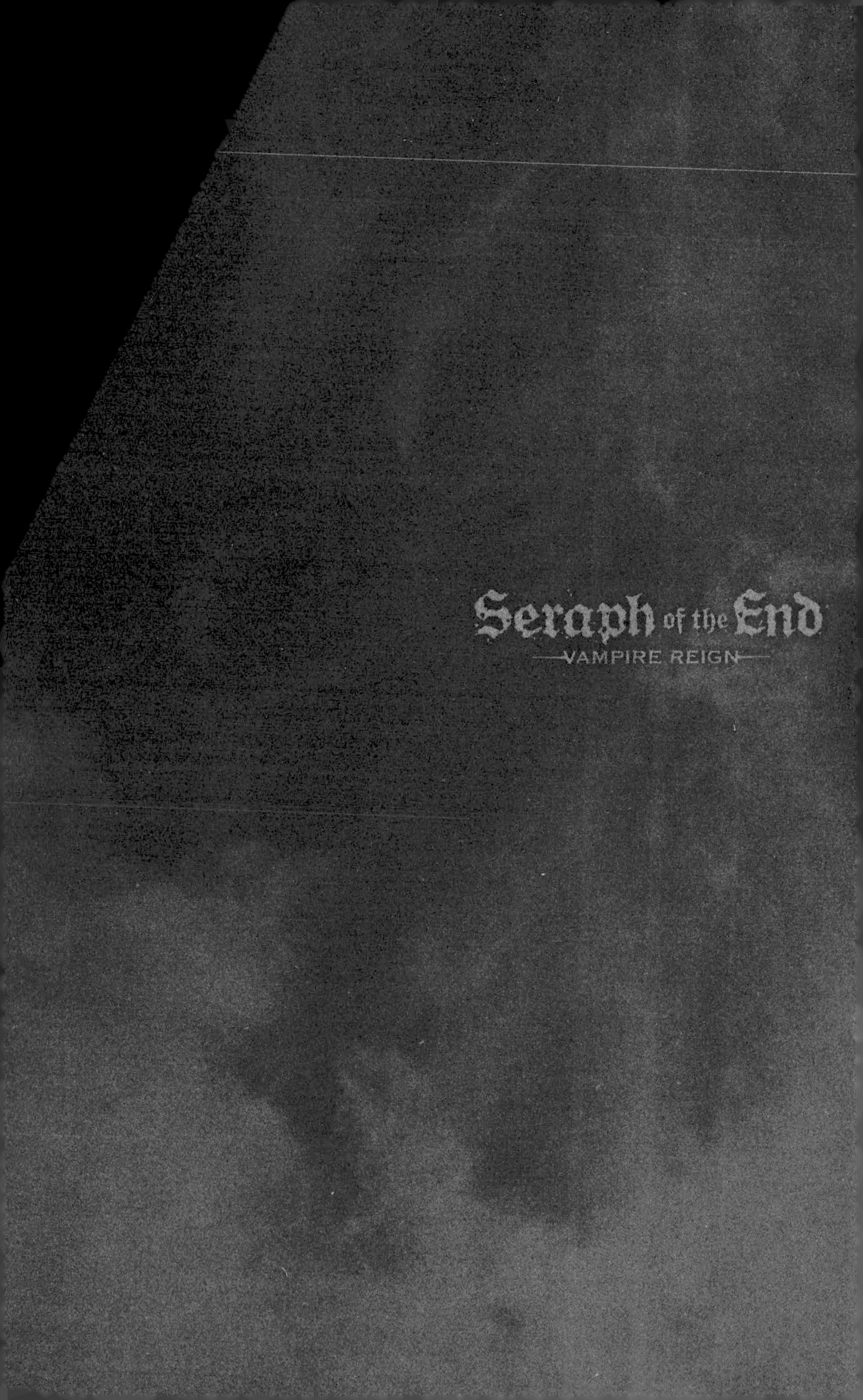
Seraph of the End
VAMPIRE REIGN

GRAAAAAAAAA!!!

ZWISH

CHAPTER 61
Who Is More Bored?

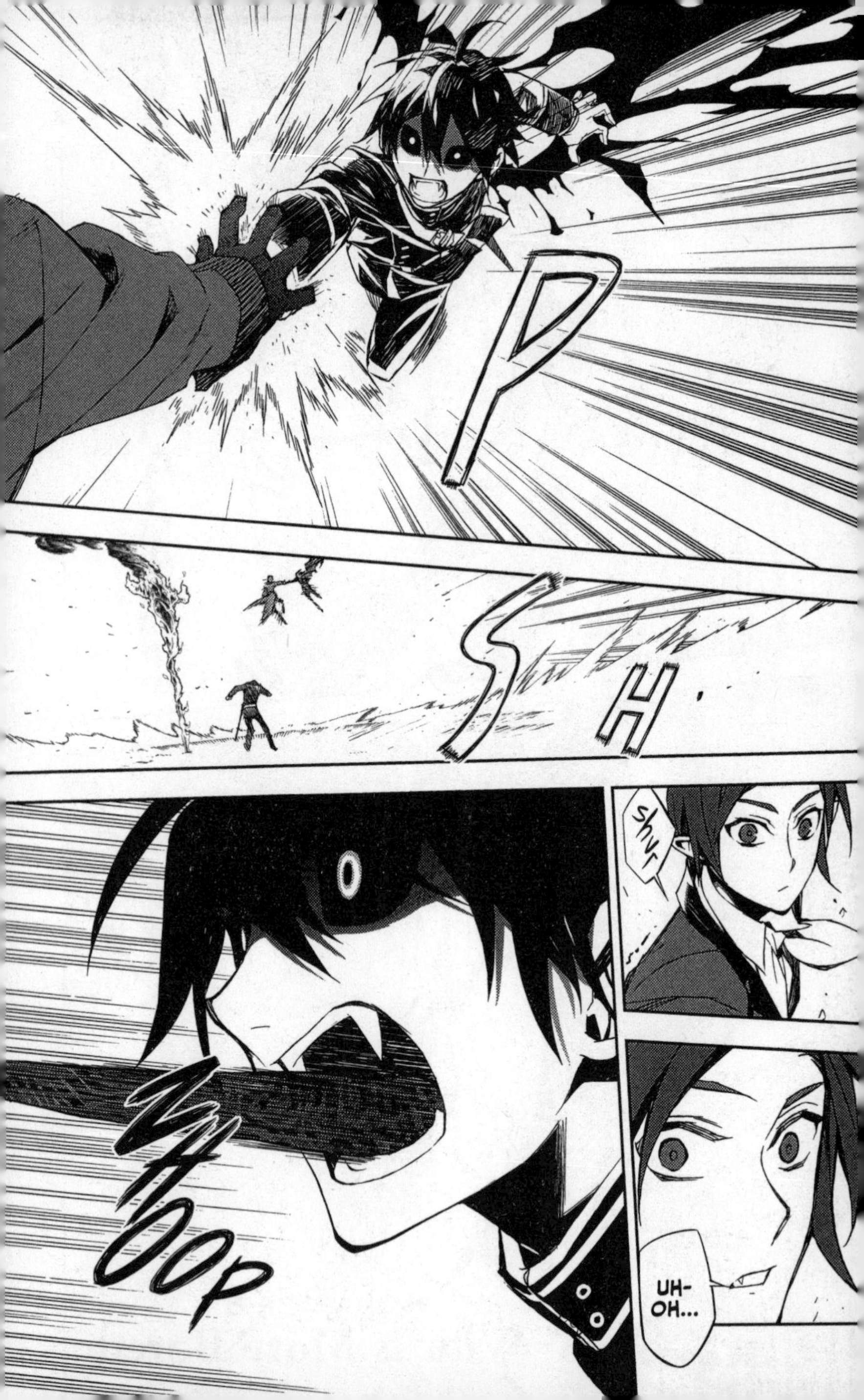

P
SH
shur
WHOOP
UH-
OH...

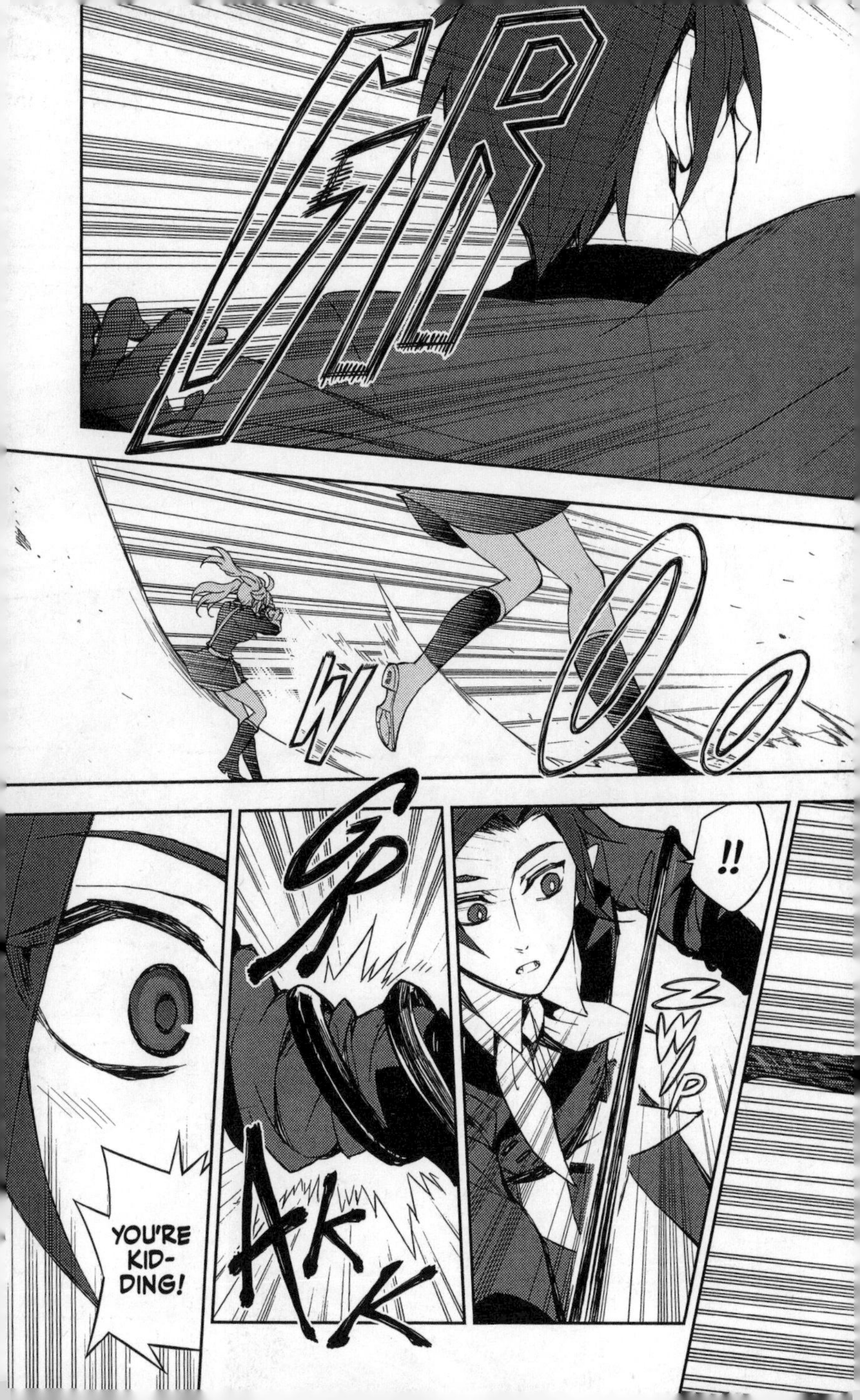
!!
YOU'RE KID-DING!

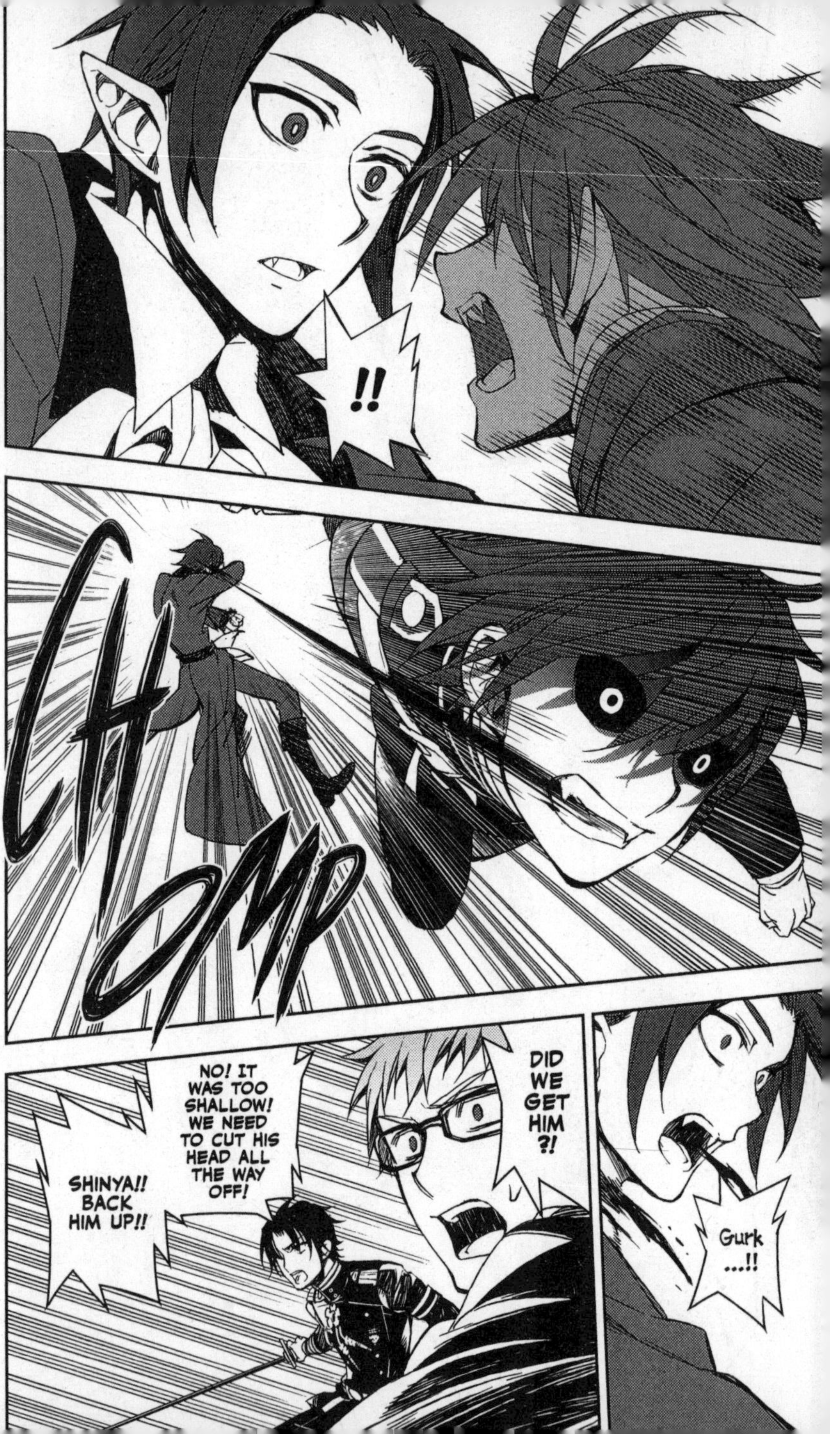
!!
CHOMP
Gurk ...!!
DID WE GET HIM?!
NO! IT WAS TOO SHALLOW! WE NEED TO CUT HIS HEAD ALL THE WAY OFF!
SHINYA!! BACK HIM UP!!

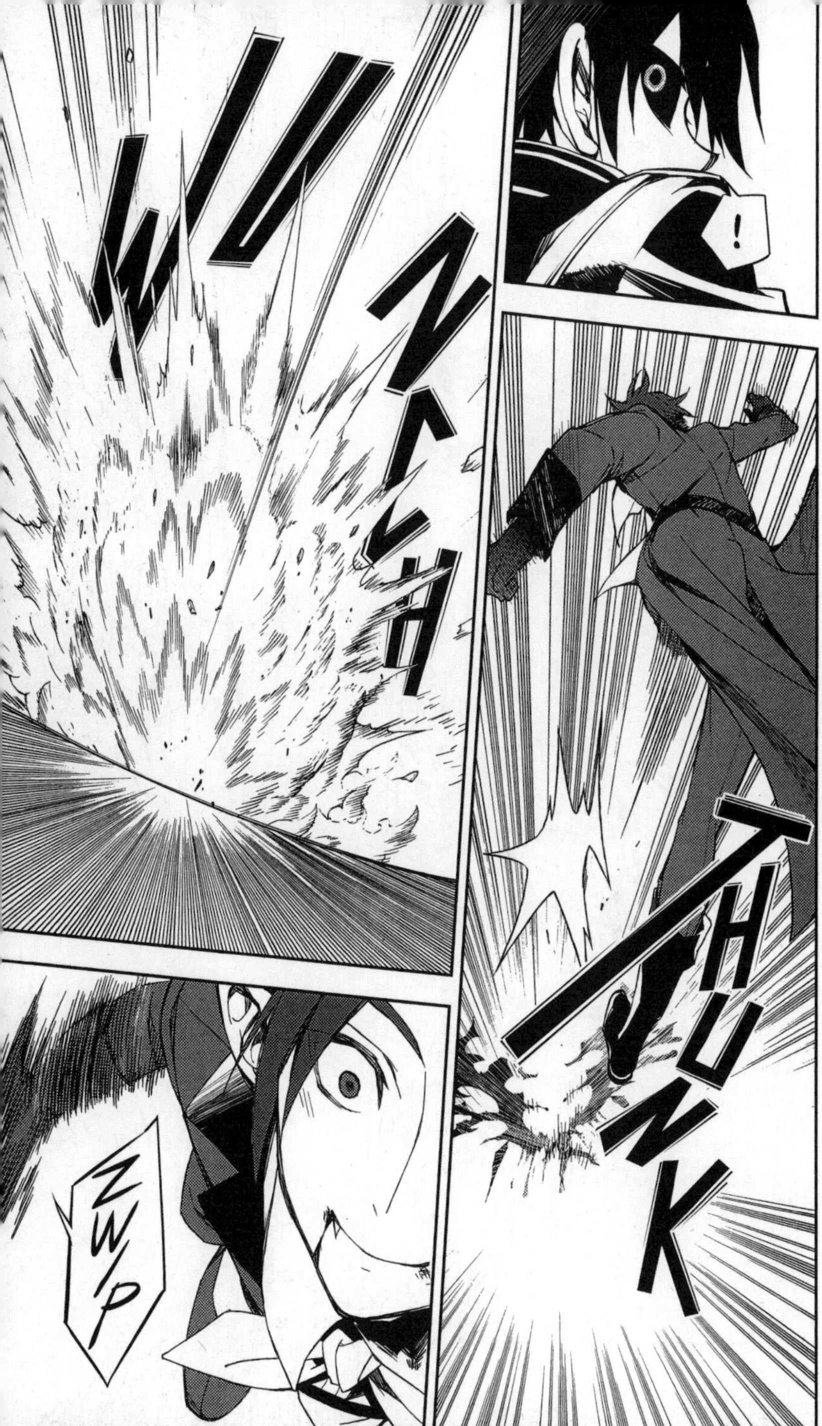
!
THUNK
WUNNNH
ZWIP

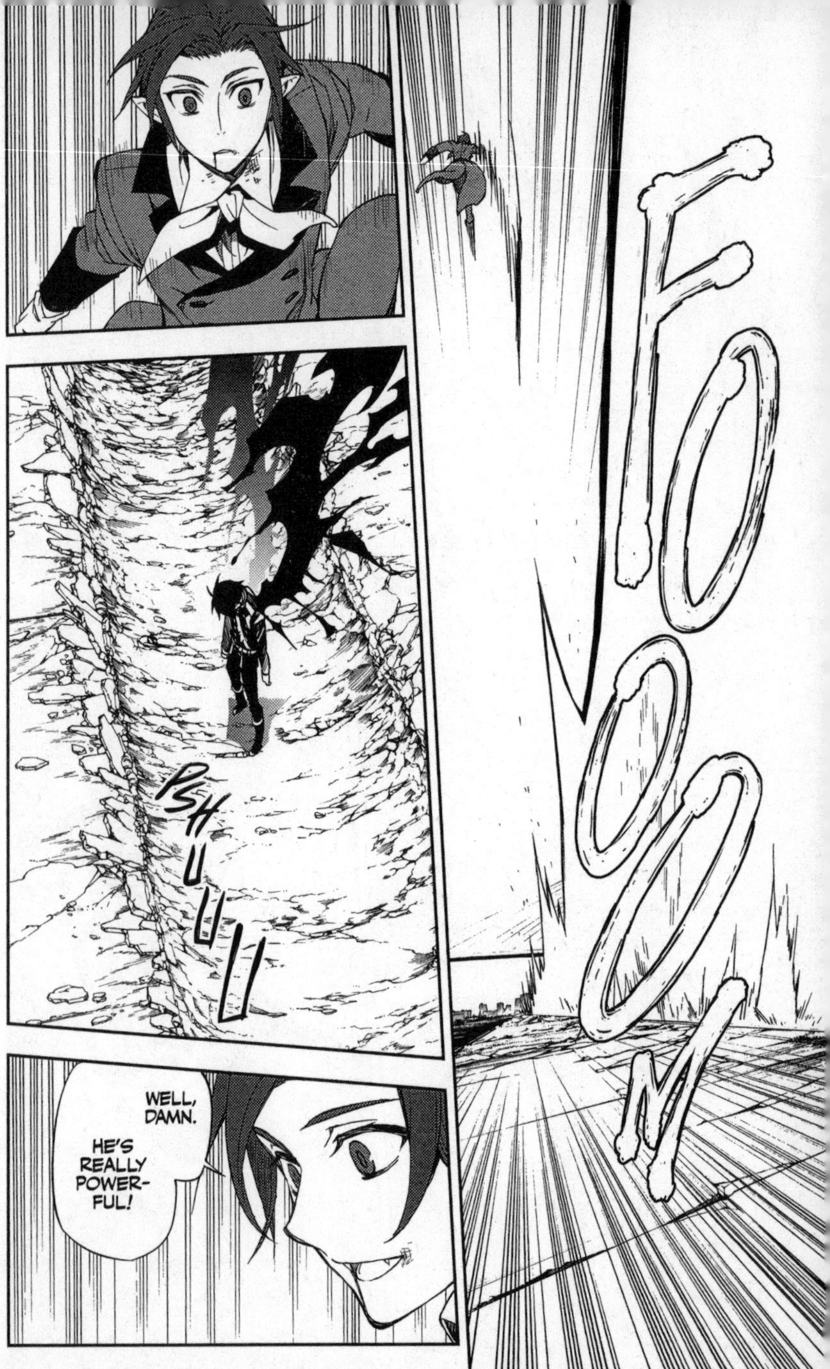
FOOOM
PSHUUU
WELL, DAMN.
HE'S REALLY POWER-FUL!

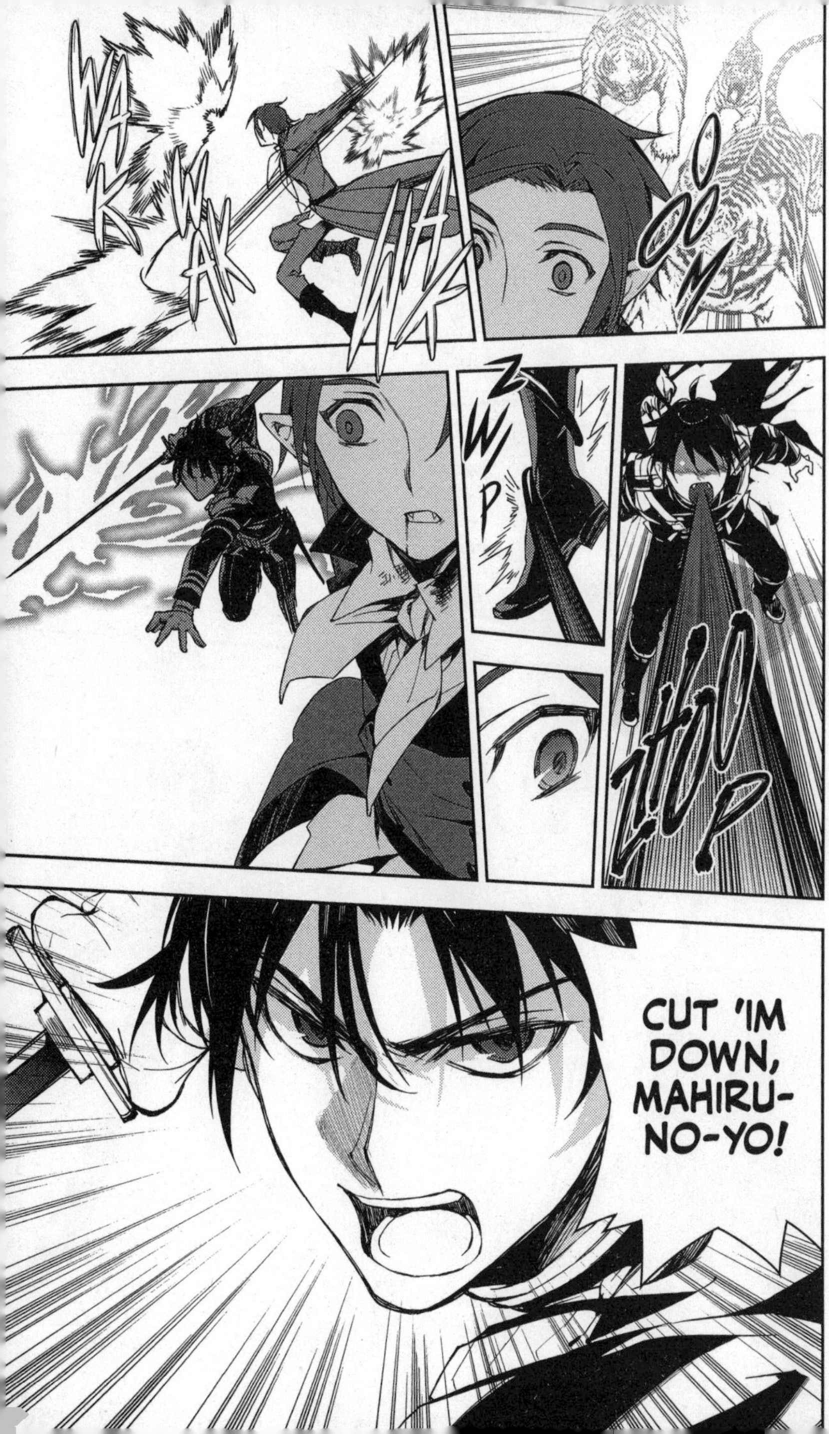
OOOOM
WHAK
WHAK
WHAK
ZHOOP
ZWIP
CUT 'IM DOWN, MAHIRU-NO-YO!

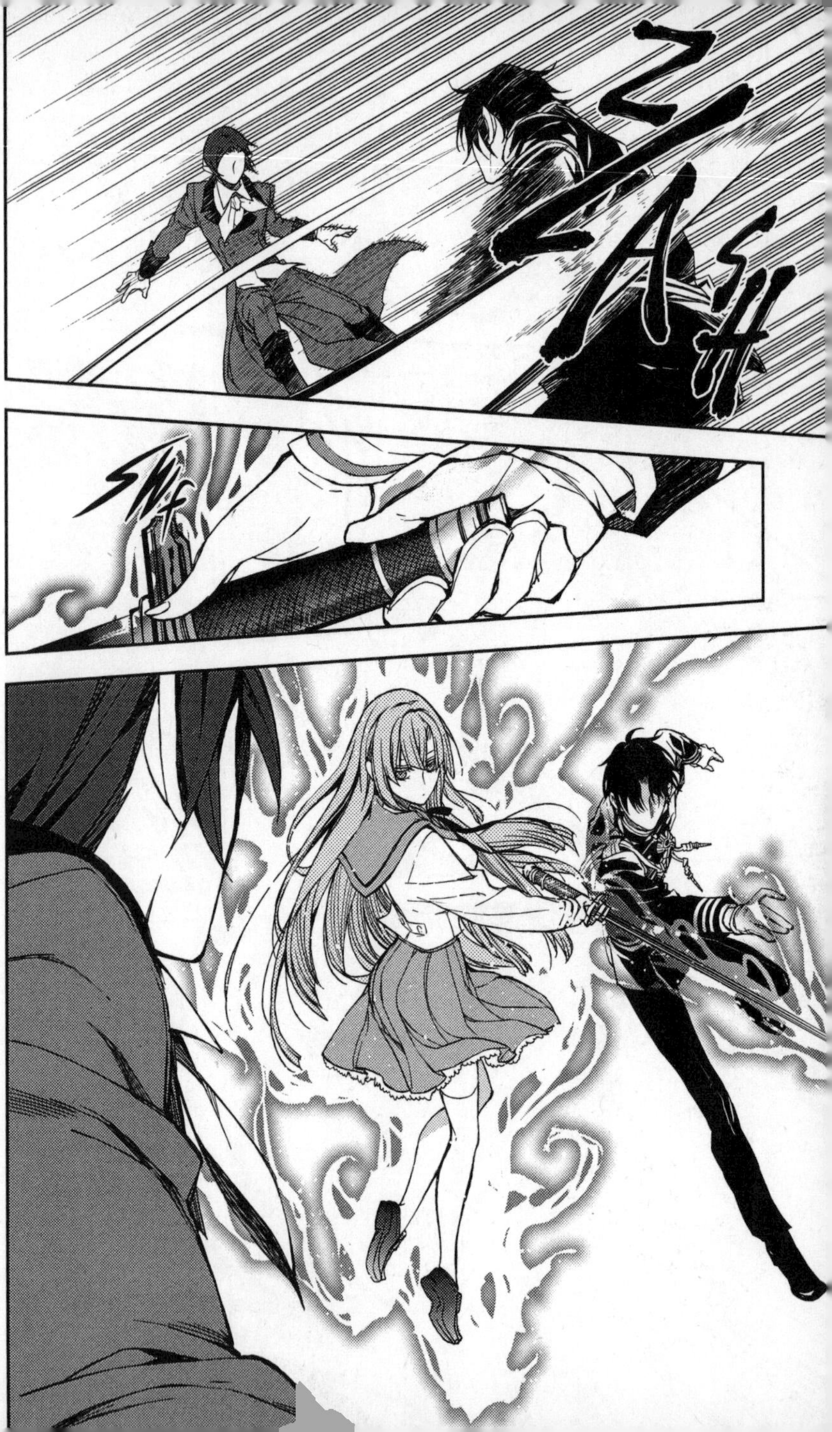
ZASH
SHF

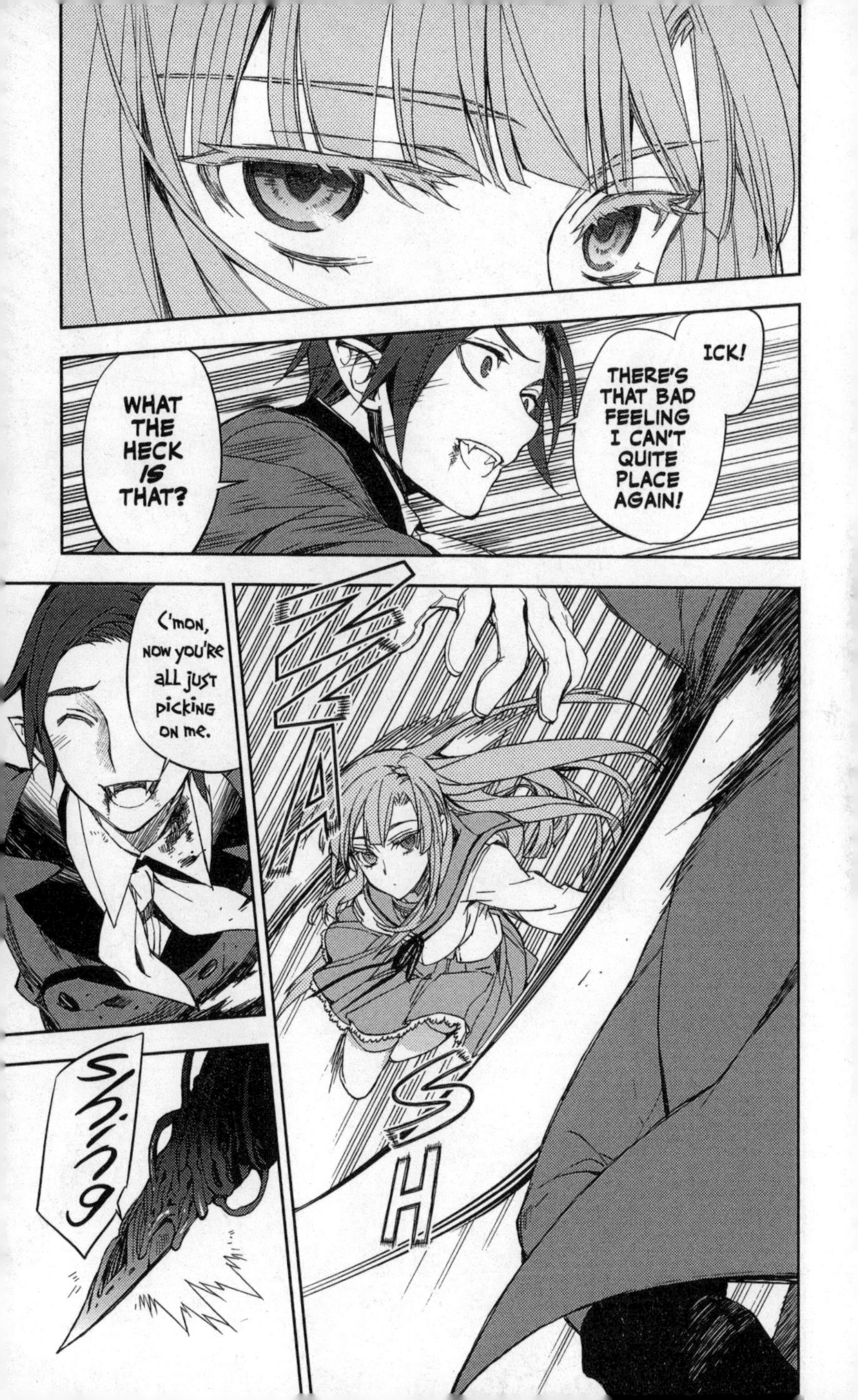
ICK!
THERE'S THAT BAD FEELING I CAN'T QUITE PLACE AGAIN!
WHAT THE HECK *IS* THAT?
WHASH
C'mon, now you're all just picking on me.
shing

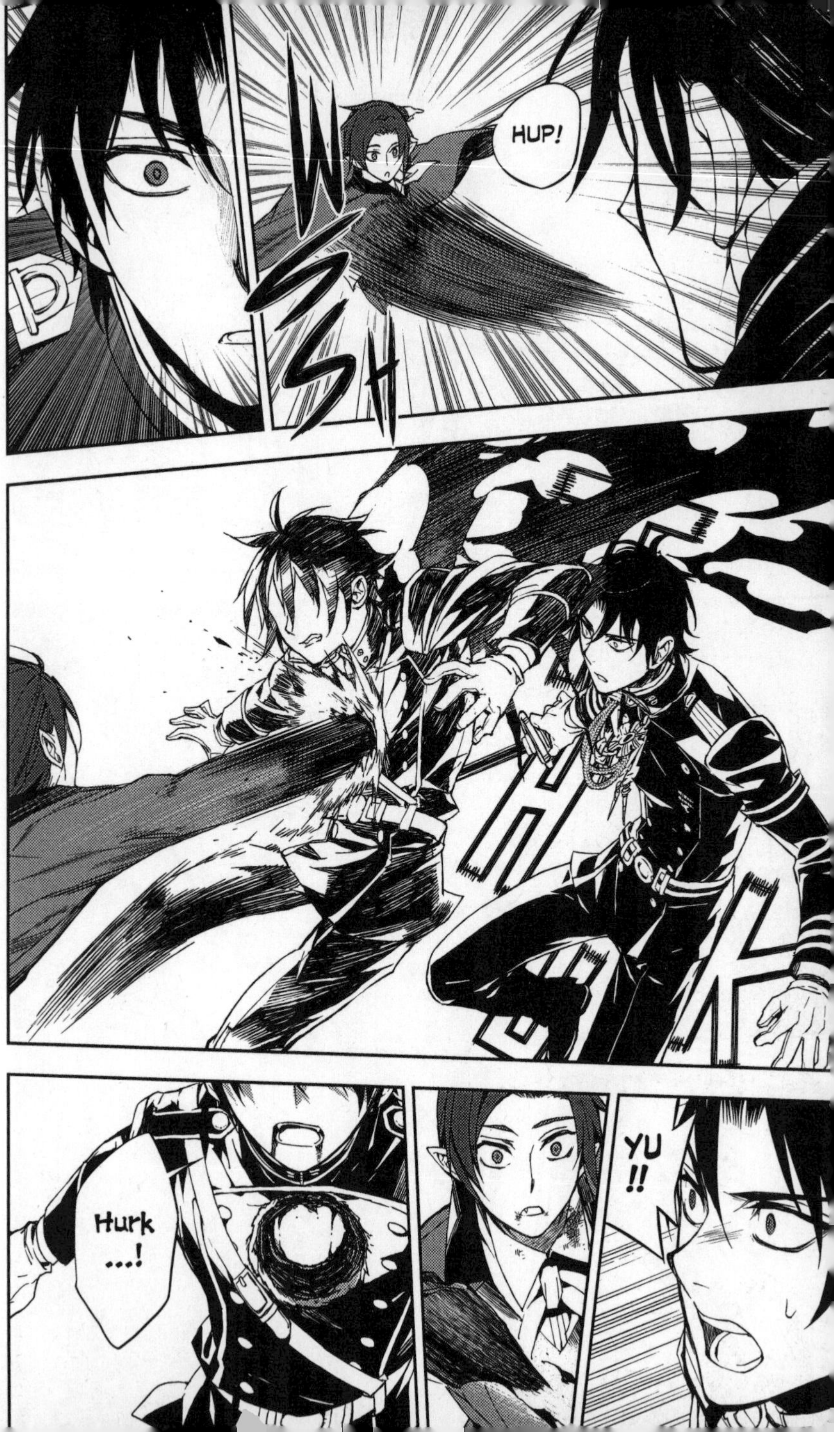
HUP!
WSSH
HK
YU!!
Hurk...!

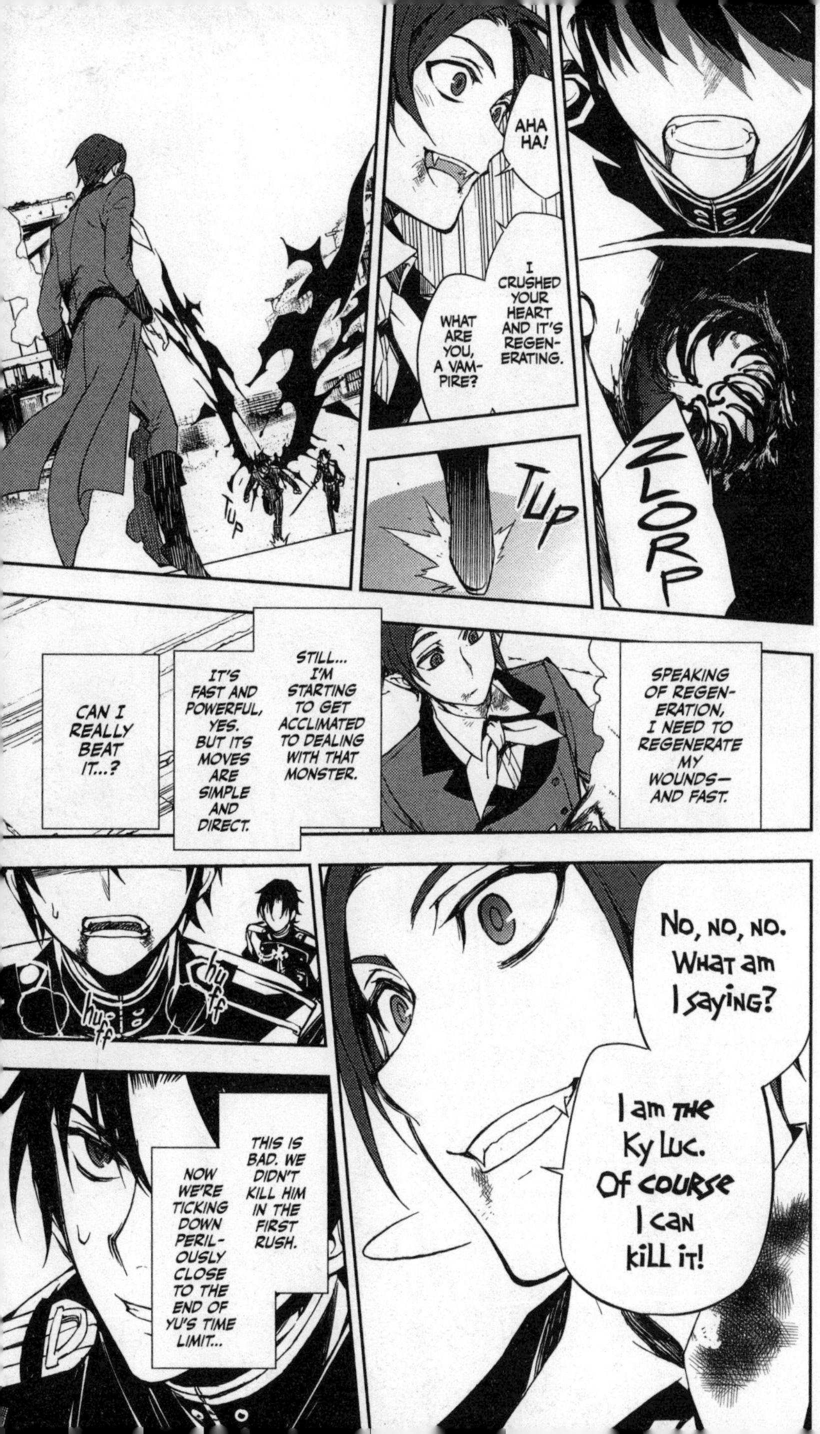
ZLORP
AHA HA!
I CRUSHED YOUR HEART AND IT'S REGEN-ERATING.
WHAT ARE YOU, A VAM-PIRE?
TUP
TUP
SPEAKING OF REGEN-ERATION, I NEED TO REGENERATE MY WOUNDS— AND FAST.
STILL... I'M STARTING TO GET ACCLIMATED TO DEALING WITH THAT MONSTER.
IT'S FAST AND POWERFUL, YES. BUT ITS MOVES ARE SIMPLE AND DIRECT.
CAN I REALLY BEAT IT...?
No, no, no. What am I saying?
I am the Ky Luc. Of course I can kill it!
huff huff
THIS IS BAD. WE DIDN'T KILL HIM IN THE FIRST RUSH.
NOW WE'RE TICKING DOWN PERIL-OUSLY CLOSE TO THE END OF YU'S TIME LIMIT...

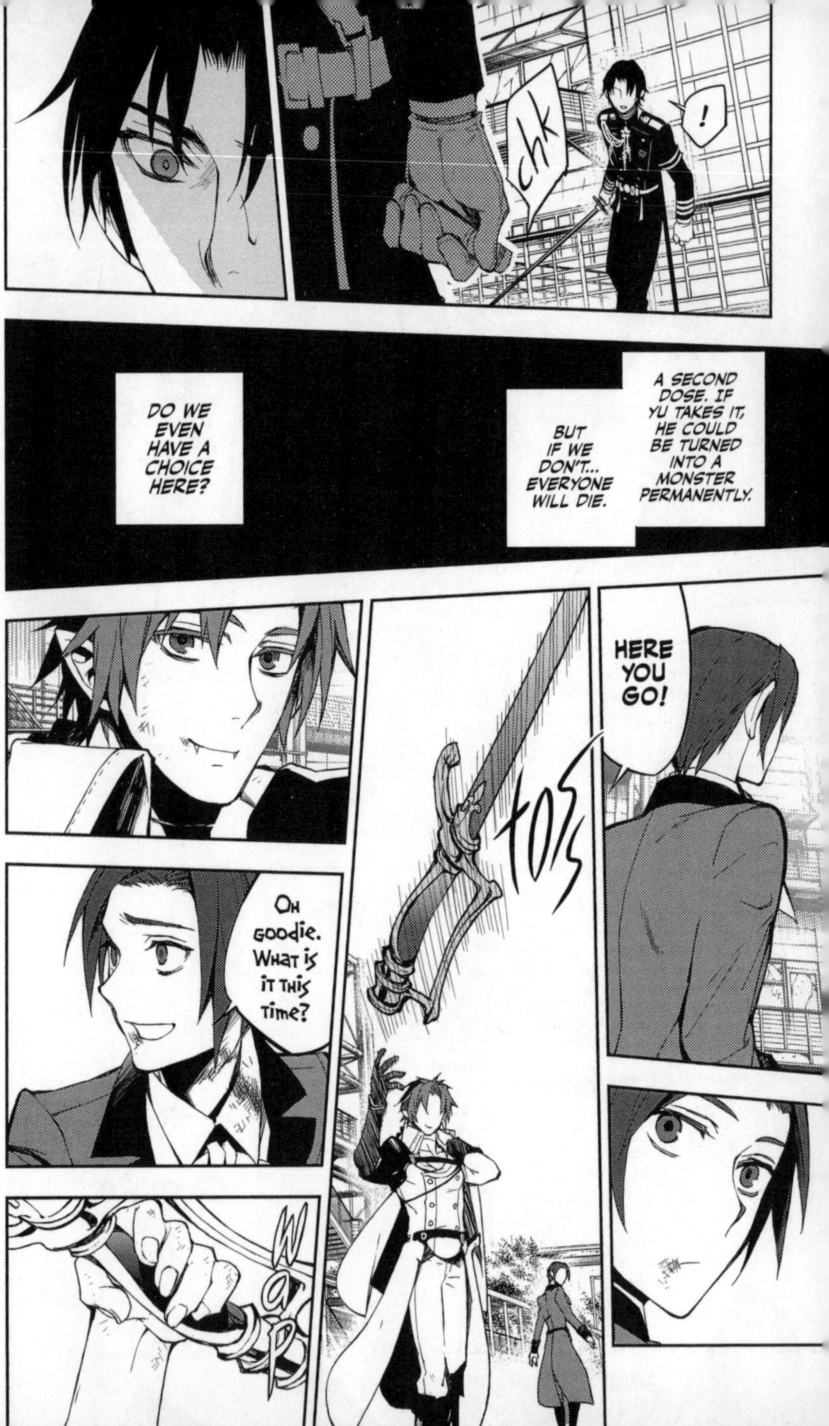
!
chk
A SECOND DOSE. IF YU TAKES IT, HE COULD BE TURNED INTO A MONSTER PERMANENTLY.
BUT IF WE DON'T... EVERYONE WILL DIE.
DO WE EVEN HAVE A CHOICE HERE?
HERE YOU GO!
toss
Oh goodie. What is it this time?
Wap

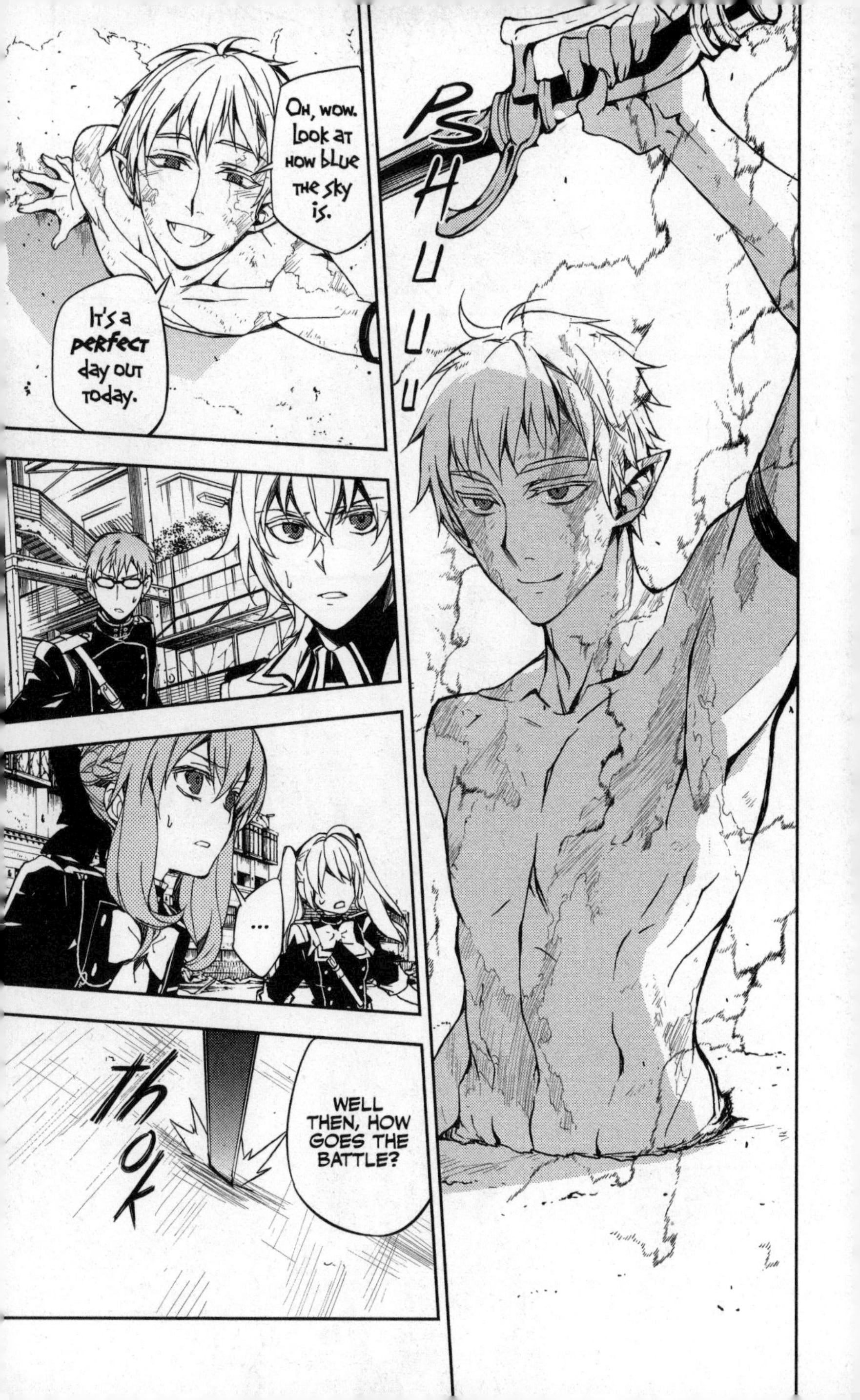
PSHUUUU
Oh, wow. Look at how blue the sky is.
It's a perfect day out today.
...
thok
WELL THEN, HOW GOES THE BATTLE?

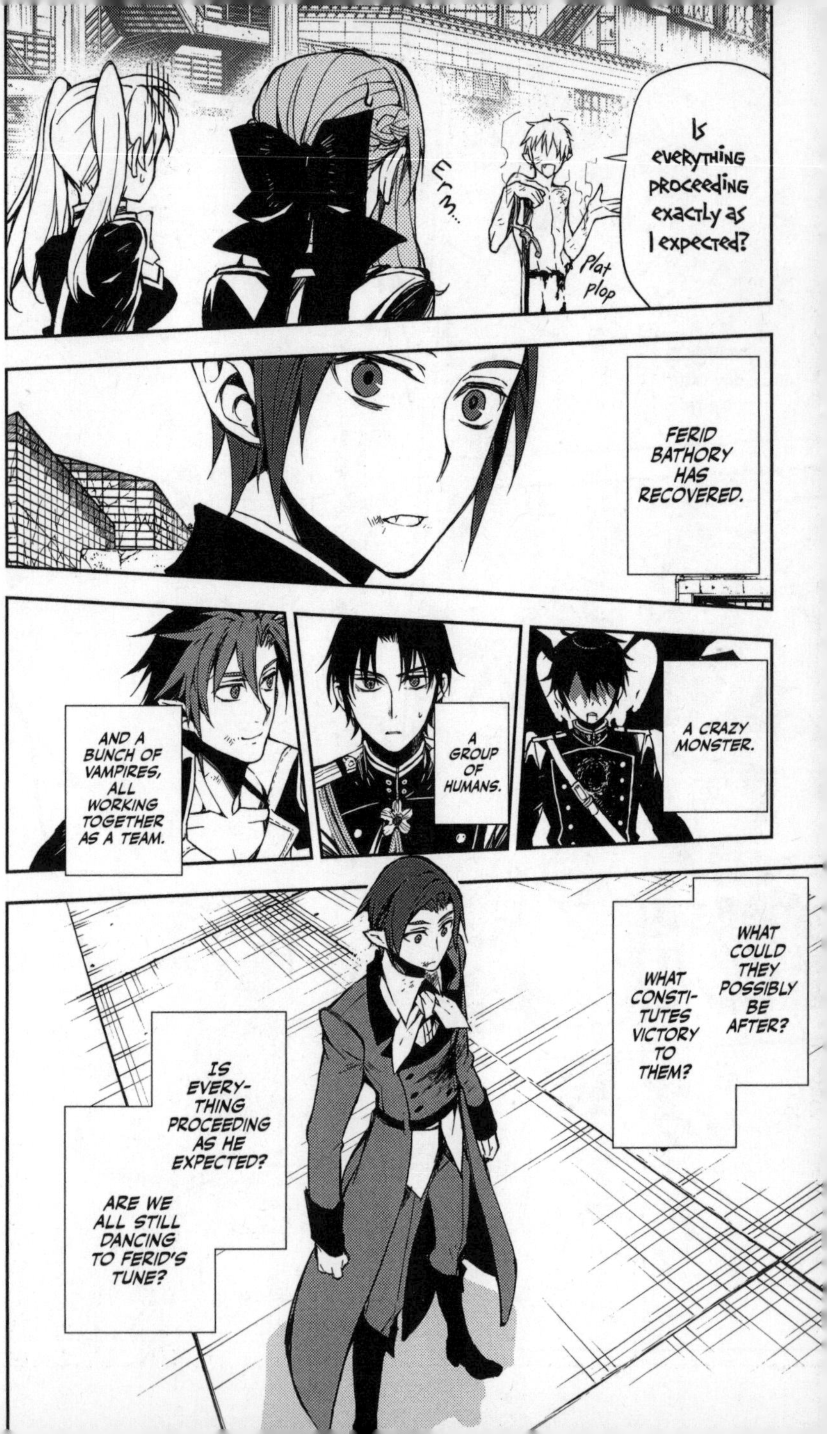
Is everything proceeding exactly as I expected?
Erm...
Plat plop
FERID BATHORY HAS RECOVERED.
A CRAZY MONSTER.
A GROUP OF HUMANS.
AND A BUNCH OF VAMPIRES, ALL WORKING TOGETHER AS A TEAM.
WHAT COULD THEY POSSIBLY BE AFTER?
WHAT CONSTITUTES VICTORY TO THEM?
IS EVERYTHING PROCEEDING AS HE EXPECTED?
ARE WE ALL STILL DANCING TO FERID'S TUNE?

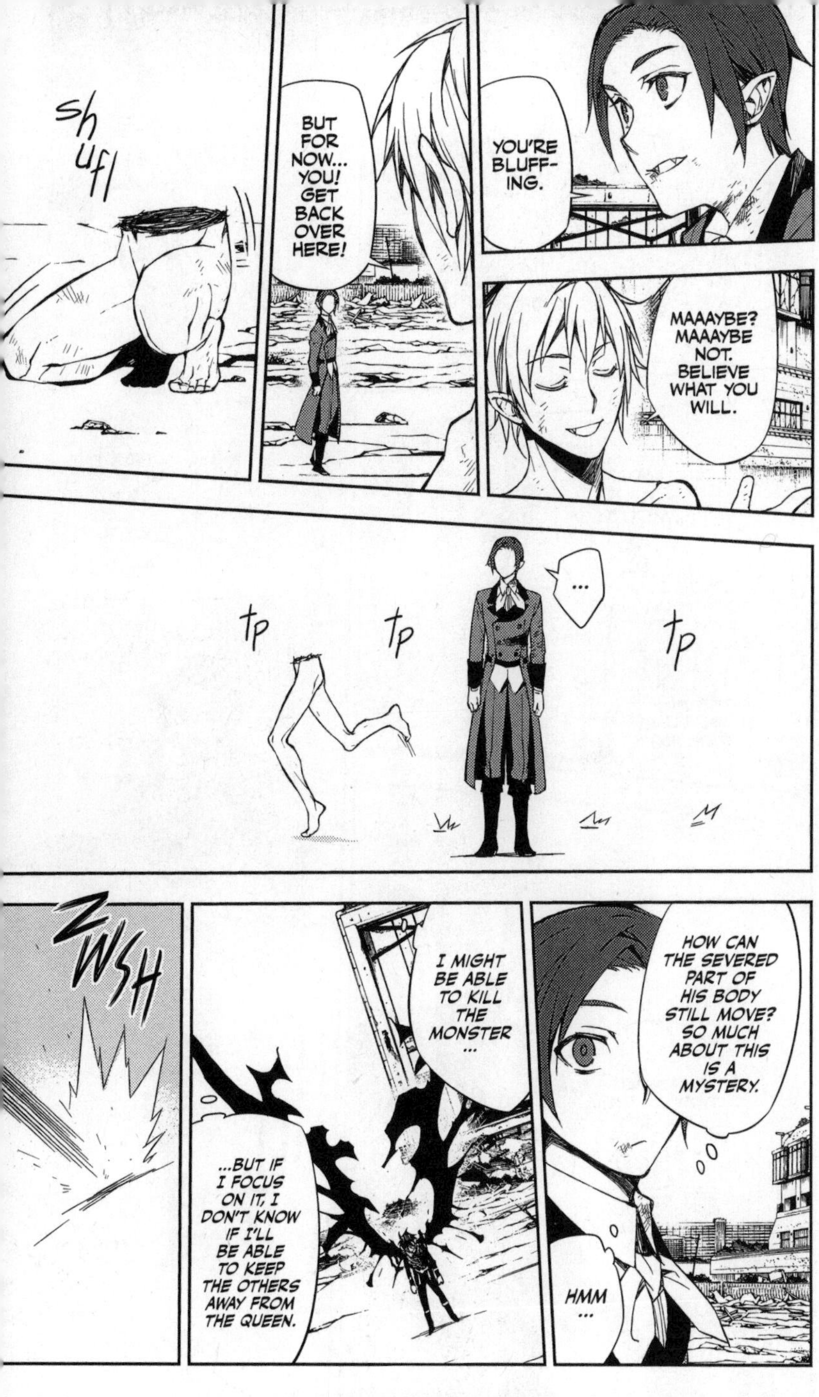
YOU'RE BLUFF-ING.
MAAAYBE? MAAAYBE NOT. BELIEVE WHAT YOU WILL.
BUT FOR NOW... YOU! GET BACK OVER HERE!
shufl
tp
...
tp
tp
HOW CAN THE SEVERED PART OF HIS BODY STILL MOVE? SO MUCH ABOUT THIS IS A MYSTERY.
HMM...
I MIGHT BE ABLE TO KILL THE MONSTER...
...BUT IF I FOCUS ON IT, I DON'T KNOW IF I'LL BE ABLE TO KEEP THE OTHERS AWAY FROM THE QUEEN.
ZWSH

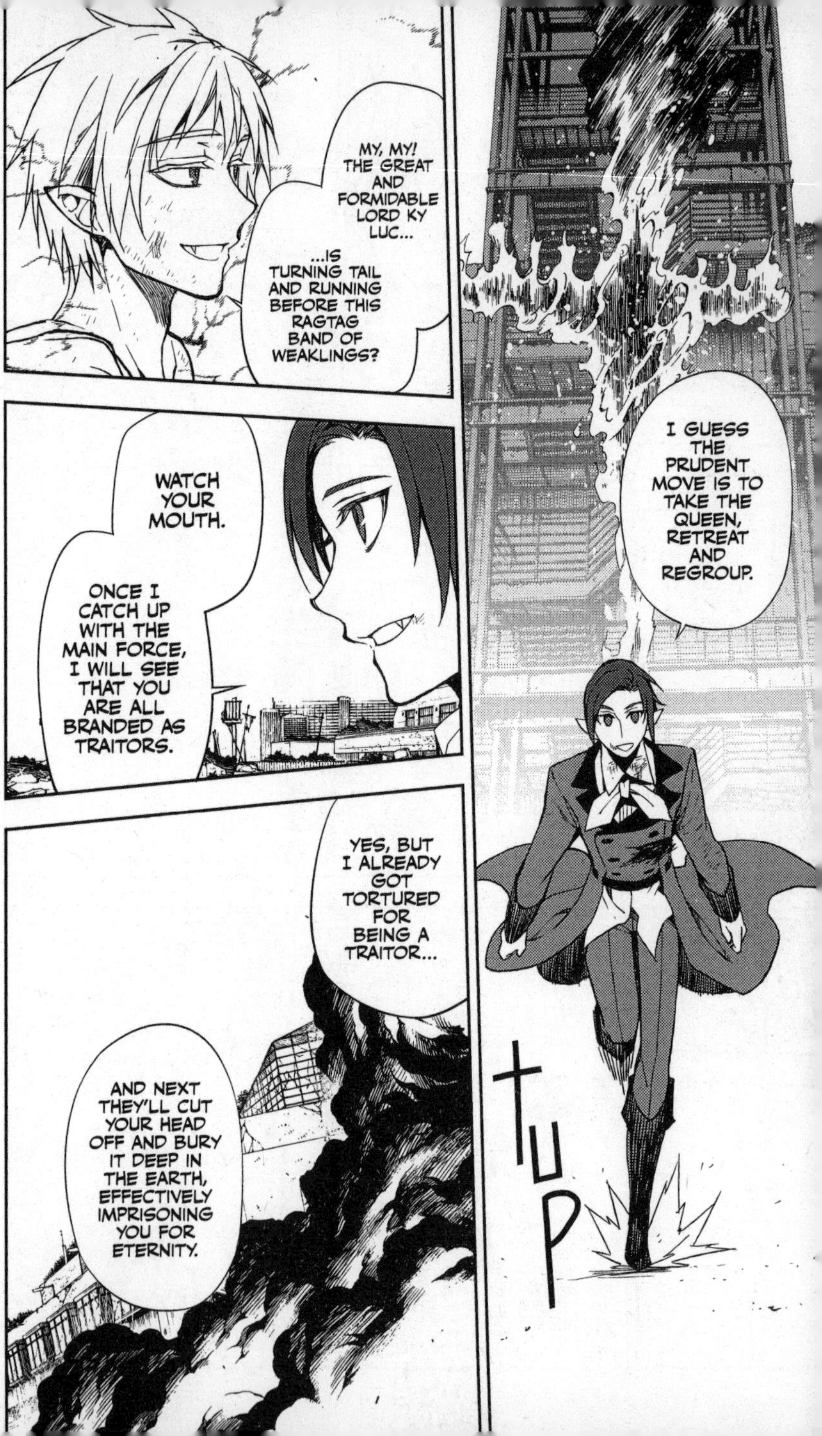
I GUESS THE PRUDENT MOVE IS TO TAKE THE QUEEN, RETREAT AND REGROUP.
TUP
MY, MY! THE GREAT AND FORMIDABLE LORD KY LUC...
...IS TURNING TAIL AND RUNNING BEFORE THIS RAGTAG BAND OF WEAKLINGS?
WATCH YOUR MOUTH.
ONCE I CATCH UP WITH THE MAIN FORCE, I WILL SEE THAT YOU ARE ALL BRANDED AS TRAITORS.
YES, BUT I ALREADY GOT TORTURED FOR BEING A TRAITOR...
AND NEXT THEY'LL CUT YOUR HEAD OFF AND BURY IT DEEP IN THE EARTH, EFFECTIVELY IMPRISONING YOU FOR ETERNITY.

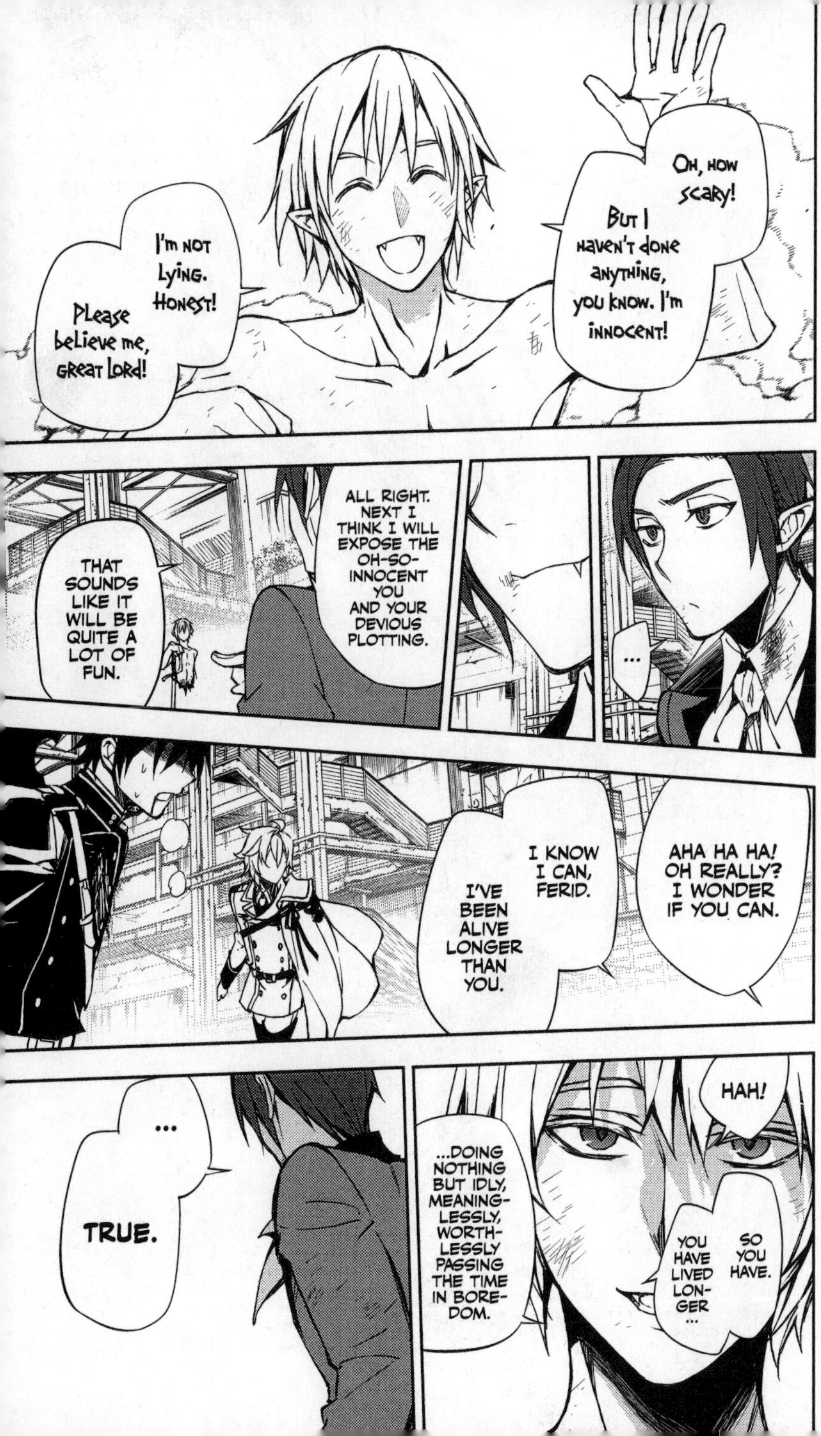
Oh, how scary! But I haven't done anything, you know. I'm innocent!
I'm not lying. Honest! Please believe me, great Lord!
...
ALL RIGHT. NEXT I THINK I WILL EXPOSE THE OH-SO-INNOCENT YOU AND YOUR DEVIOUS PLOTTING.
THAT SOUNDS LIKE IT WILL BE QUITE A LOT OF FUN.
AHA HA HA! OH REALLY? I WONDER IF YOU CAN.
I KNOW I CAN, FERID.
I'VE BEEN ALIVE LONGER THAN YOU.
HAH!
SO YOU HAVE.
YOU HAVE LIVED LONGER...
...DOING NOTHING BUT IDLY, MEANINGLESSLY, WORTHLESSLY PASSING THE TIME IN BOREDOM.
...
TRUE.

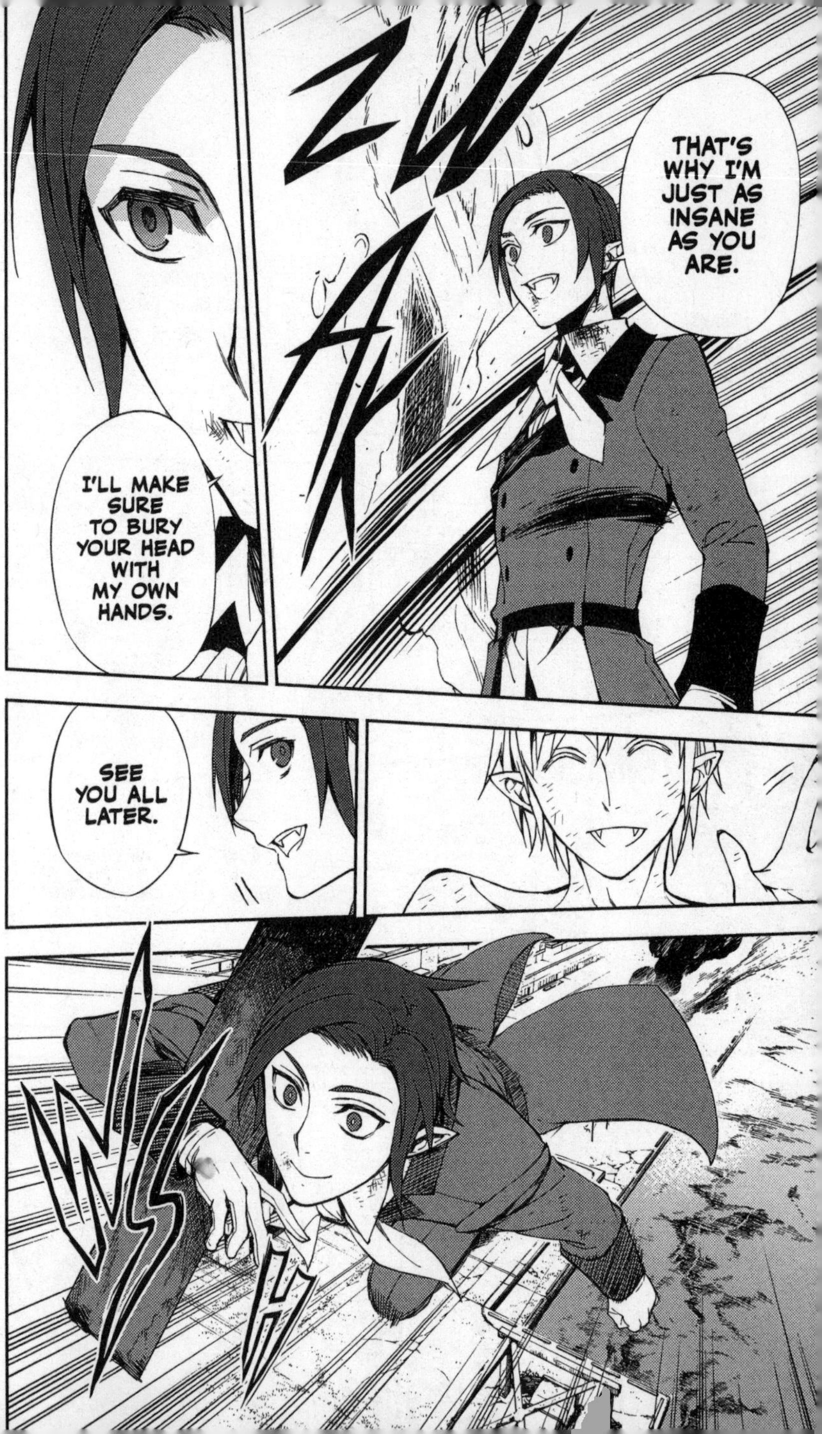
THAT'S WHY I'M JUST AS INSANE AS YOU ARE.
ZWAK
I'LL MAKE SURE TO BURY YOUR HEAD WITH MY OWN HANDS.
SEE YOU ALL LATER.

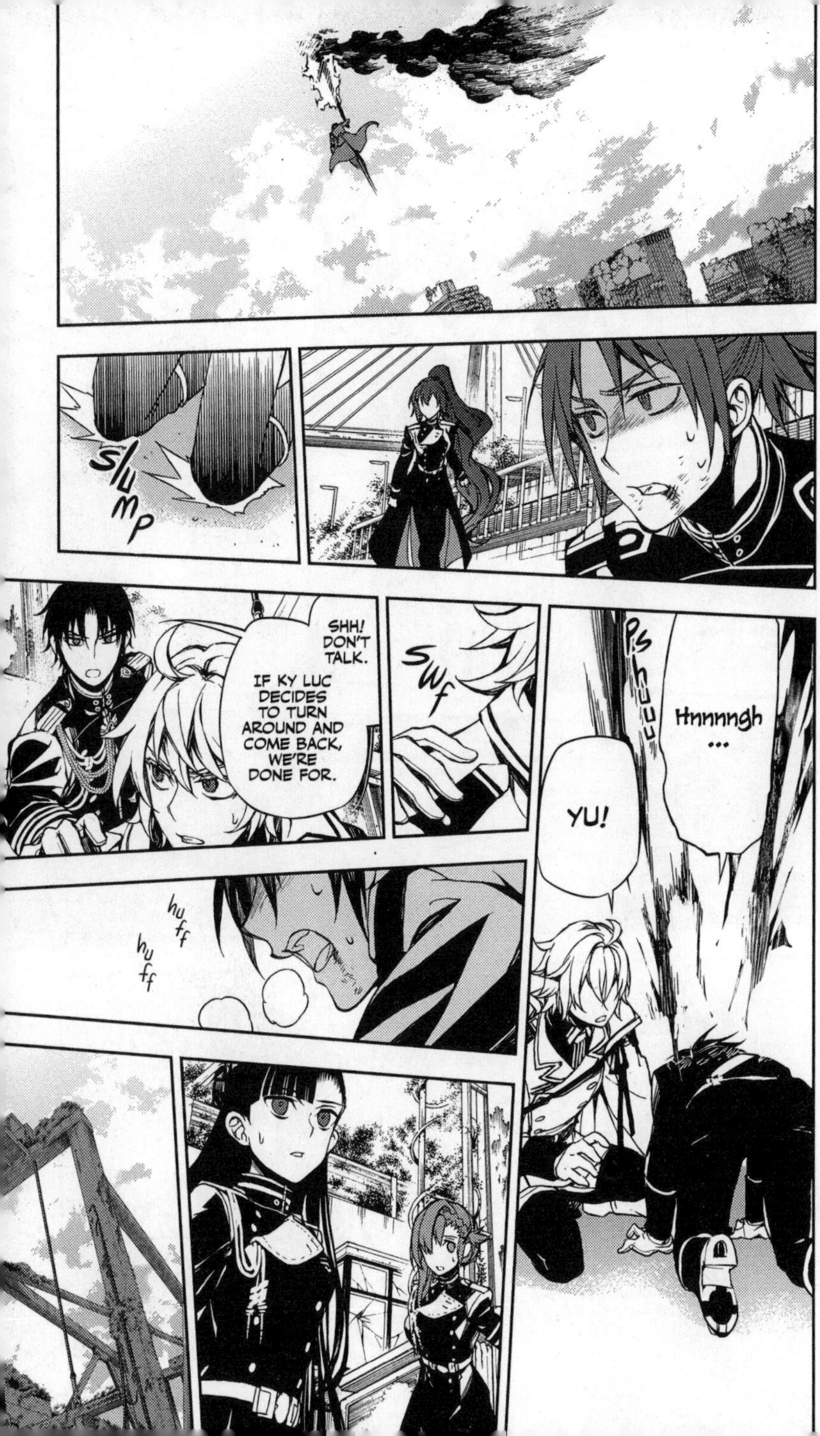
slump
Pshuuu
Hnnnngh...
YU!
Swf
SHH! DON'T TALK.
IF KY LUC DECIDES TO TURN AROUND AND COME BACK, WE'RE DONE FOR.
huff huff

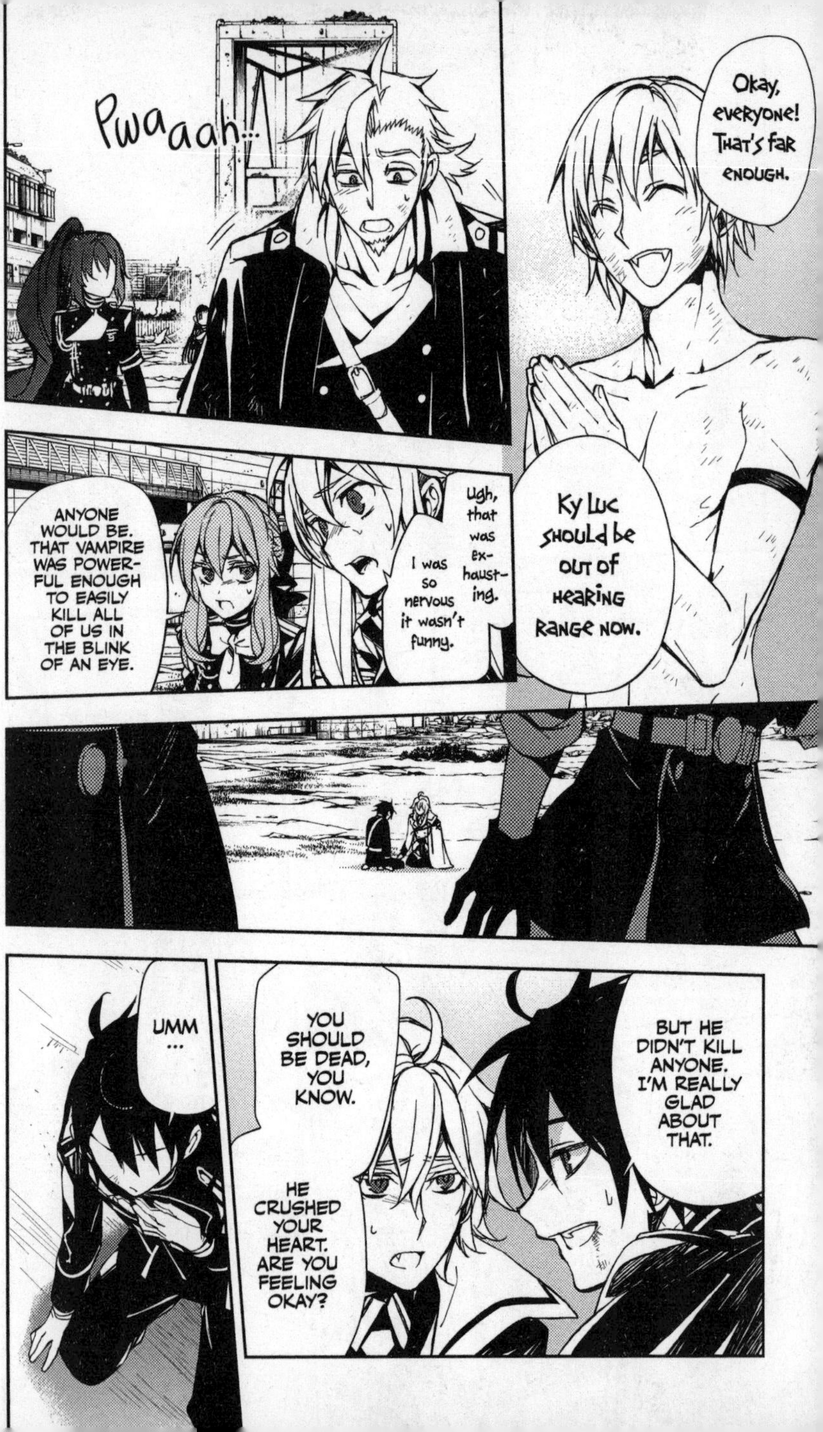
Okay, everyone! That's far enough.
Ky Luc should be out of hearing range now.
Pwaaaah...
Ugh, that was exhausting.
I was so nervous it wasn't funny.
ANYONE WOULD BE. THAT VAMPIRE WAS POWERFUL ENOUGH TO EASILY KILL ALL OF US IN THE BLINK OF AN EYE.
BUT HE DIDN'T KILL ANYONE. I'M REALLY GLAD ABOUT THAT.
YOU SHOULD BE DEAD, YOU KNOW.
HE CRUSHED YOUR HEART. ARE YOU FEELING OKAY?
UMM ...

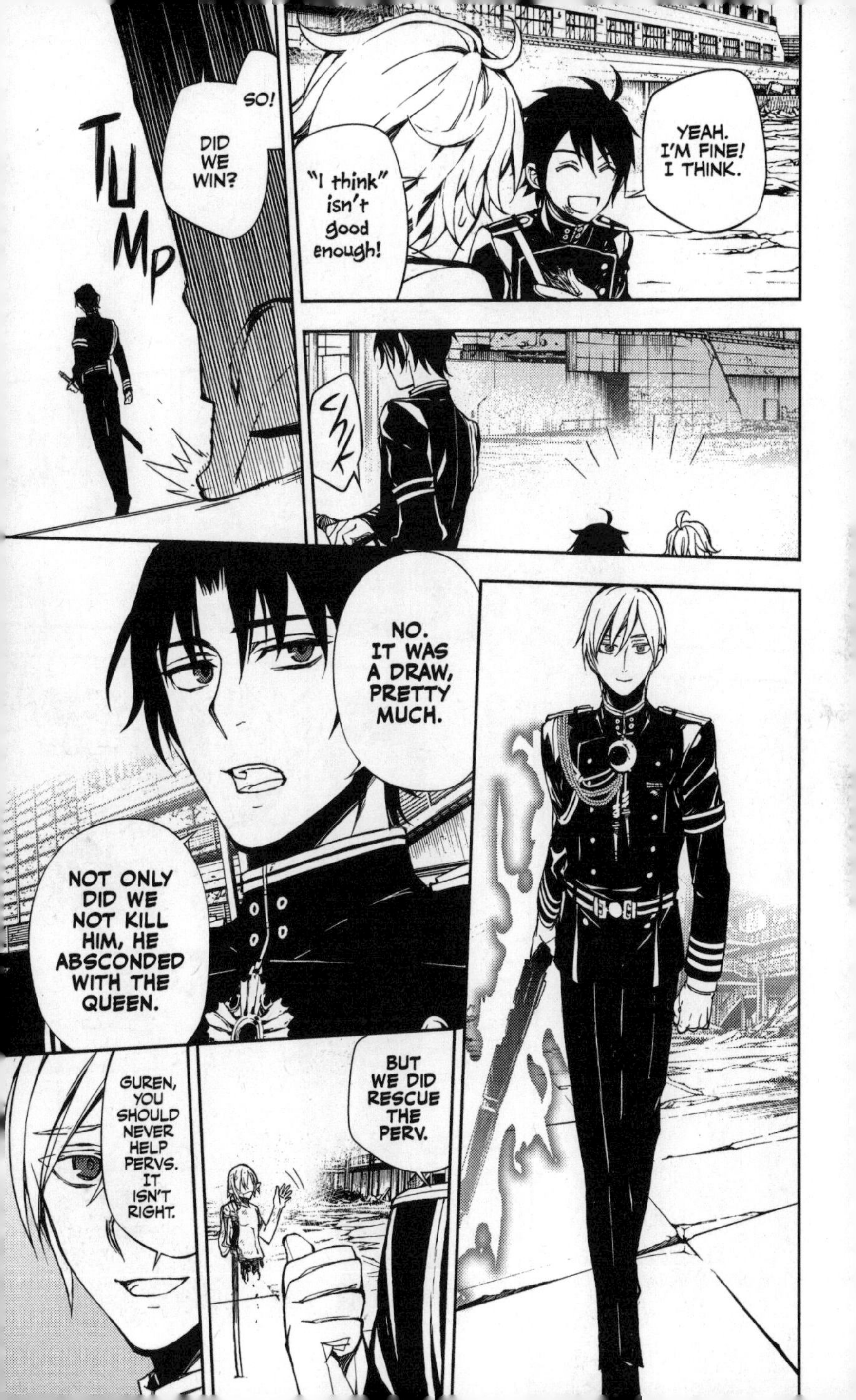
YEAH. I'M FINE! I THINK.
"I think" isn't good enough!
CRIK
SO!
DID WE WIN?
TUMP
NO. IT WAS A DRAW, PRETTY MUCH.
NOT ONLY DID WE NOT KILL HIM, HE ABSCONDED WITH THE QUEEN.
BUT WE DID RESCUE THE PERV.
GUREN, YOU SHOULD NEVER HELP PERVS. IT ISN'T RIGHT.

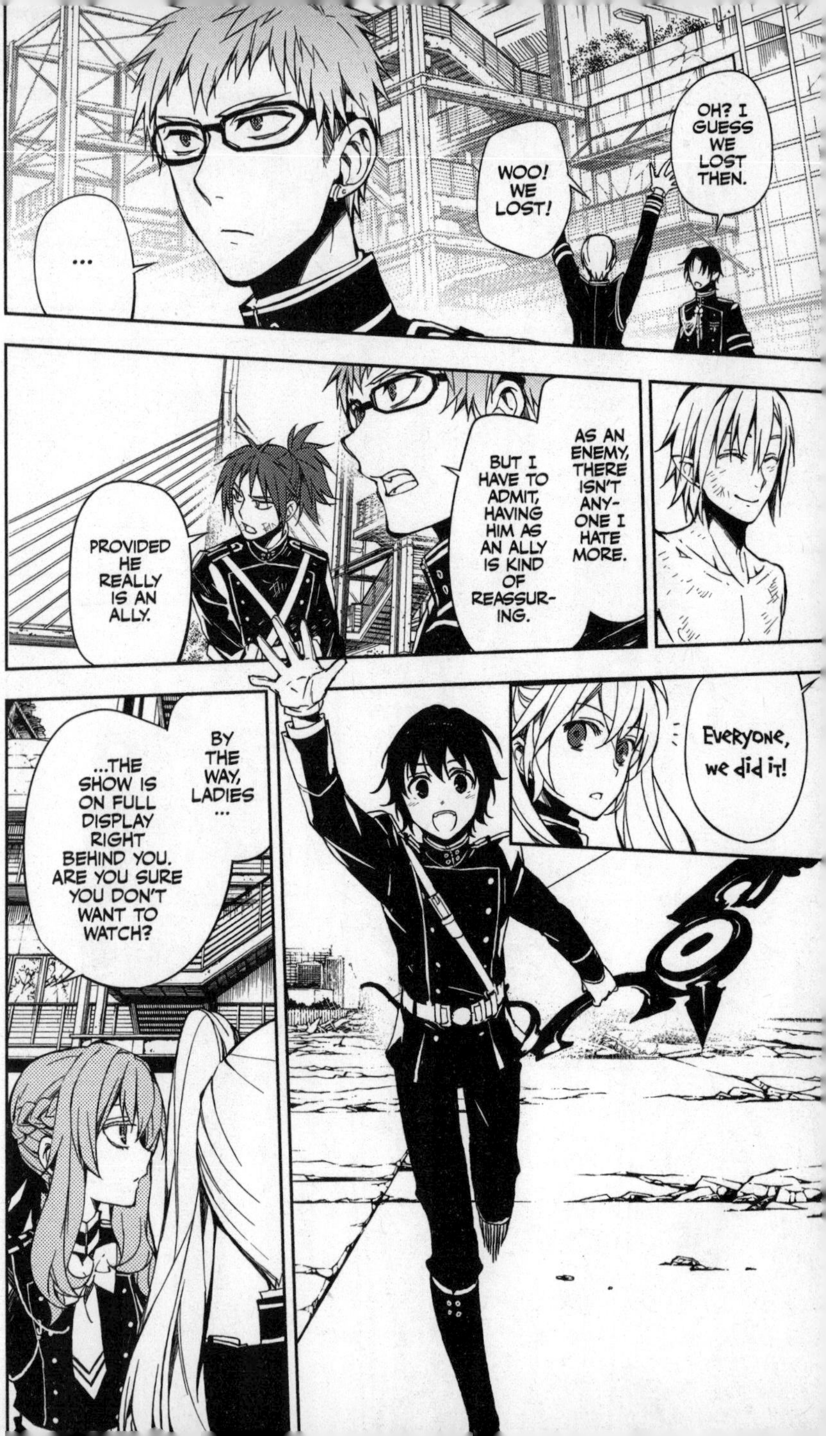
OH? I GUESS WE LOST THEN.
WOO! WE LOST!
...
AS AN ENEMY, THERE ISN'T ANYONE I HATE MORE.
BUT I HAVE TO ADMIT, HAVING HIM AS AN ALLY IS KIND OF REASSURING.
PROVIDED HE REALLY IS AN ALLY.
Everyone, we did it!
BY THE WAY, LADIES...
...THE SHOW IS ON FULL DISPLAY RIGHT BEHIND YOU. ARE YOU SURE YOU DON'T WANT TO WATCH?

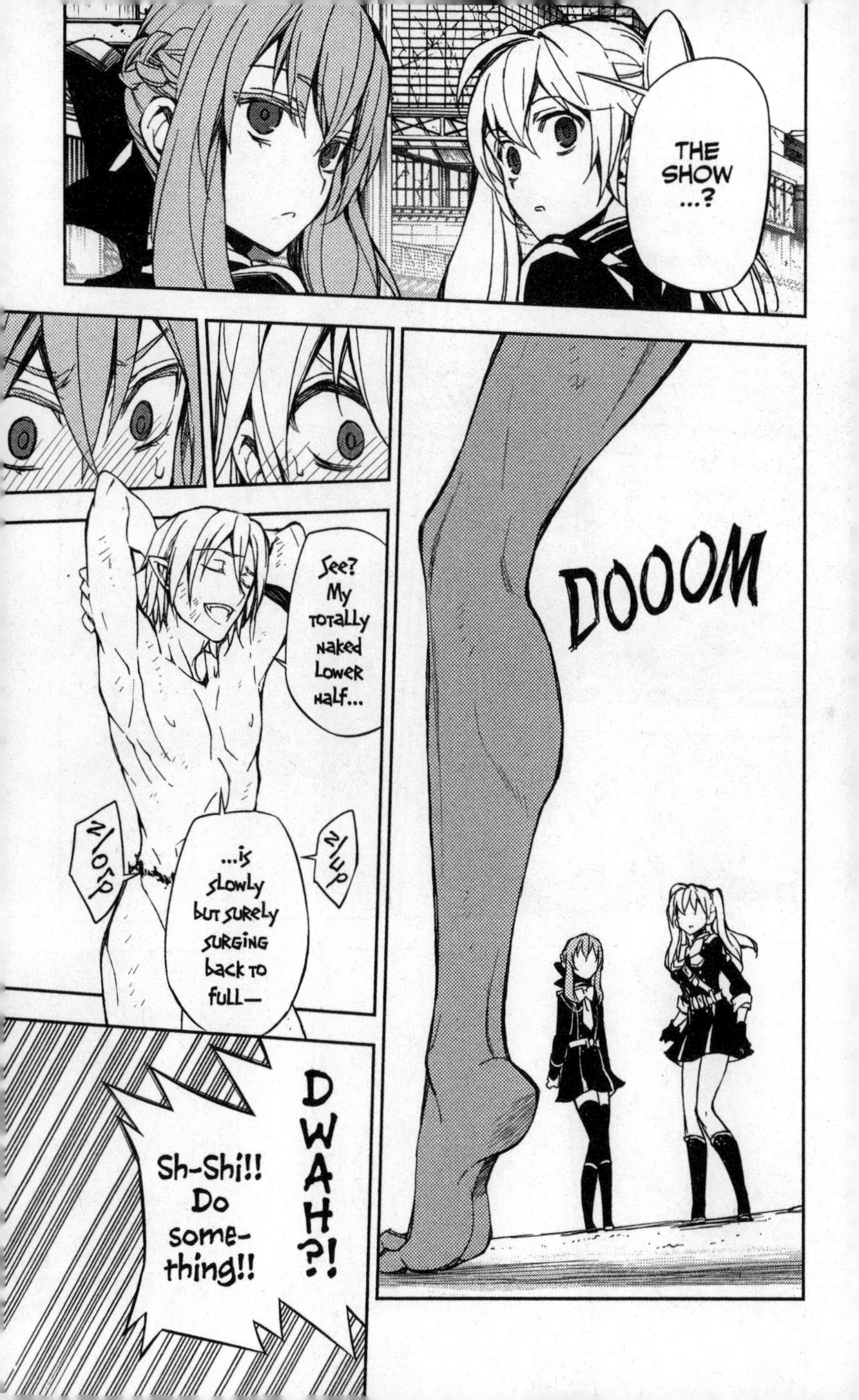
THE SHOW ...?
DOOOM
See? My totally naked lower half...
zlup
...is slowly but surely surging back to full—
zlorp
DWAH?!
Sh-Shi!! Do some-thing!!

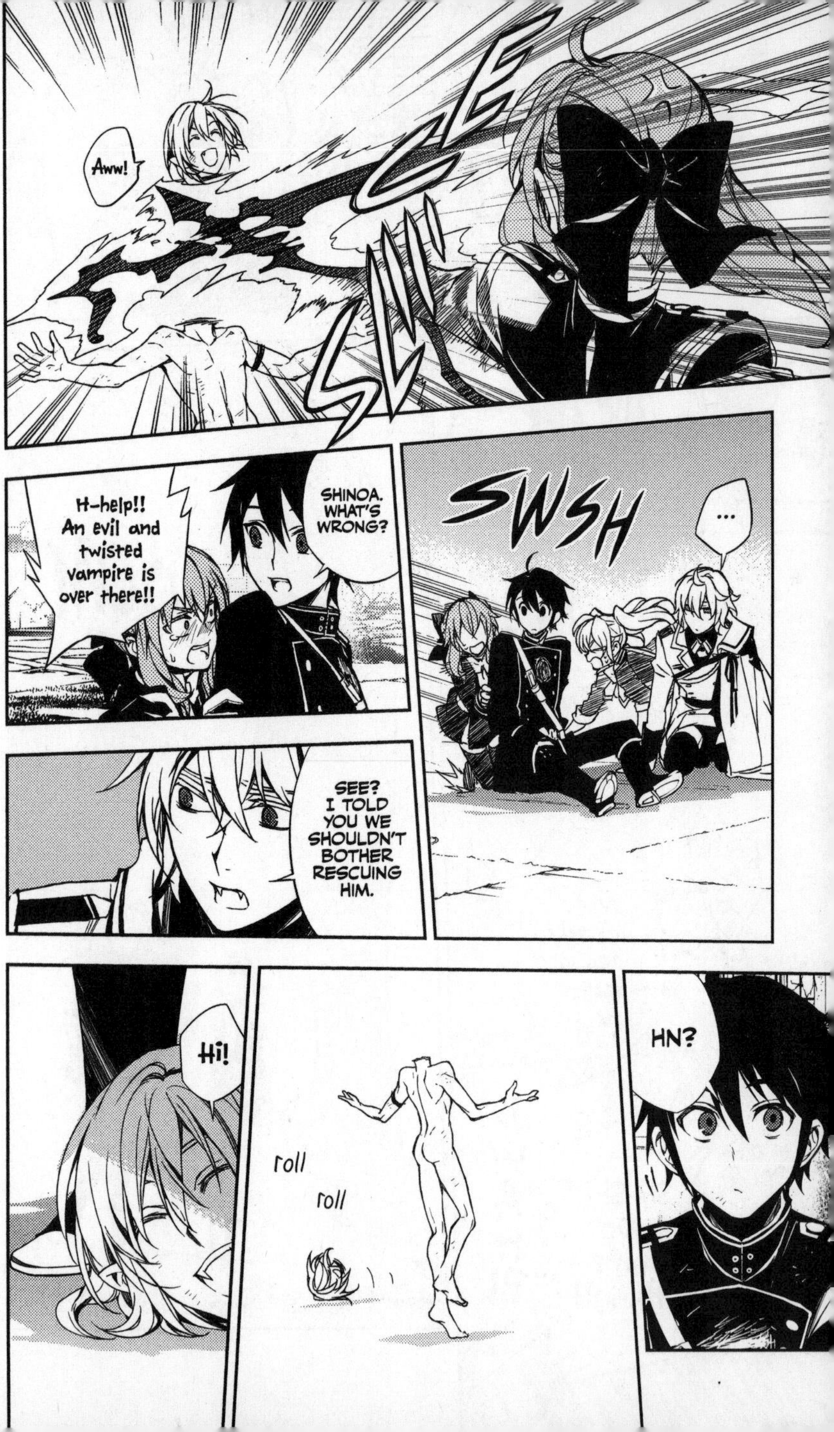
SLICE
Aww!
SWSH
...
SHINOA. WHAT'S WRONG?
H-help!! An evil and twisted vampire is over there!!
SEE? I TOLD YOU WE SHOULDN'T BOTHER RESCUING HIM.
HN?
roll
roll
Hi!

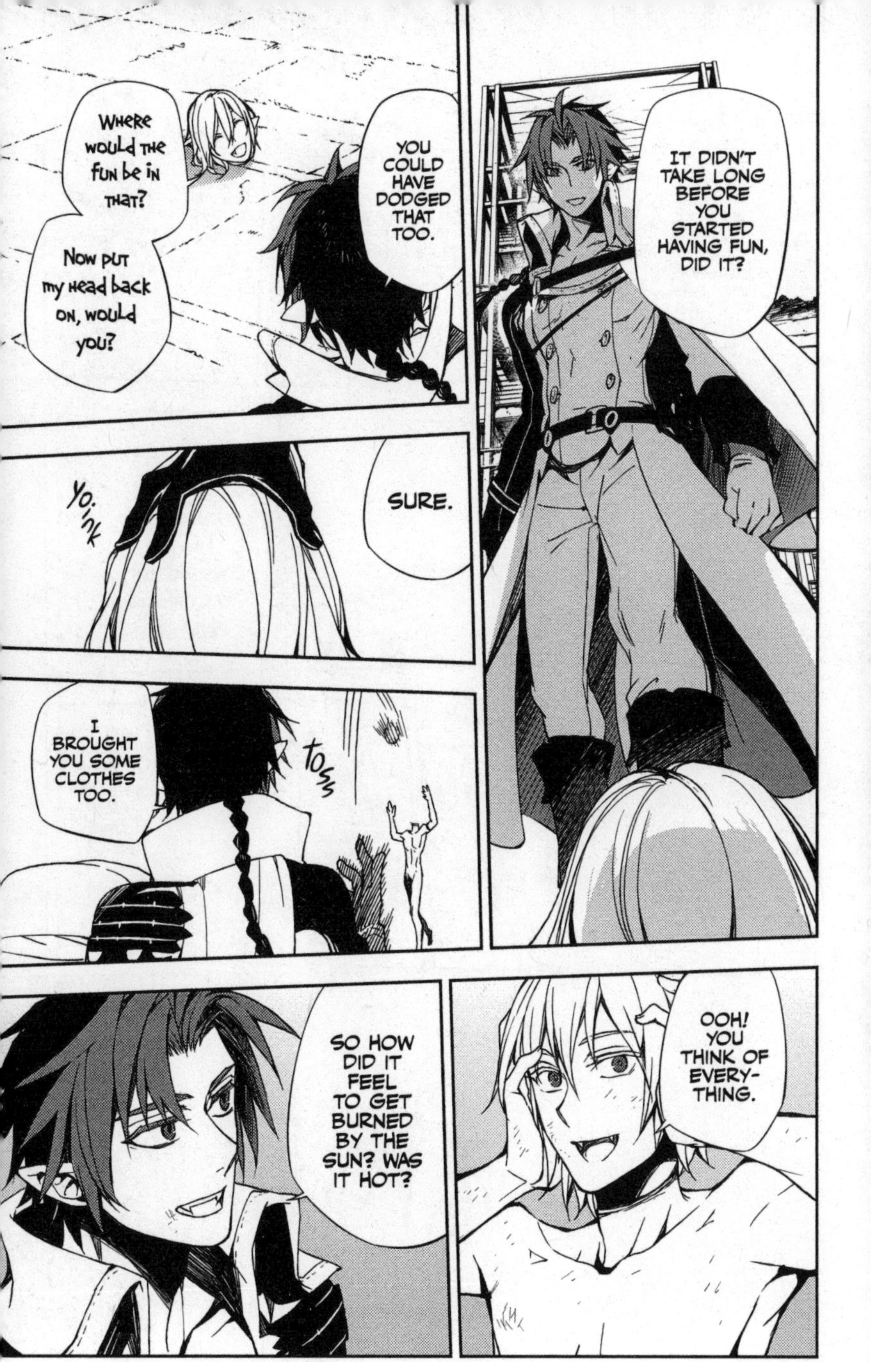
IT DIDN'T TAKE LONG BEFORE YOU STARTED HAVING FUN, DID IT?
YOU COULD HAVE DODGED THAT TOO.
Where would the fun be in that?
Now put my head back on, would you?
SURE.
yoink
toss
I BROUGHT YOU SOME CLOTHES TOO.
OOH! YOU THINK OF EVERY-THING.
SO HOW DID IT FEEL TO GET BURNED BY THE SUN? WAS IT HOT?

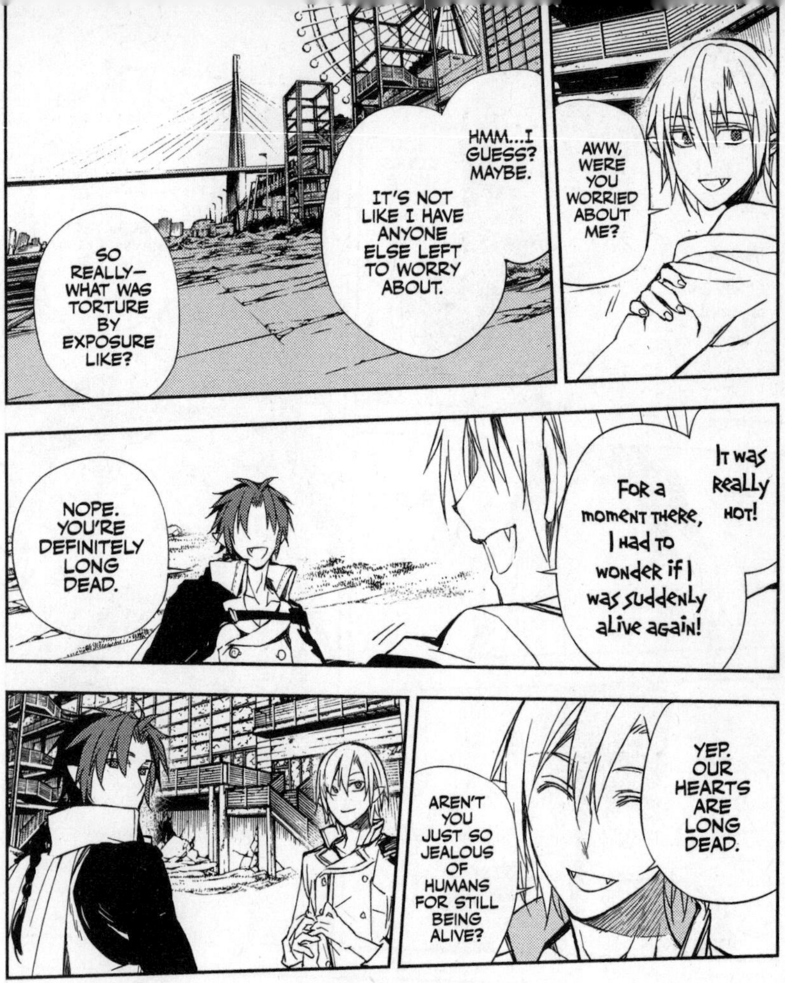
AWW, WERE YOU WORRIED ABOUT ME?
HMM...I GUESS? MAYBE.
IT'S NOT LIKE I HAVE ANYONE ELSE LEFT TO WORRY ABOUT.
SO REALLY—WHAT WAS TORTURE BY EXPOSURE LIKE?
It was really hot!
For a moment there, I had to wonder if I was suddenly alive again!
NOPE. YOU'RE DEFINITELY LONG DEAD.
YEP. OUR HEARTS ARE LONG DEAD.
AREN'T YOU JUST SO JEALOUS OF HUMANS FOR STILL BEING ALIVE?

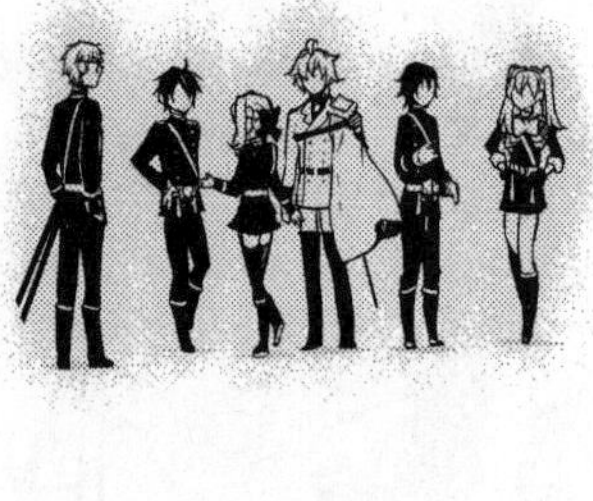

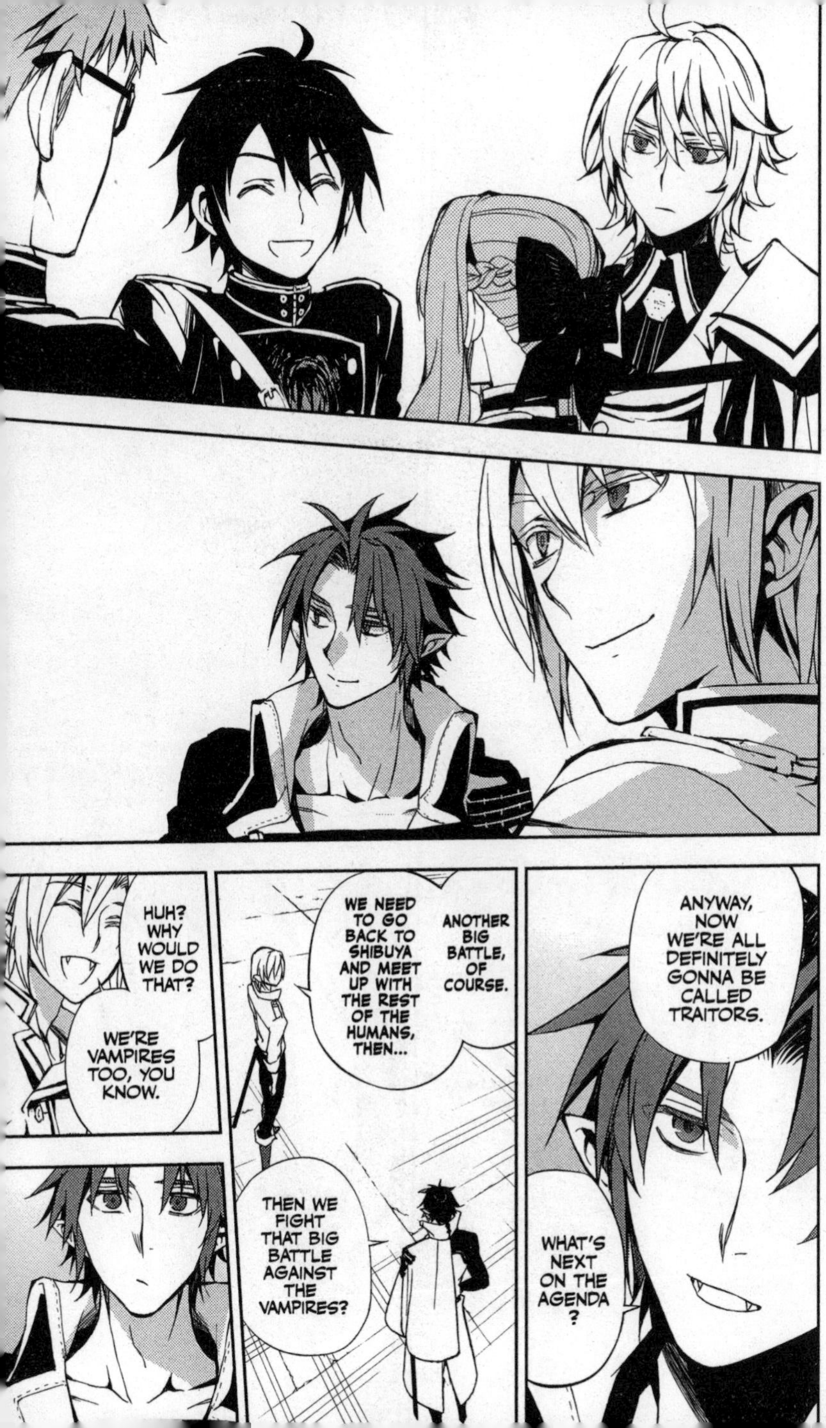
ANYWAY, NOW WE'RE ALL DEFINITELY GONNA BE CALLED TRAITORS.
WHAT'S NEXT ON THE AGENDA?
ANOTHER BIG BATTLE, OF COURSE.
WE NEED TO GO BACK TO SHIBUYA AND MEET UP WITH THE REST OF THE HUMANS, THEN...
THEN WE FIGHT THAT BIG BATTLE AGAINST THE VAMPIRES?
HUH? WHY WOULD WE DO THAT?
WE'RE VAMPIRES TOO, YOU KNOW.

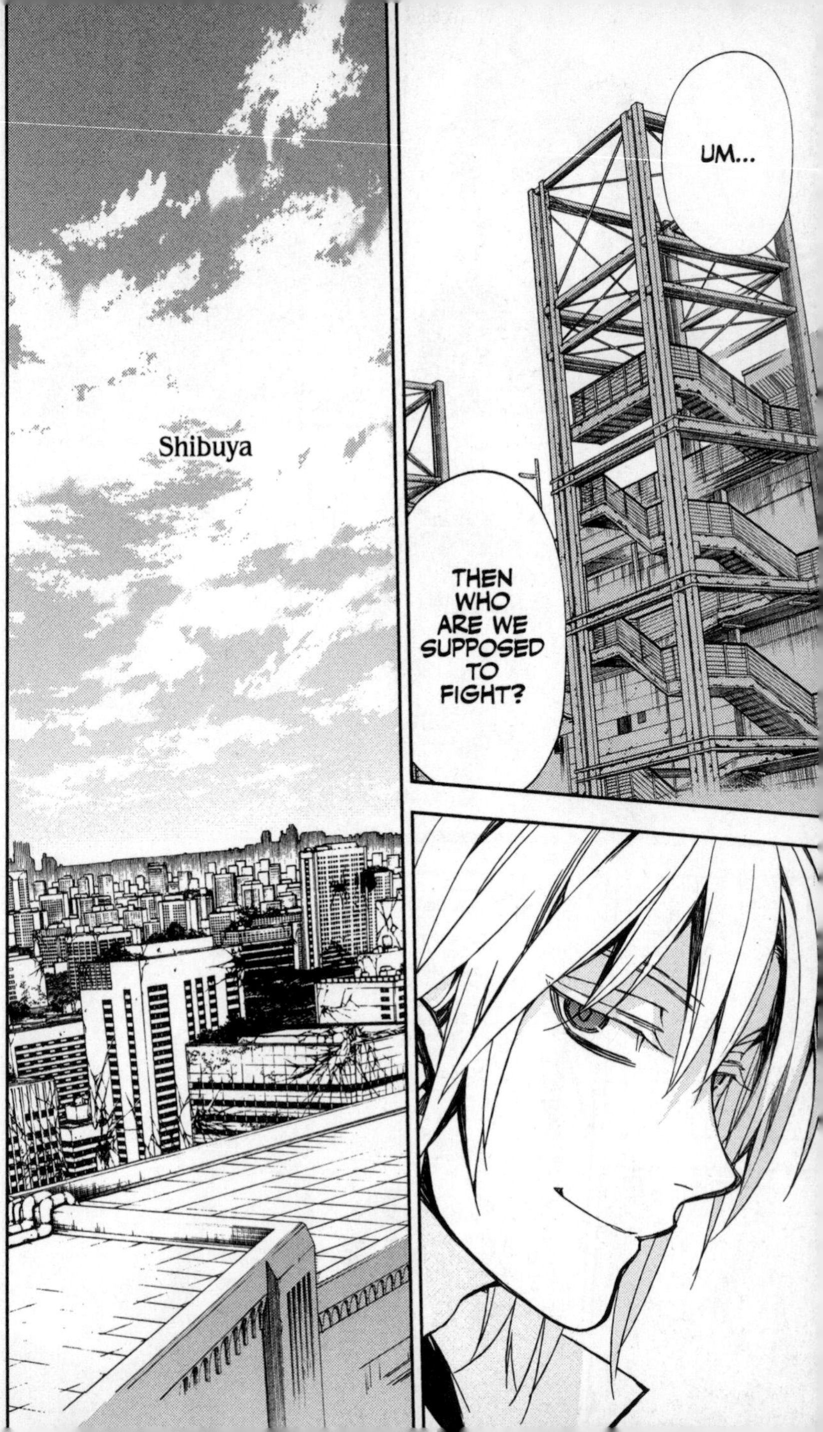
UM...
THEN WHO ARE WE SUPPOSED TO FIGHT?
Shibuya

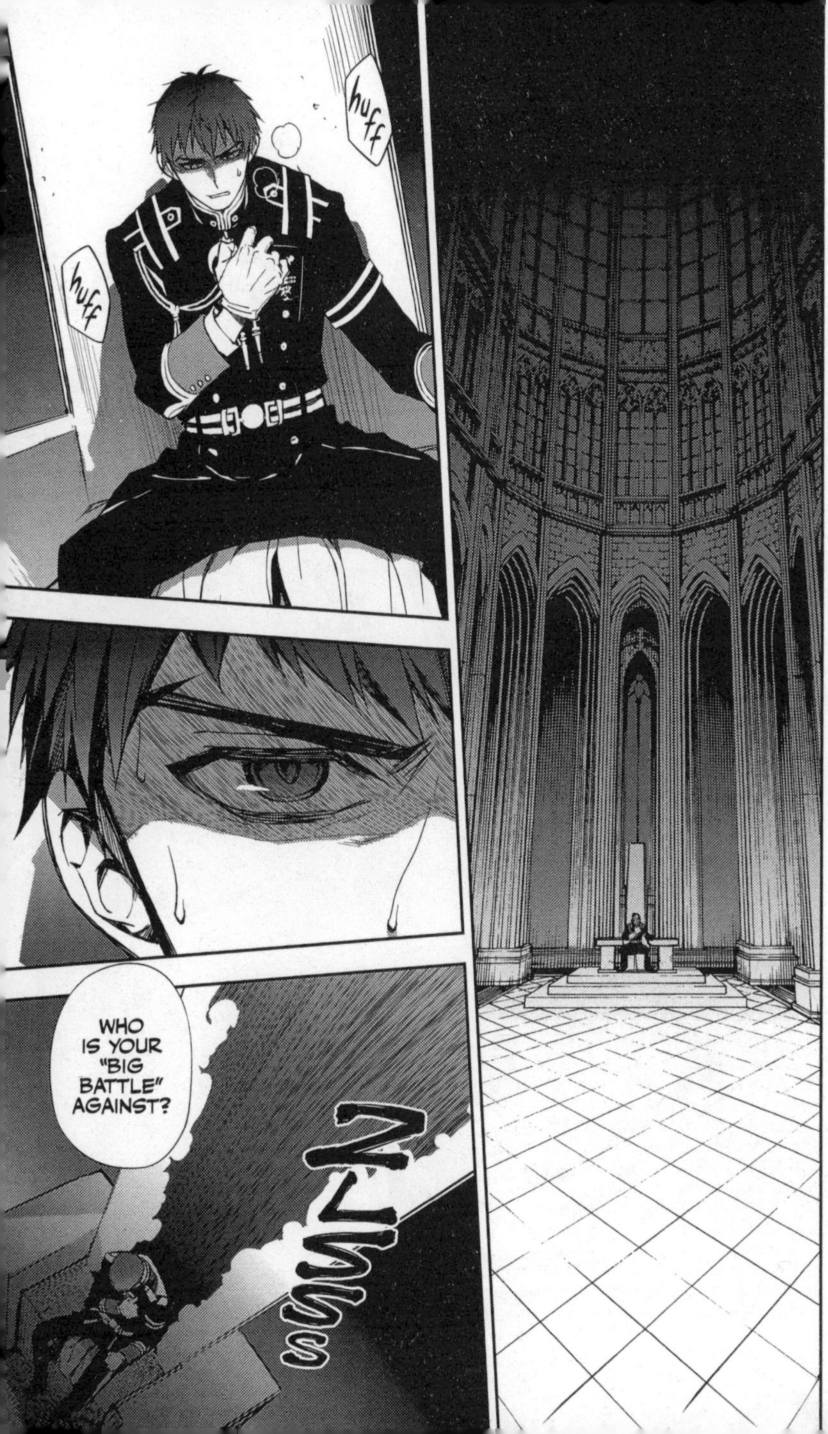
huff
huff
WHO IS YOUR "BIG BATTLE" AGAINST?

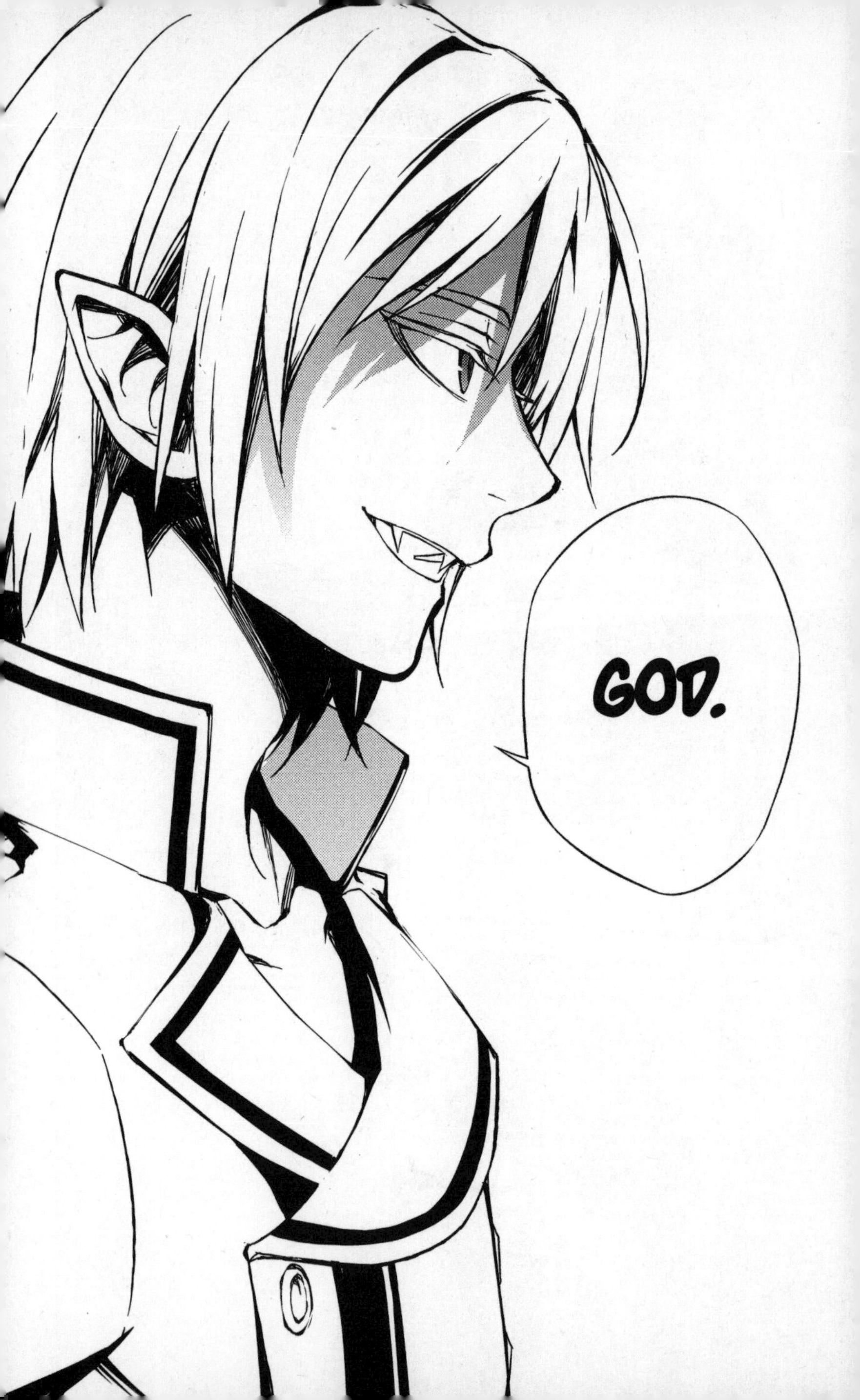
GOD.

Seraph of the End

VAMPIRE REIGN

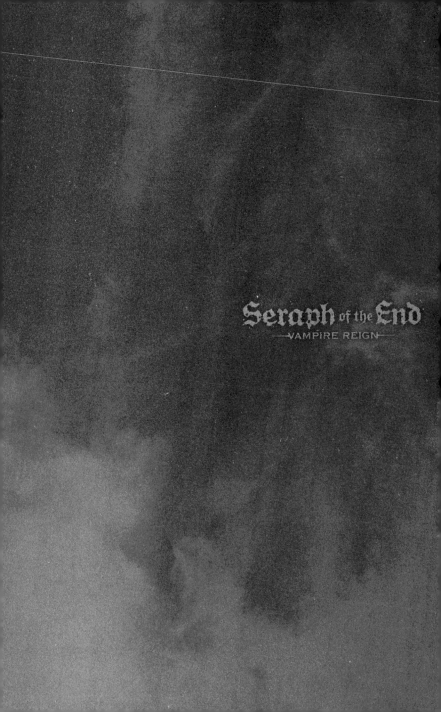

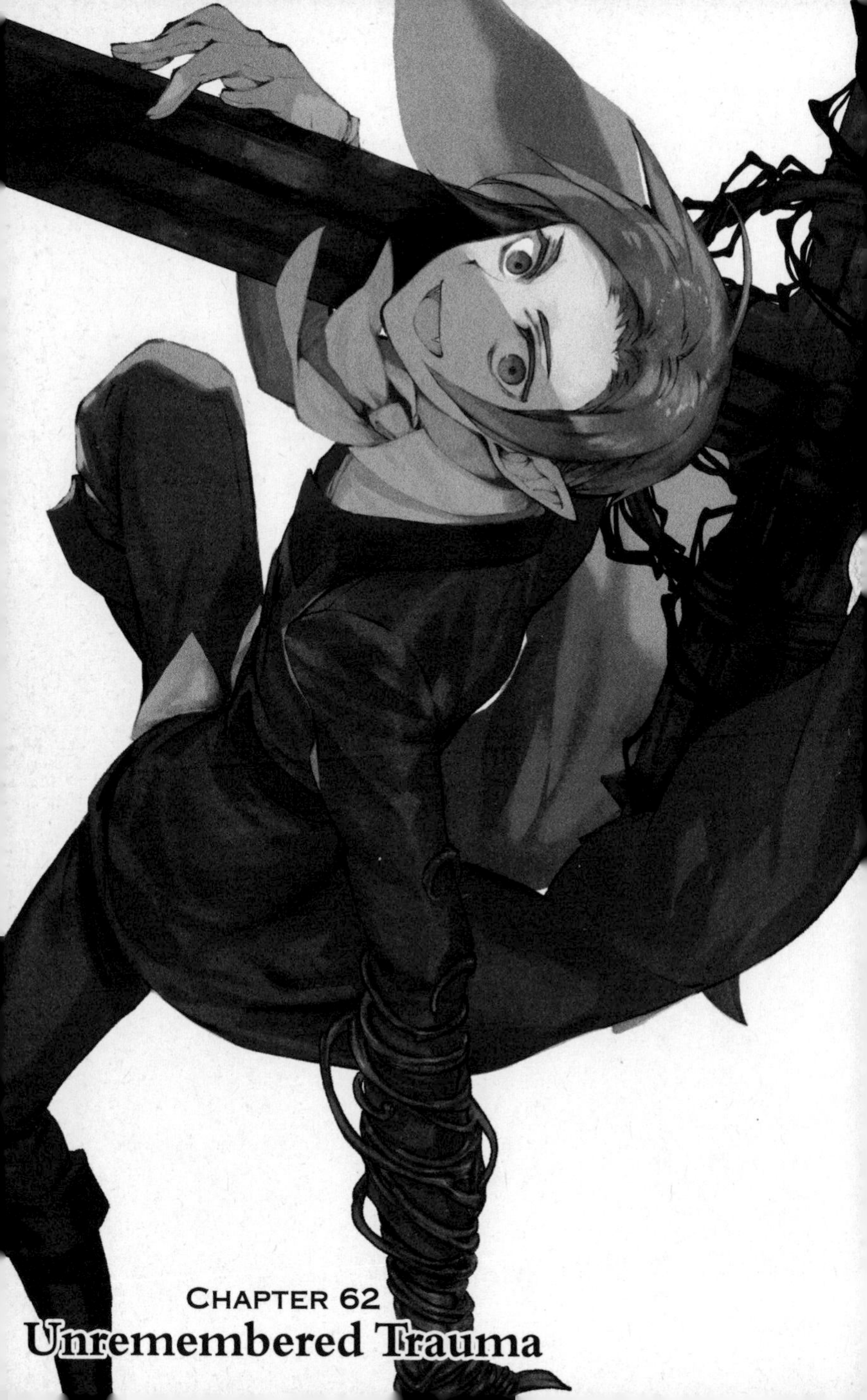

CHAPTER 62

Unremembered Trauma

Seraph of the End
VAMPIRE REIGN

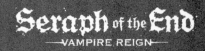

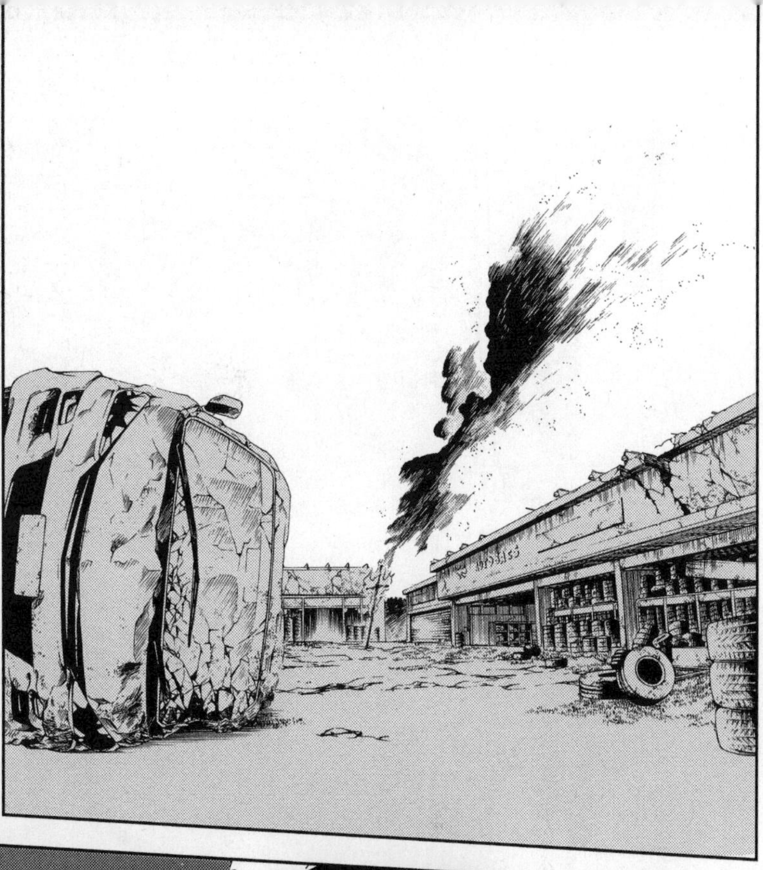
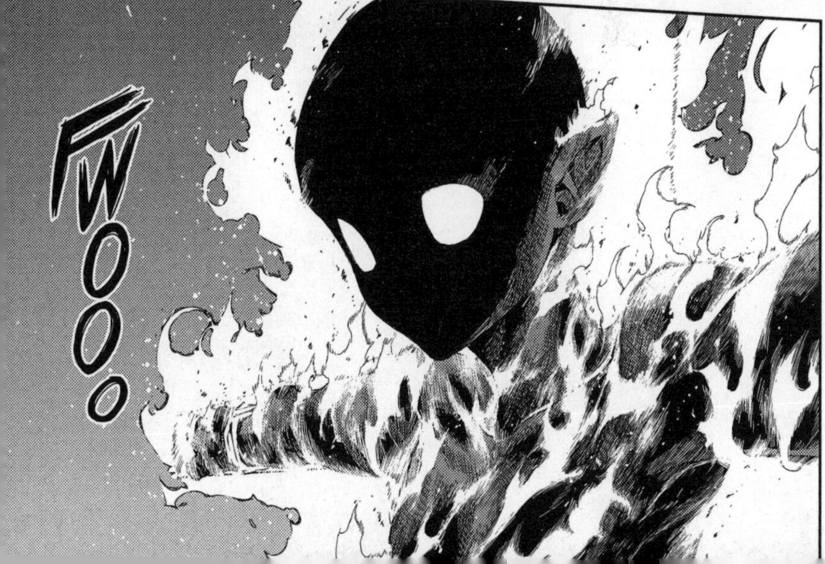
FWOOOO

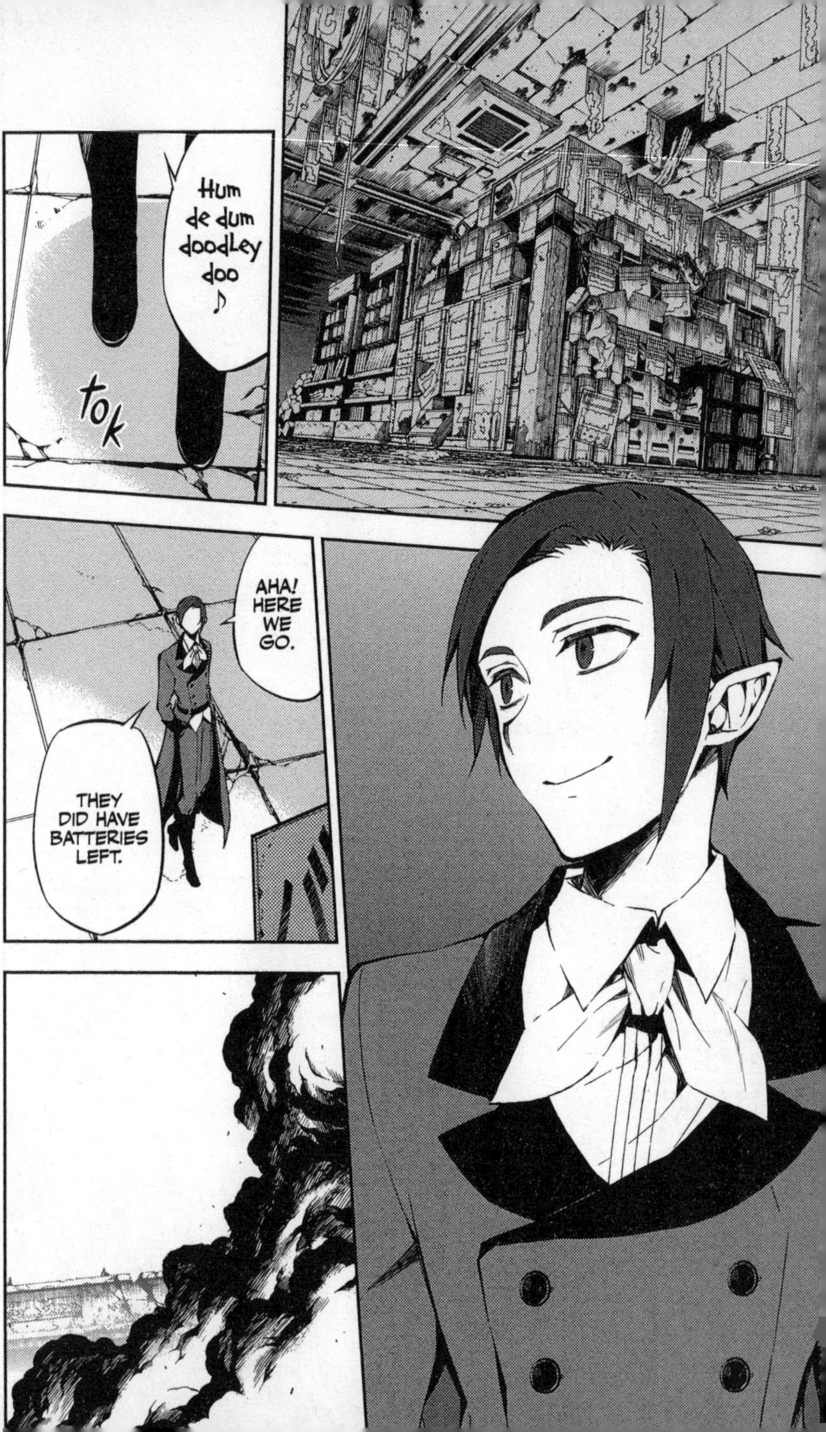
Hum de dum doodLey doo ♪
tok
AHA! HERE WE GO.
THEY DID HAVE BATTERIES LEFT.

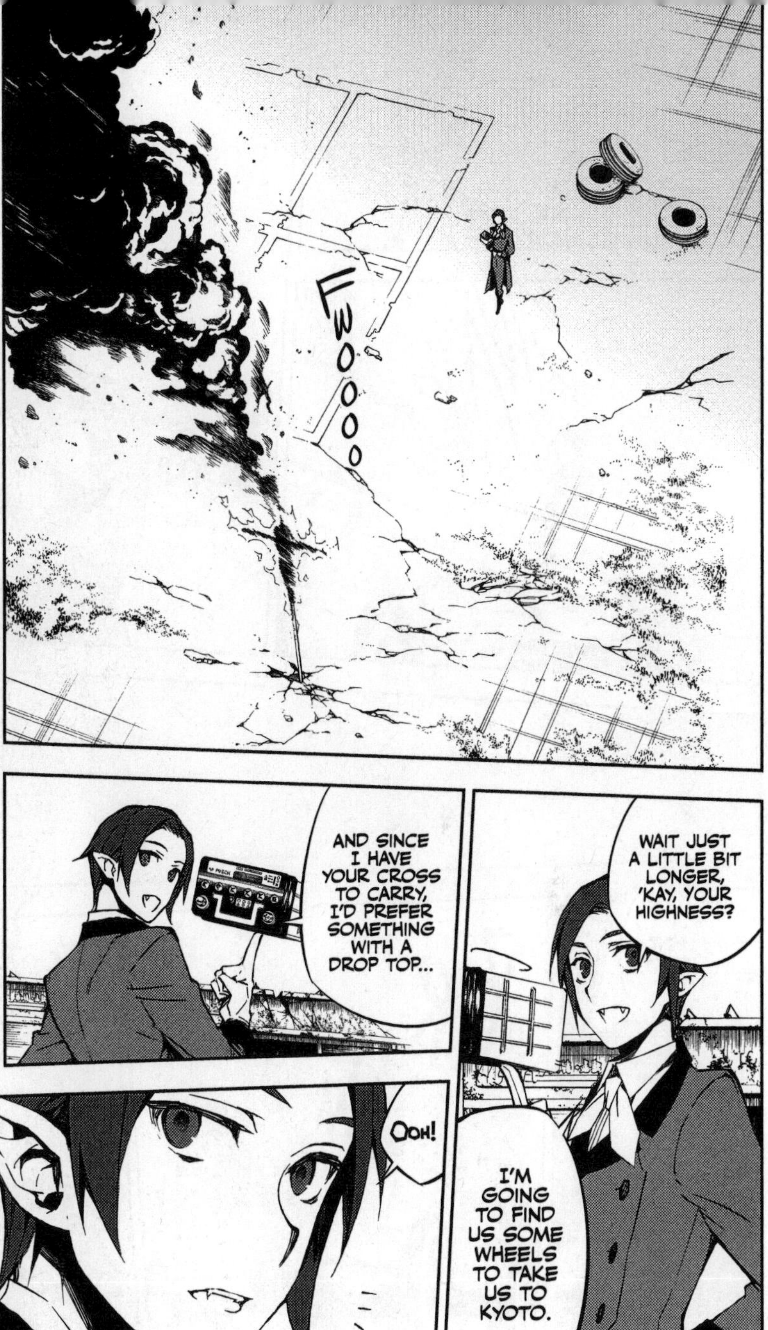
FWOOOOO
WAIT JUST A LITTLE BIT LONGER, 'KAY, YOUR HIGHNESS?
I'M GOING TO FIND US SOME WHEELS TO TAKE US TO KYOTO.
AND SINCE I HAVE YOUR CROSS TO CARRY, I'D PREFER SOMETHING WITH A DROP TOP...
OOH!

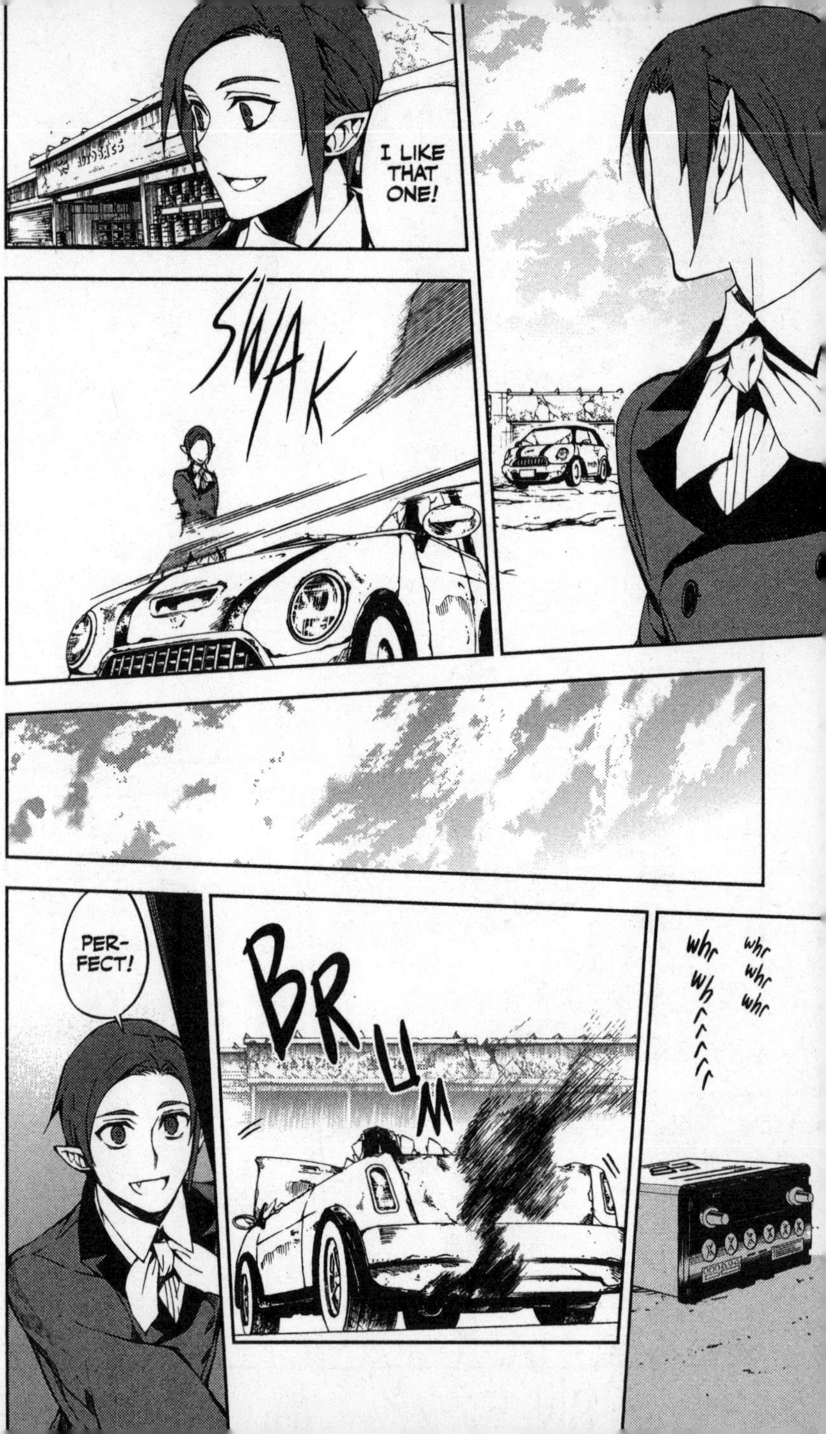
I LIKE THAT ONE!
SWAK
whr whr whr whr
whr whr whrrrrrr
BRUUM
PER-FECT!

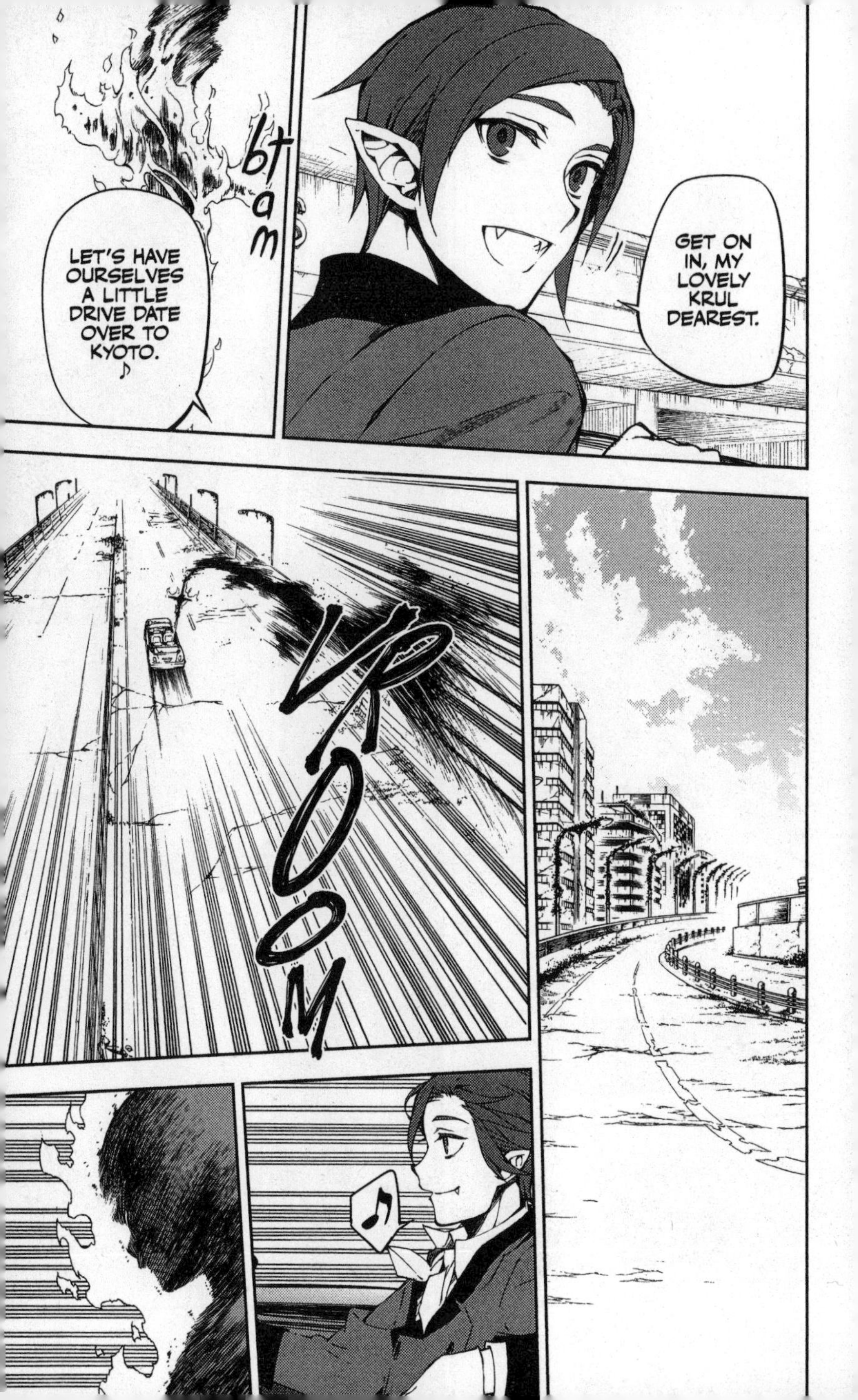
GET ON IN, MY LOVELY KRUL DEAREST.
btam
LET'S HAVE OURSELVES A LITTLE DRIVE DATE OVER TO KYOTO. ♪
VROOOM
♪

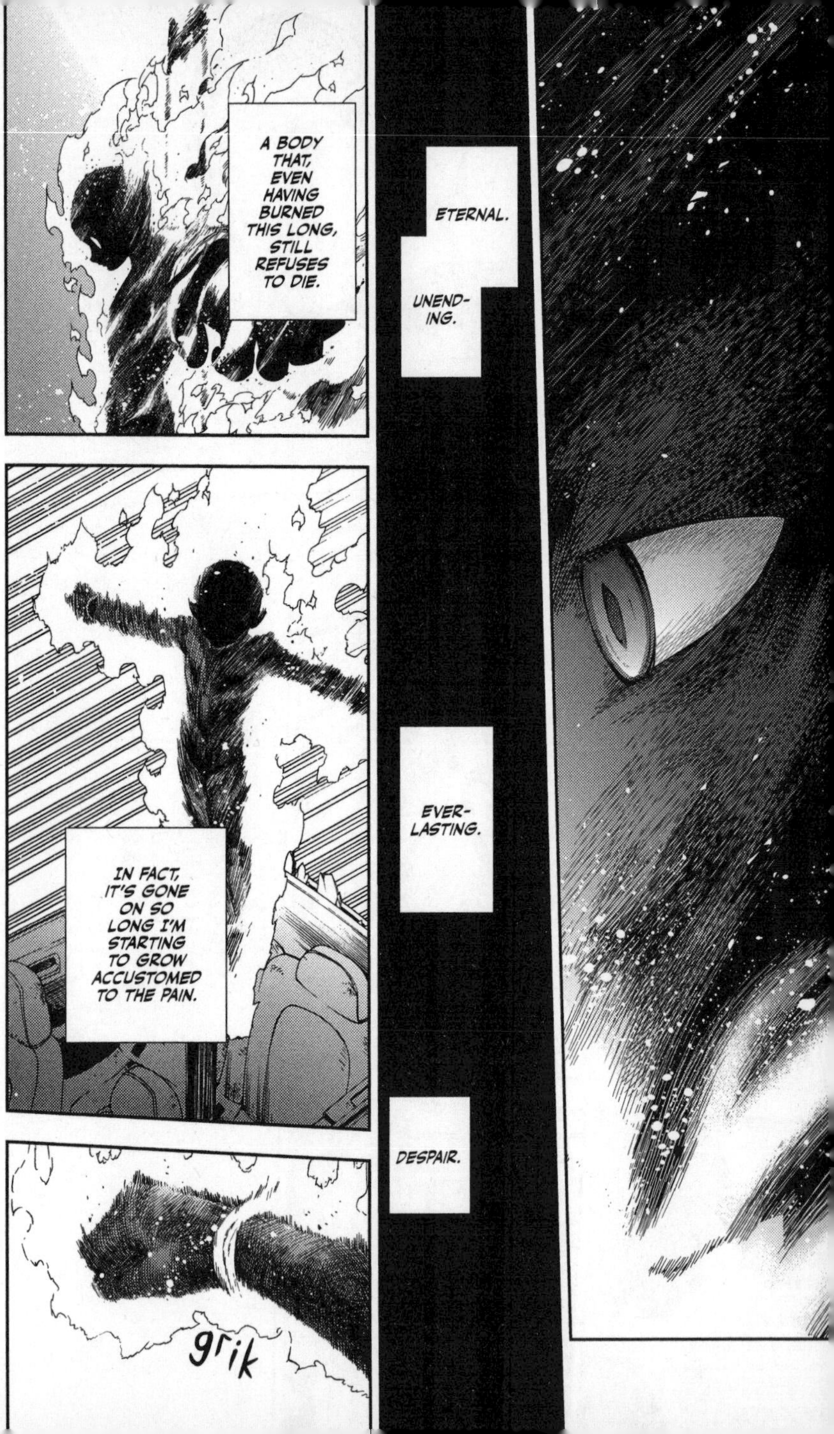
ETERNAL.
UNEND-ING.
EVER-LASTING.
DESPAIR.
A BODY THAT, EVEN HAVING BURNED THIS LONG, STILL REFUSES TO DIE.
IN FACT, IT'S GONE ON SO LONG I'M STARTING TO GROW ACCUSTOMED TO THE PAIN.
grik

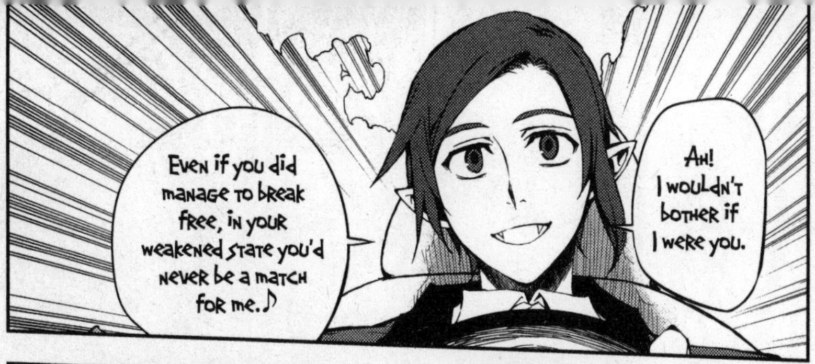
Ah! I wouldn't bother if I were you.
Even if you did manage to break free, in your weakened state you'd never be a match for me.♪

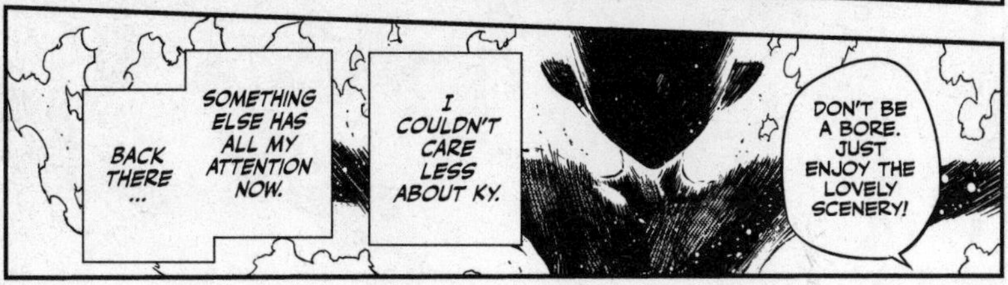
DON'T BE A BORE. JUST ENJOY THE LOVELY SCENERY!
I COULDN'T CARE LESS ABOUT KY.
SOMETHING ELSE HAS ALL MY ATTENTION NOW.
BACK THERE ...

I SENSED MY BROTHER.

ASHERA.

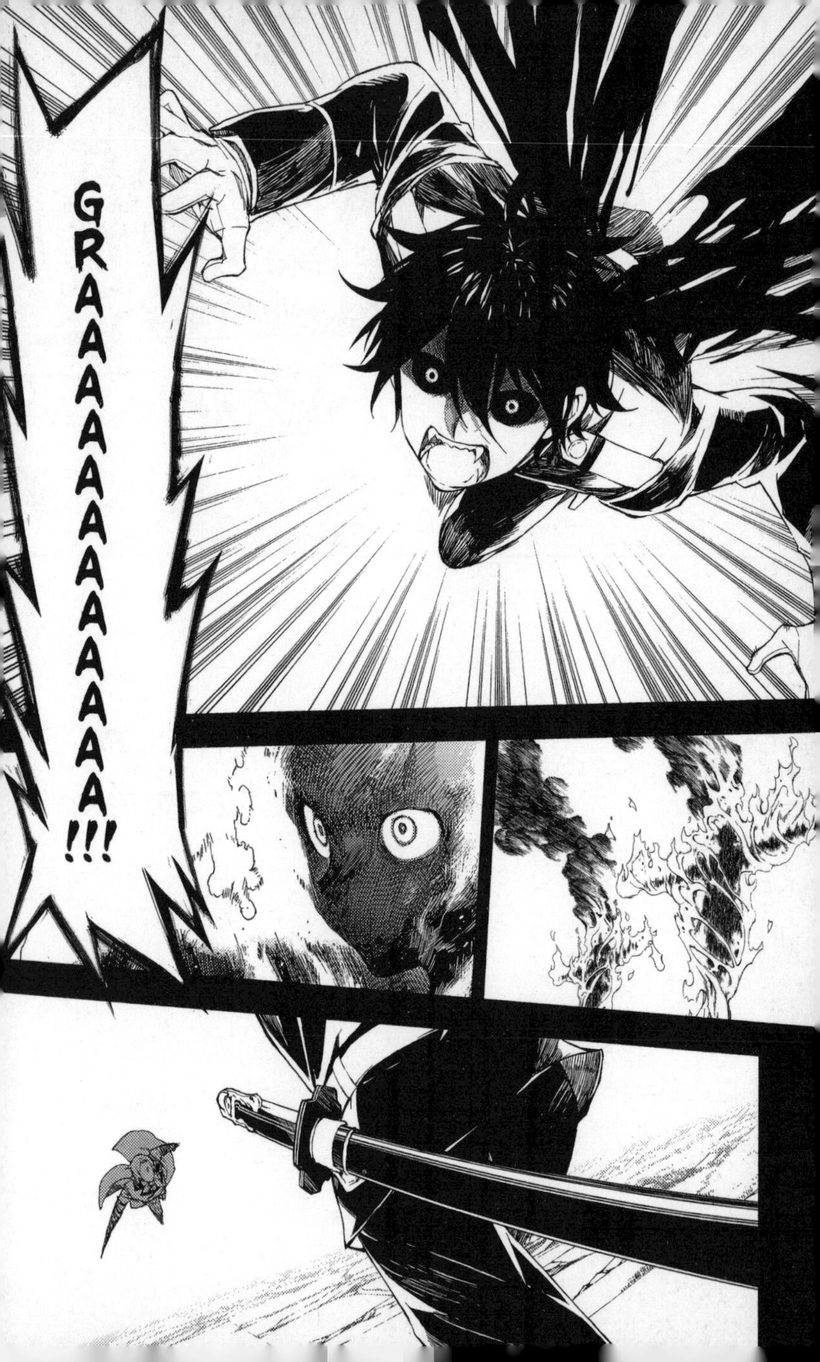
GRAAAAAAAAAAAAA!!!

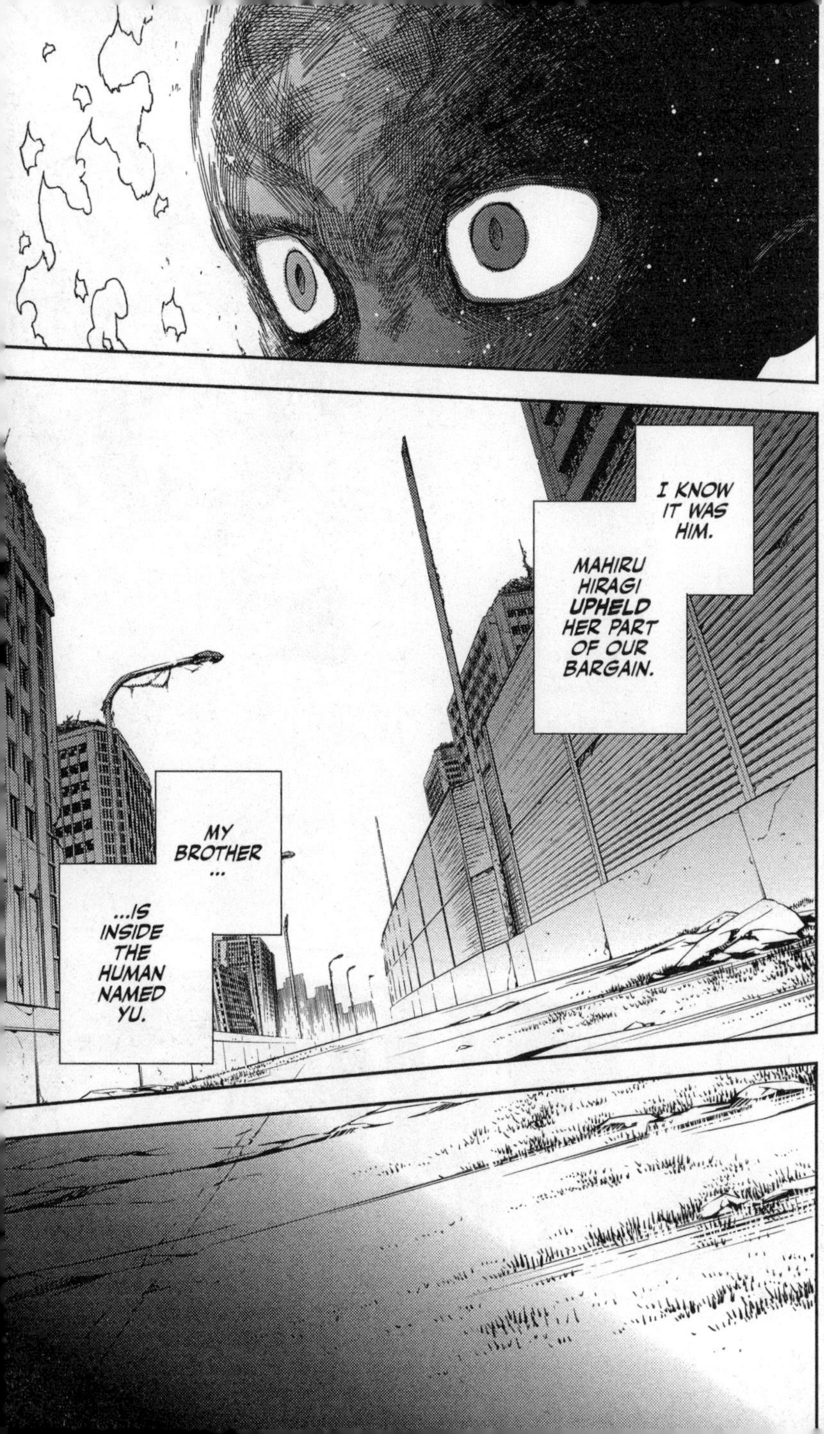
I KNOW IT WAS HIM.
MAHIRU HIRAGI UPHELD HER PART OF OUR BARGAIN.
MY BROTHER ...
...IS INSIDE THE HUMAN NAMED YU.

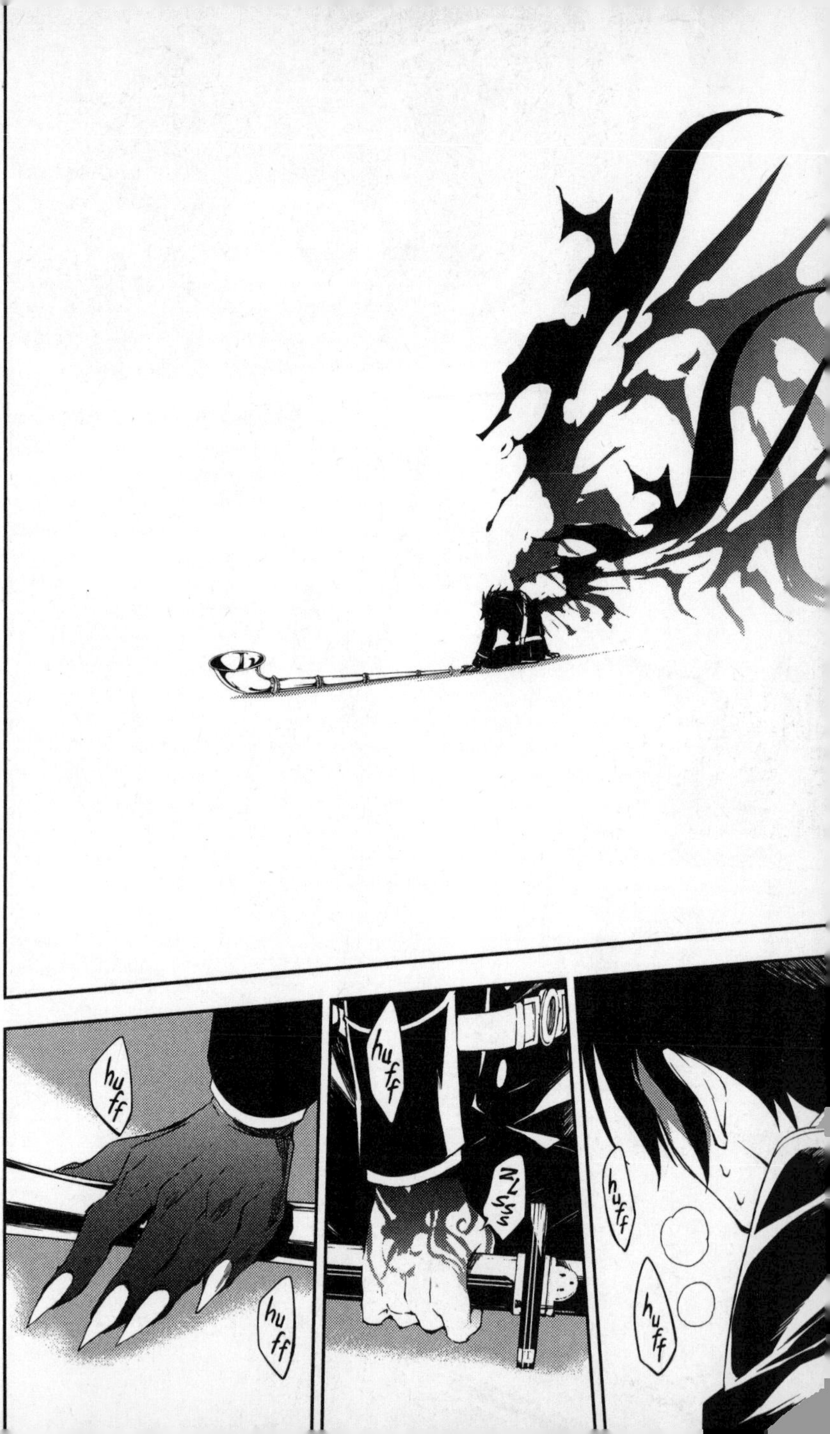
huff
huff
huff
SSSZZ
huff
huff

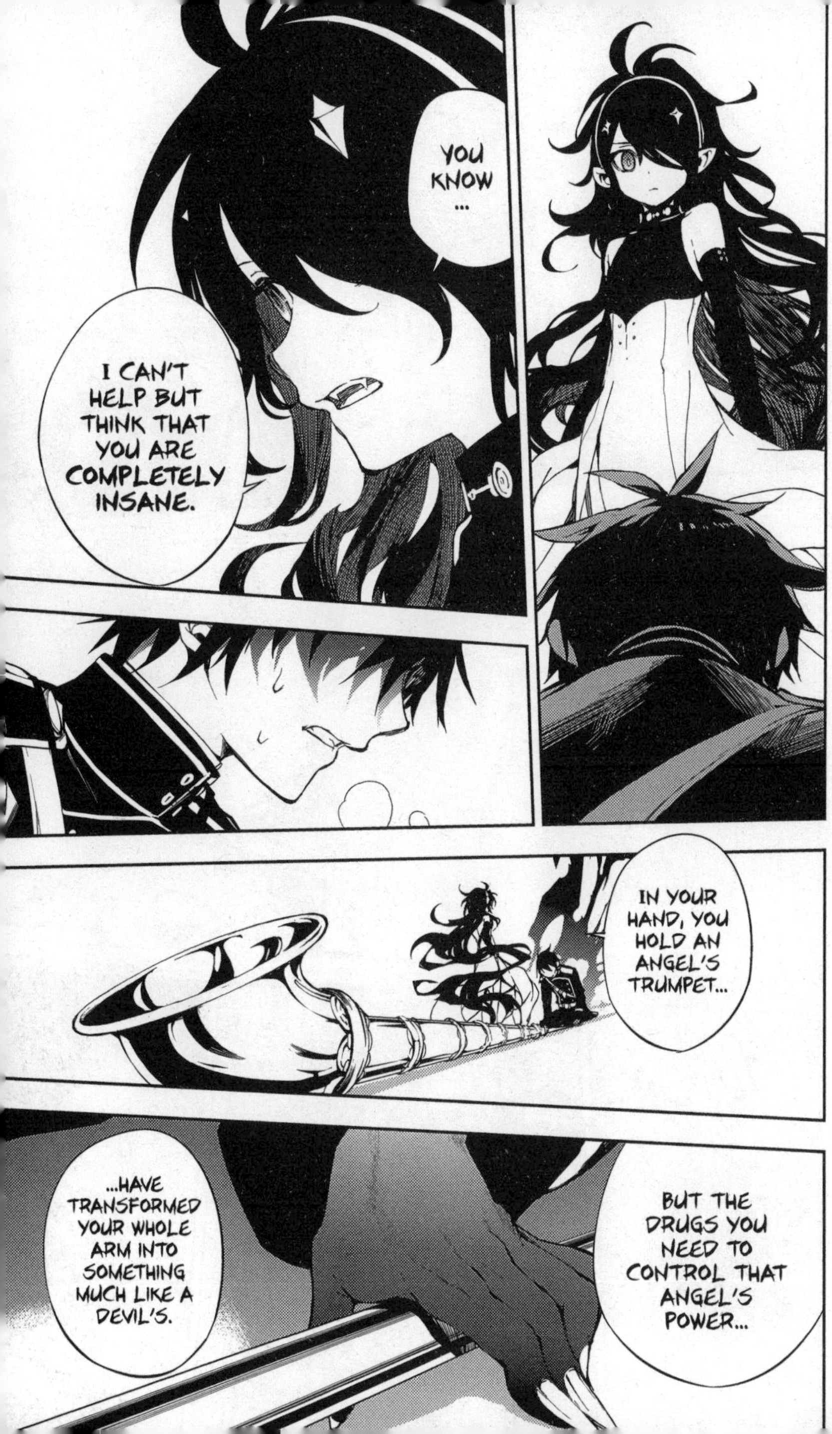
YOU KNOW...
I CAN'T HELP BUT THINK THAT YOU ARE COMPLETELY INSANE.
IN YOUR HAND, YOU HOLD AN ANGEL'S TRUMPET...
BUT THE DRUGS YOU NEED TO CONTROL THAT ANGEL'S POWER...
...HAVE TRANSFORMED YOUR WHOLE ARM INTO SOMETHING MUCH LIKE A DEVIL'S.

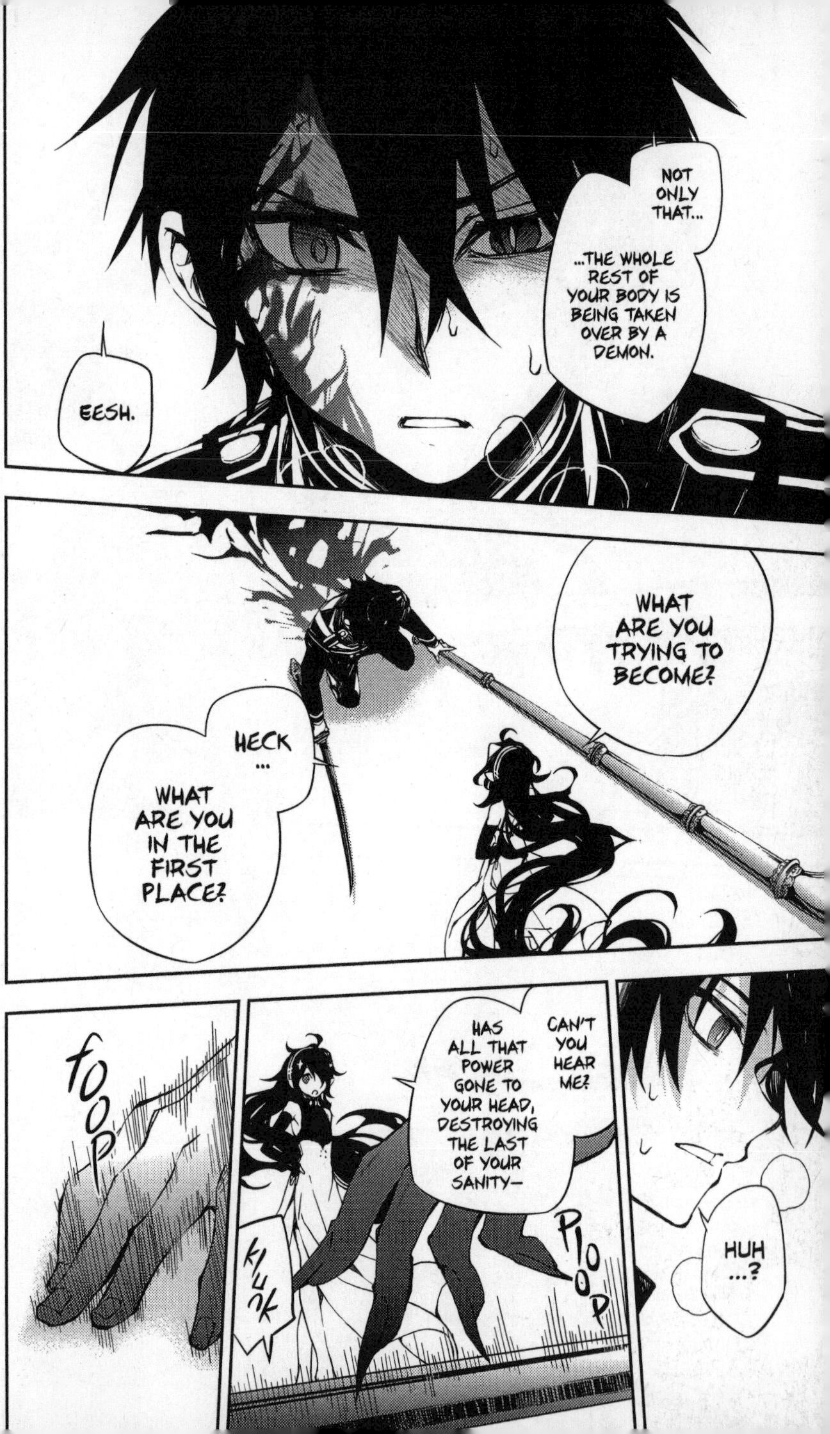
NOT ONLY THAT...
...THE WHOLE REST OF YOUR BODY IS BEING TAKEN OVER BY A DEMON.
EESH.
WHAT ARE YOU TRYING TO BECOME?
HECK... WHAT ARE YOU IN THE FIRST PLACE?
HUH...?
CAN'T YOU HEAR ME?
HAS ALL THAT POWER GONE TO YOUR HEAD, DESTROYING THE LAST OF YOUR SANITY—
PLOOP
KLUNK
FOOP

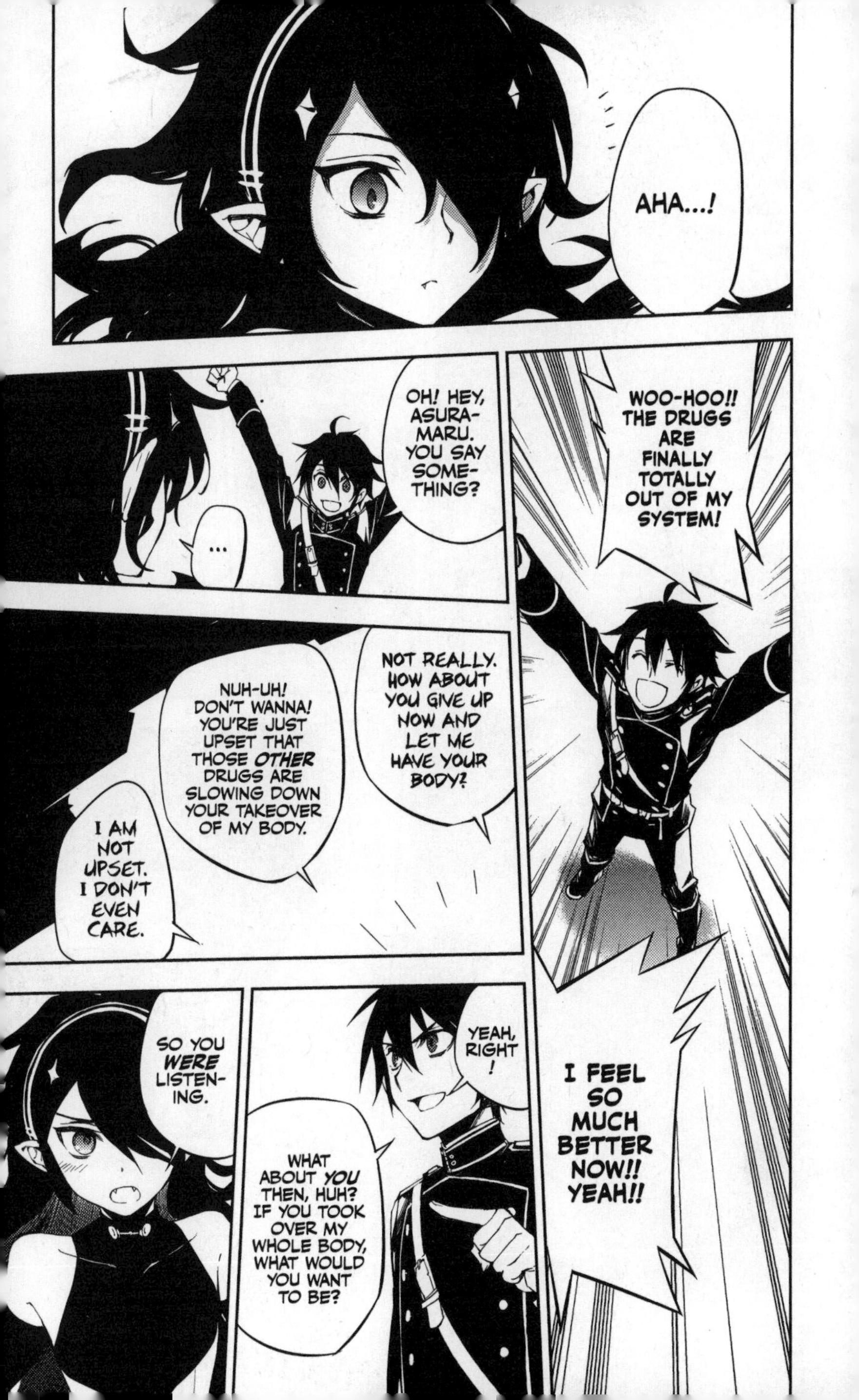
AHA...!
WOO-HOO!! THE DRUGS ARE FINALLY TOTALLY OUT OF MY SYSTEM!
I FEEL SO MUCH BETTER NOW!! YEAH!!
OH! HEY, ASURA-MARU. YOU SAY SOME-THING?
...
NOT REALLY. HOW ABOUT YOU GIVE UP NOW AND LET ME HAVE YOUR BODY?
NUH-UH! DON'T WANNA! YOU'RE JUST UPSET THAT THOSE *OTHER* DRUGS ARE SLOWING DOWN YOUR TAKEOVER OF MY BODY.
I AM NOT UPSET. I DON'T EVEN CARE.
YEAH, RIGHT!
WHAT ABOUT *YOU* THEN, HUH? IF YOU TOOK OVER MY WHOLE BODY, WHAT WOULD YOU WANT TO BE?
SO YOU *WERE* LISTEN-ING.

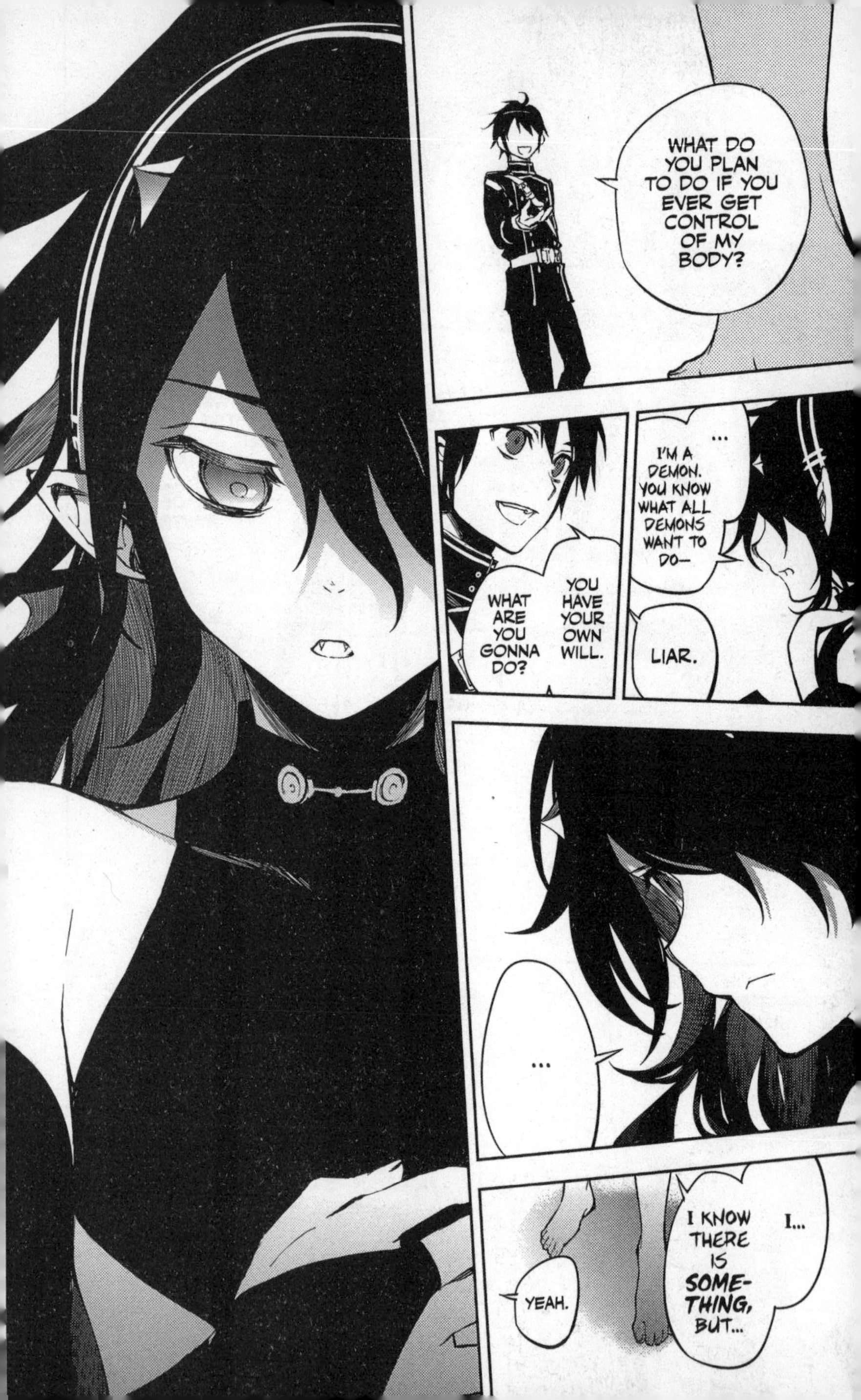
WHAT DO YOU PLAN TO DO IF YOU EVER GET CONTROL OF MY BODY?
...
I'M A DEMON. YOU KNOW WHAT ALL DEMONS WANT TO DO—
LIAR.
YOU HAVE YOUR OWN WILL.
WHAT ARE YOU GONNA DO?
...
I...
I KNOW THERE IS SOMETHING, BUT...
YEAH.

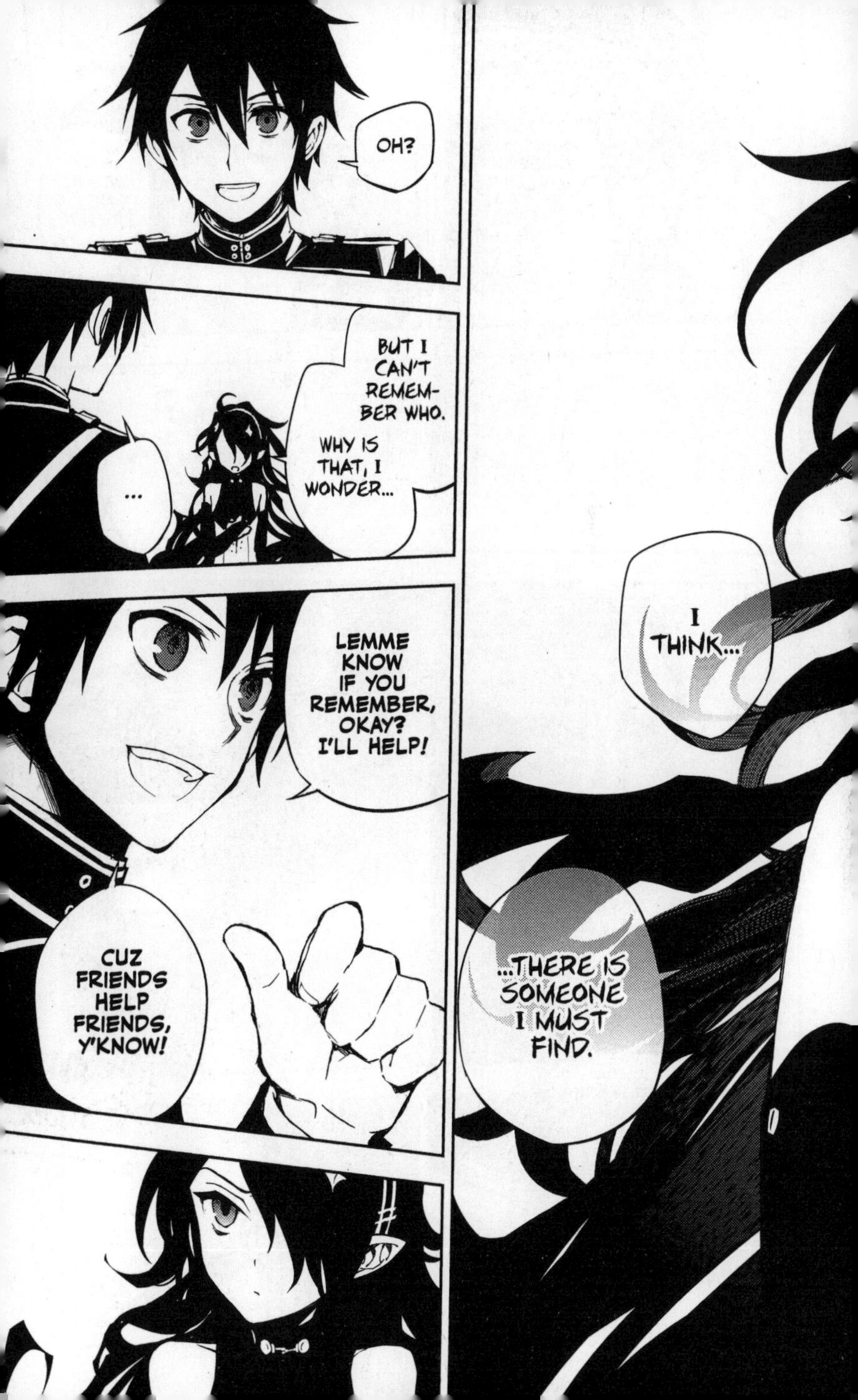
I THINK...
...THERE IS SOMEONE I MUST FIND.
OH?
BUT I CAN'T REMEMBER WHO.
WHY IS THAT, I WONDER...
...
LEMME KNOW IF YOU REMEMBER, OKAY? I'LL HELP!
CUZ FRIENDS HELP FRIENDS, Y'KNOW!

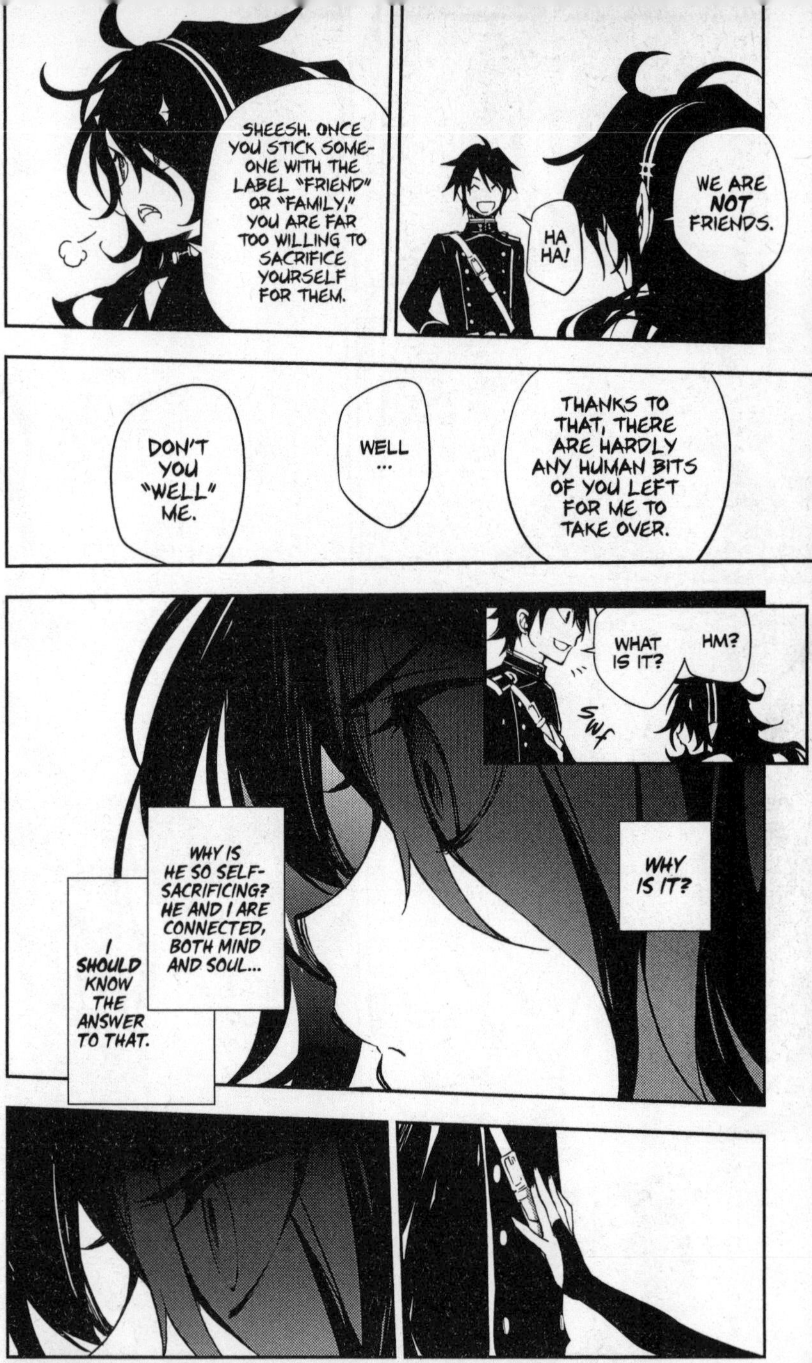
WE ARE NOT FRIENDS.
HA HA!
SHEESH. ONCE YOU STICK SOME-ONE WITH THE LABEL "FRIEND" OR "FAMILY," YOU ARE FAR TOO WILLING TO SACRIFICE YOURSELF FOR THEM.
THANKS TO THAT, THERE ARE HARDLY ANY HUMAN BITS OF YOU LEFT FOR ME TO TAKE OVER.
WELL ...
DON'T YOU "WELL" ME.
HM?
WHAT IS IT?
SWF
WHY IS IT?
WHY IS HE SO SELF-SACRIFICING? HE AND I ARE CONNECTED, BOTH MIND AND SOUL...
I SHOULD KNOW THE ANSWER TO THAT.

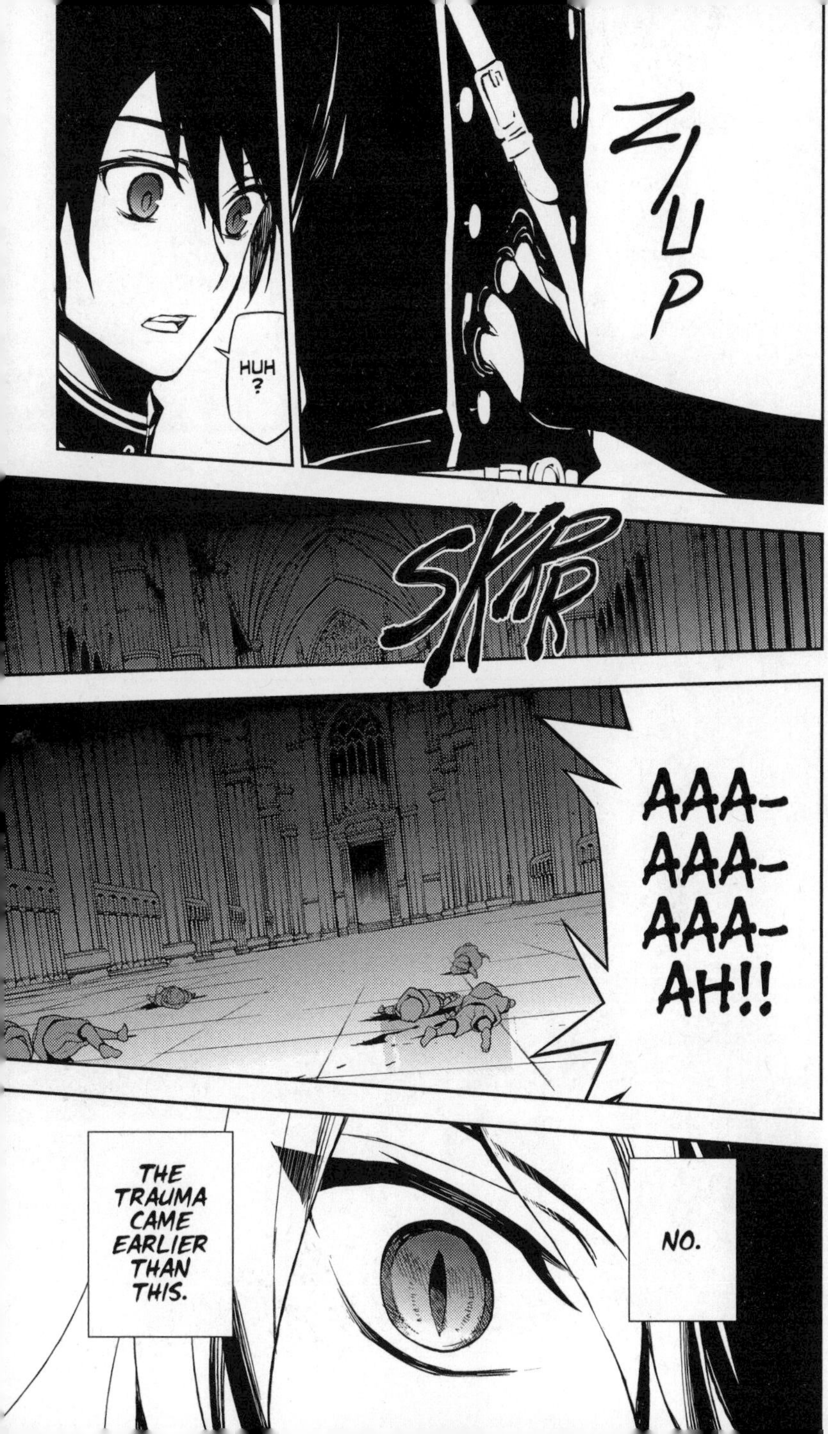
ZIUP
HUH?
SKRR
AAA-AAA-AAA-AH!!
NO.
THE TRAUMA CAME EARLIER THAN THIS.

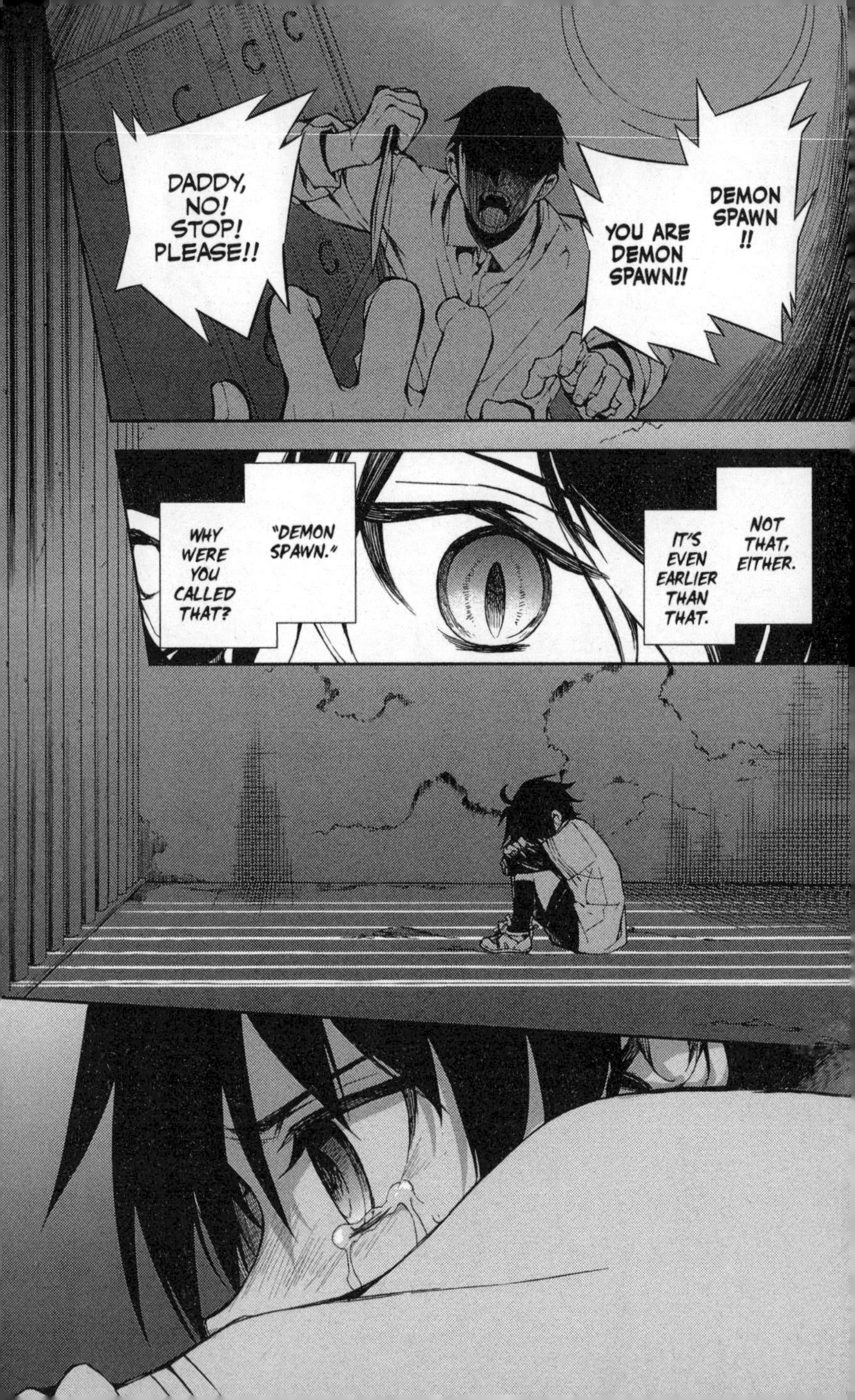
DEMON SPAWN!!
YOU ARE DEMON SPAWN!!
DADDY, NO! STOP! PLEASE!!
NOT THAT, EITHER.
IT'S EVEN EARLIER THAN THAT.
"DEMON SPAWN."
WHY WERE YOU CALLED THAT?

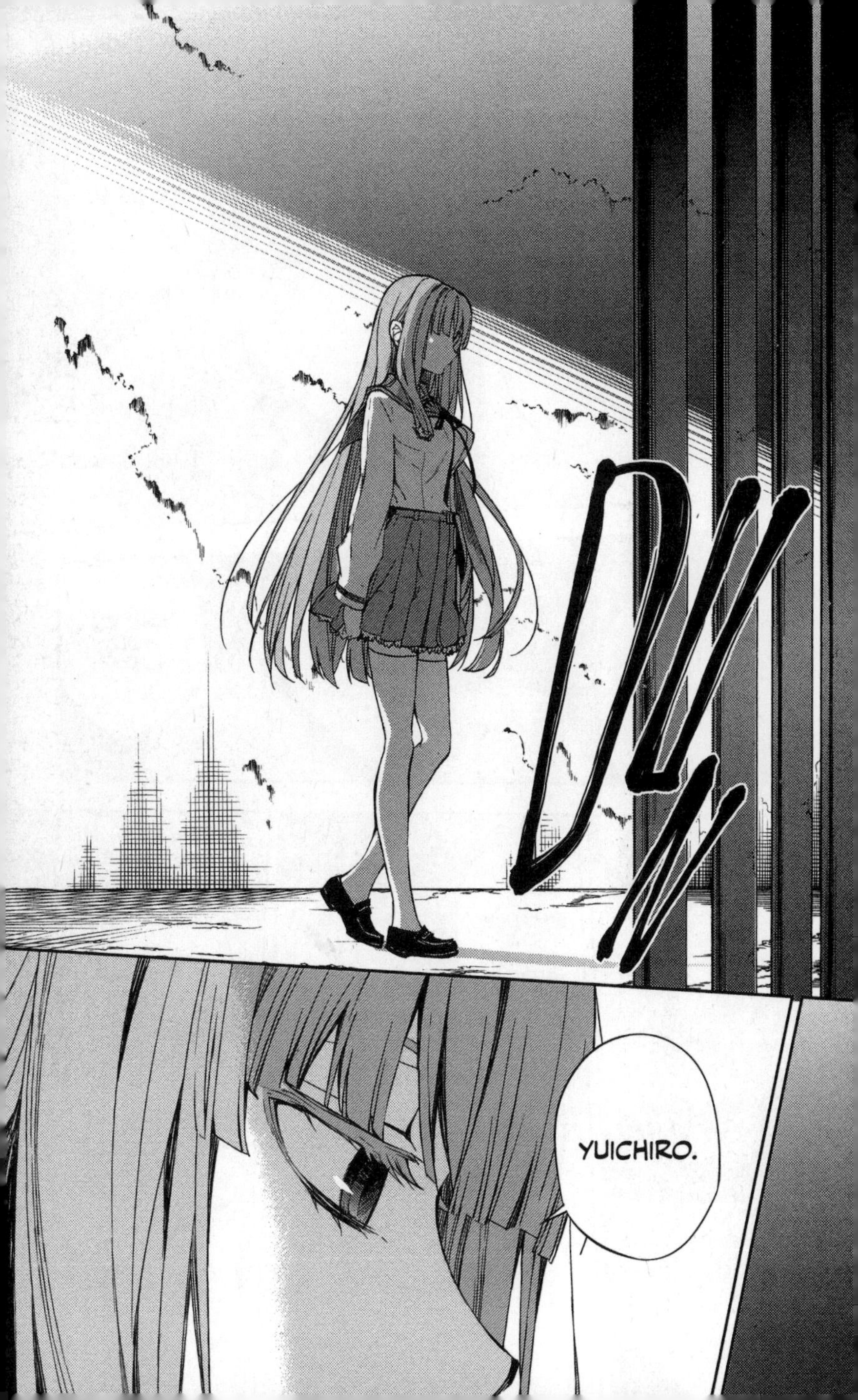
YUICHIRO.

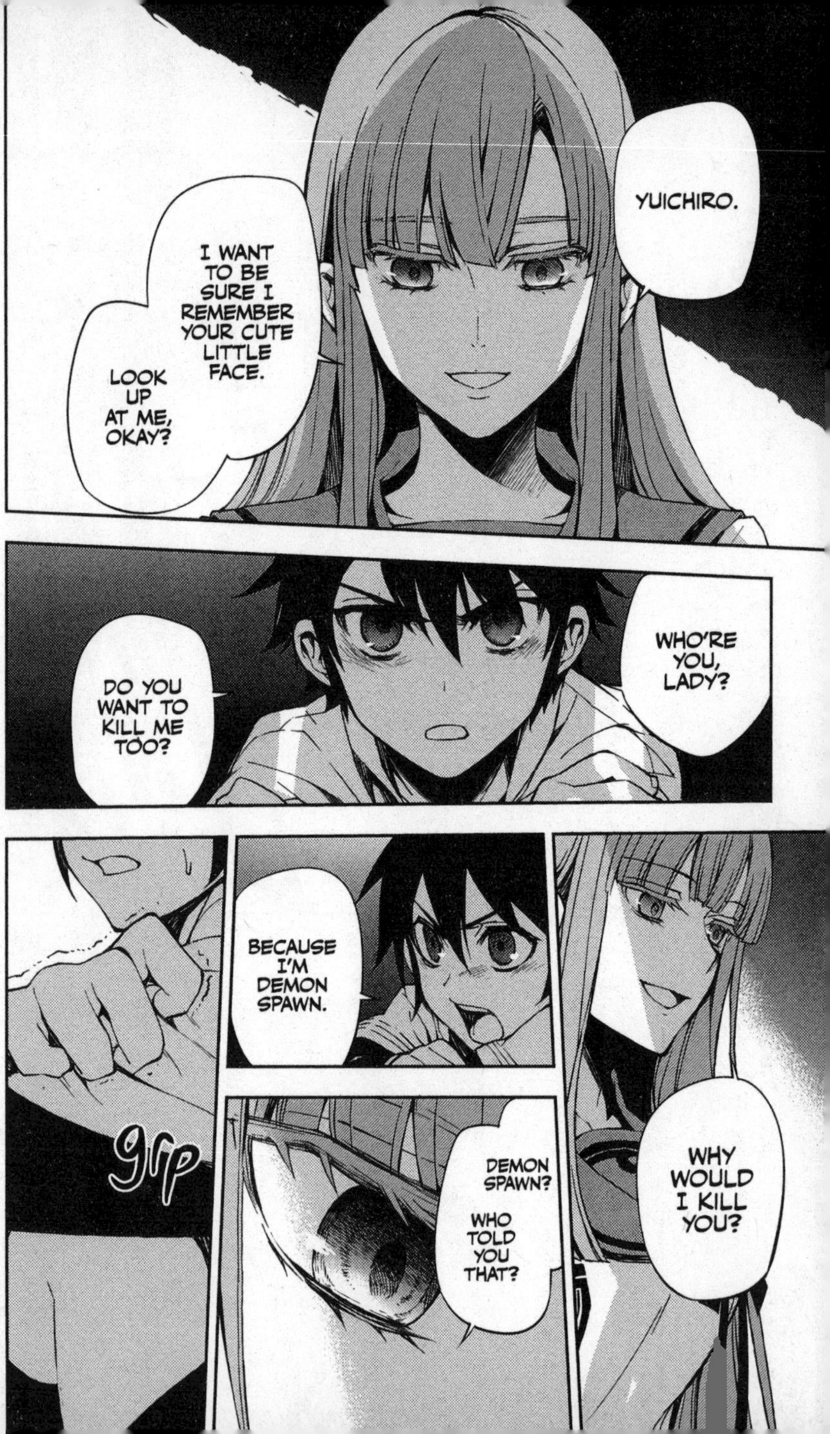
YUICHIRO.
I WANT TO BE SURE I REMEMBER YOUR CUTE LITTLE FACE.
LOOK UP AT ME, OKAY?
WHO'RE YOU, LADY?
DO YOU WANT TO KILL ME TOO?
WHY WOULD I KILL YOU?
BECAUSE I'M DEMON SPAWN.
DEMON SPAWN?
WHO TOLD YOU THAT?
grp

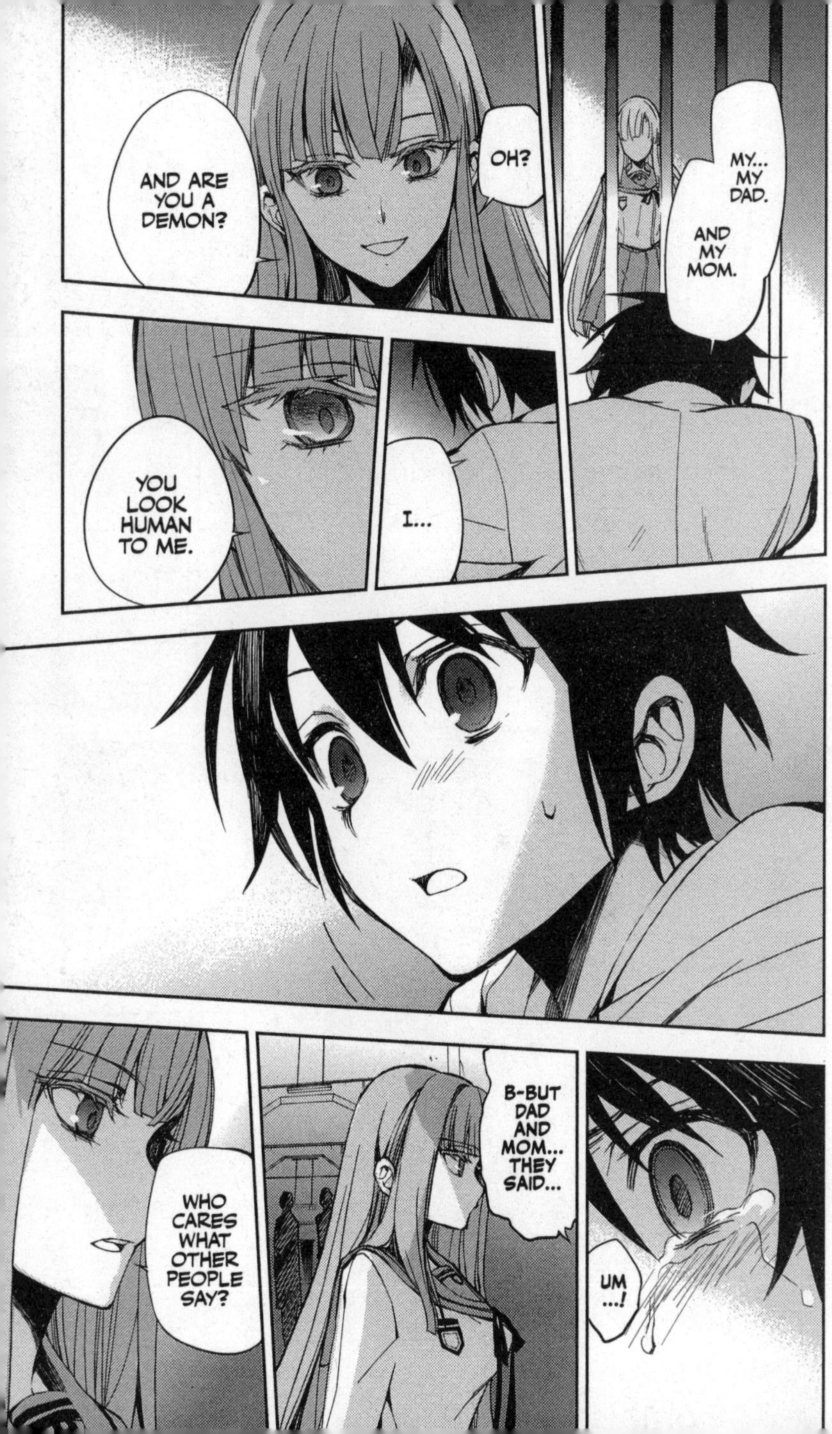
MY... MY DAD.
AND MY MOM.
OH?
AND ARE YOU A DEMON?
I...
YOU LOOK HUMAN TO ME.
UM ...!
B-BUT DAD AND MOM... THEY SAID...
WHO CARES WHAT OTHER PEOPLE SAY?

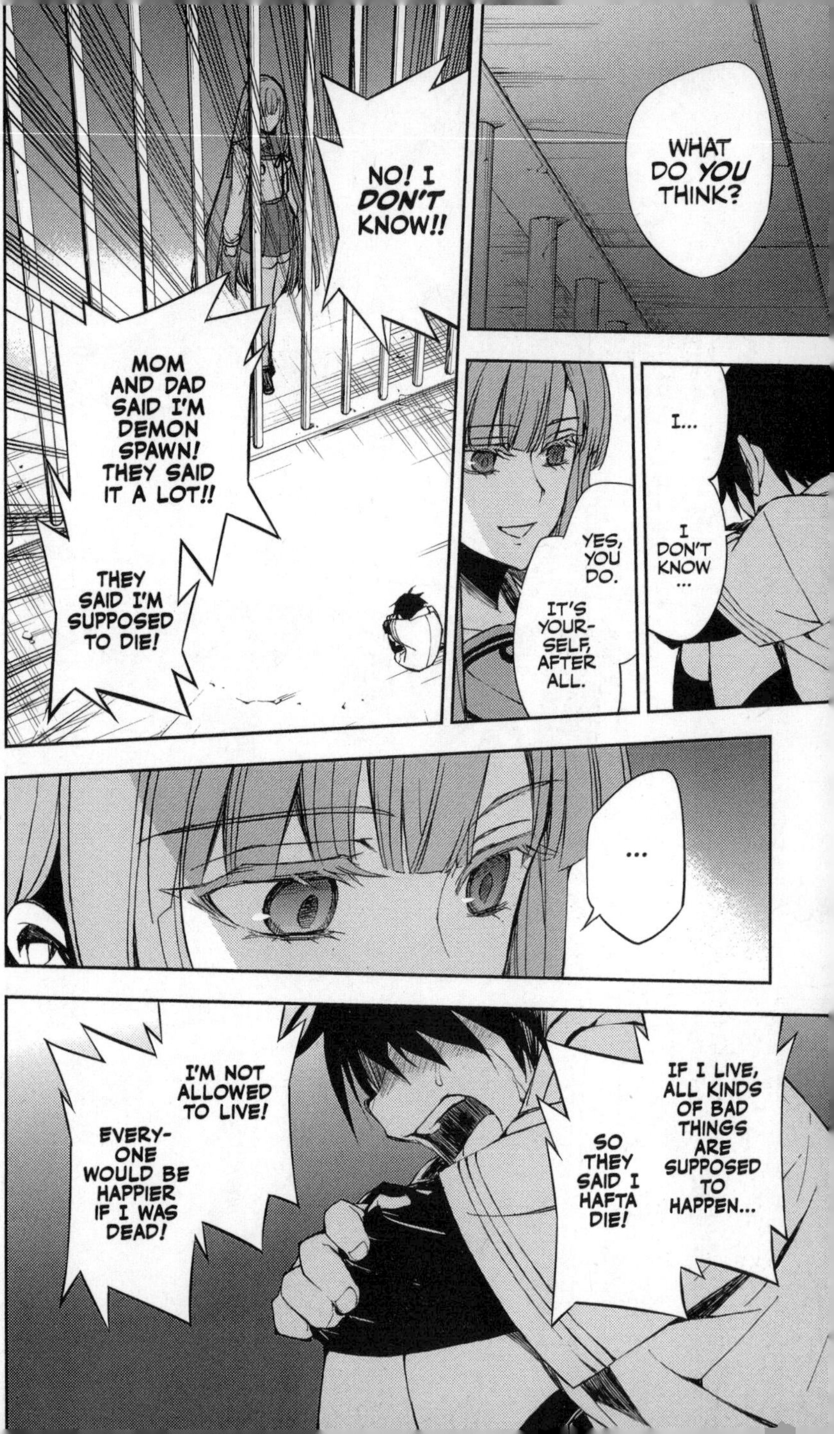

WHAT DO YOU THINK?
I...
I DON'T KNOW...
YES, YOU DO.
IT'S YOURSELF, AFTER ALL.
NO! I DON'T KNOW!!
MOM AND DAD SAID I'M DEMON SPAWN! THEY SAID IT A LOT!!
THEY SAID I'M SUPPOSED TO DIE!
...
IF I LIVE, ALL KINDS OF BAD THINGS ARE SUPPOSED TO HAPPEN...
SO THEY SAID I HAFTA DIE!
I'M NOT ALLOWED TO LIVE!
EVERYONE WOULD BE HAPPIER IF I WAS DEAD!

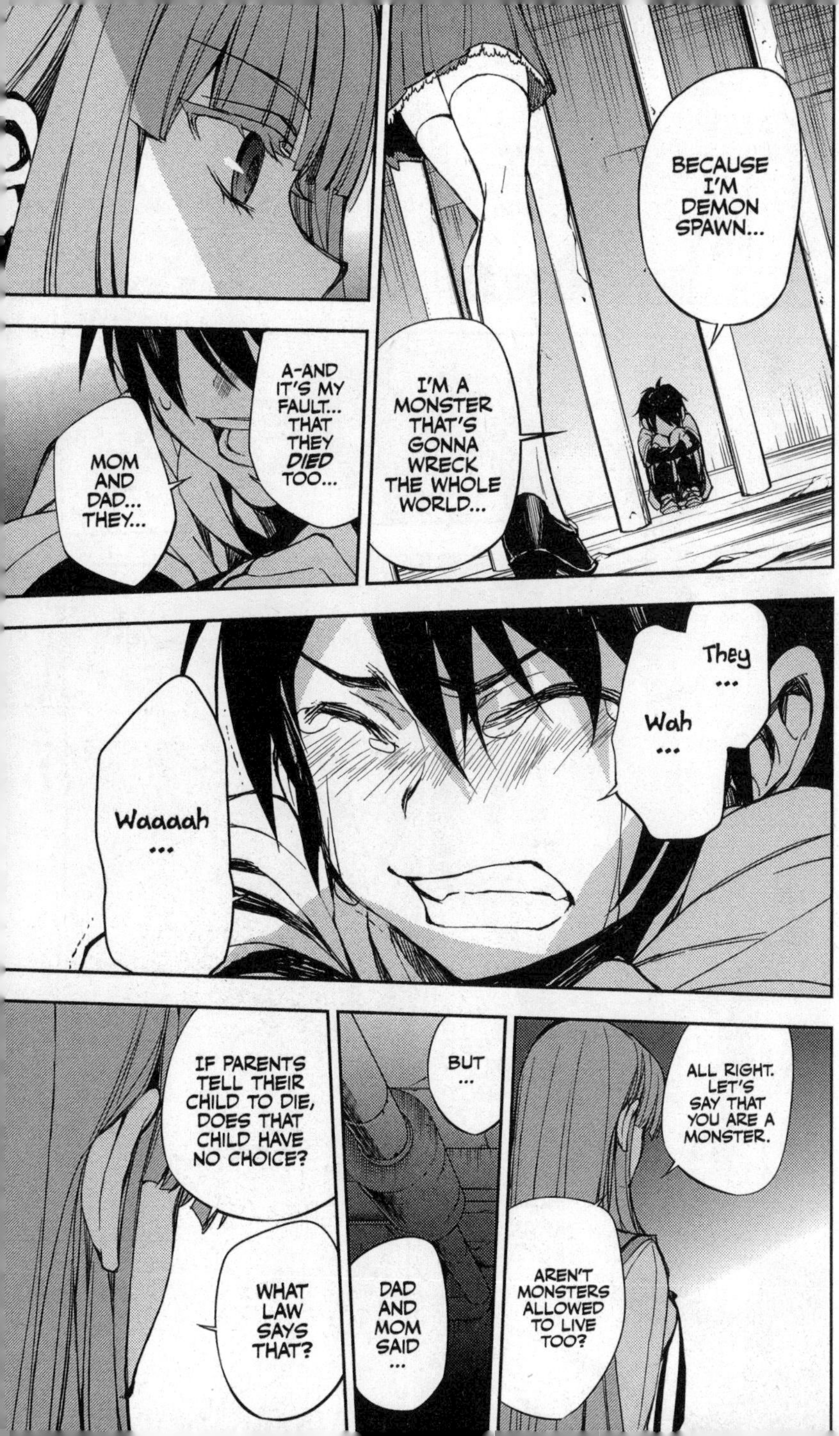
BECAUSE I'M DEMON SPAWN...
I'M A MONSTER THAT'S GONNA WRECK THE WHOLE WORLD...
A-AND IT'S MY FAULT... THAT THEY *DIED* TOO...
MOM AND DAD... THEY...
They... Wah...
Waaaah...
ALL RIGHT. LET'S SAY THAT YOU ARE A MONSTER.
AREN'T MONSTERS ALLOWED TO LIVE TOO?
BUT...
DAD AND MOM SAID...
IF PARENTS TELL THEIR CHILD TO DIE, DOES THAT CHILD HAVE NO CHOICE?
WHAT LAW SAYS THAT?

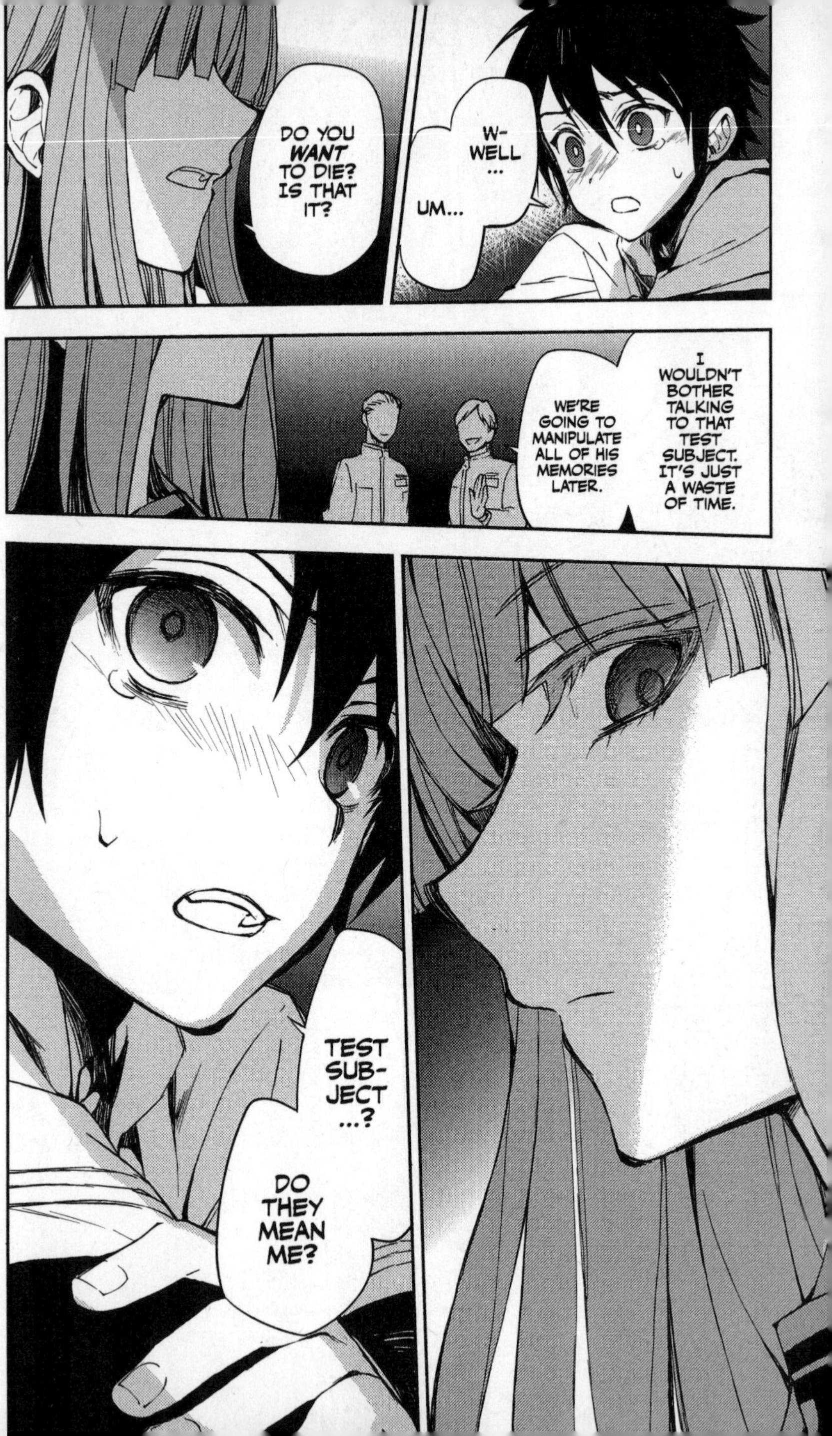
W-WELL...
UM...
DO YOU *WANT* TO DIE? IS THAT IT?
I WOULDN'T BOTHER TALKING TO THAT TEST SUBJECT. IT'S JUST A WASTE OF TIME.
WE'RE GOING TO MANIPULATE ALL OF HIS MEMORIES LATER.
TEST SUB-JECT...?
DO THEY MEAN ME?

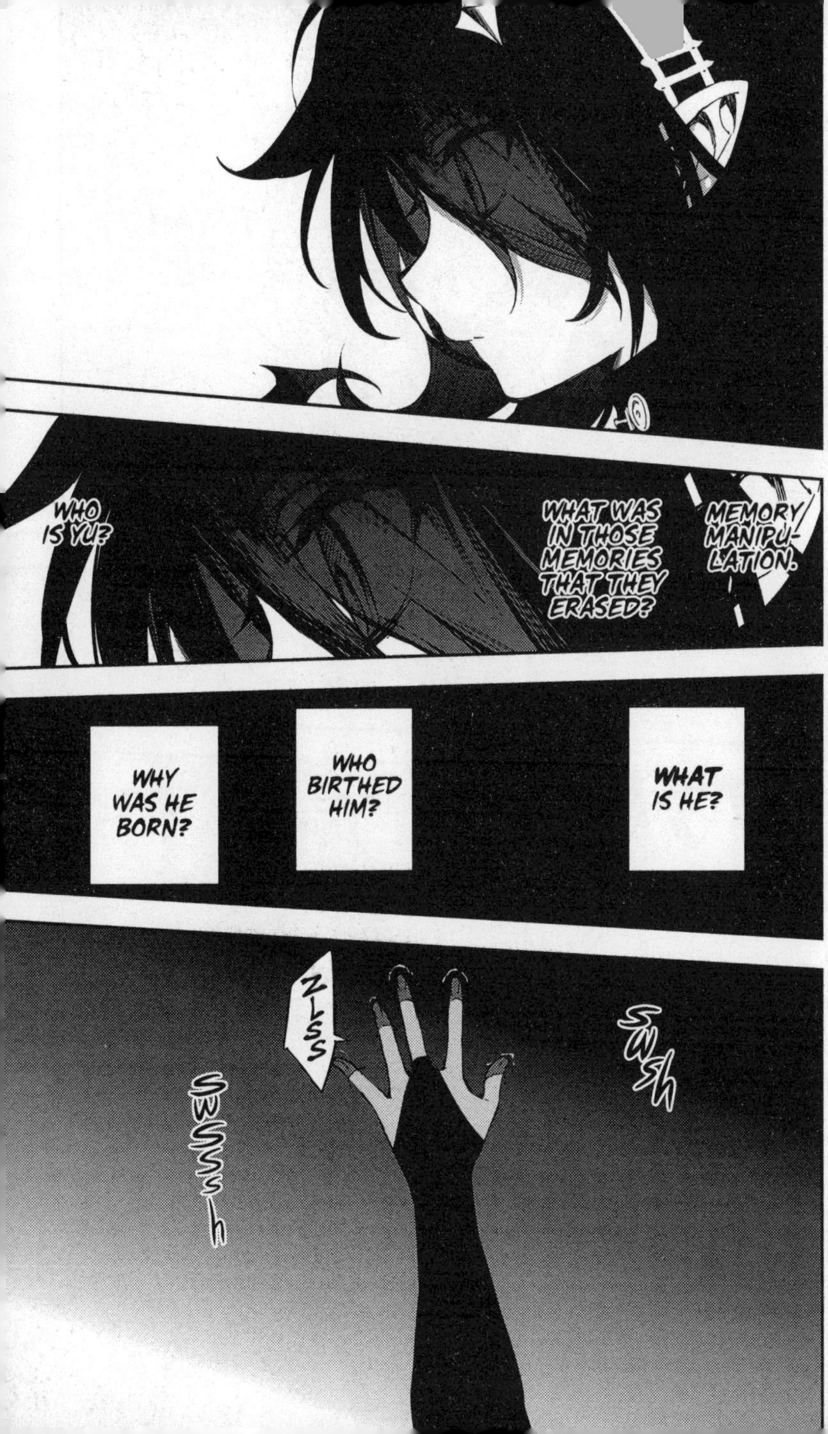
MEMORY MANIPULATION.
WHAT WAS IN THOSE MEMORIES THAT THEY ERASED?
WHO IS YU?
WHAT IS HE?
WHO BIRTHED HIM?
WHY WAS HE BORN?
SWSH
ZLSS
SWSSSH

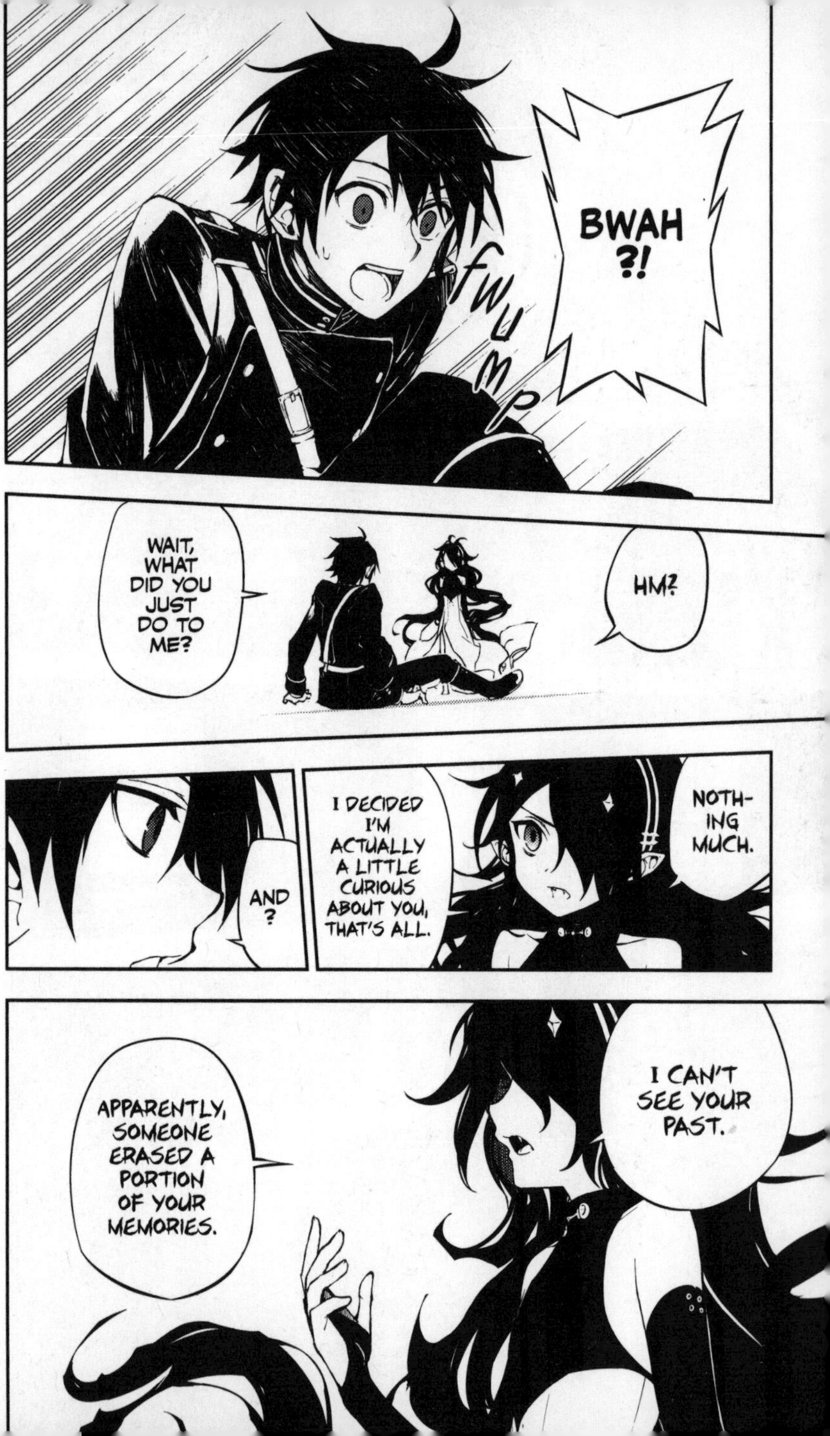
BWAH ?!
fwump
HM?
WAIT, WHAT DID YOU JUST DO TO ME?
NOTHING MUCH.
I DECIDED I'M ACTUALLY A LITTLE CURIOUS ABOUT YOU, THAT'S ALL.
AND ?
I CAN'T SEE YOUR PAST.
APPARENTLY, SOMEONE ERASED A PORTION OF YOUR MEMORIES.

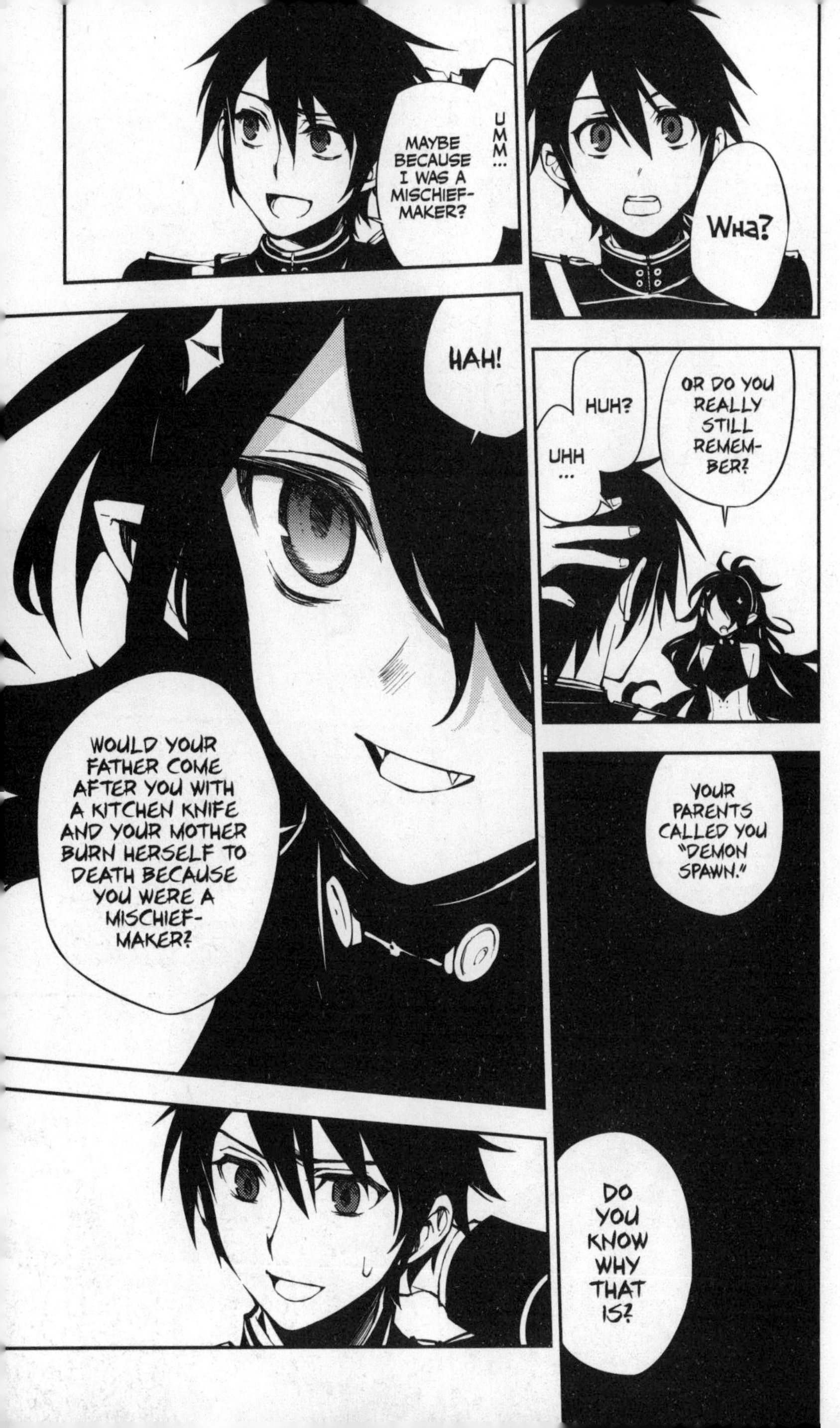
WHA?
UMM...
MAYBE BECAUSE I WAS A MISCHIEF-MAKER?
HAH!
OR DO YOU REALLY STILL REMEMBER?
HUH?
UHH...
WOULD YOUR FATHER COME AFTER YOU WITH A KITCHEN KNIFE AND YOUR MOTHER BURN HERSELF TO DEATH BECAUSE YOU WERE A MISCHIEF-MAKER?
YOUR PARENTS CALLED YOU "DEMON SPAWN."
DO YOU KNOW WHY THAT IS?

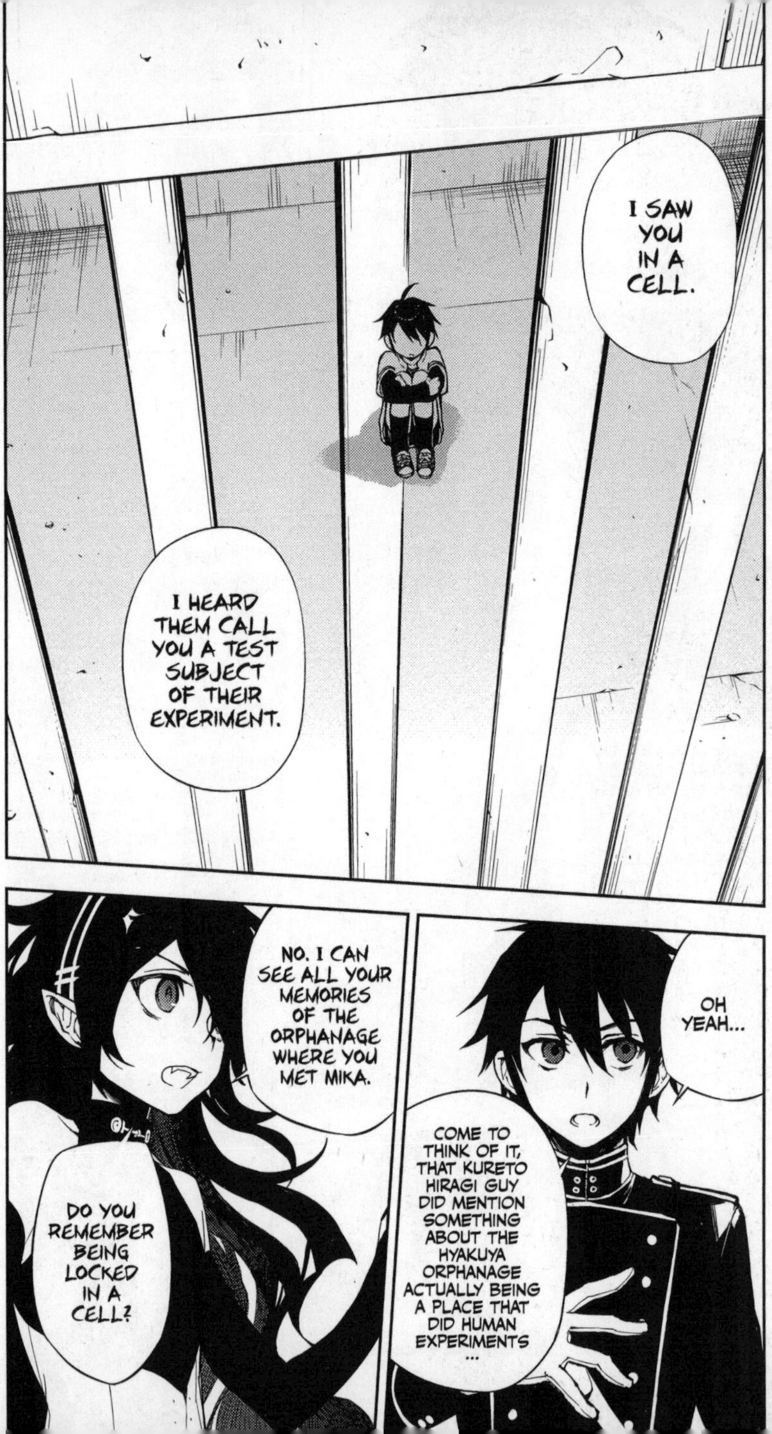
I SAW YOU IN A CELL.
I HEARD THEM CALL YOU A TEST SUBJECT OF THEIR EXPERIMENT.
OH YEAH...
COME TO THINK OF IT, THAT KURETO HIRAGI GUY DID MENTION SOMETHING ABOUT THE HYAKUYA ORPHANAGE ACTUALLY BEING A PLACE THAT DID HUMAN EXPERIMENTS ...
NO. I CAN SEE ALL YOUR MEMORIES OF THE ORPHANAGE WHERE YOU MET MIKA.
DO YOU REMEMBER BEING LOCKED IN A CELL?

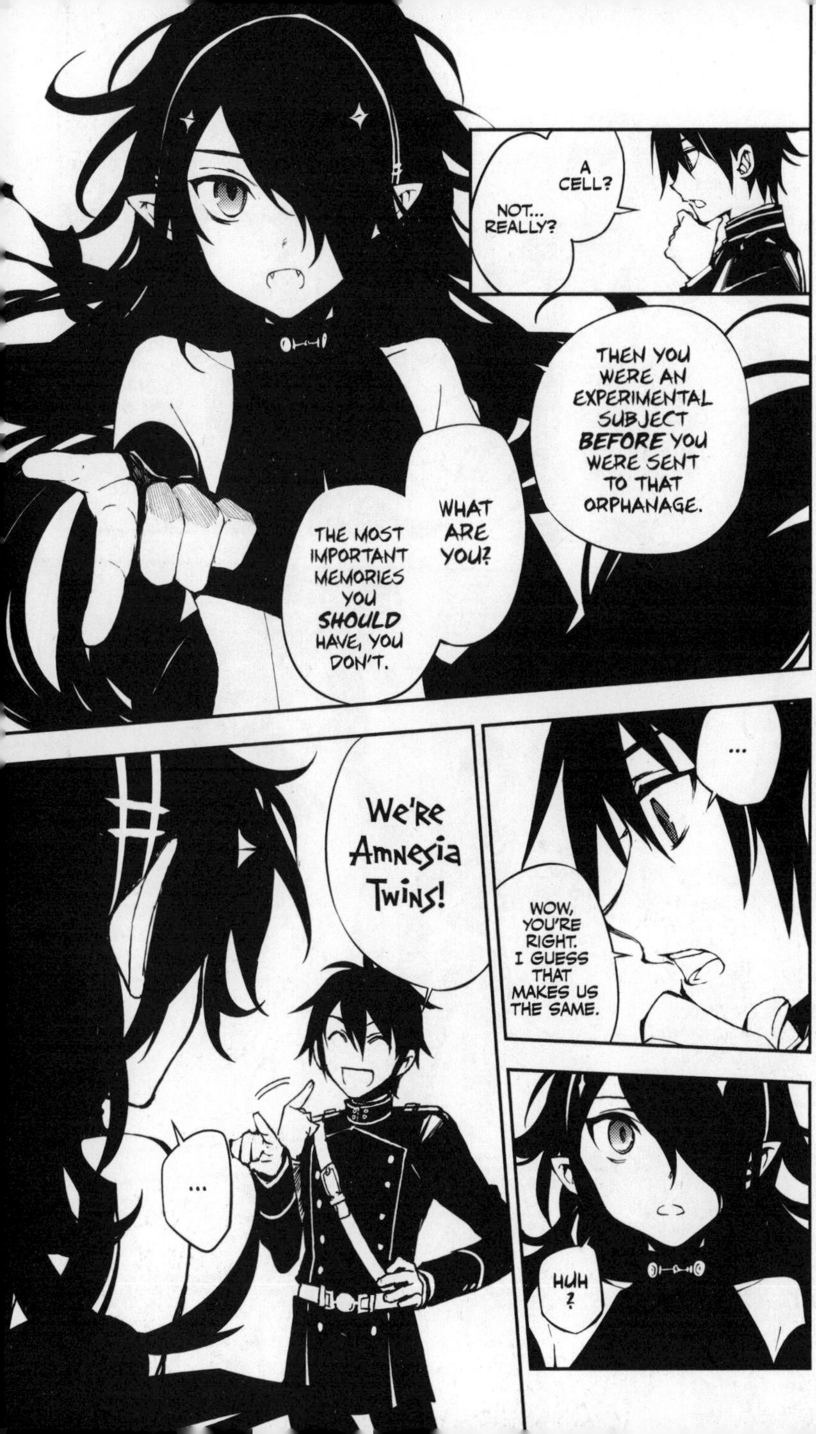
A CELL?
NOT... REALLY?
THEN YOU WERE AN EXPERIMENTAL SUBJECT BEFORE YOU WERE SENT TO THAT ORPHANAGE.
WHAT ARE YOU?
THE MOST IMPORTANT MEMORIES YOU SHOULD HAVE, YOU DON'T.
...
WOW, YOU'RE RIGHT. I GUESS THAT MAKES US THE SAME.
HUH?
We're Amnesia Twins!
...

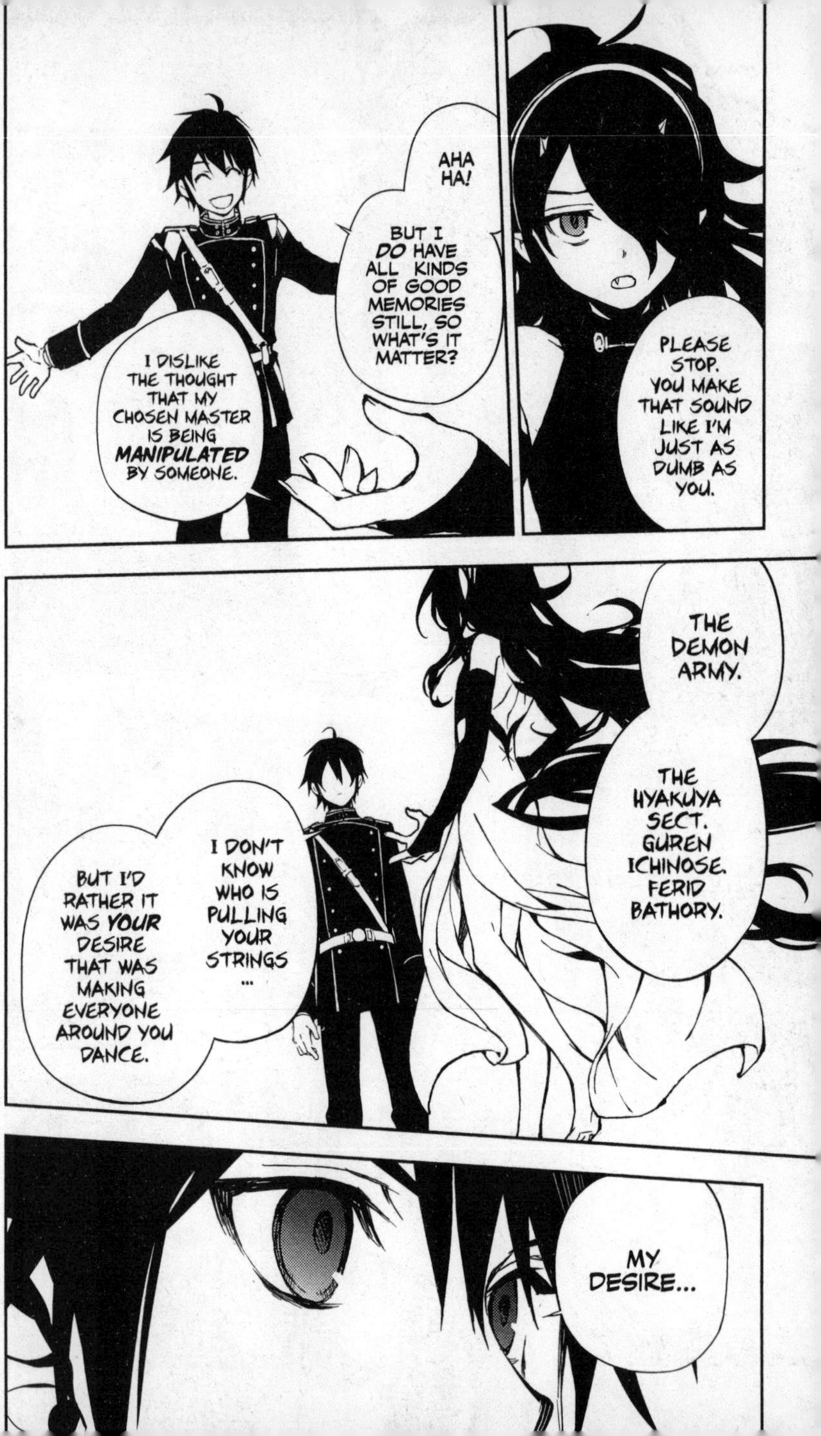

PLEASE STOP. YOU MAKE THAT SOUND LIKE I'M JUST AS DUMB AS YOU.
AHA HA!
BUT I DO HAVE ALL KINDS OF GOOD MEMORIES STILL, SO WHAT'S IT MATTER?
I DISLIKE THE THOUGHT THAT MY CHOSEN MASTER IS BEING MANIPULATED BY SOMEONE.
THE DEMON ARMY.
THE HYAKUYA SECT. GUREN ICHINOSE. FERID BATHORY.
I DON'T KNOW WHO IS PULLING YOUR STRINGS...
BUT I'D RATHER IT WAS YOUR DESIRE THAT WAS MAKING EVERYONE AROUND YOU DANCE.
MY DESIRE...

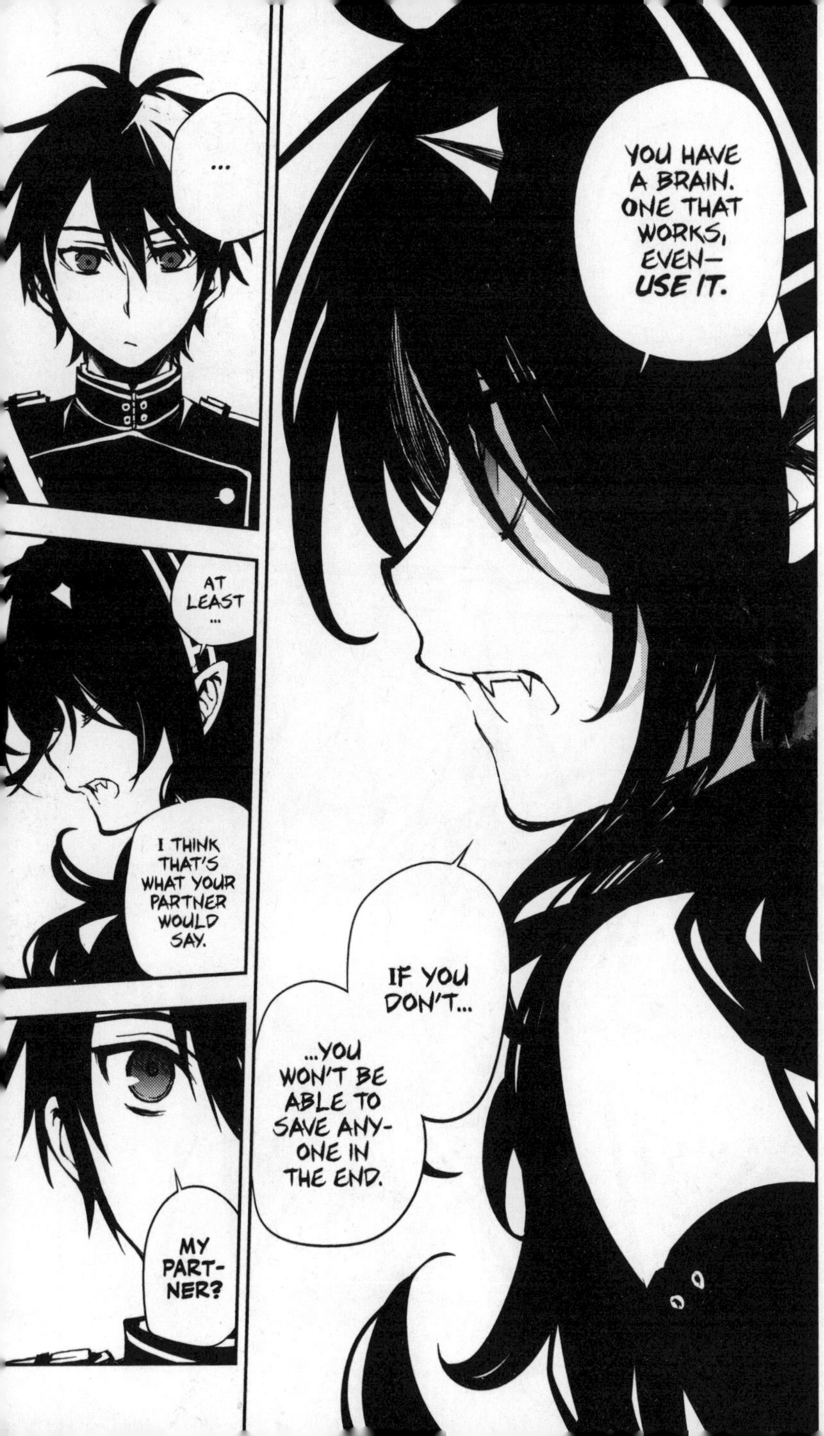
YOU HAVE A BRAIN. ONE THAT WORKS, EVEN— USE IT.
IF YOU DON'T...
...YOU WON'T BE ABLE TO SAVE ANY-ONE IN THE END.
...
AT LEAST ...
I THINK THAT'S WHAT YOUR PARTNER WOULD SAY.
MY PART-NER?

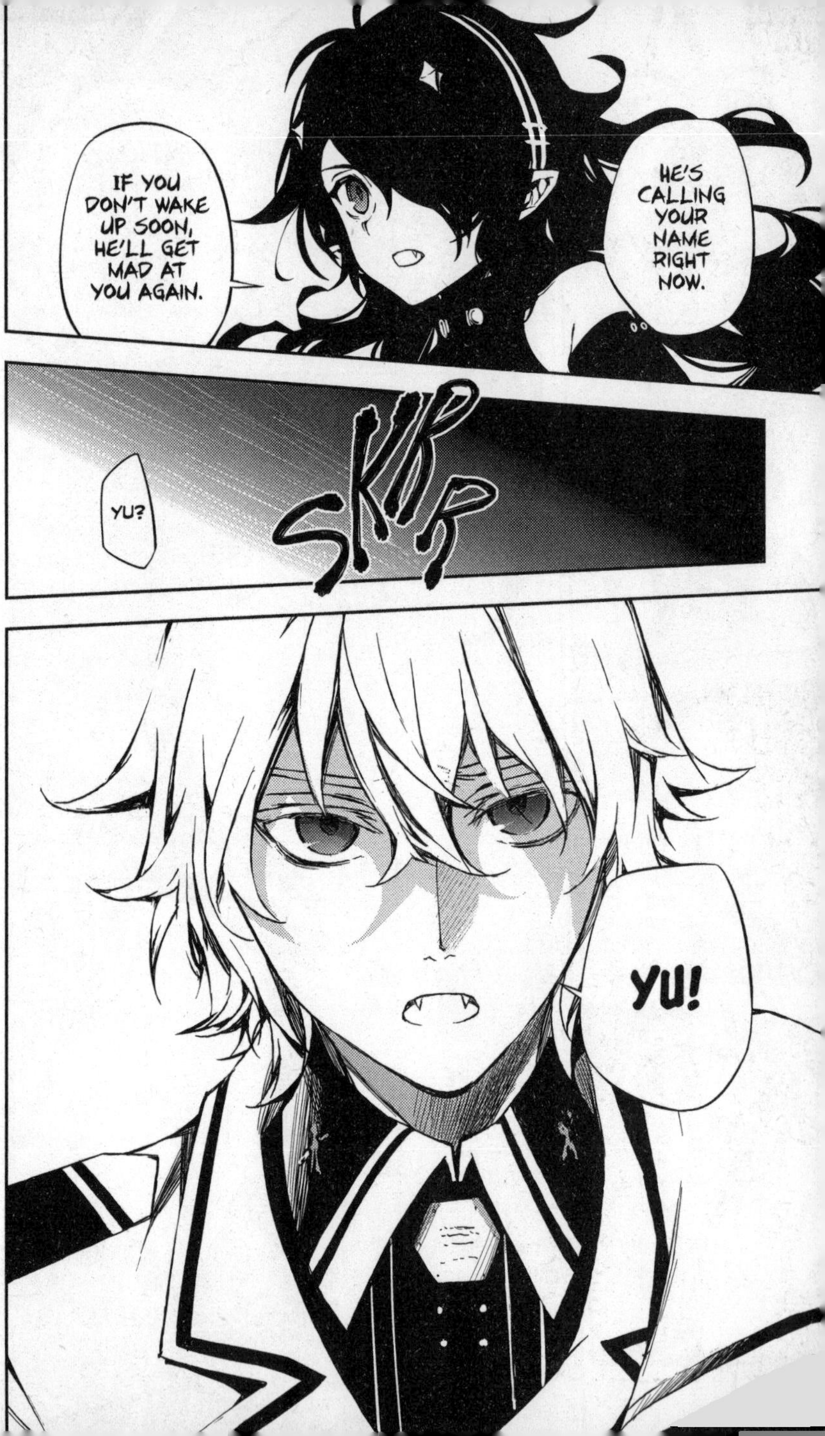
HE'S CALLING YOUR NAME RIGHT NOW.
IF YOU DON'T WAKE UP SOON, HE'LL GET MAD AT YOU AGAIN.
SKRR
YU?
YU!

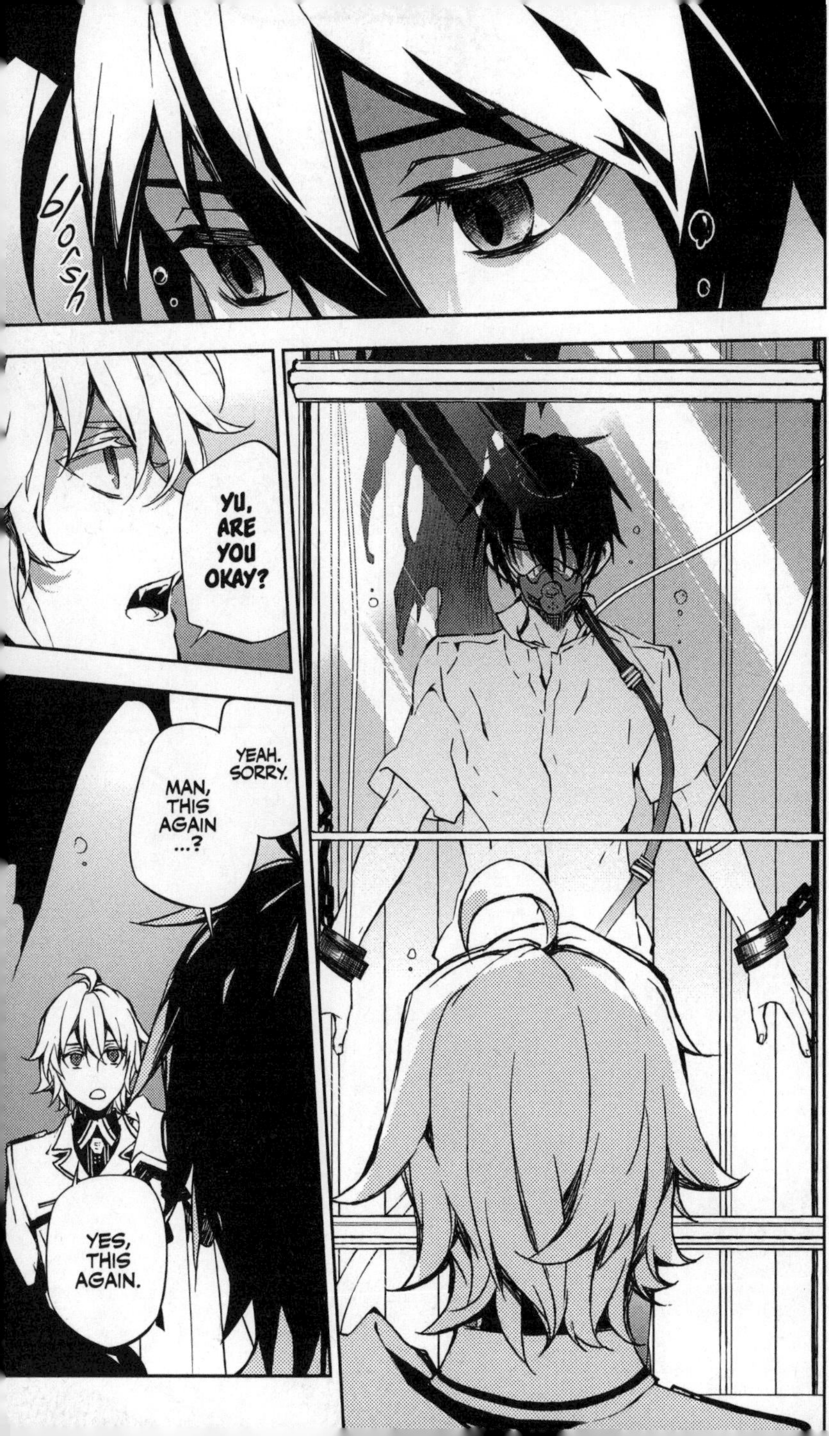
blorsh
YU, ARE YOU OKAY?
YEAH. SORRY.
MAN, THIS AGAIN ...?
YES, THIS AGAIN.

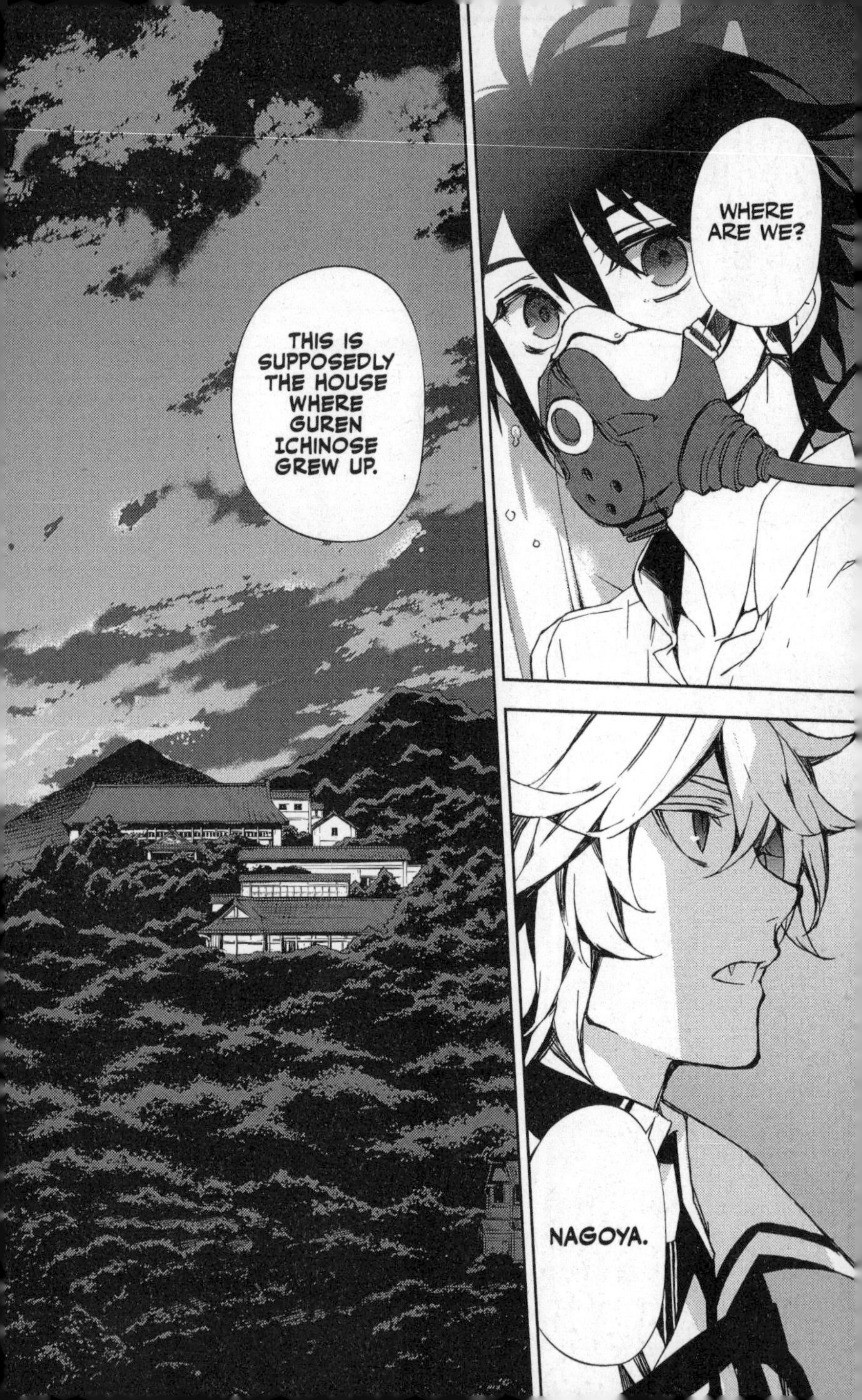
WHERE ARE WE?
NAGOYA.
THIS IS SUPPOSEDLY THE HOUSE WHERE GUREN ICHINOSE GREW UP.

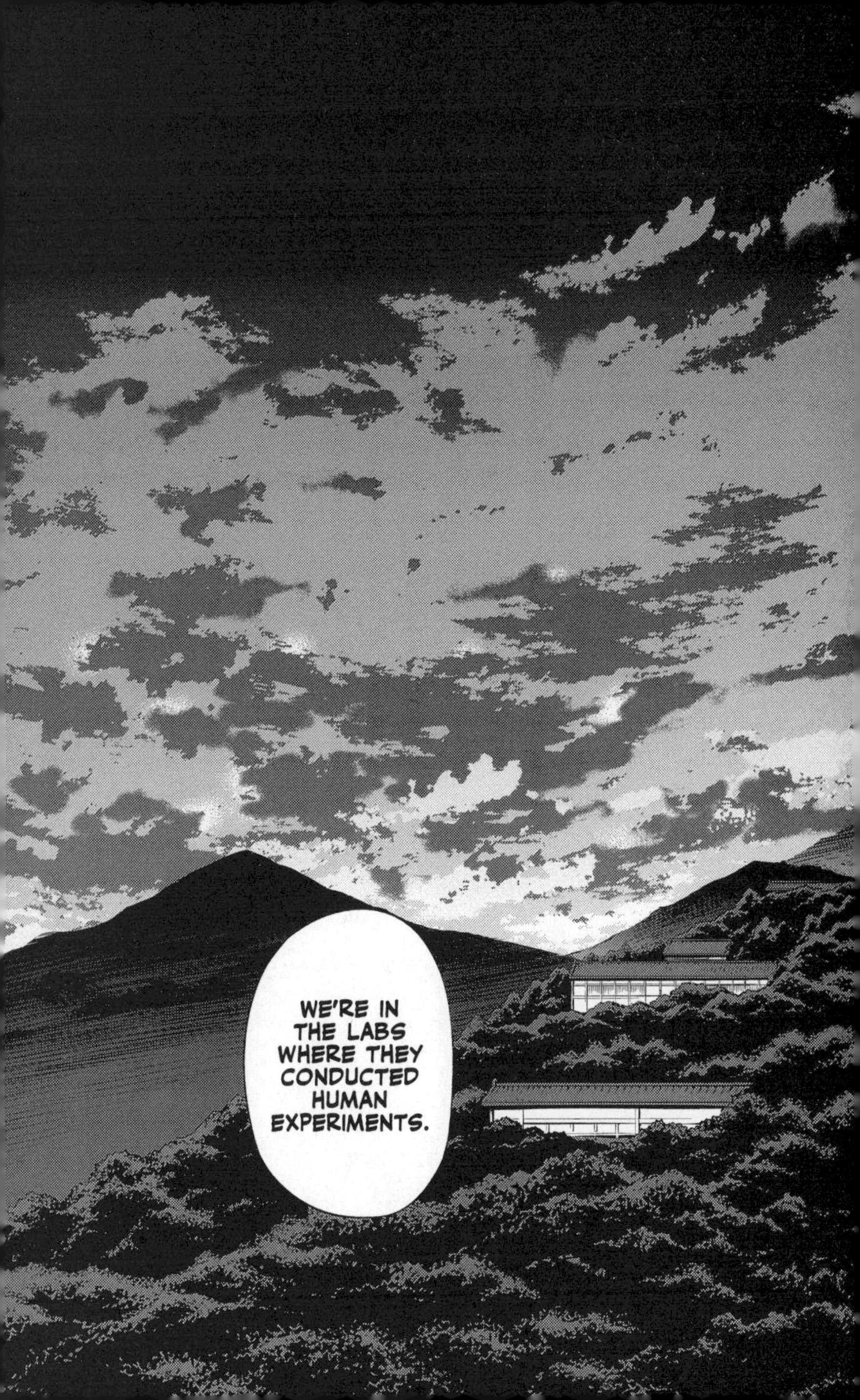
WE'RE IN THE LABS WHERE THEY CONDUCTED HUMAN EXPERIMENTS.

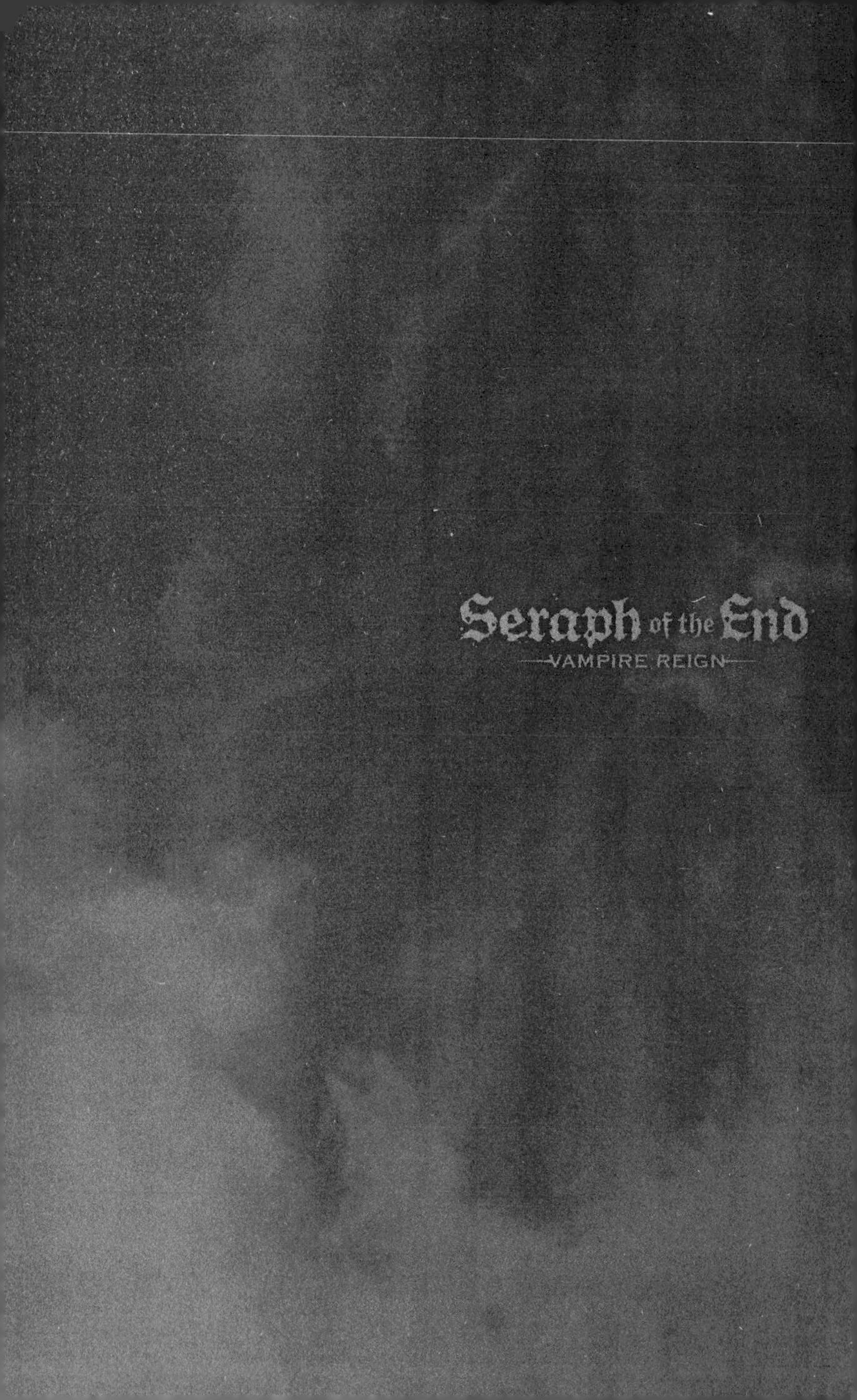
Seraph of the End
VAMPIRE REIGN

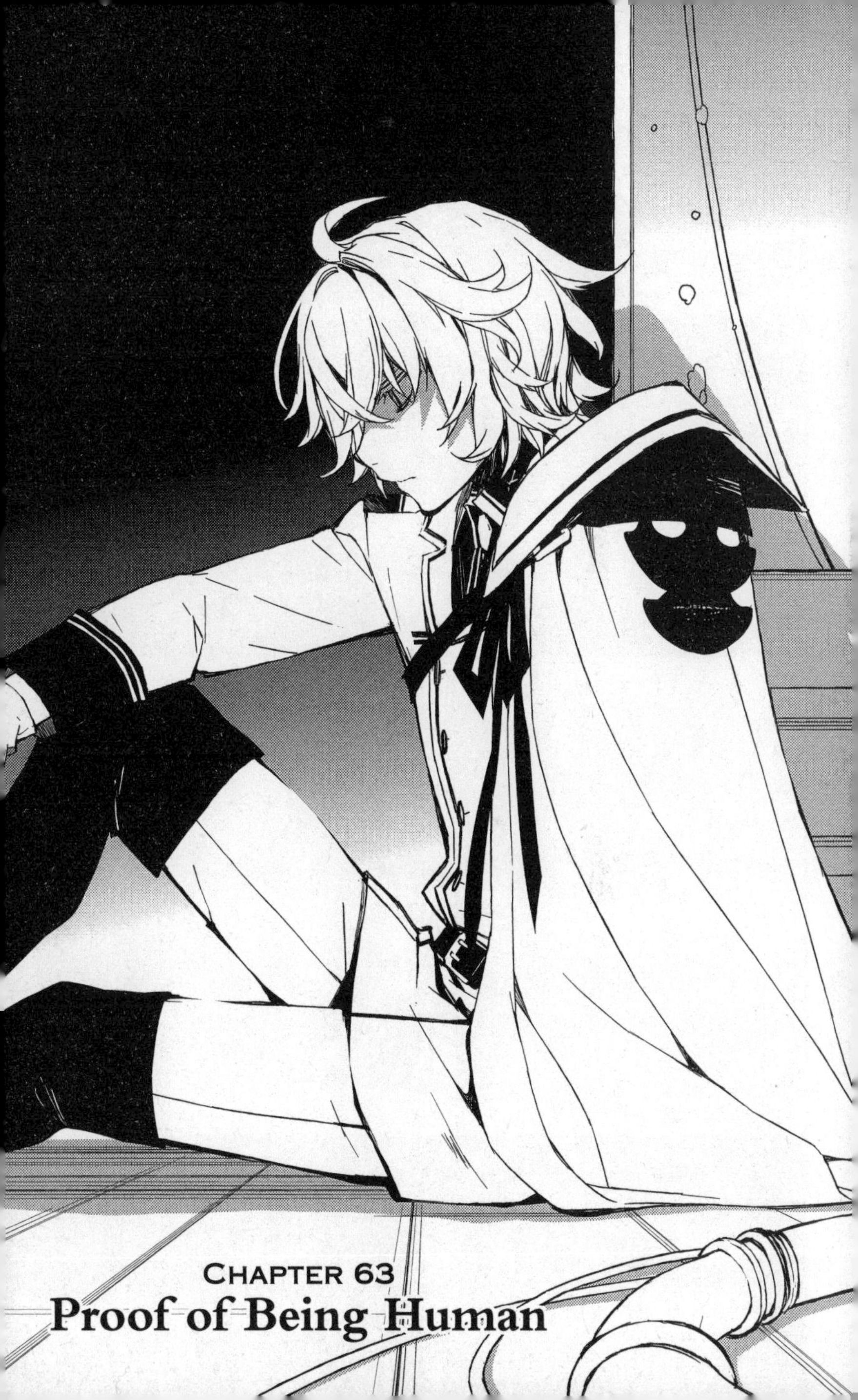

Chapter 63
Proof of Being Human

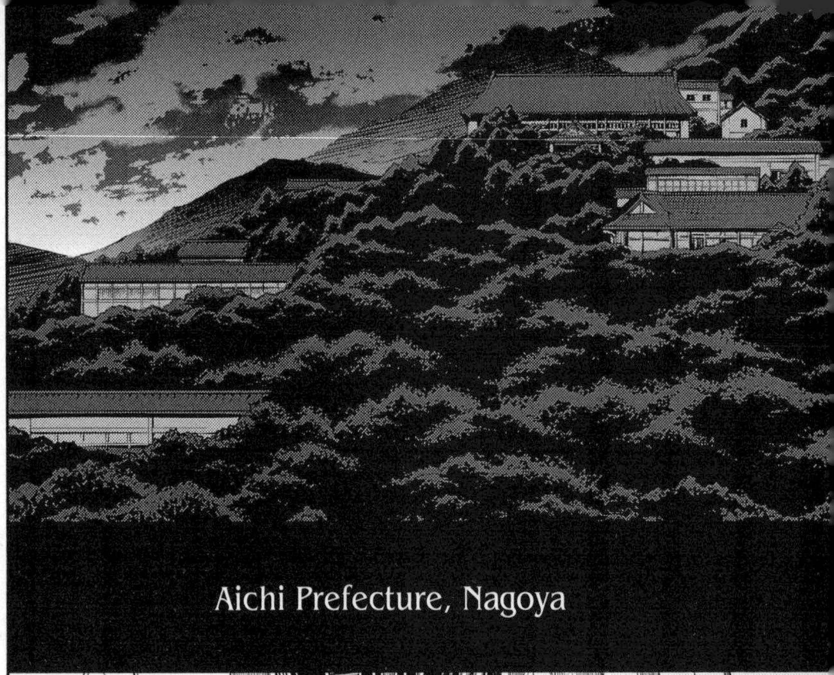
Aichi Prefecture, Nagoya

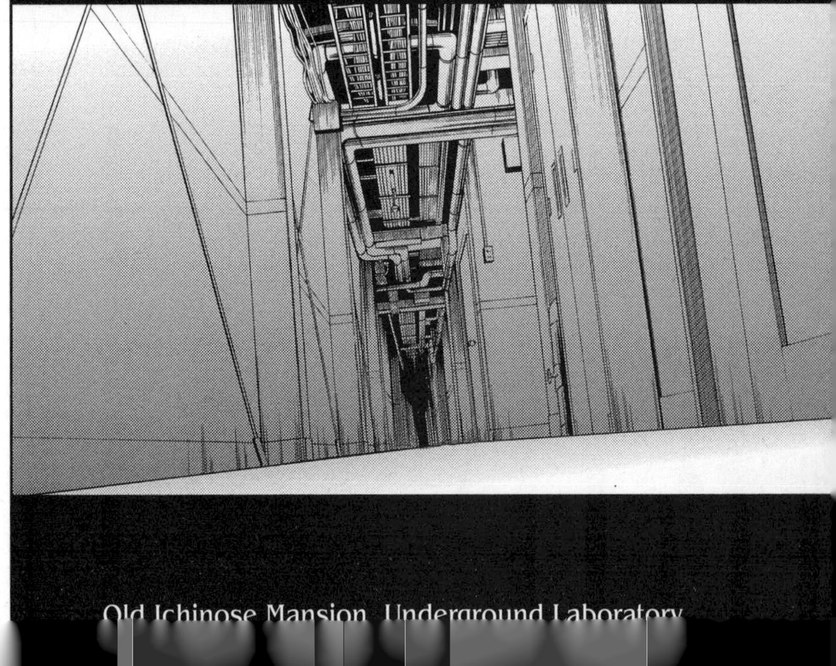
Old Ichinose Mansion, Underground Laboratory

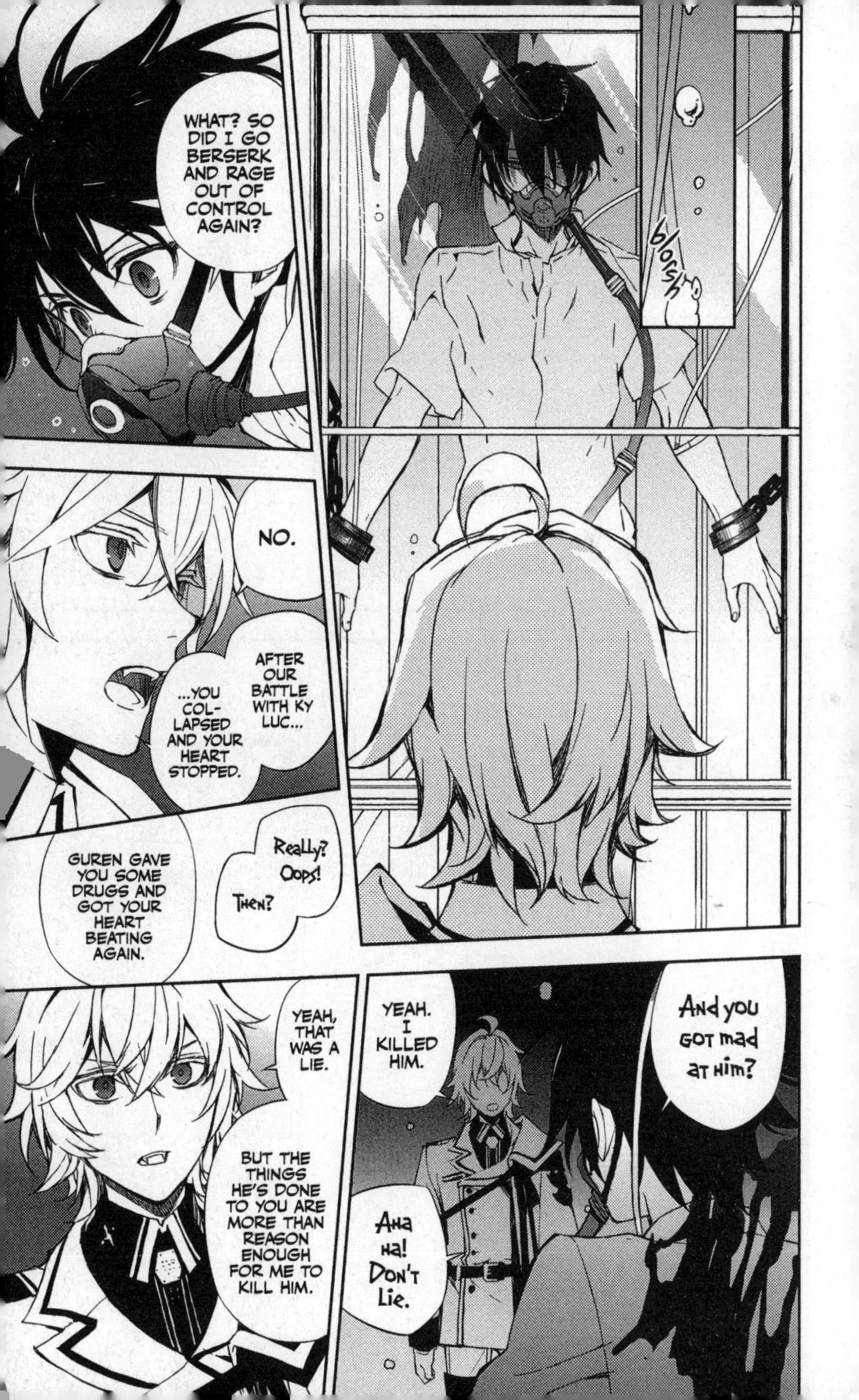
blorsh
WHAT? SO DID I GO BERSERK AND RAGE OUT OF CONTROL AGAIN?
NO.
AFTER OUR BATTLE WITH KY LUC...
...YOU COL-LAPSED AND YOUR HEART STOPPED.
Really? Oops!
Then?
GUREN GAVE YOU SOME DRUGS AND GOT YOUR HEART BEATING AGAIN.
And you got mad at him?
YEAH. I KILLED HIM.
Aha ha! Don't Lie.
YEAH, THAT WAS A LIE.
BUT THE THINGS HE'S DONE TO YOU ARE MORE THAN REASON ENOUGH FOR ME TO KILL HIM.

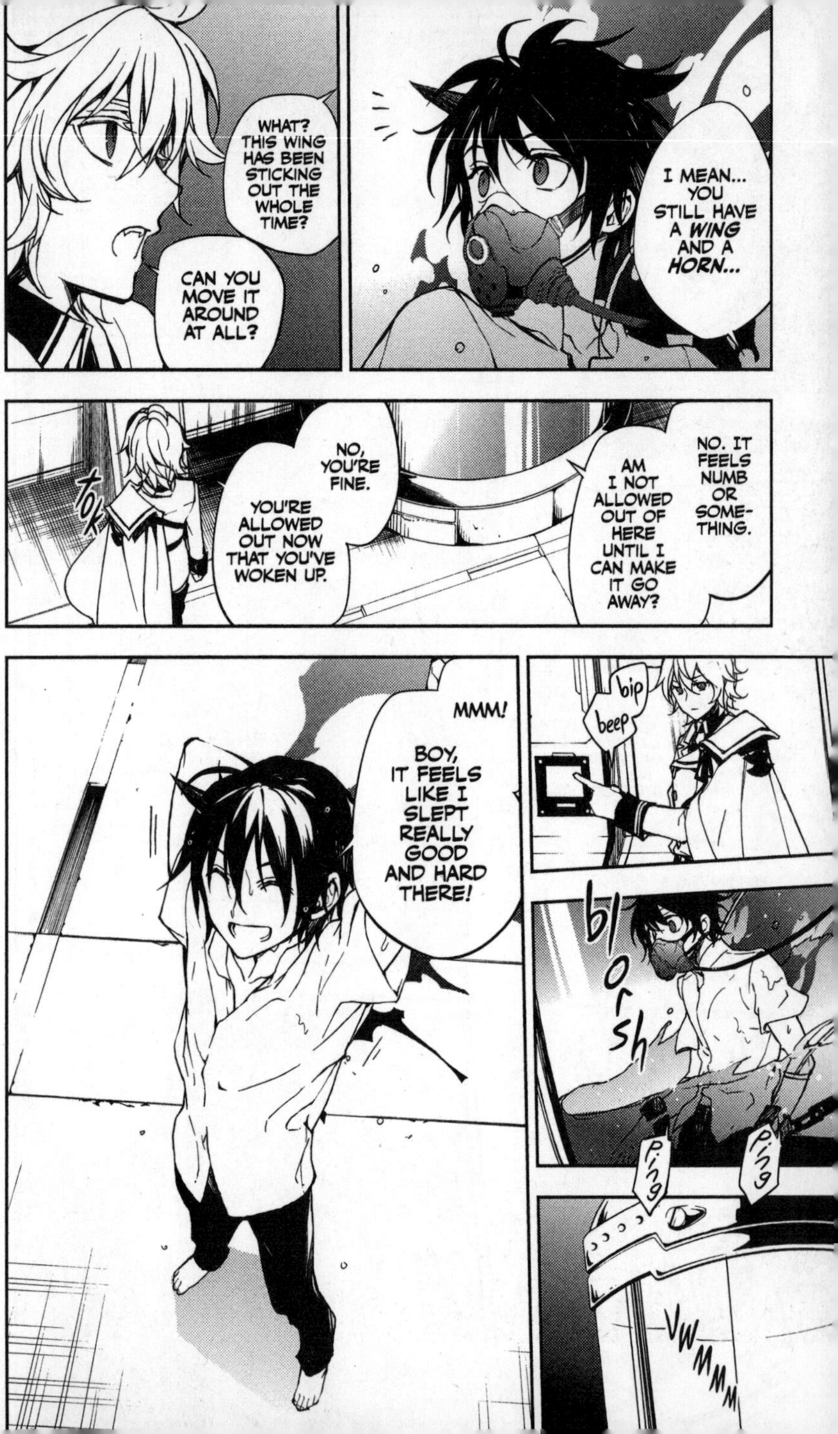
I MEAN... YOU STILL HAVE A *WING* AND A *HORN*...
WHAT? THIS WING HAS BEEN STICKING OUT THE WHOLE TIME?
CAN YOU MOVE IT AROUND AT ALL?
NO. IT FEELS NUMB OR SOME-THING.
AM I NOT ALLOWED OUT OF HERE UNTIL I CAN MAKE IT GO AWAY?
NO, YOU'RE FINE.
YOU'RE ALLOWED OUT NOW THAT YOU'VE WOKEN UP.
tok
bip
beep
blorsh
ping
ping
VWMMMM
MMM!
BOY, IT FEELS LIKE I SLEPT REALLY GOOD AND HARD THERE!

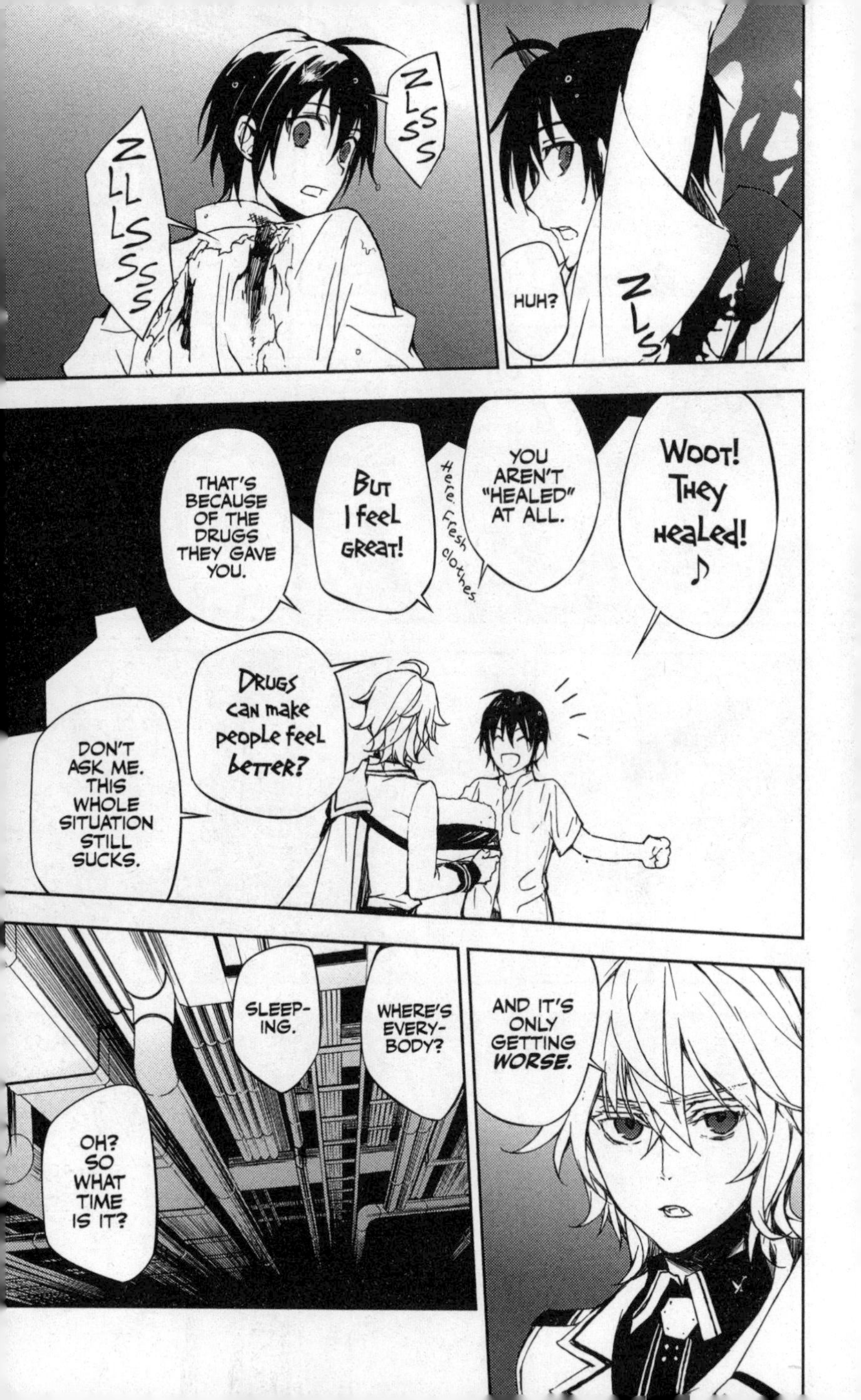
HUH?
ZLLS
ZLSSS
ZLLLSSSS
WOOT! THEY HEALED! ♪
YOU AREN'T "HEALED" AT ALL.
Here. Fresh clothes.
BUT I FEEL GREAT!
THAT'S BECAUSE OF THE DRUGS THEY GAVE YOU.
DRUGS CAN MAKE PEOPLE FEEL BETTER?
DON'T ASK ME. THIS WHOLE SITUATION STILL SUCKS.
AND IT'S ONLY GETTING WORSE.
WHERE'S EVERYBODY?
SLEEP-ING.
OH? SO WHAT TIME IS IT?

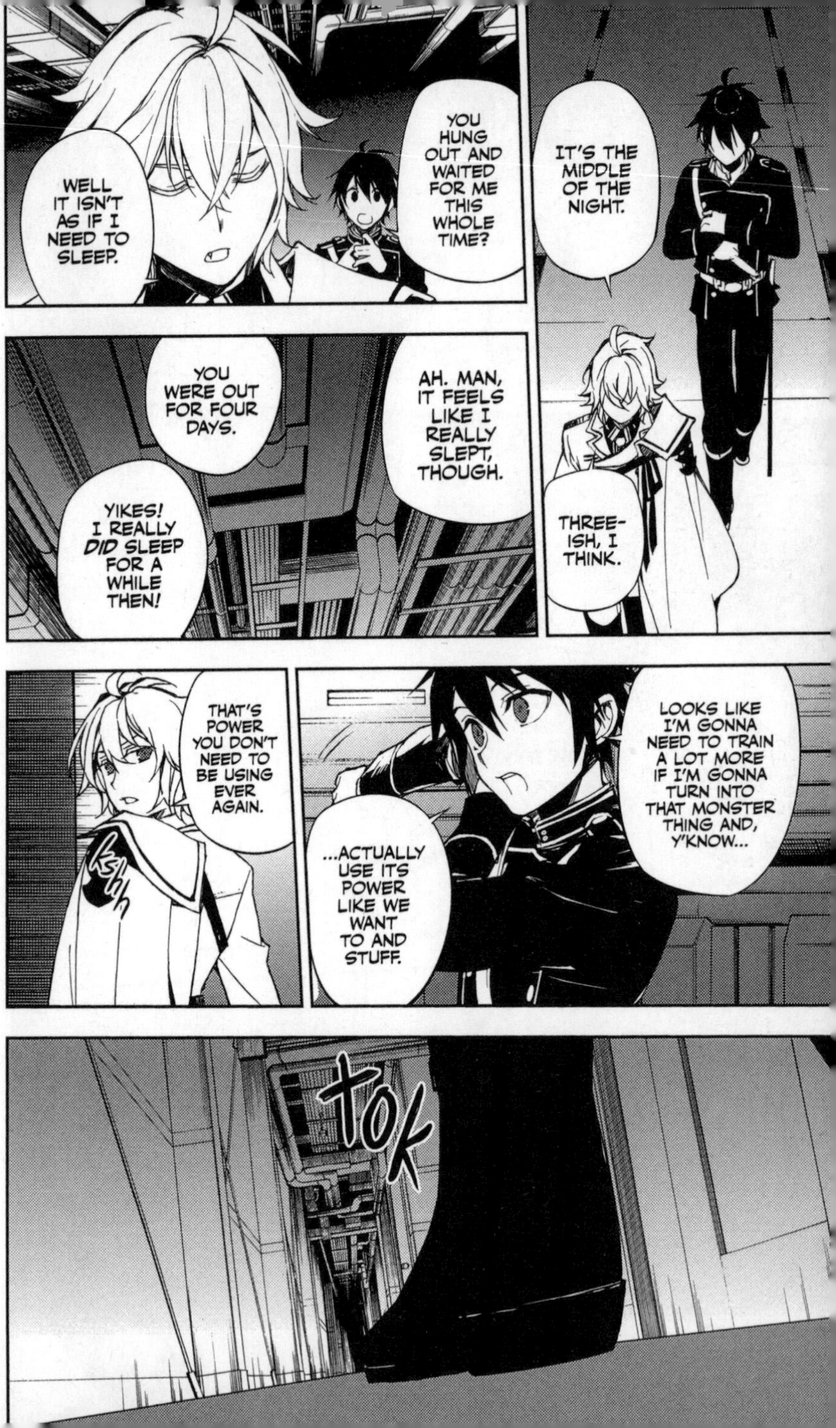

IT'S THE MIDDLE OF THE NIGHT.
THREE-ISH, I THINK.
YOU HUNG OUT AND WAITED FOR ME THIS WHOLE TIME?
WELL IT ISN'T AS IF I NEED TO SLEEP.
AH. MAN, IT FEELS LIKE I REALLY SLEPT, THOUGH.
YOU WERE OUT FOR FOUR DAYS.
YIKES! I REALLY *DID* SLEEP FOR A WHILE THEN!
LOOKS LIKE I'M GONNA NEED TO TRAIN A LOT MORE IF I'M GONNA TURN INTO THAT MONSTER THING AND, Y'KNOW...
...ACTUALLY USE ITS POWER LIKE WE WANT TO AND STUFF.
THAT'S POWER YOU DON'T NEED TO BE USING EVER AGAIN.
kshh
TOK

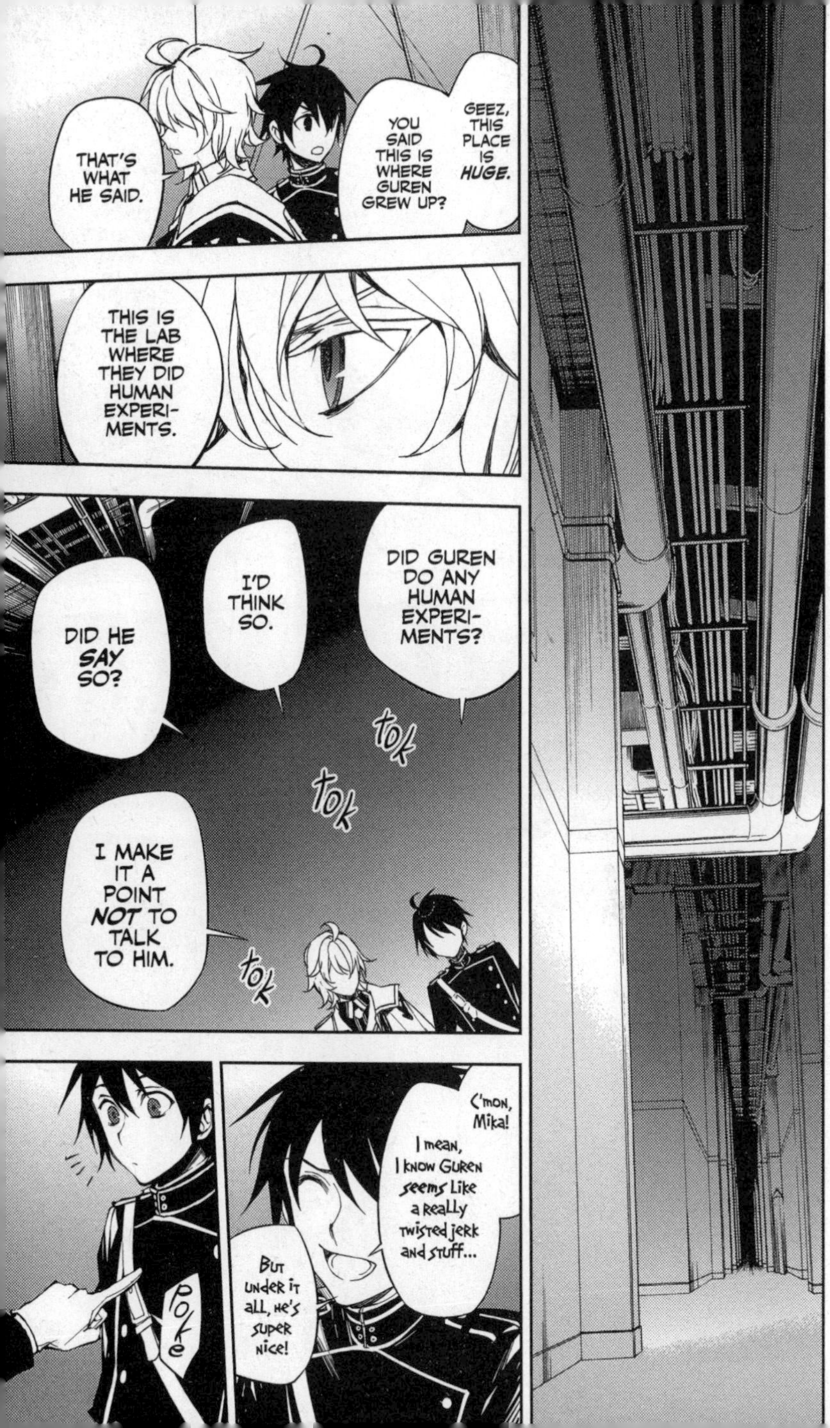
GEEZ, THIS PLACE IS *HUGE.*
YOU SAID THIS IS WHERE GUREN GREW UP?
THAT'S WHAT HE SAID.
THIS IS THE LAB WHERE THEY DID HUMAN EXPERIMENTS.
DID GUREN DO ANY HUMAN EXPERIMENTS?
I'D THINK SO.
DID HE *SAY* SO?
tok
tok
I MAKE IT A POINT *NOT* TO TALK TO HIM.
tok
C'mon, Mika!
I mean, I know Guren *seems* like a really twisted jerk and stuff...
But under it all, he's super nice!
Poke

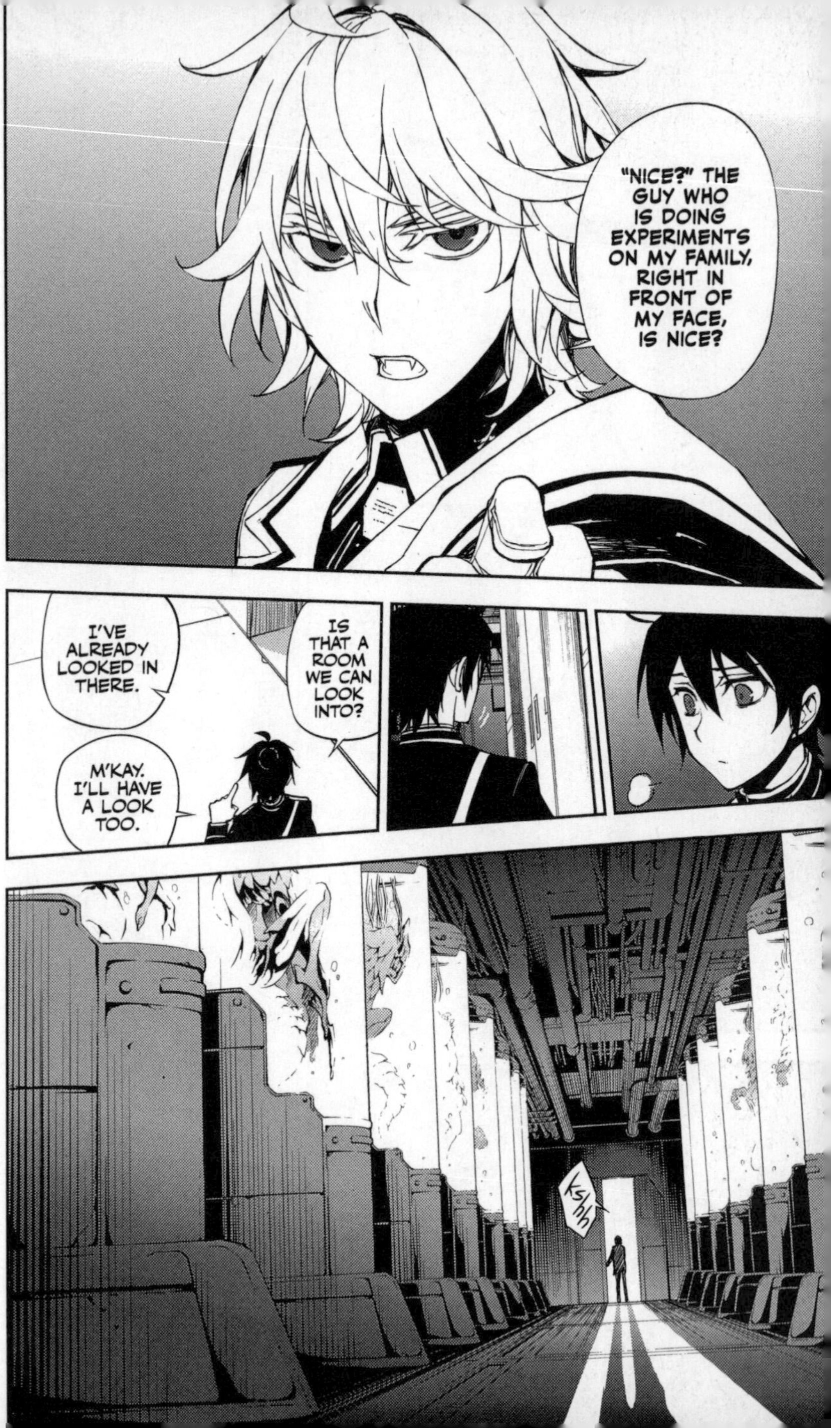
"NICE?" THE GUY WHO IS DOING EXPERIMENTS ON MY FAMILY, RIGHT IN FRONT OF MY FACE, IS NICE?
IS THAT A ROOM WE CAN LOOK INTO?
I'VE ALREADY LOOKED IN THERE.
M'KAY. I'LL HAVE A LOOK TOO.
KSHH

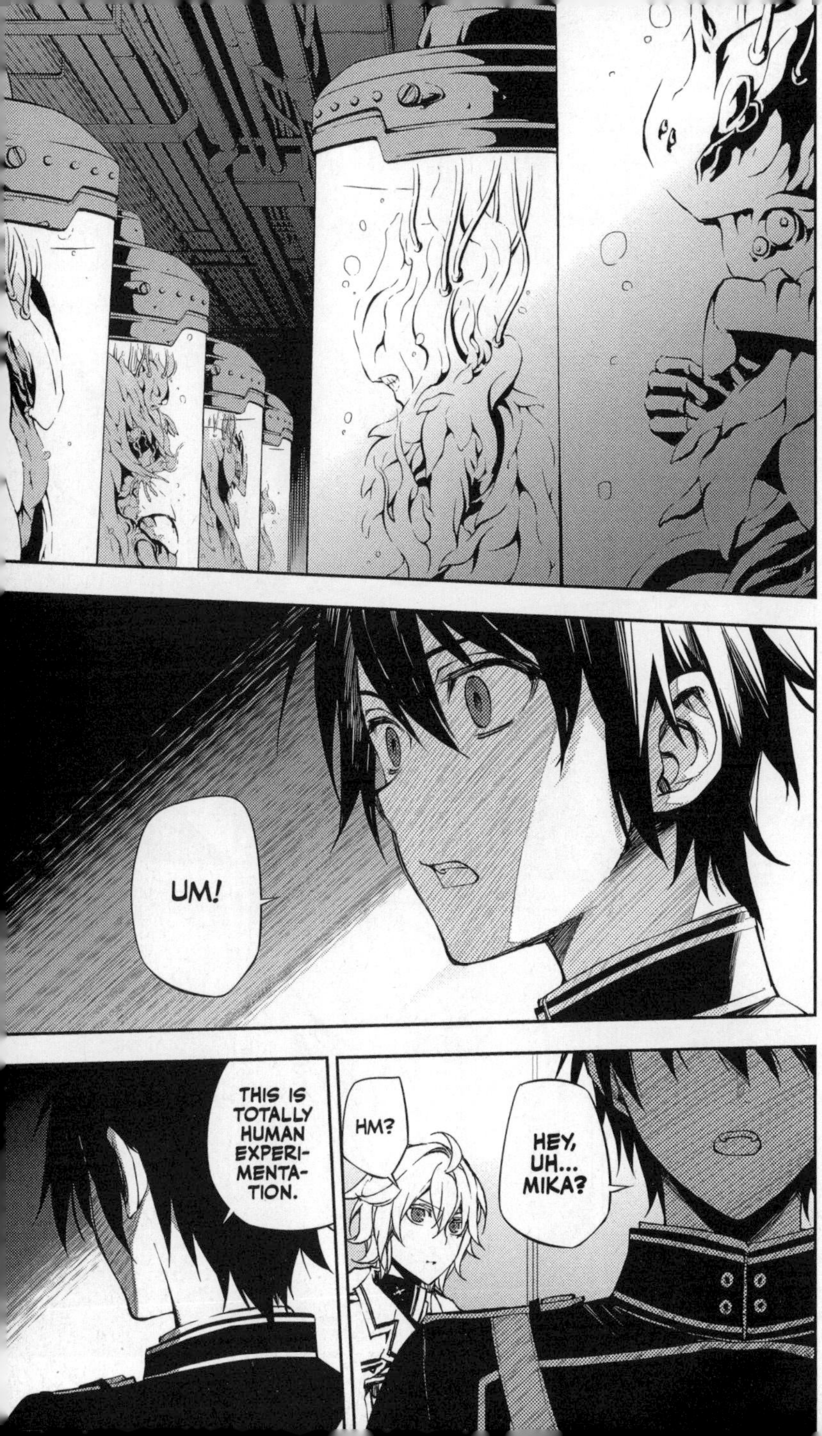
UM!
HEY, UH... MIKA?
HM?
THIS IS TOTALLY HUMAN EXPERIMENTATION.

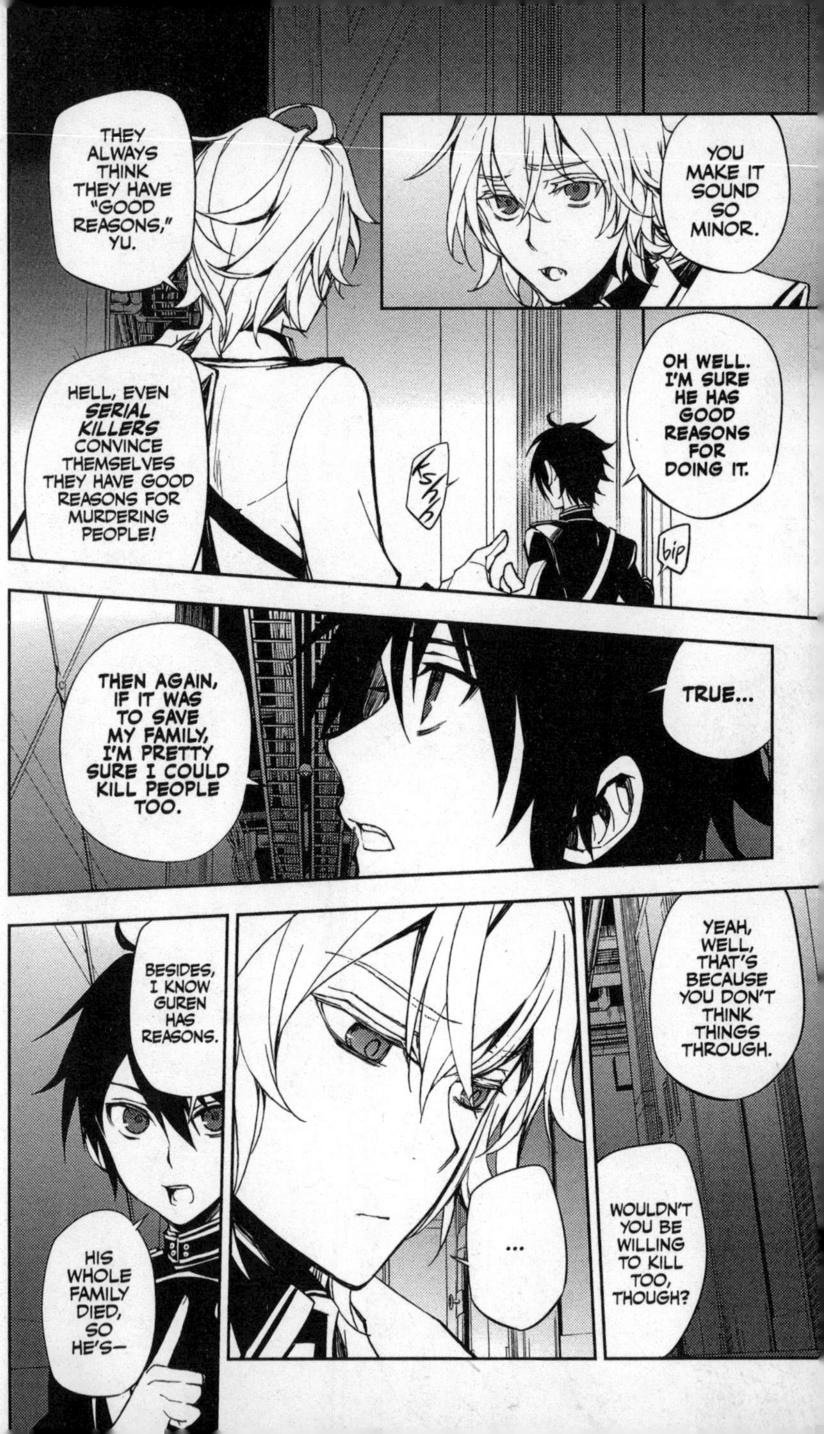
YOU MAKE IT SOUND SO MINOR.
OH WELL. I'M SURE HE HAS GOOD REASONS FOR DOING IT.
bip
kshh
THEY ALWAYS THINK THEY HAVE "GOOD REASONS," YU.
HELL, EVEN *SERIAL KILLERS* CONVINCE THEMSELVES THEY HAVE GOOD REASONS FOR MURDERING PEOPLE!
TRUE...
THEN AGAIN, IF IT WAS TO SAVE MY FAMILY, I'M PRETTY SURE I COULD KILL PEOPLE TOO.
YEAH, WELL, THAT'S BECAUSE YOU DON'T THINK THINGS THROUGH.
WOULDN'T YOU BE WILLING TO KILL TOO, THOUGH?
...
BESIDES, I KNOW GUREN HAS REASONS.
HIS WHOLE FAMILY DIED, SO HE'S—

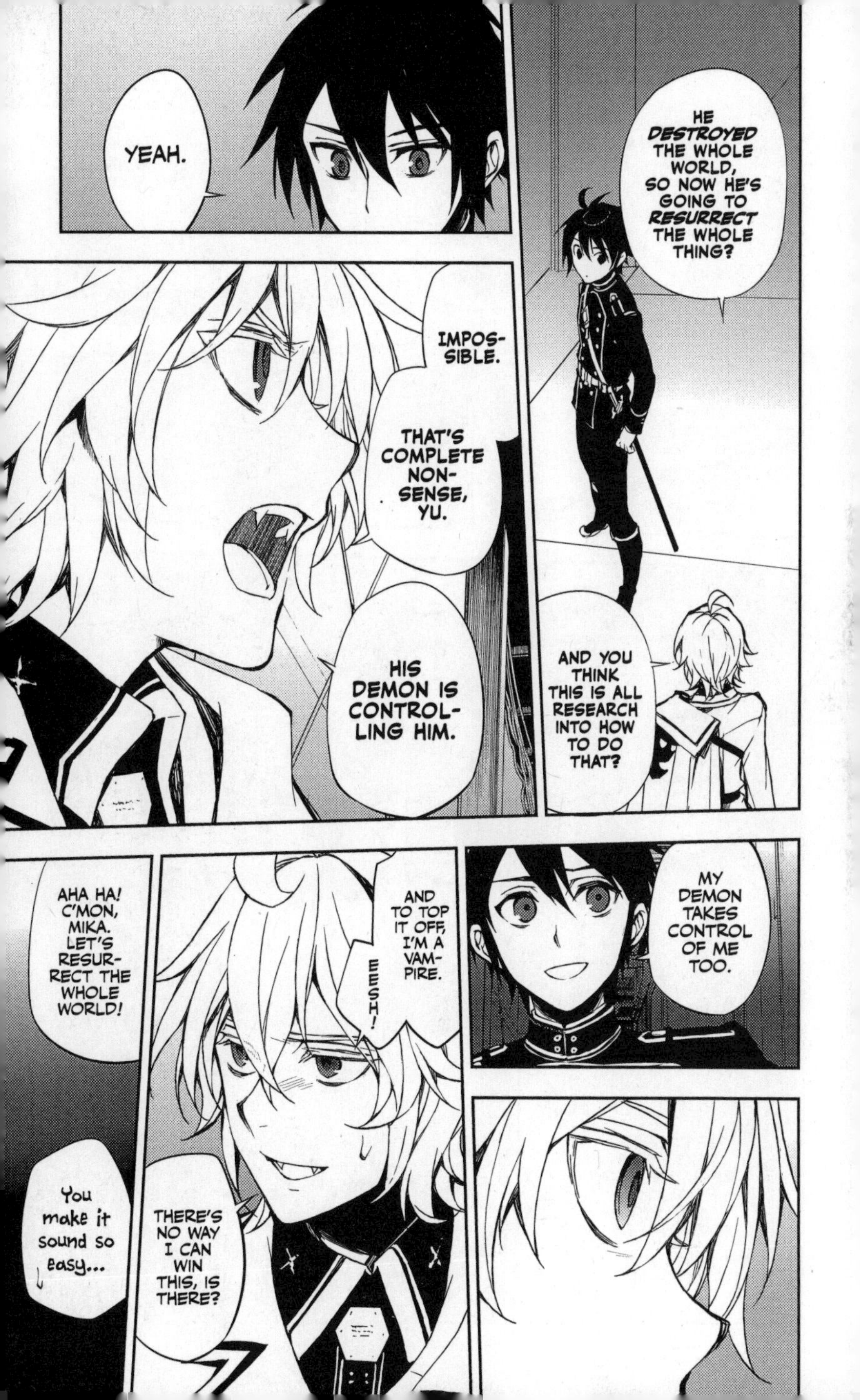
HE DESTROYED THE WHOLE WORLD, SO NOW HE'S GOING TO RESURRECT THE WHOLE THING?
AND YOU THINK THIS IS ALL RESEARCH INTO HOW TO DO THAT?
YEAH.
IMPOSSIBLE.
THAT'S COMPLETE NONSENSE, YU.
HIS DEMON IS CONTROLLING HIM.
MY DEMON TAKES CONTROL OF ME TOO.
AND TO TOP IT OFF, I'M A VAMPIRE.
EESH!
THERE'S NO WAY I CAN WIN THIS, IS THERE?
AHA HA! C'MON, MIKA. LET'S RESURRECT THE WHOLE WORLD!
You make it sound so easy...

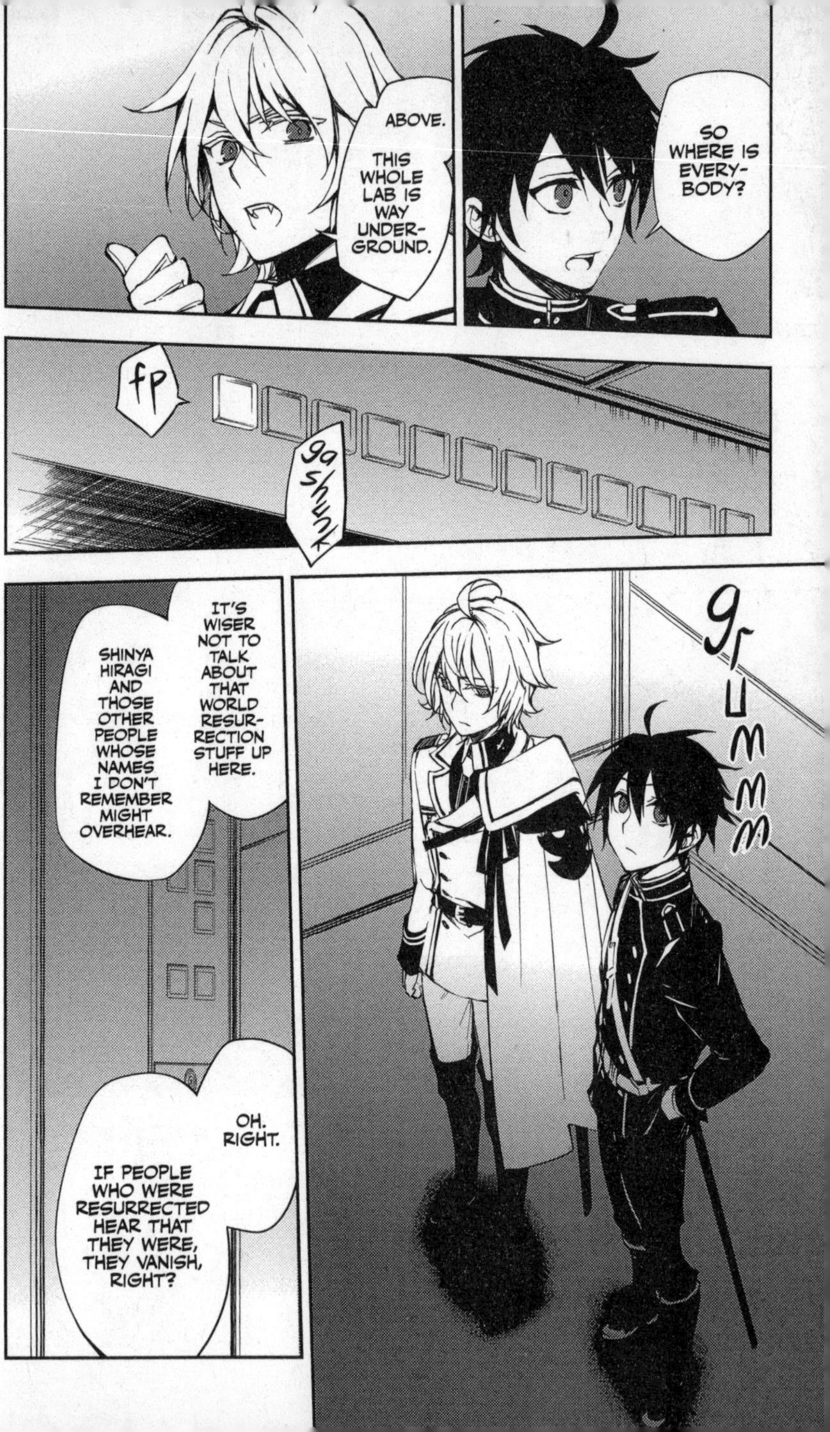
SO WHERE IS EVERY-BODY?
ABOVE.
THIS WHOLE LAB IS WAY UNDER-GROUND.
fp
ga shunk
grummm
IT'S WISER NOT TO TALK ABOUT THAT WORLD RESUR-RECTION STUFF UP HERE.
SHINYA HIRAGI AND THOSE OTHER PEOPLE WHOSE NAMES I DON'T REMEMBER MIGHT OVERHEAR.
OH. RIGHT.
IF PEOPLE WHO WERE RESURRECTED HEAR THAT THEY WERE, THEY VANISH, RIGHT?

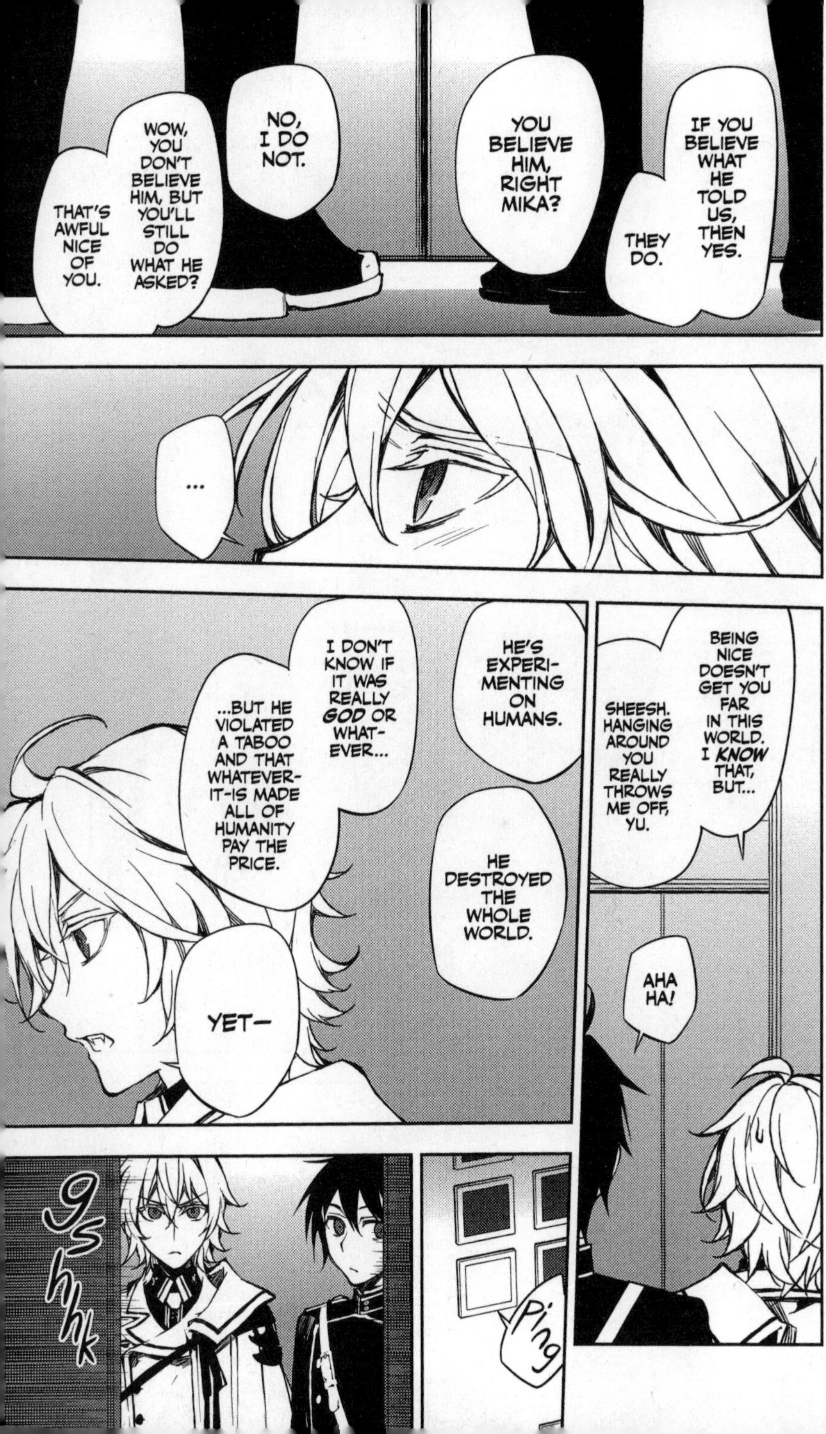
IF YOU BELIEVE WHAT HE TOLD US, THEN YES.
THEY DO.
YOU BELIEVE HIM, RIGHT MIKA?
NO, I DO NOT.
WOW, YOU DON'T BELIEVE HIM, BUT YOU'LL STILL DO WHAT HE ASKED?
THAT'S AWFUL NICE OF YOU.
...
BEING NICE DOESN'T GET YOU FAR IN THIS WORLD. I *KNOW* THAT, BUT...
SHEESH. HANGING AROUND YOU REALLY THROWS ME OFF, YU.
AHA HA!
HE'S EXPERIMENTING ON HUMANS.
I DON'T KNOW IF IT WAS REALLY *GOD* OR WHATEVER...
...BUT HE VIOLATED A TABOO AND THAT WHATEVER-IT-IS MADE ALL OF HUMANITY PAY THE PRICE.
HE DESTROYED THE WHOLE WORLD.
YET—
Ping
gshhk

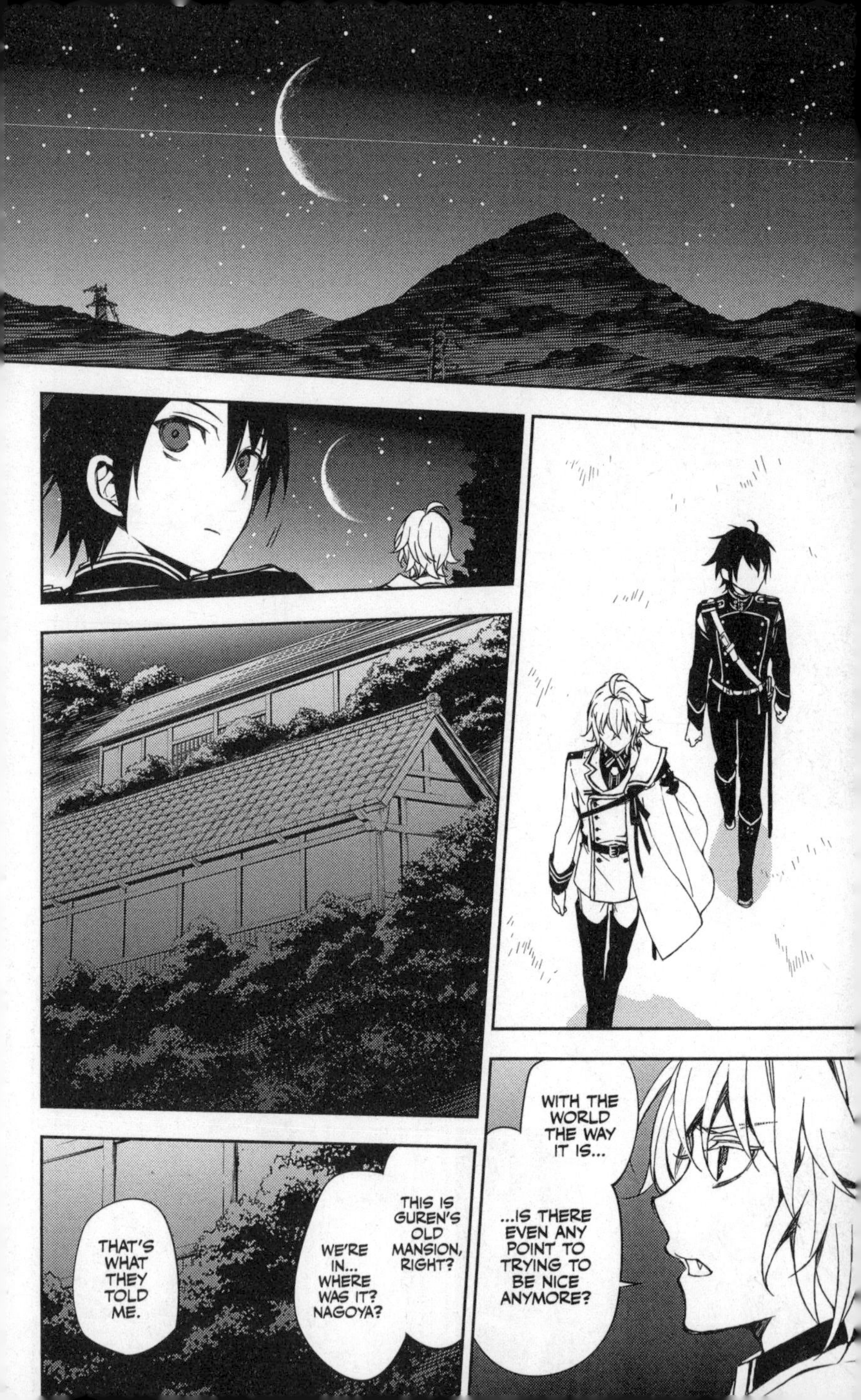
WITH THE WORLD THE WAY IT IS...
...IS THERE EVEN ANY POINT TO TRYING TO BE NICE ANYMORE?
THIS IS GUREN'S OLD MANSION, RIGHT?
WE'RE IN... WHERE WAS IT? NAGOYA?
THAT'S WHAT THEY TOLD ME.

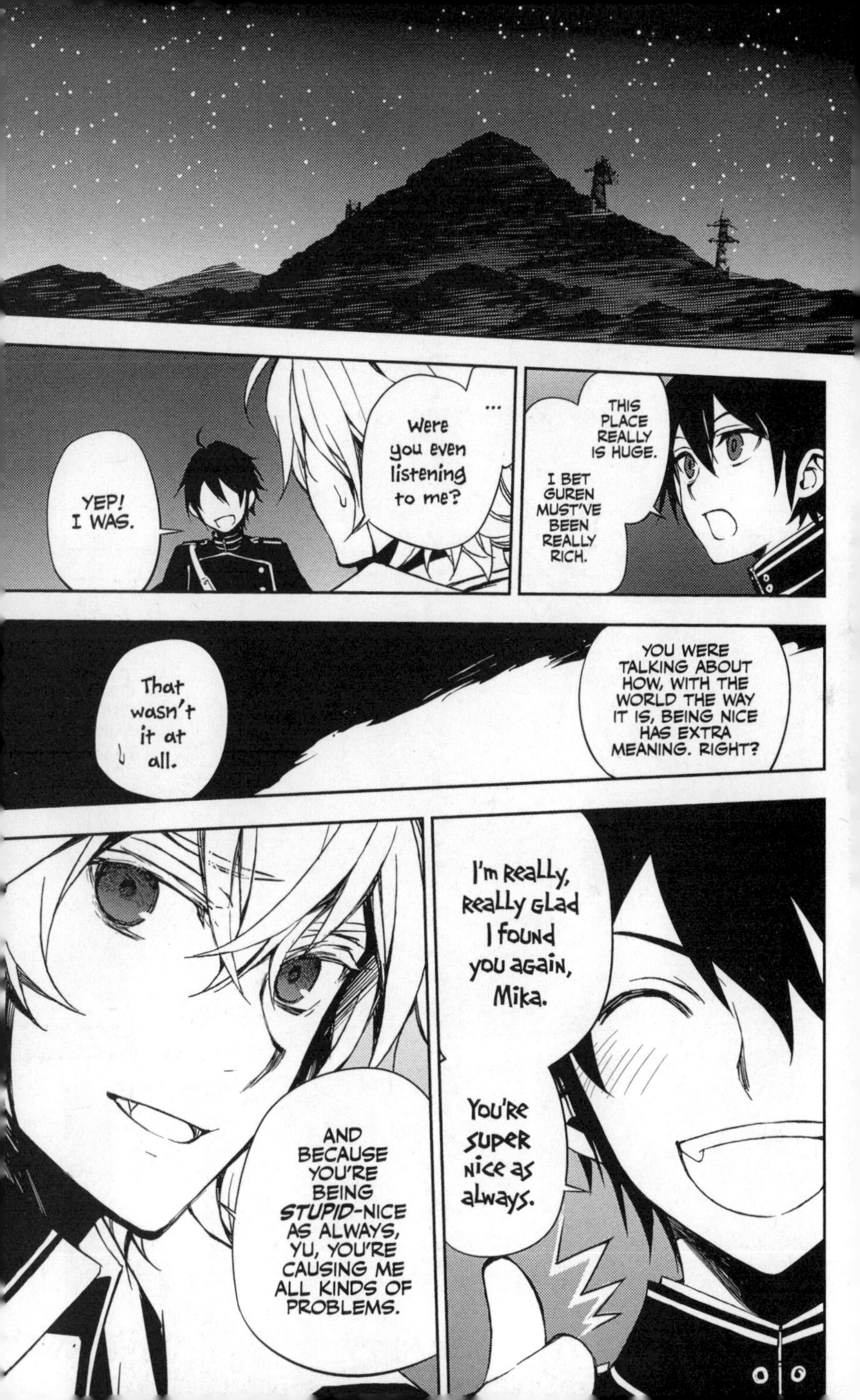
THIS PLACE REALLY IS HUGE.
I BET GUREN MUST'VE BEEN REALLY RICH.
...
Were you even listening to me?
YEP! I WAS.
YOU WERE TALKING ABOUT HOW, WITH THE WORLD THE WAY IT IS, BEING NICE HAS EXTRA MEANING. RIGHT?
That wasn't it at all.
I'm really, really glad I found you again, Mika.
You're super nice as always.
AND BECAUSE YOU'RE BEING STUPID-NICE AS ALWAYS, YU, YOU'RE CAUSING ME ALL KINDS OF PROBLEMS.

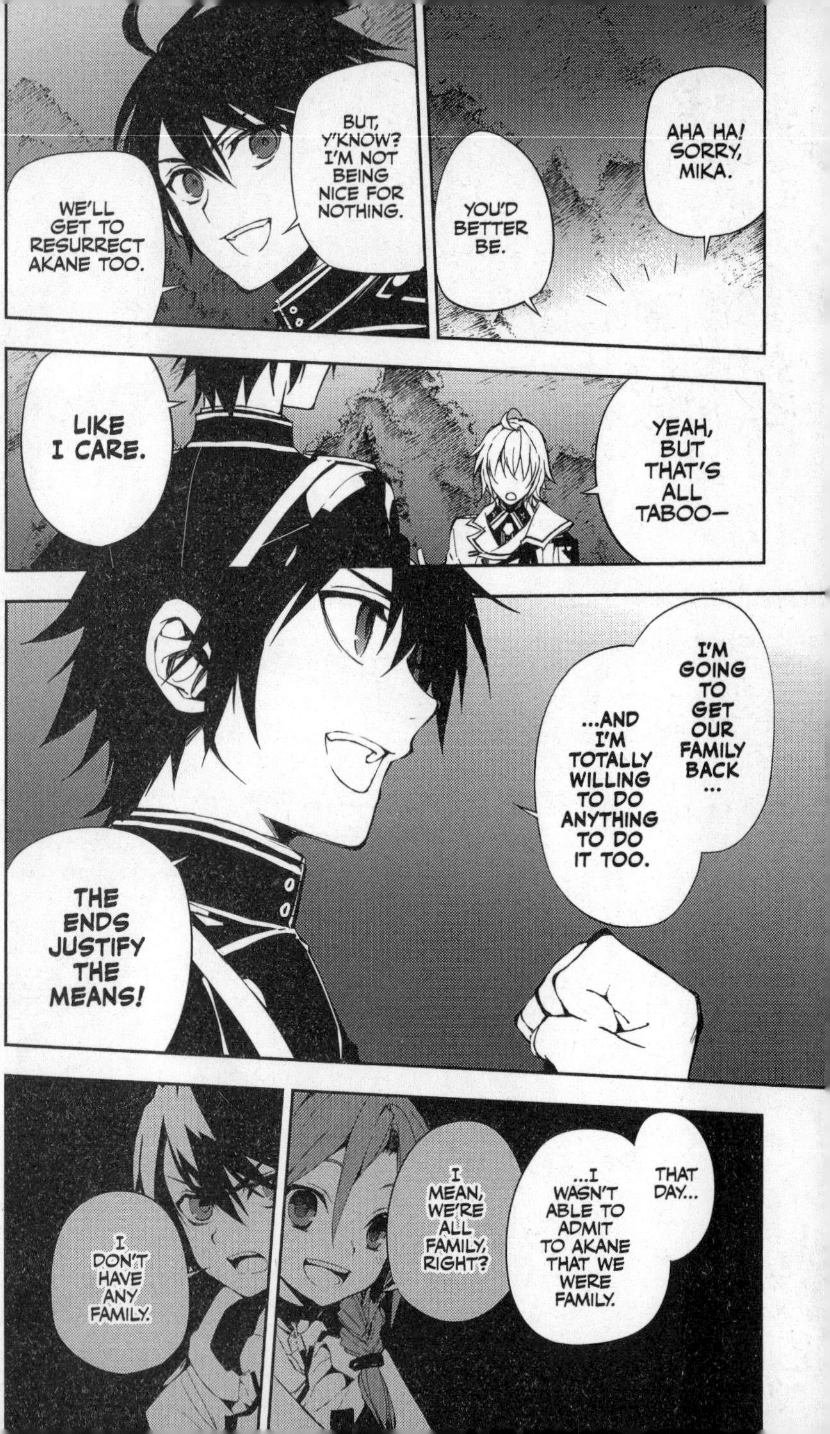
AHA HA! SORRY, MIKA.
YOU'D BETTER BE.
BUT, Y'KNOW? I'M NOT BEING NICE FOR NOTHING.
WE'LL GET TO RESURRECT AKANE TOO.
YEAH, BUT THAT'S ALL TABOO—
LIKE I CARE.
I'M GOING TO GET OUR FAMILY BACK...
...AND I'M TOTALLY WILLING TO DO ANYTHING TO DO IT TOO.
THE ENDS JUSTIFY THE MEANS!
THAT DAY...
...I WASN'T ABLE TO ADMIT TO AKANE THAT WE WERE FAMILY.
I MEAN, WE'RE ALL FAMILY, RIGHT?
I DON'T HAVE ANY FAMILY.

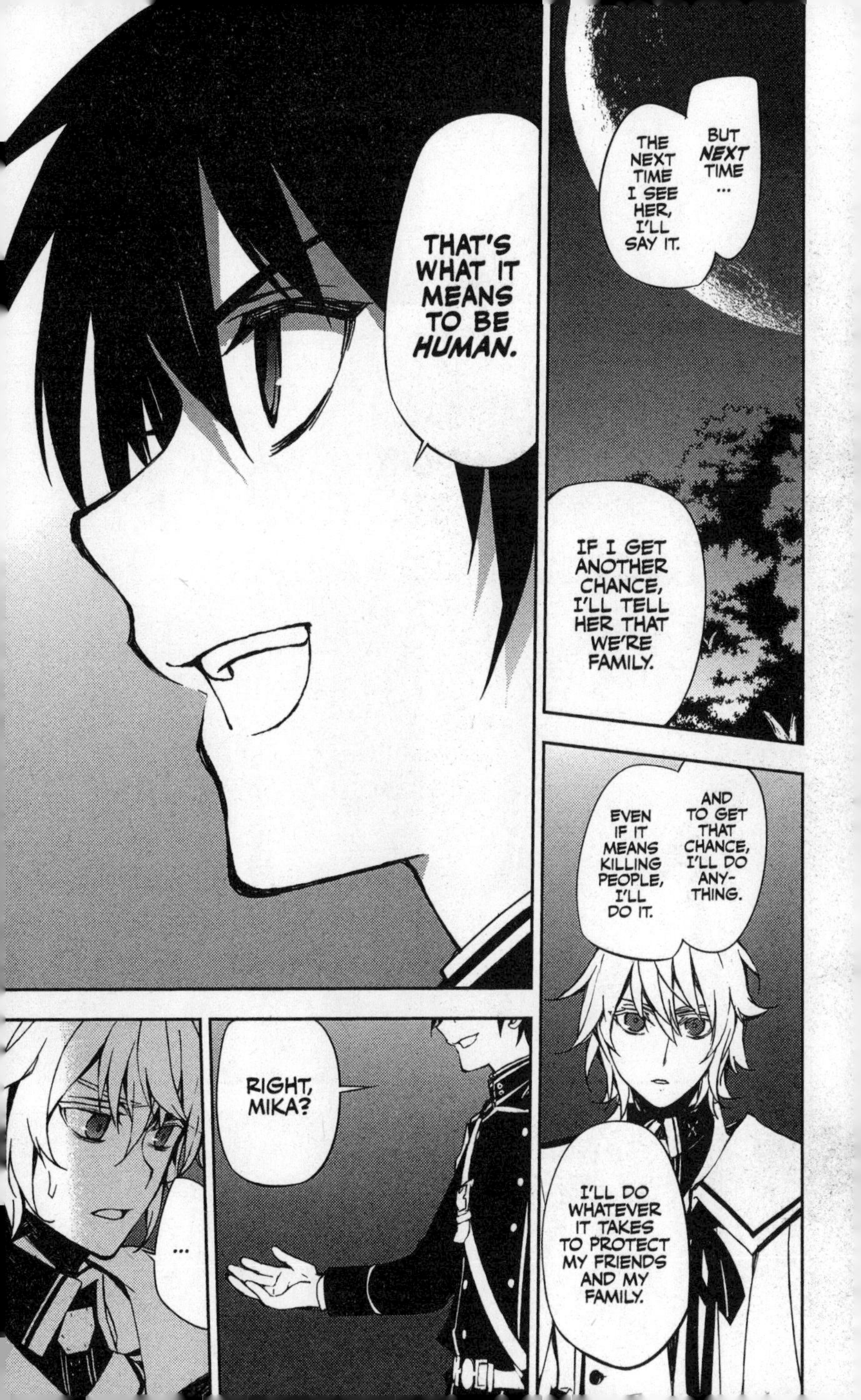

BUT *NEXT* TIME...
THE NEXT TIME I SEE HER, I'LL SAY IT.
IF I GET ANOTHER CHANCE, I'LL TELL HER THAT WE'RE FAMILY.
AND TO GET THAT CHANCE, I'LL DO ANY-THING.
EVEN IF IT MEANS KILLING PEOPLE, I'LL DO IT.
THAT'S WHAT IT MEANS TO BE *HUMAN*.
I'LL DO WHATEVER IT TAKES TO PROTECT MY FRIENDS AND MY FAMILY.
RIGHT, MIKA?
...

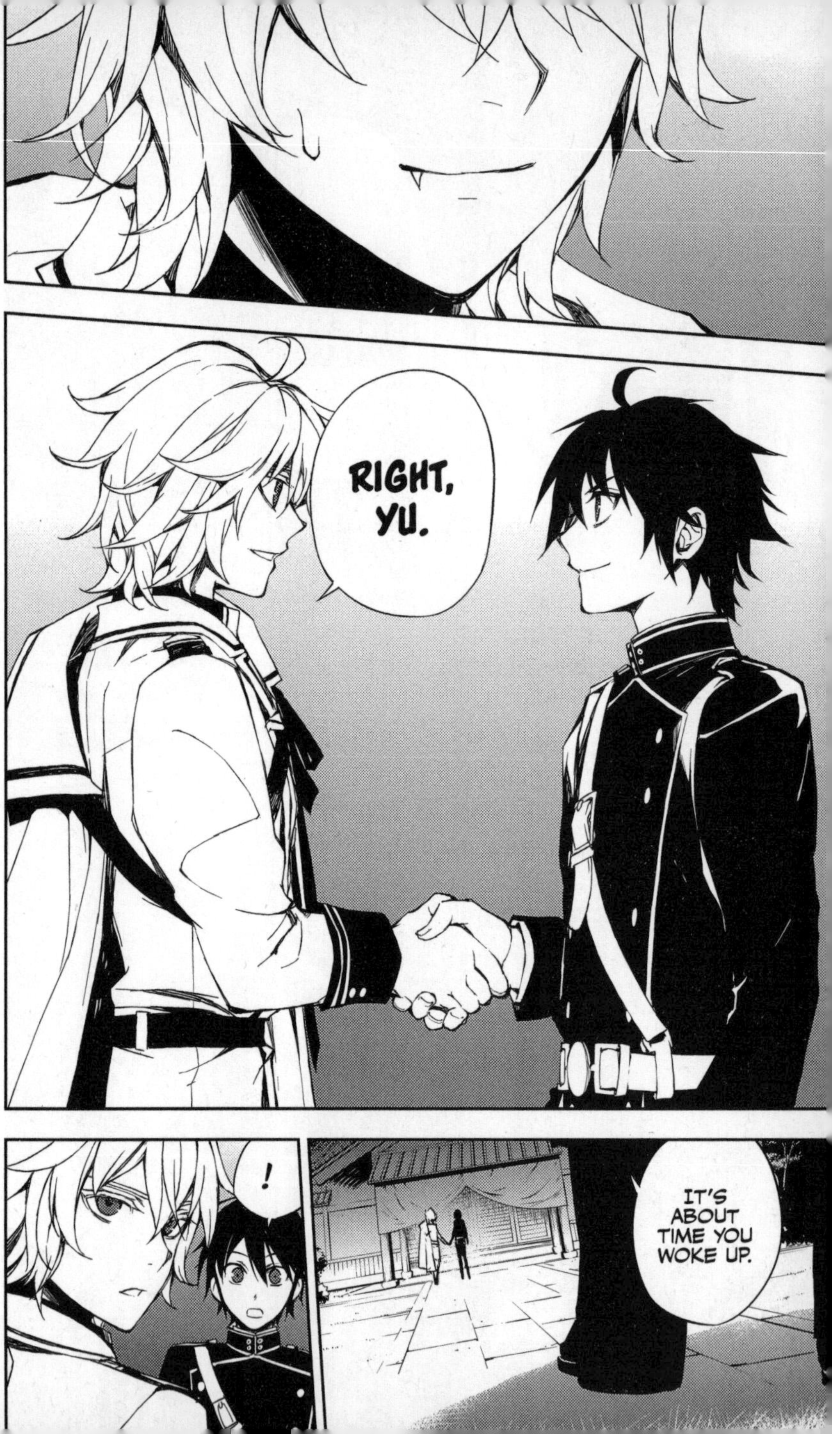
RIGHT, YU.
IT'S ABOUT TIME YOU WOKE UP.
!

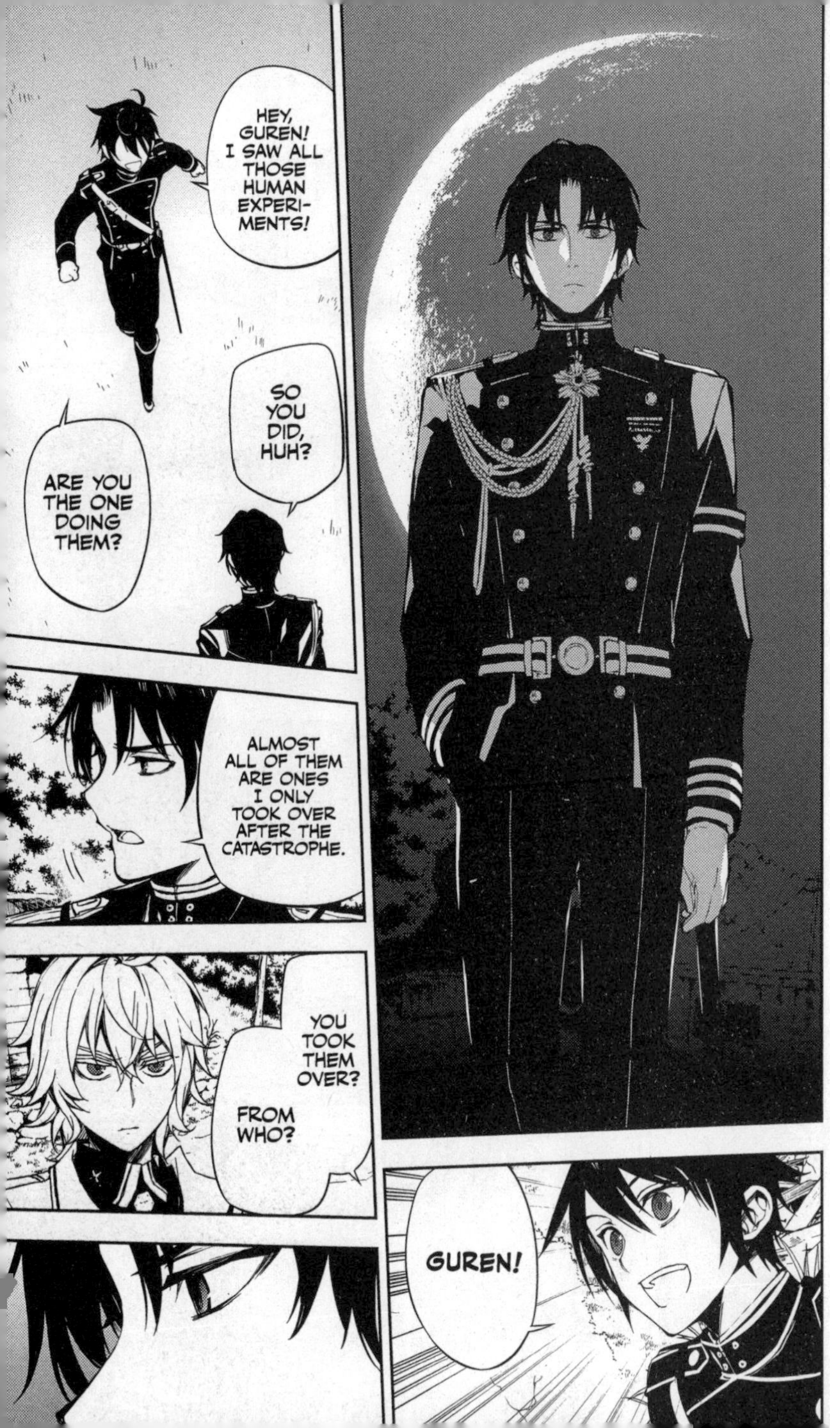
HEY, GUREN! I SAW ALL THOSE HUMAN EXPERI-MENTS!
SO YOU DID, HUH?
ARE YOU THE ONE DOING THEM?
ALMOST ALL OF THEM ARE ONES I ONLY TOOK OVER AFTER THE CATASTROPHE.
YOU TOOK THEM OVER?
FROM WHO?
GUREN!

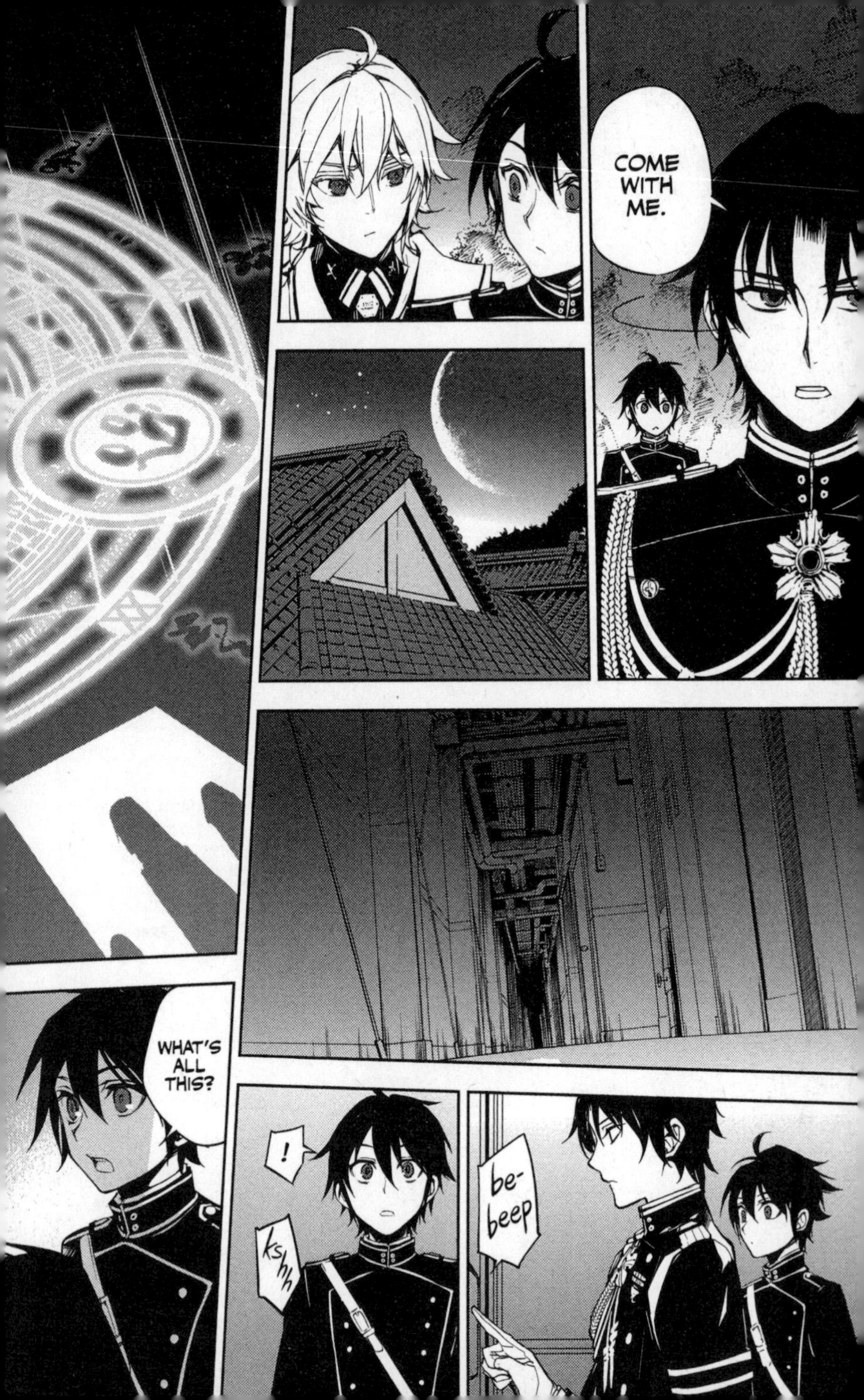
COME WITH ME.
be-beep
!
kshh
WHAT'S ALL THIS?

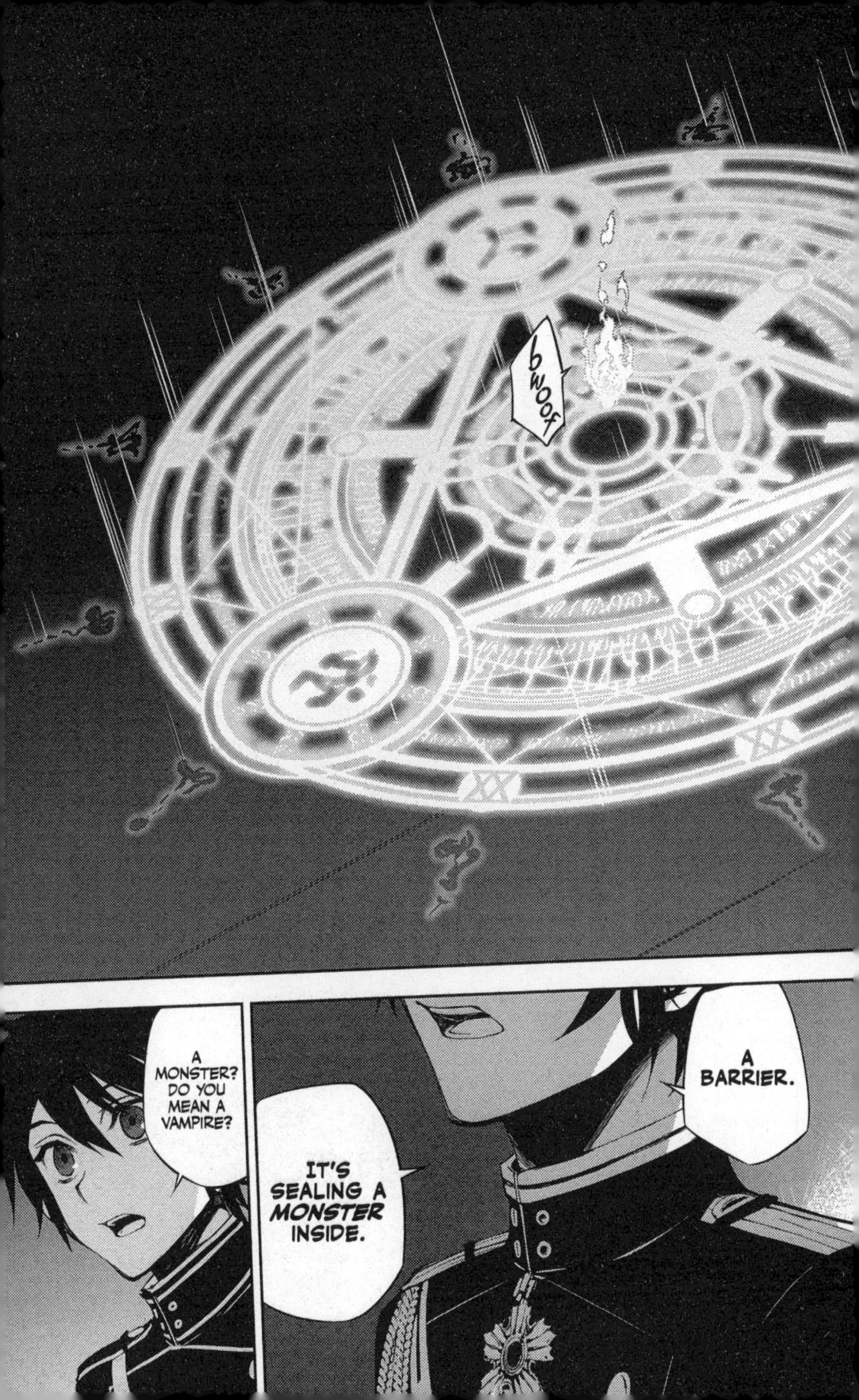
bwoof
A BARRIER.
IT'S SEALING A *MONSTER* INSIDE.
A MONSTER? DO YOU MEAN A VAMPIRE?

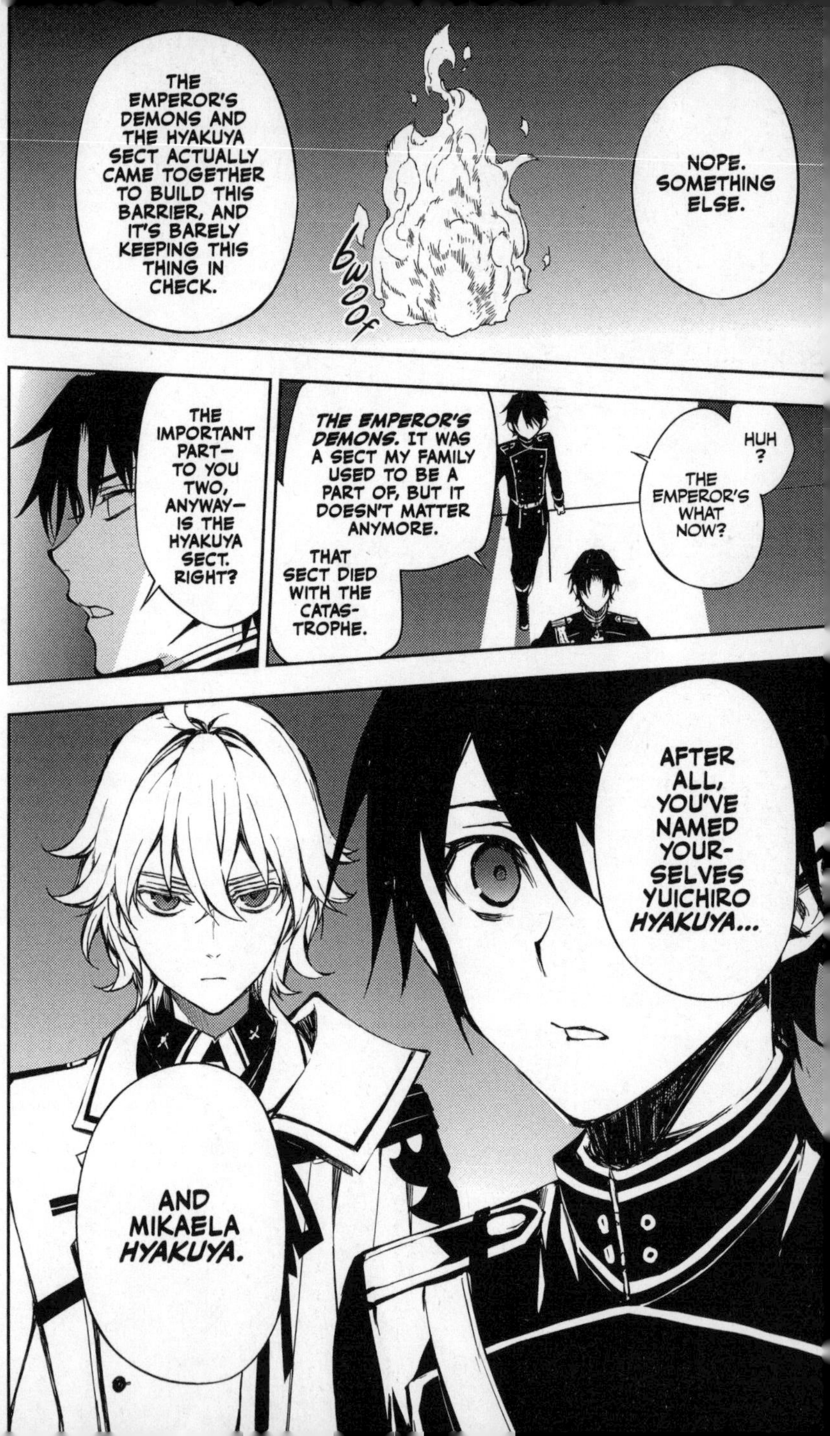
NOPE. SOMETHING ELSE.
BWOOF
THE EMPEROR'S DEMONS AND THE HYAKUYA SECT ACTUALLY CAME TOGETHER TO BUILD THIS BARRIER, AND IT'S BARELY KEEPING THIS THING IN CHECK.
HUH?
THE EMPEROR'S WHAT NOW?
THE EMPEROR'S DEMONS. IT WAS A SECT MY FAMILY USED TO BE A PART OF, BUT IT DOESN'T MATTER ANYMORE.
THAT SECT DIED WITH THE CATAS-TROPHE.
THE IMPORTANT PART—TO YOU TWO, ANYWAY—IS THE HYAKUYA SECT. RIGHT?
AFTER ALL, YOU'VE NAMED YOUR-SELVES YUICHIRO *HYAKUYA*...
AND MIKAELA *HYAKUYA.*

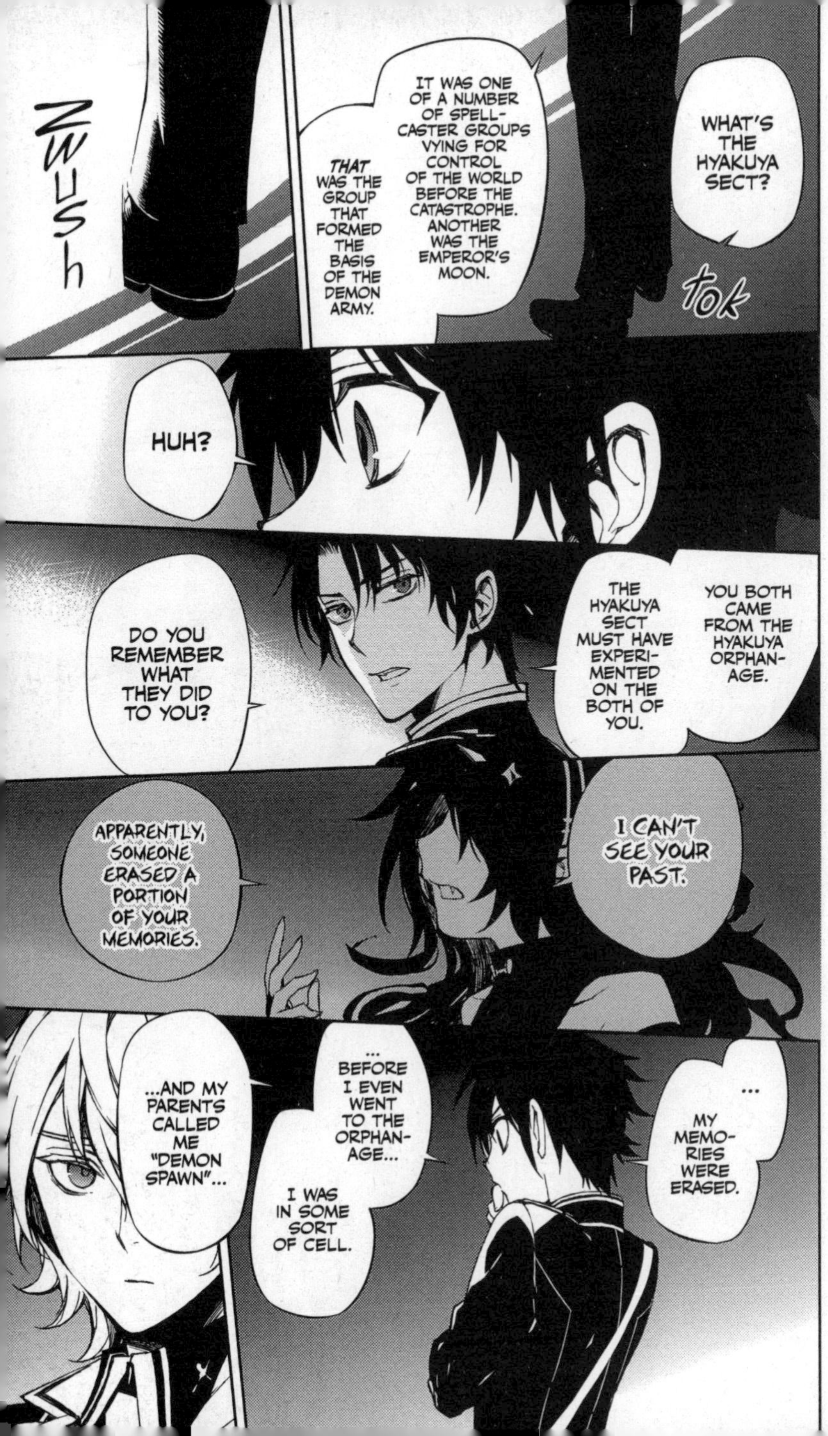
WHAT'S THE HYAKUYA SECT?
tok
IT WAS ONE OF A NUMBER OF SPELL-CASTER GROUPS VYING FOR CONTROL OF THE WORLD BEFORE THE CATASTROPHE. ANOTHER WAS THE EMPEROR'S MOON.
THAT WAS THE GROUP THAT FORMED THE BASIS OF THE DEMON ARMY.
ZWUSH
HUH?
YOU BOTH CAME FROM THE HYAKUYA ORPHANAGE.
THE HYAKUYA SECT MUST HAVE EXPERIMENTED ON THE BOTH OF YOU.
DO YOU REMEMBER WHAT THEY DID TO YOU?
I CAN'T SEE YOUR PAST.
APPARENTLY, SOMEONE ERASED A PORTION OF YOUR MEMORIES.
... MY MEMORIES WERE ERASED.
... BEFORE I EVEN WENT TO THE ORPHANAGE...
I WAS IN SOME SORT OF CELL.
...AND MY PARENTS CALLED ME "DEMON SPAWN"...

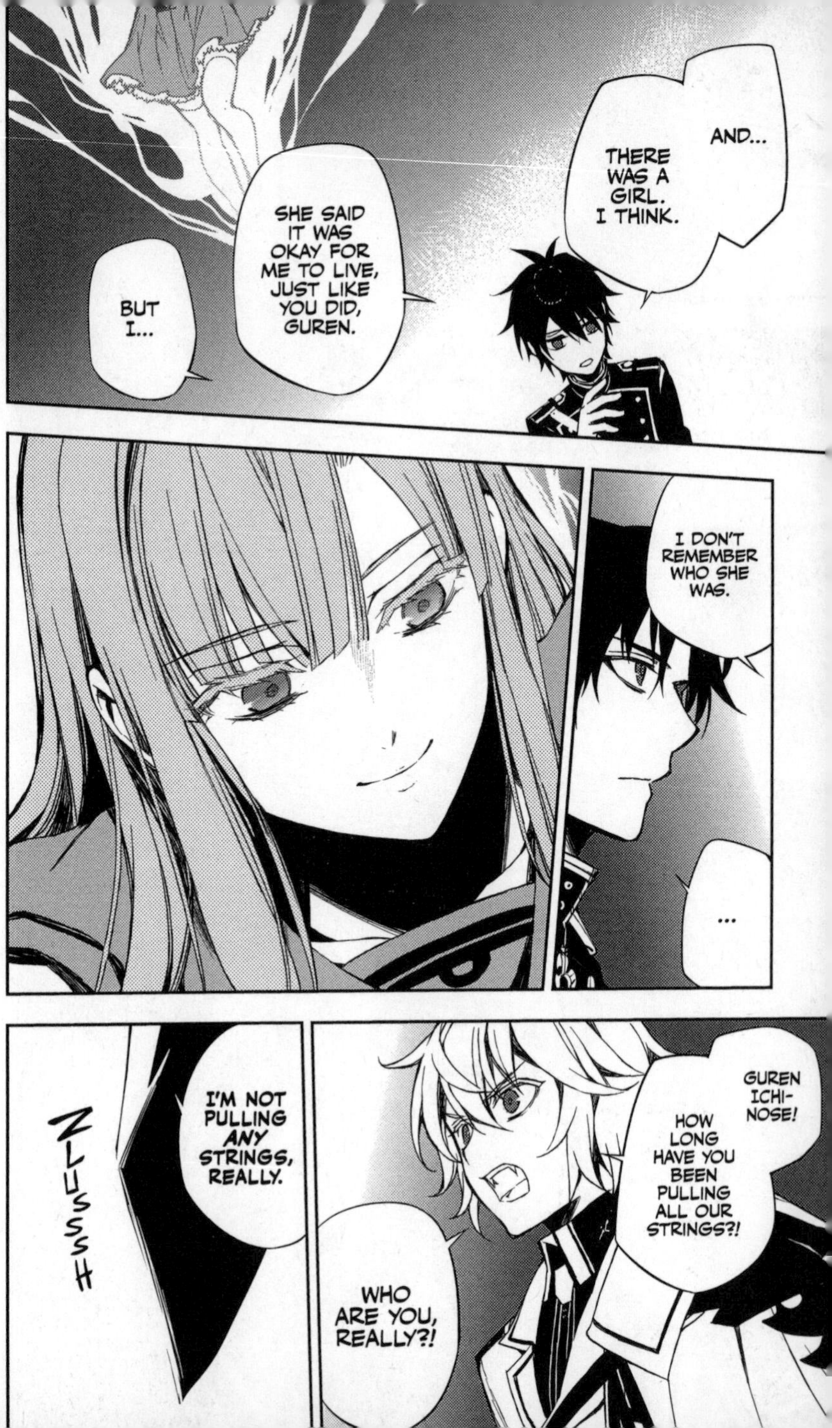
AND... THERE WAS A GIRL. I THINK.
SHE SAID IT WAS OKAY FOR ME TO LIVE, JUST LIKE YOU DID, GUREN.
BUT I...
I DON'T REMEMBER WHO SHE WAS.
...
GUREN ICHI-NOSE!
HOW LONG HAVE YOU BEEN PULLING ALL OUR STRINGS?!
WHO ARE YOU, REALLY?!
I'M NOT PULLING *ANY* STRINGS, REALLY.
ZLUSSSH

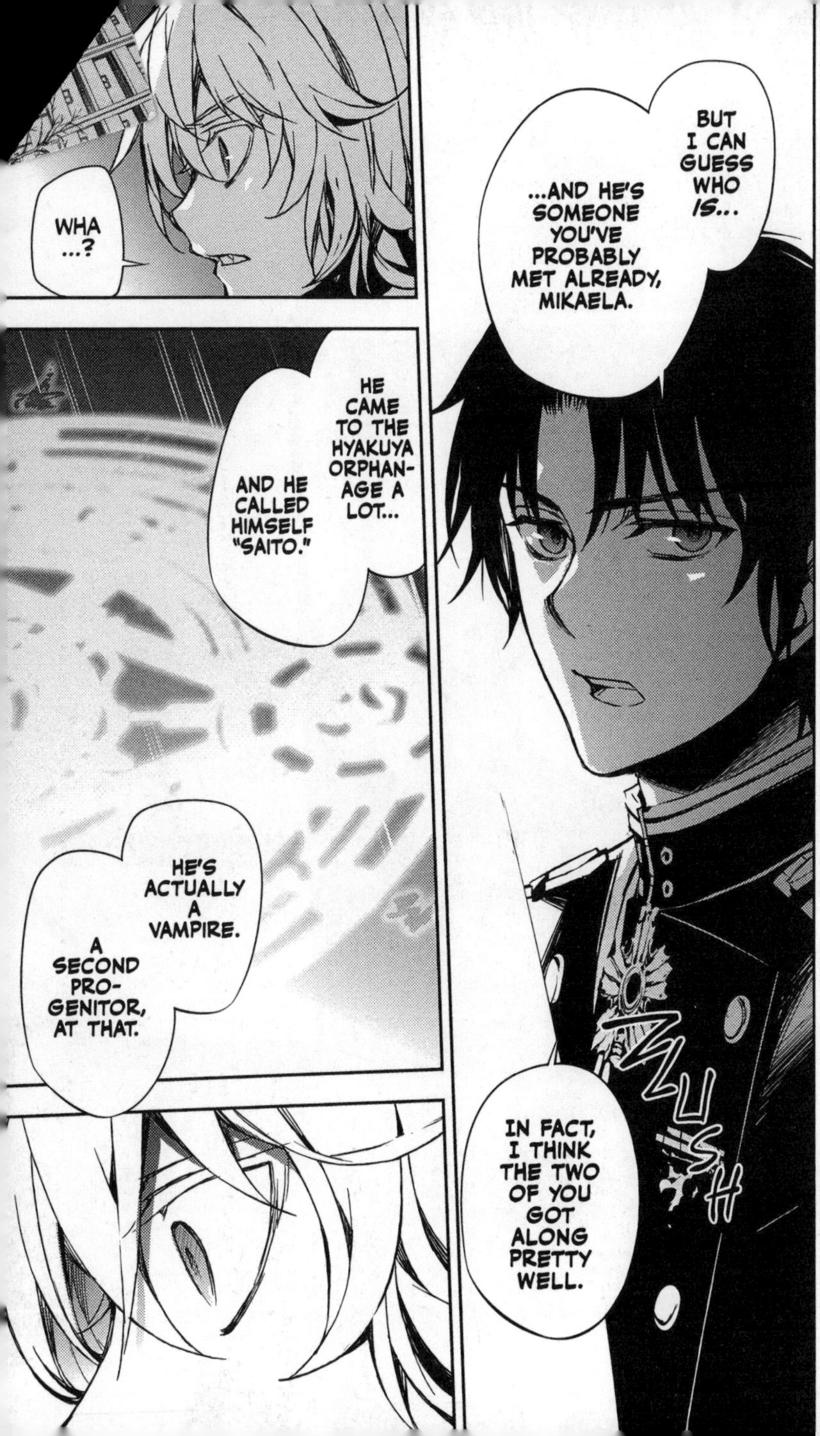
BUT I CAN GUESS WHO *IS*...
...AND HE'S SOMEONE YOU'VE PROBABLY MET ALREADY, MIKAELA.
ZZUSH
IN FACT, I THINK THE TWO OF YOU GOT ALONG PRETTY WELL.
WHA ...?
HE CAME TO THE HYAKUYA ORPHANAGE A LOT...
AND HE CALLED HIMSELF "SAITO."
HE'S ACTUALLY A VAMPIRE.
A SECOND PROGENITOR, AT THAT.

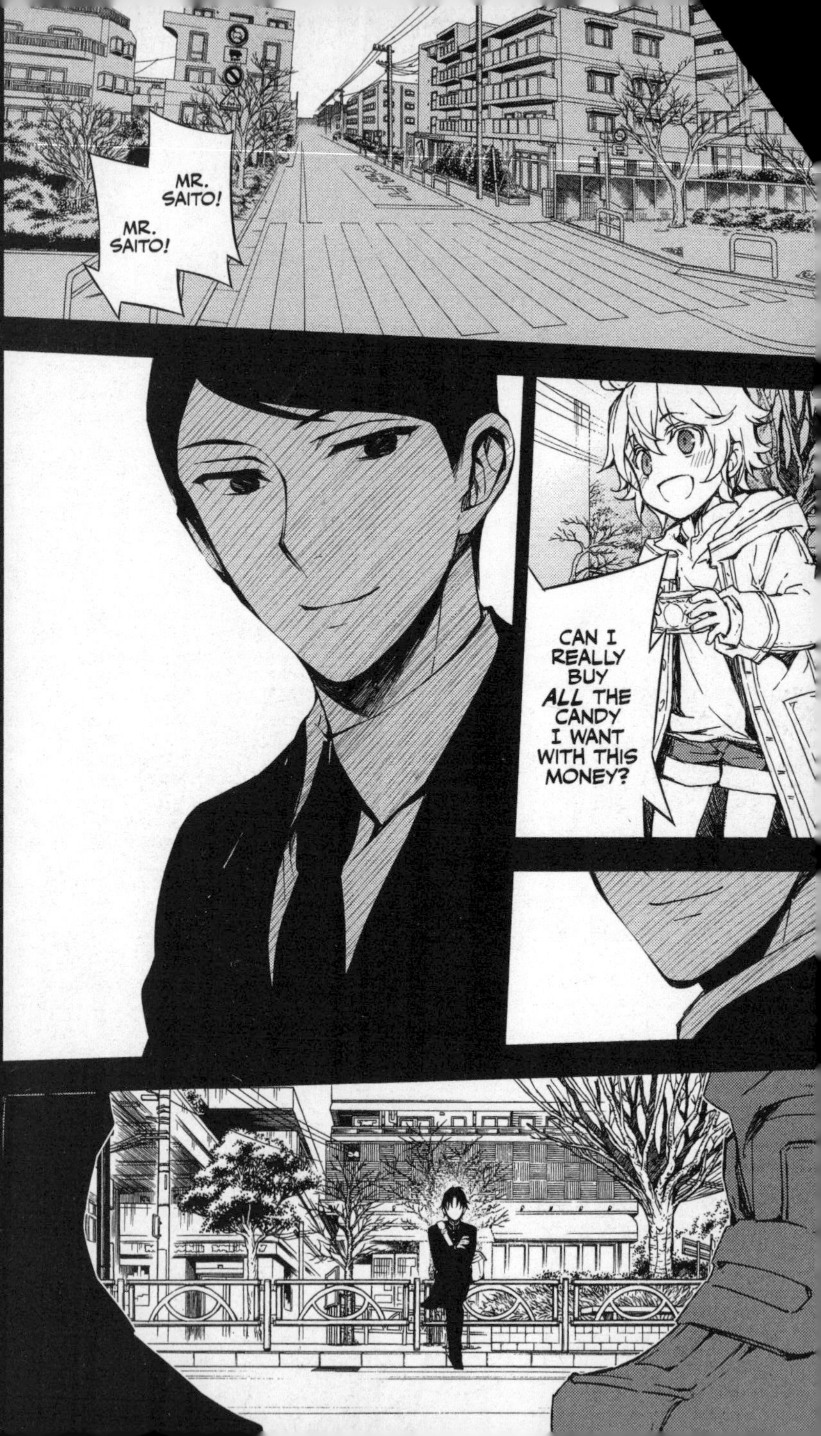
MR. SAITO!
MR. SAITO!
CAN I REALLY BUY ALL THE CANDY I WANT WITH THIS MONEY?

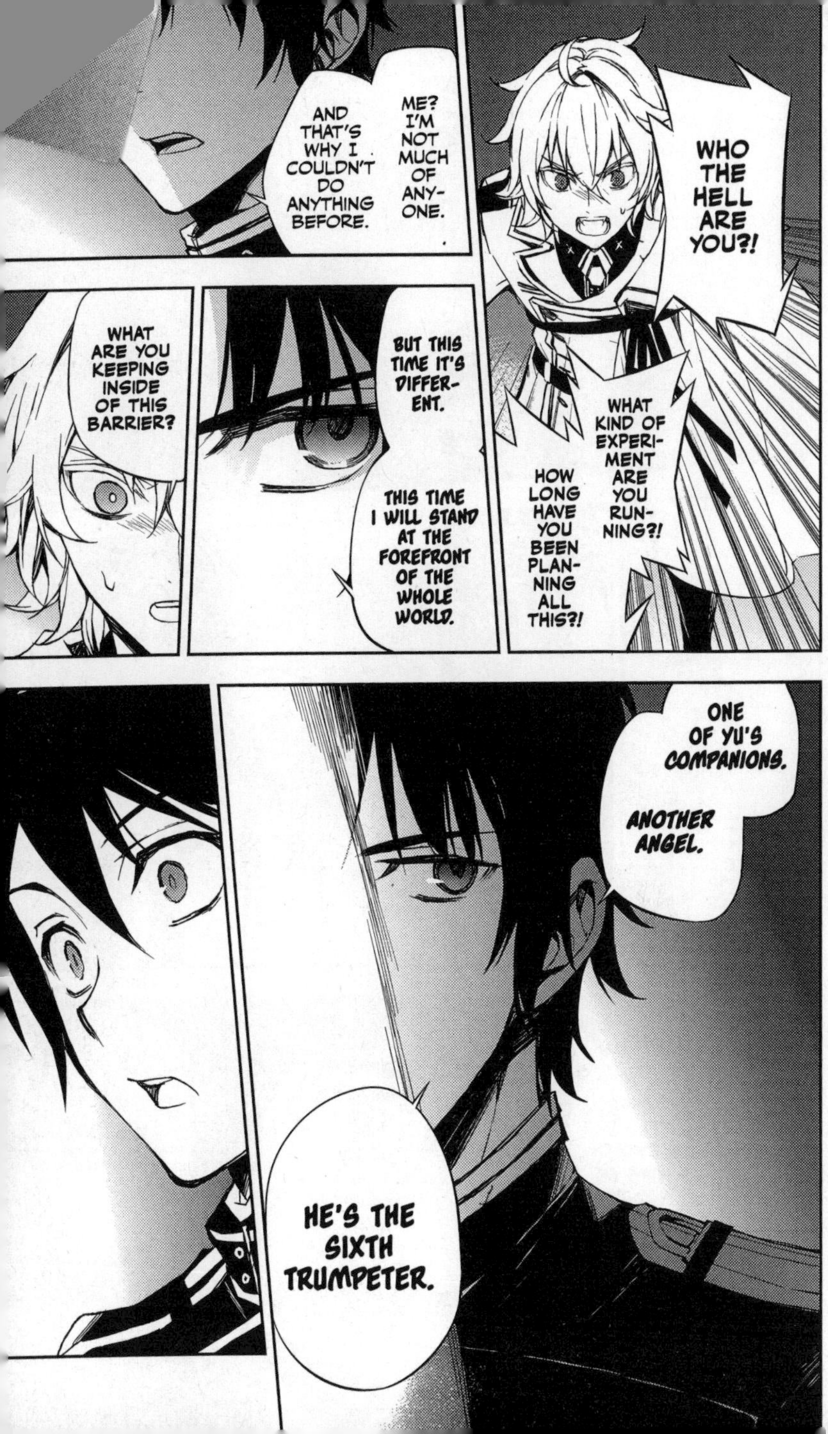
WHO THE HELL ARE YOU?!
WHAT KIND OF EXPERIMENT ARE YOU RUNNING?!
HOW LONG HAVE YOU BEEN PLANNING ALL THIS?!
ME? I'M NOT MUCH OF ANYONE.
AND THAT'S WHY I COULDN'T DO ANYTHING BEFORE.
BUT THIS TIME IT'S DIFFERENT.
THIS TIME I WILL STAND AT THE FOREFRONT OF THE WHOLE WORLD.
WHAT ARE YOU KEEPING INSIDE OF THIS BARRIER?
ONE OF YU'S COMPANIONS.
ANOTHER ANGEL.
HE'S THE SIXTH TRUMPETER.

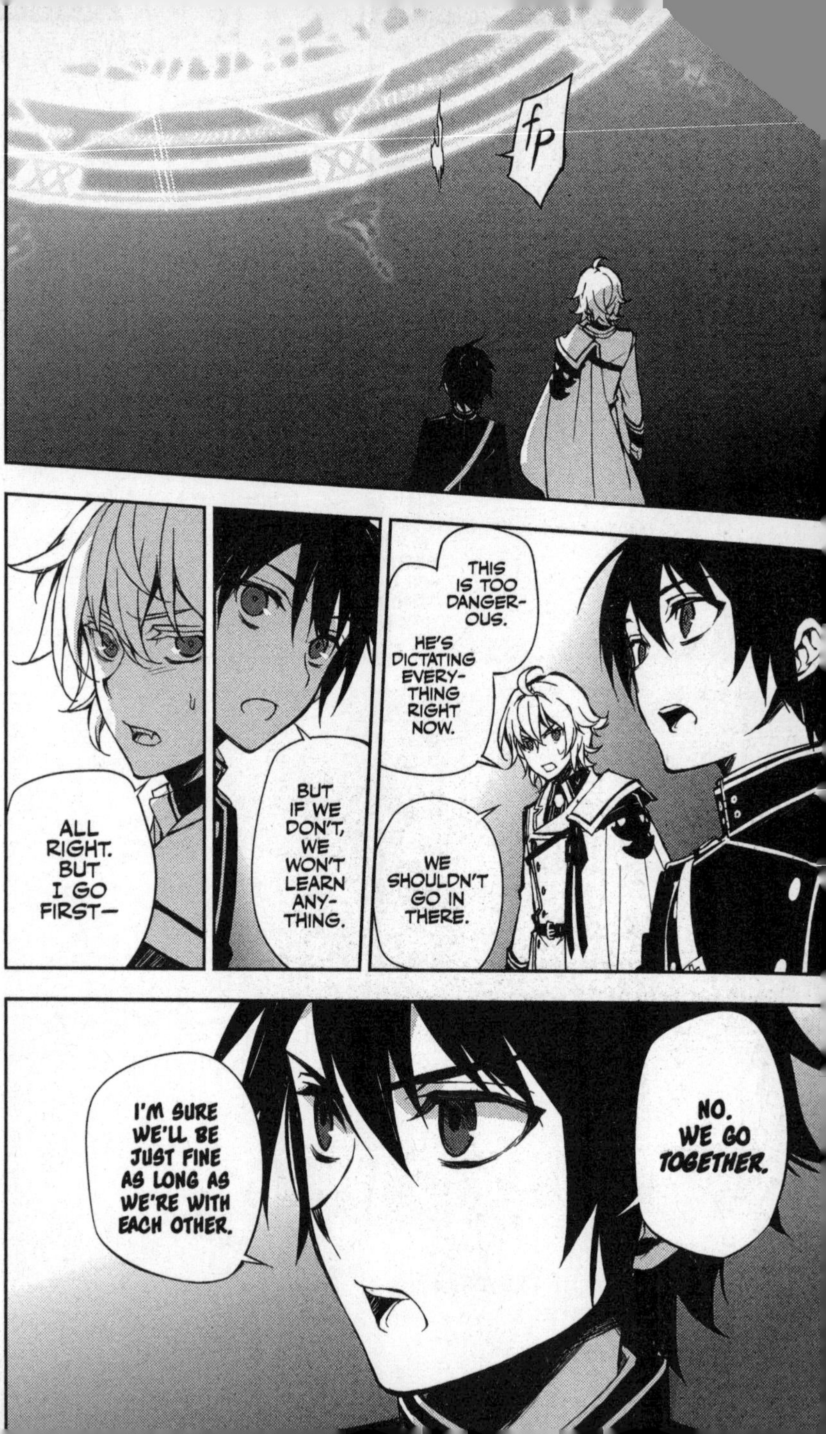
fp
THIS IS TOO DANGER-OUS.
HE'S DICTATING EVERY-THING RIGHT NOW.
WE SHOULDN'T GO IN THERE.
BUT IF WE DON'T, WE WON'T LEARN ANY-THING.
ALL RIGHT. BUT I GO FIRST—
NO. WE GO TOGETHER.
I'M SURE WE'LL BE JUST FINE AS LONG AS WE'RE WITH EACH OTHER.

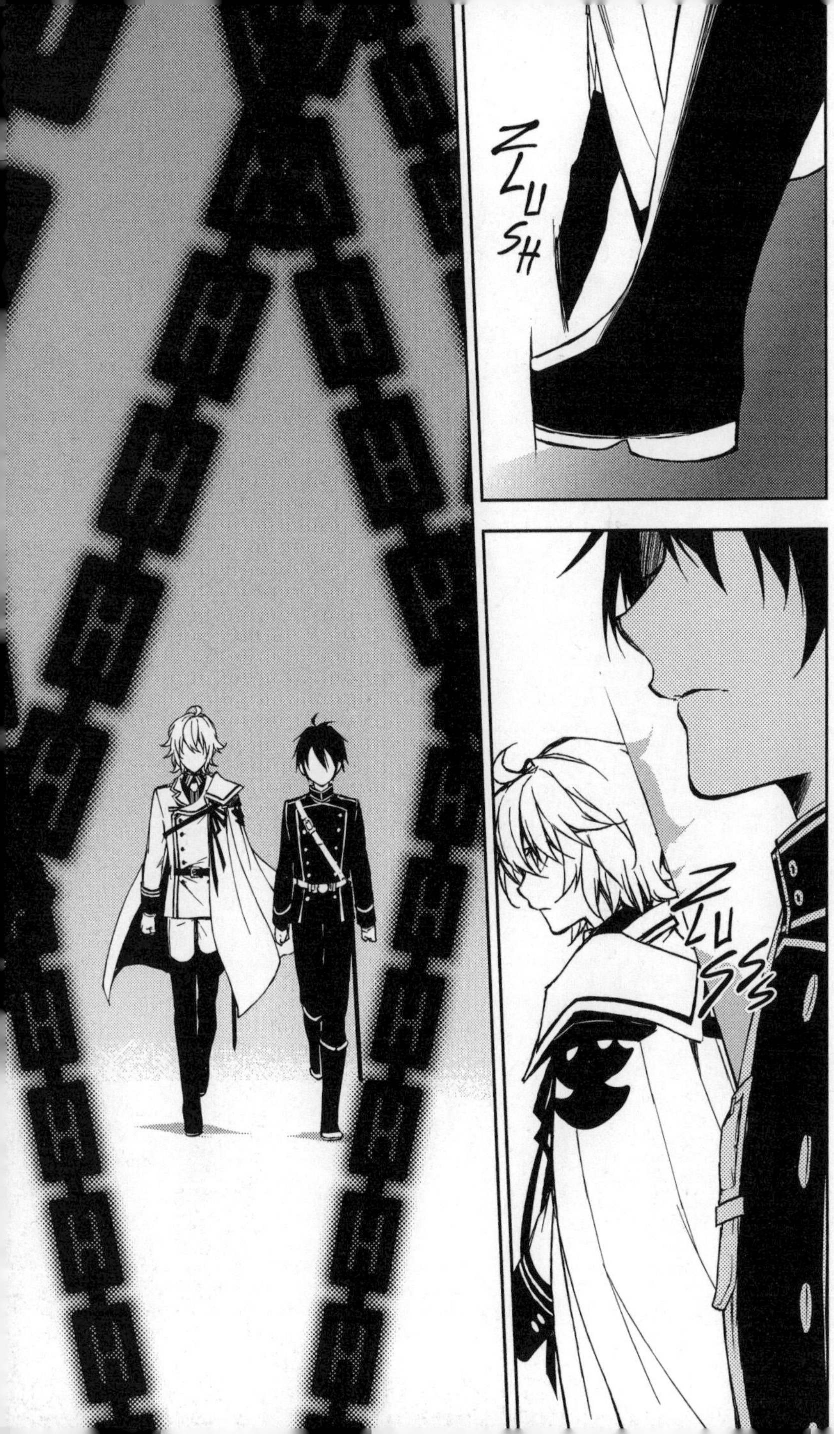
ZLUSH
ZLUSSS

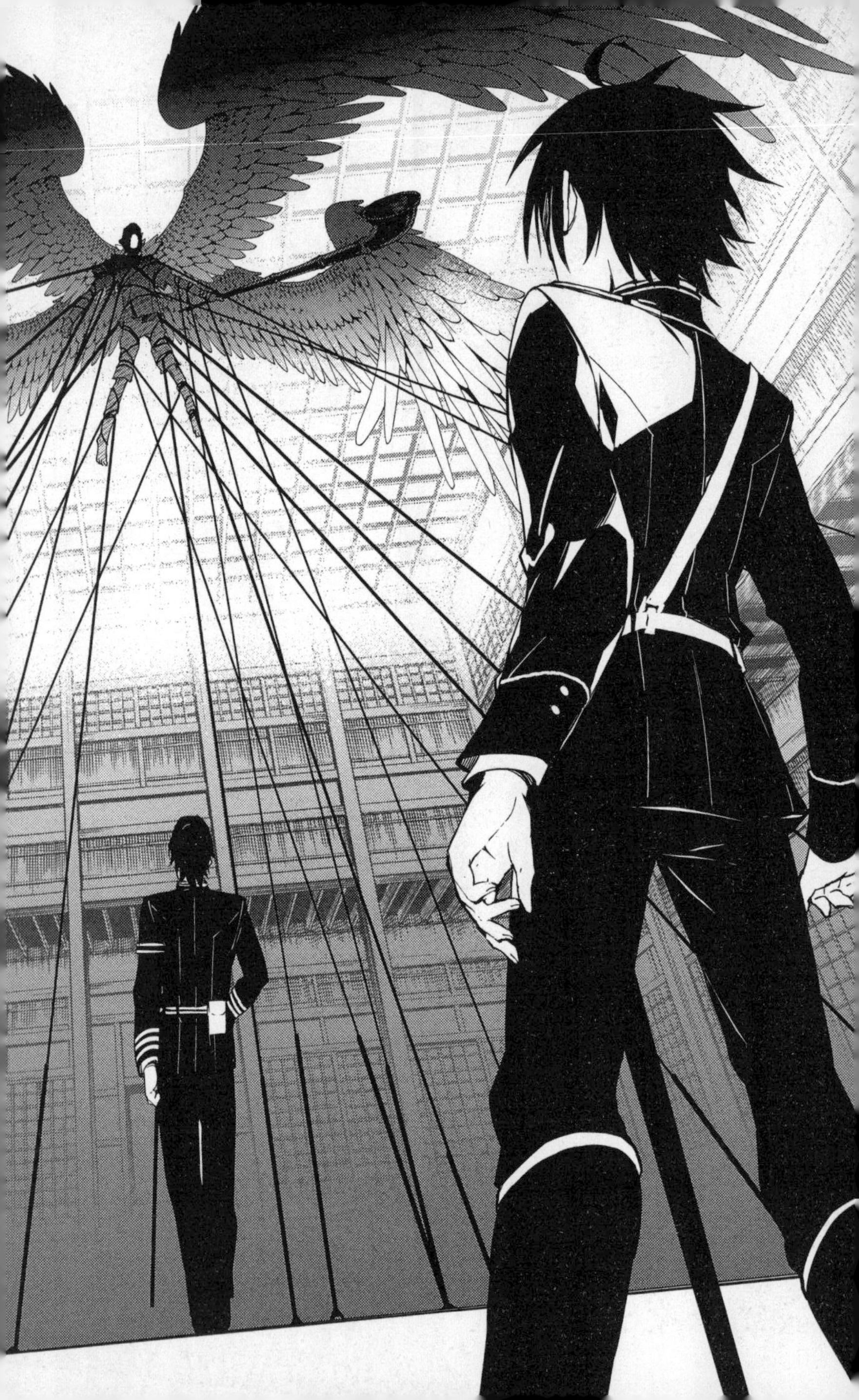

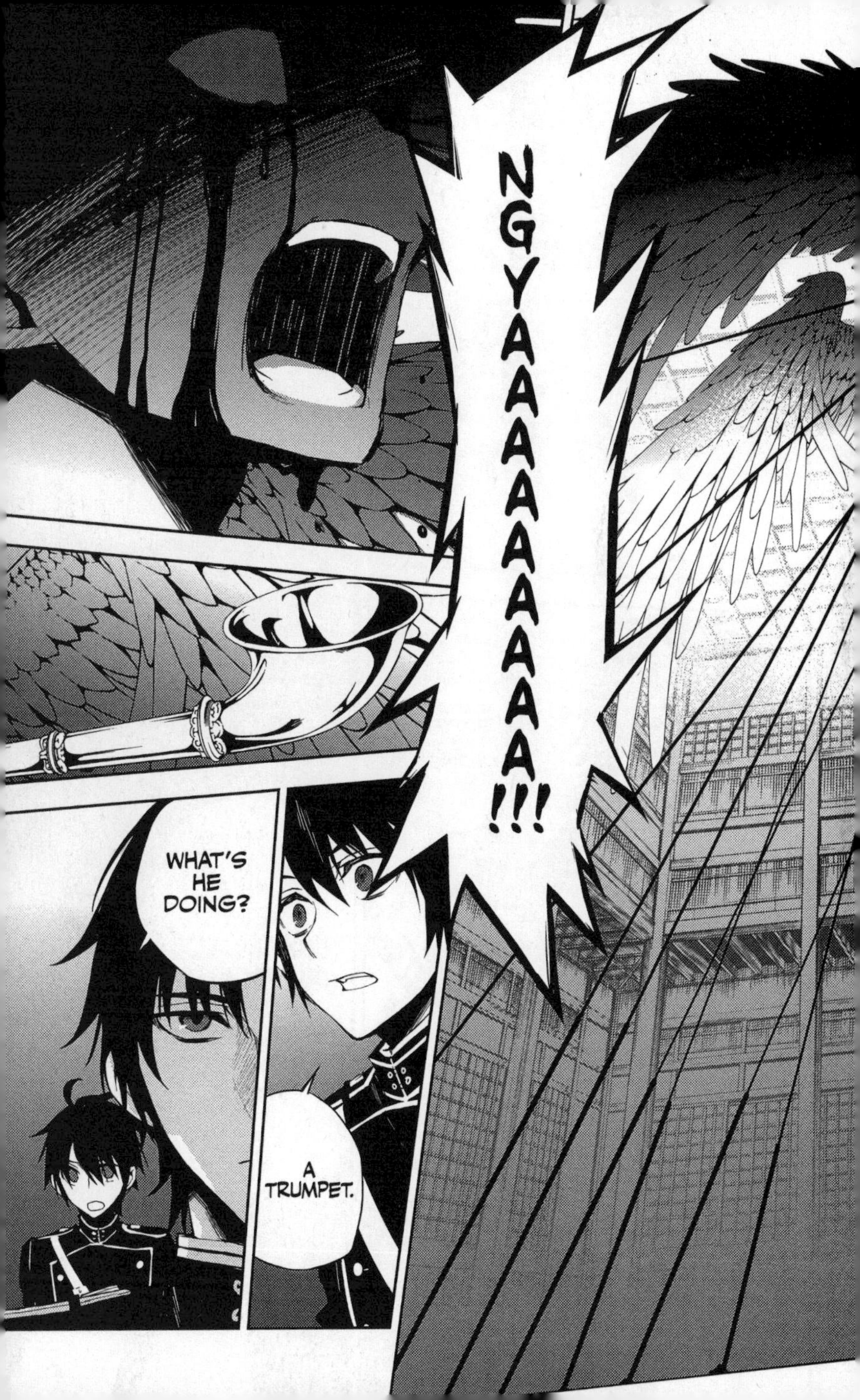
NGYAAAAAAAAAA!!!
WHAT'S HE DOING?
A TRUMPET.

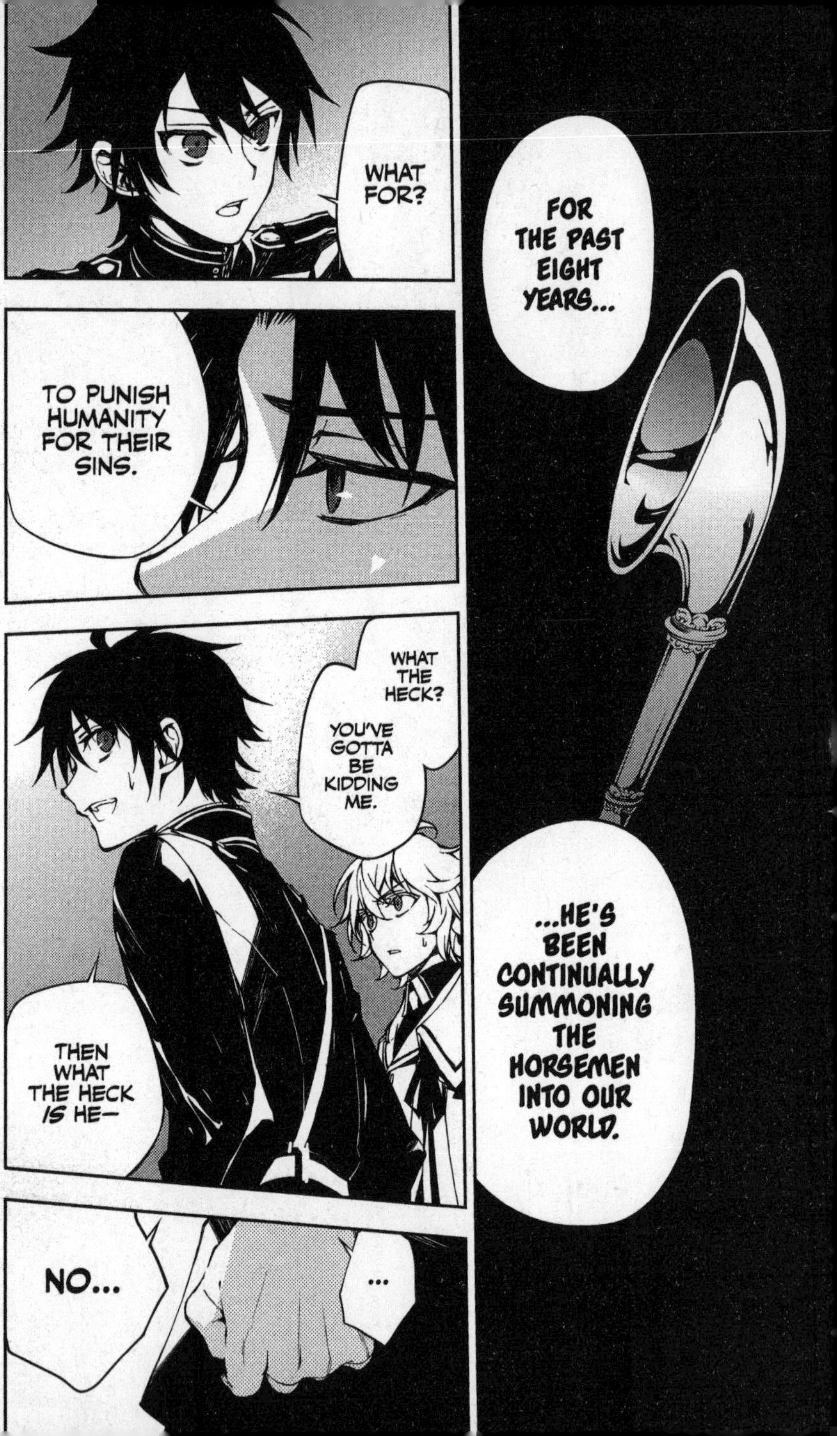
FOR THE PAST EIGHT YEARS...
...HE'S BEEN CONTINUALLY SUMMONING THE HORSEMEN INTO OUR WORLD.
WHAT FOR?
TO PUNISH HUMANITY FOR THEIR SINS.
WHAT THE HECK?
YOU'VE GOTTA BE KIDDING ME.
THEN WHAT THE HECK IS HE—
...
NO...

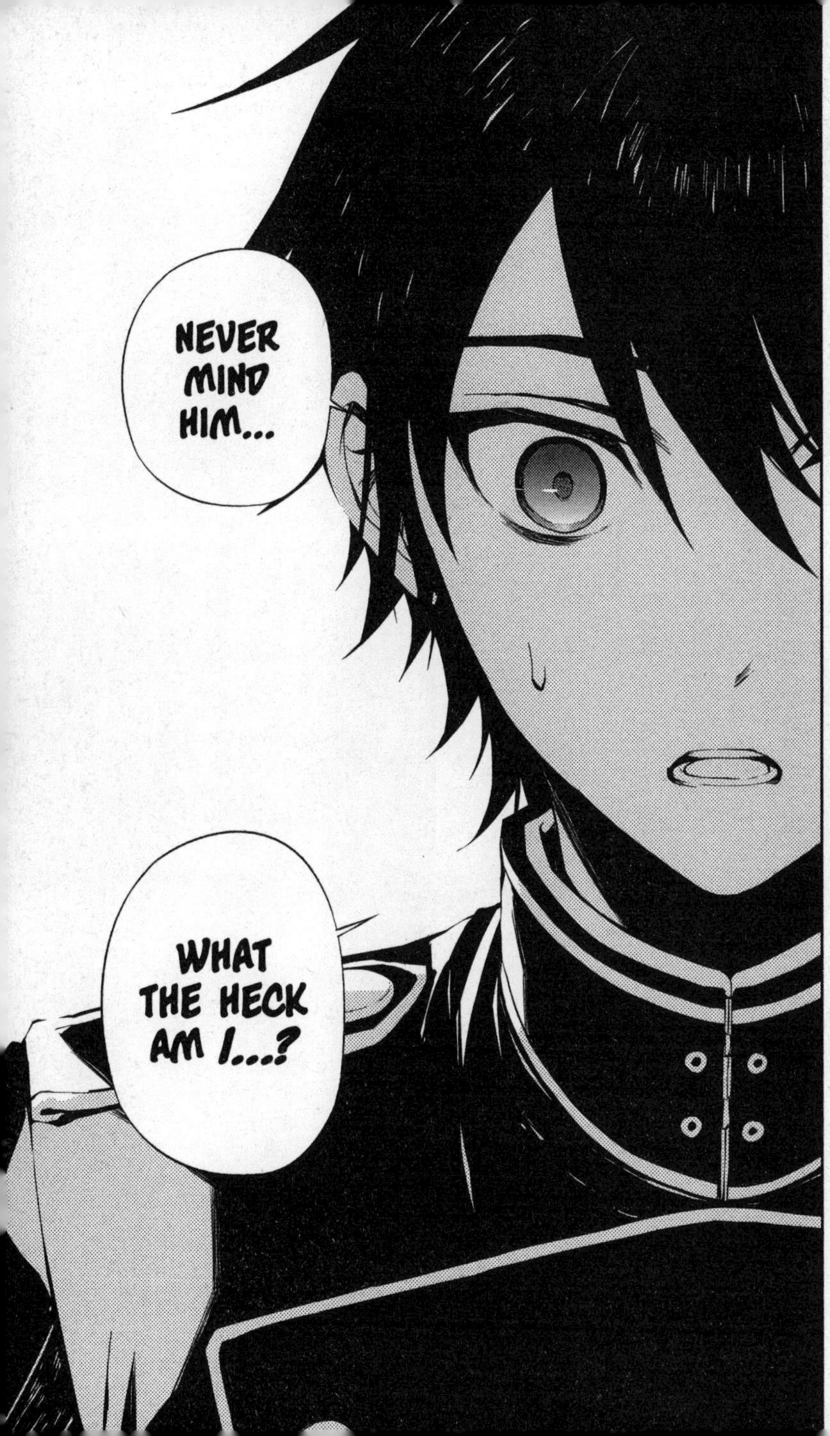
NEVER MIND HIM...
WHAT THE HECK AM I...?

Seraph of the End

VAMPIRE REIGN

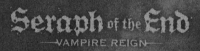

BONUS STORY

The Demon Army of Ikebukuro

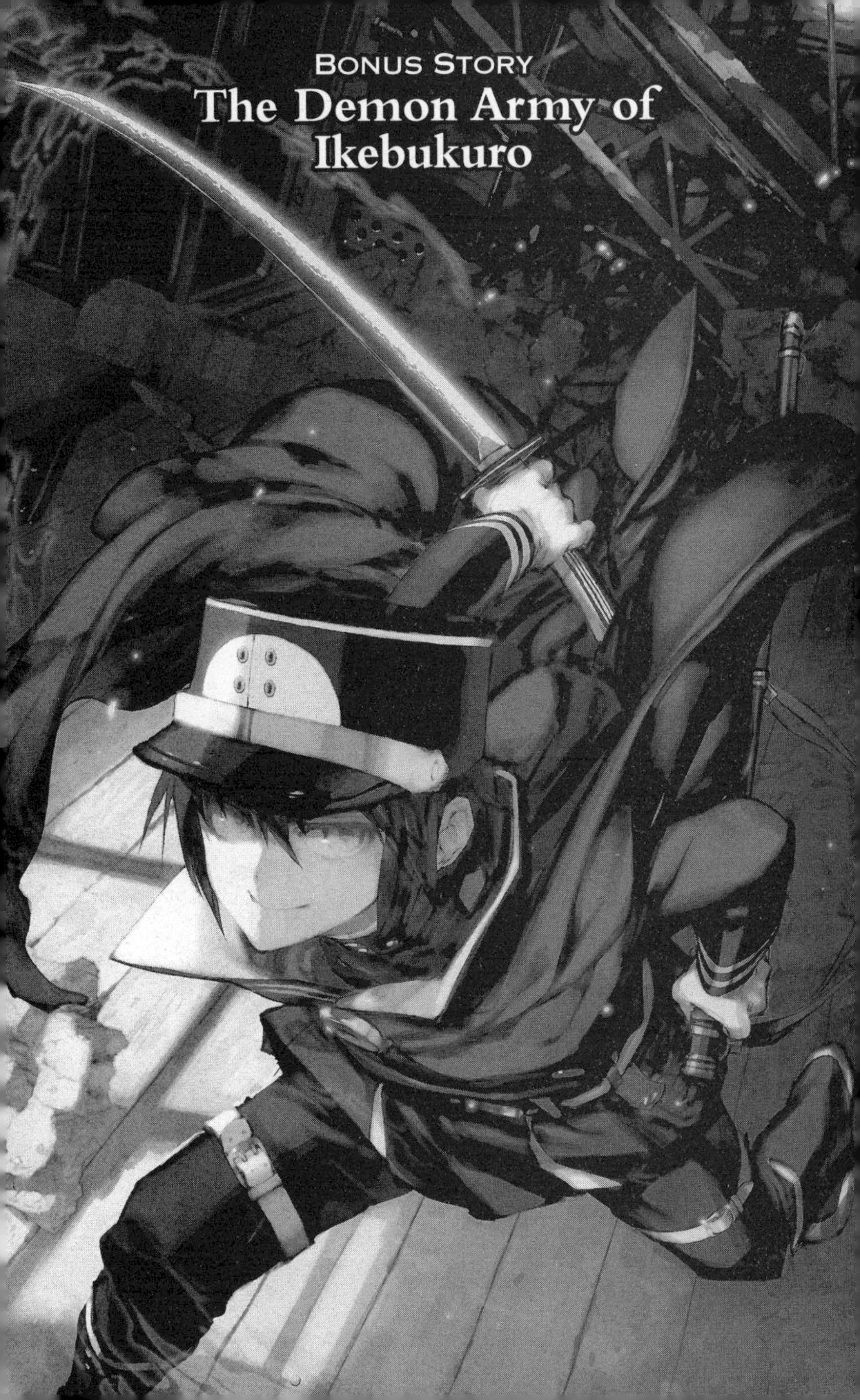

Seraph of the End
VAMPIRE REIGN

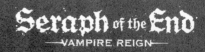

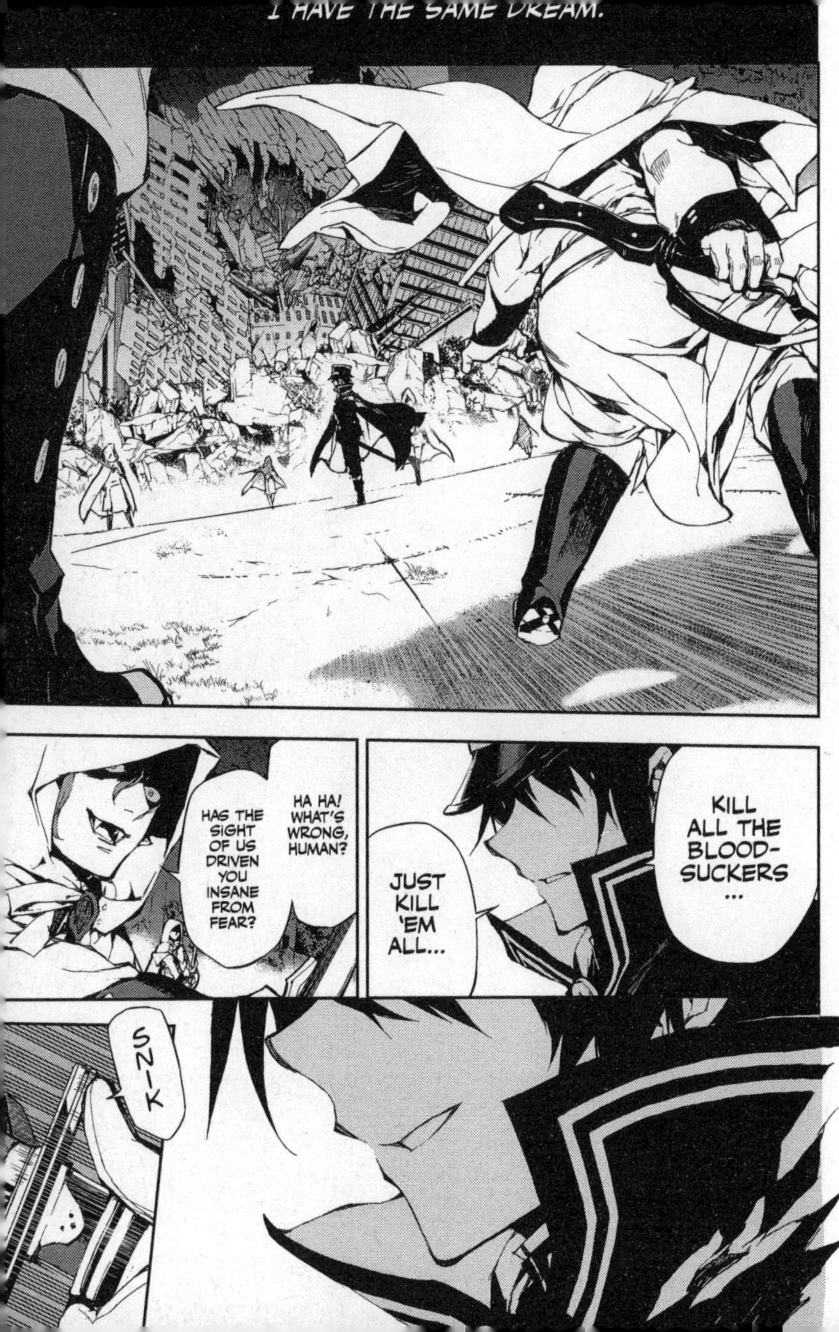
I HAVE THE SAME DREAM.
KILL ALL THE BLOOD-SUCKERS ...
JUST KILL 'EM ALL...
HA HA! WHAT'S WRONG, HUMAN?
HAS THE SIGHT OF US DRIVEN YOU INSANE FROM FEAR?
SNIK

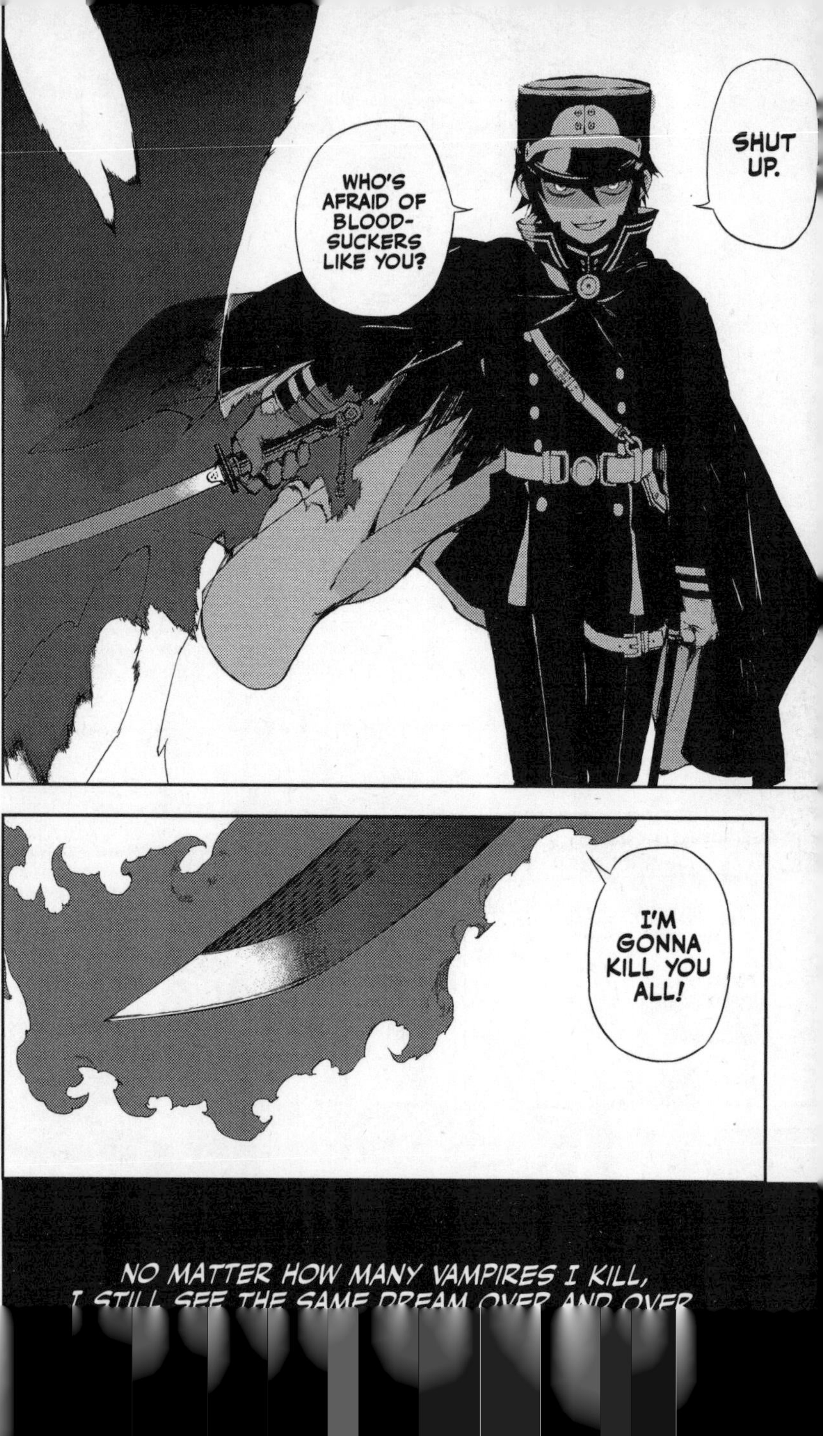
SHUT UP.
WHO'S AFRAID OF BLOOD-SUCKERS LIKE YOU?
I'M GONNA KILL YOU ALL!
NO MATTER HOW MANY VAMPIRES I KILL,
[redacted]

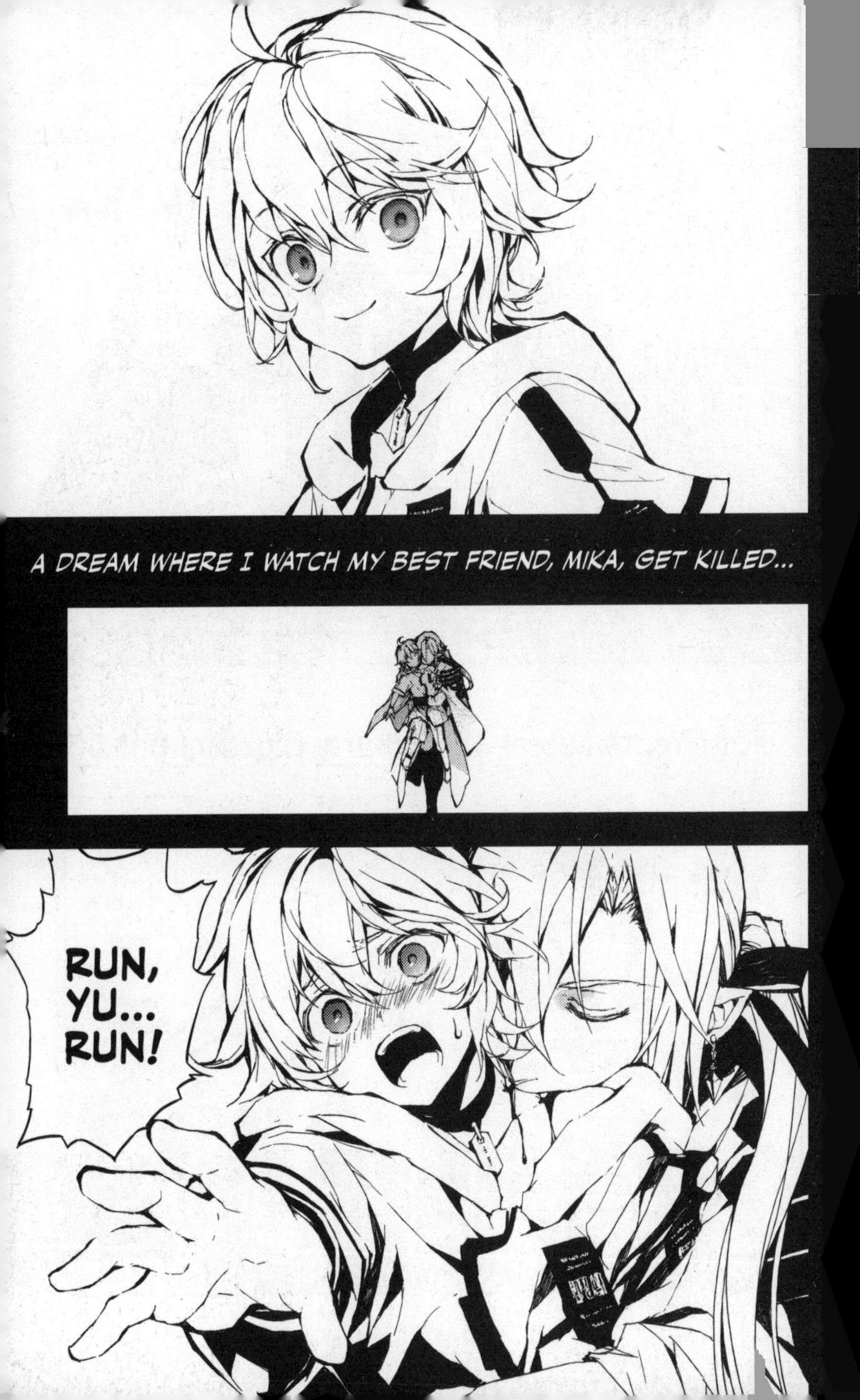
A DREAM WHERE I WATCH MY BEST FRIEND, MIKA, GET KILLED...
RUN, YU... RUN!

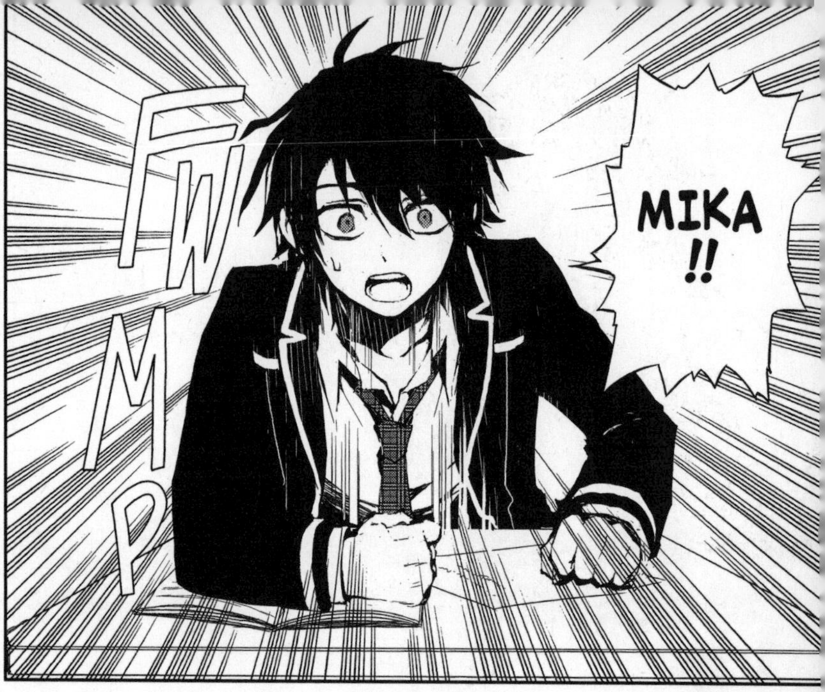
MIKA!!
FWMP

Four Years Later—Ikebukuro, High School 5

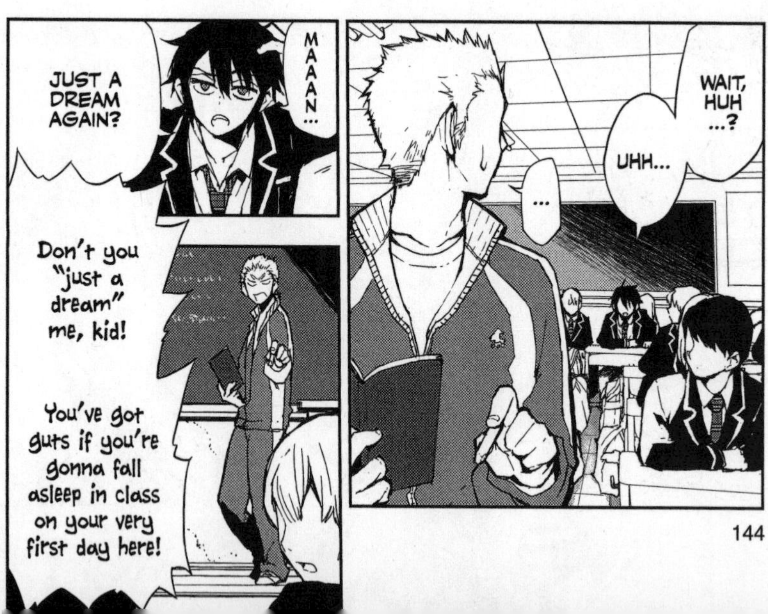
WAIT, HUH...?
UHH...
...
MAAAN...
JUST A DREAM AGAIN?
Don't you "just a dream" me, kid!
You've got guts if you're gonna fall asleep in class on your very first day here!

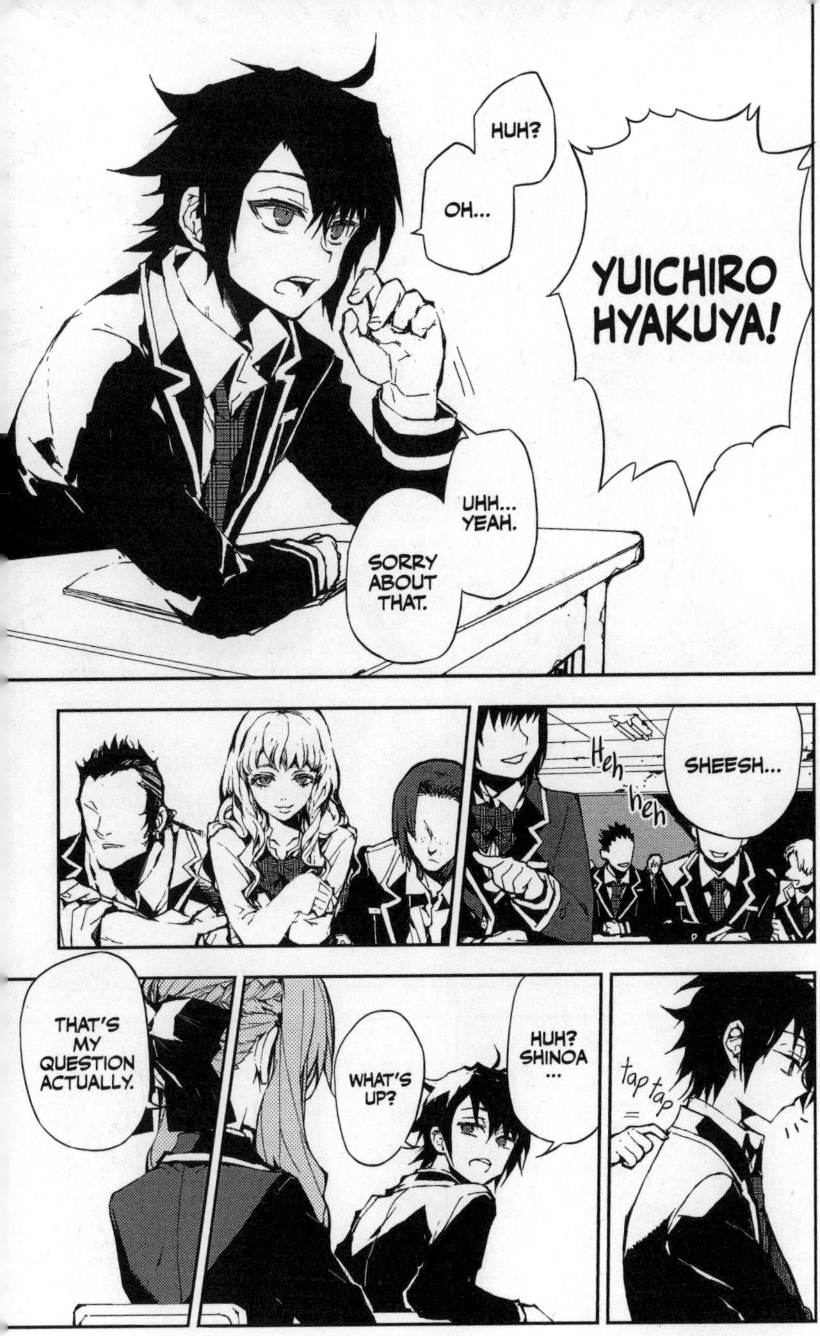
YUICHIRO HYAKUYA!
HUH?
OH...
UHH... YEAH.
SORRY ABOUT THAT.
SHEESH...
Heh heh
tap tap
HUH? SHINOA ...
WHAT'S UP?
THAT'S MY QUESTION ACTUALLY.

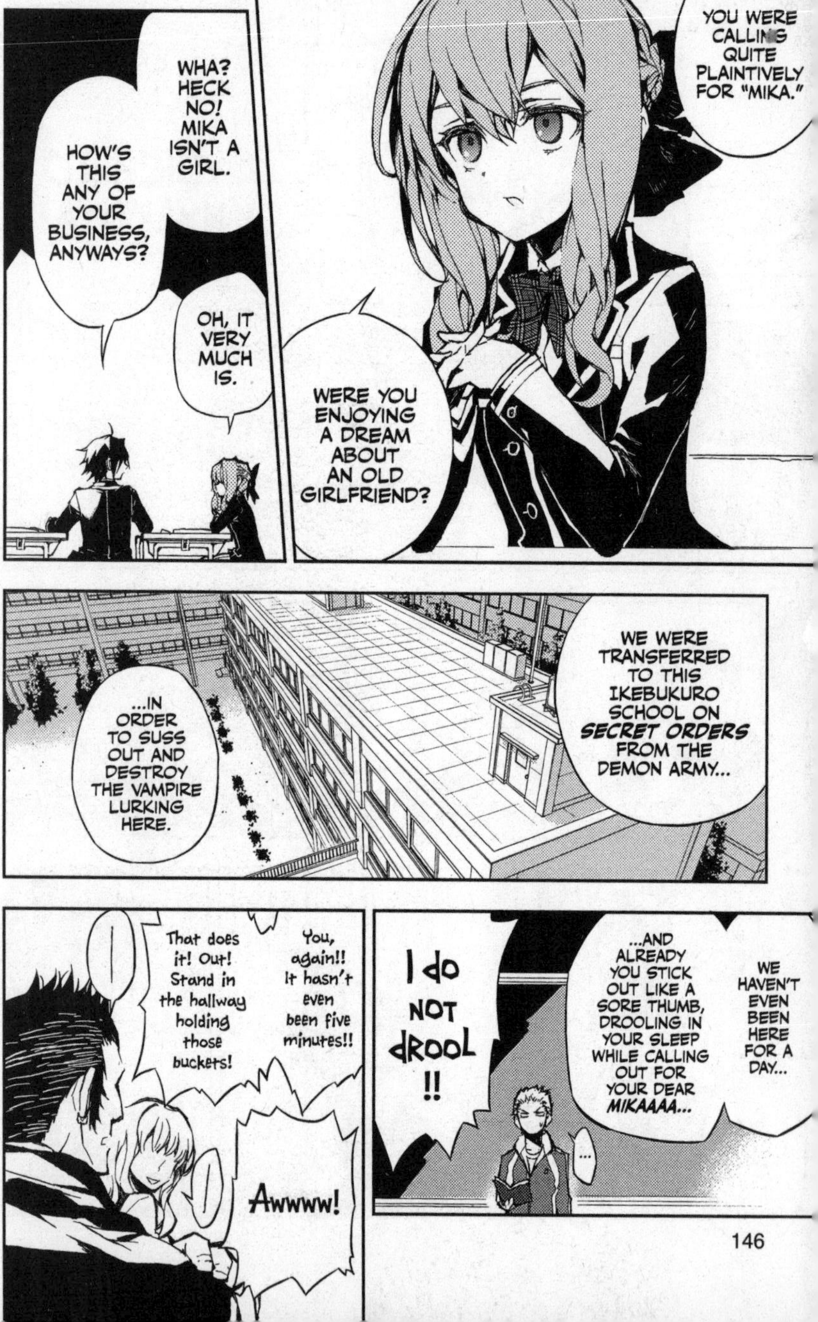
YOU WERE CALLING QUITE PLAINTIVELY FOR "MIKA."
WERE YOU ENJOYING A DREAM ABOUT AN OLD GIRLFRIEND?
WHA? HECK NO! MIKA ISN'T A GIRL.
HOW'S THIS ANY OF YOUR BUSINESS, ANYWAYS?
OH, IT VERY MUCH IS.
WE WERE TRANSFERRED TO THIS IKEBUKURO SCHOOL ON ***SECRET ORDERS*** FROM THE DEMON ARMY...
...IN ORDER TO SUSS OUT AND DESTROY THE VAMPIRE LURKING HERE.
WE HAVEN'T EVEN BEEN HERE FOR A DAY...
...AND ALREADY YOU STICK OUT LIKE A SORE THUMB, DROOLING IN YOUR SLEEP WHILE CALLING OUT FOR YOUR DEAR ***MIKAAAA...***
I do NOT drool !!
...
!
You, again!! It hasn't even been five minutes!!
That does it! Out! Stand in the hallway holding those buckets!
!
Awwww!

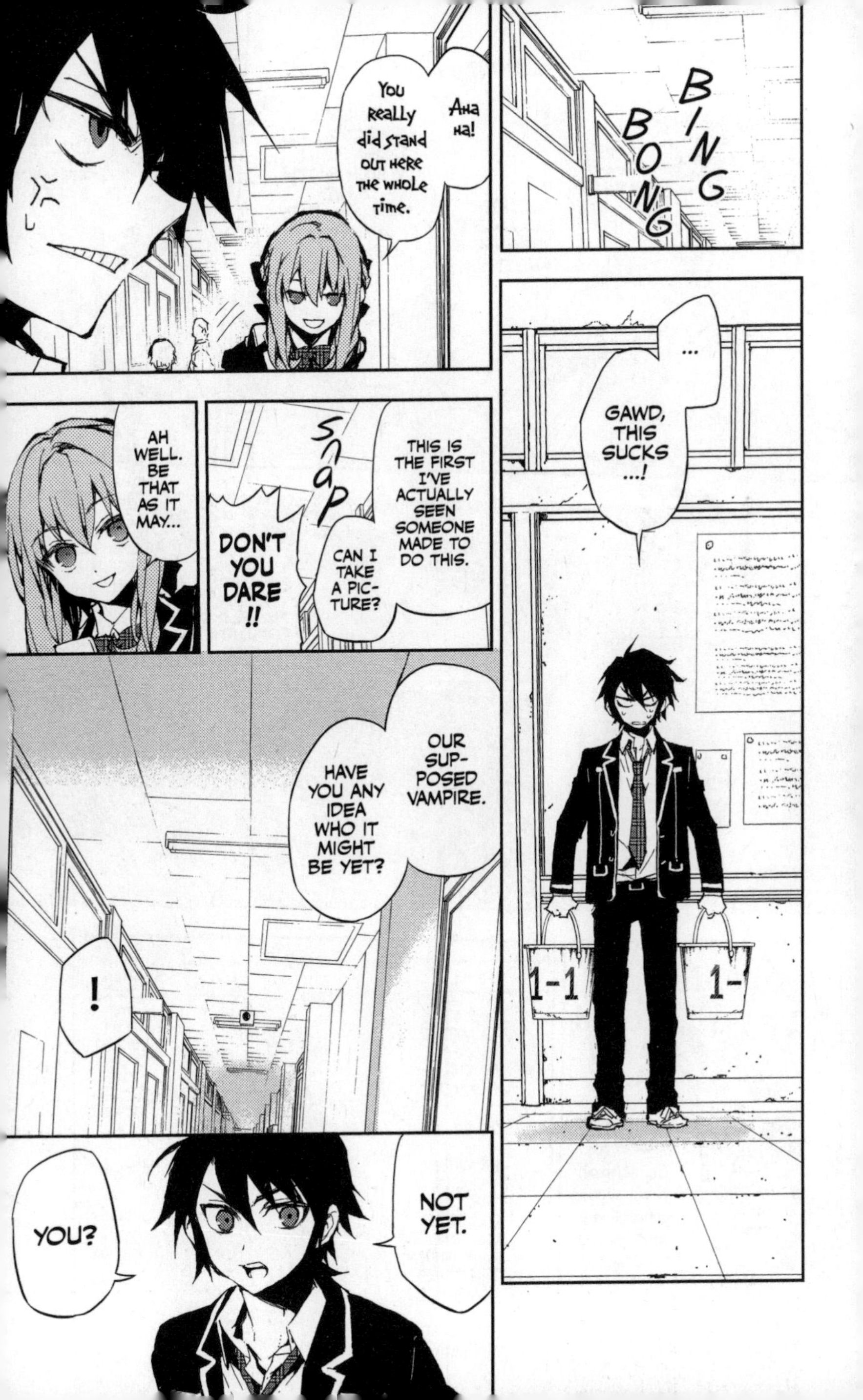
BING
BONG
...
GAWD, THIS SUCKS ...!
1-1
1-
AHA HA!
YOU REALLY DID STAND OUT HERE THE WHOLE TIME.
THIS IS THE FIRST I'VE ACTUALLY SEEN SOMEONE MADE TO DO THIS.
CAN I TAKE A PIC-TURE?
SNAP
DON'T YOU DARE!!
AH WELL. BE THAT AS IT MAY...
OUR SUP-POSED VAMPIRE.
HAVE YOU ANY IDEA WHO IT MIGHT BE YET?
!
NOT YET.
YOU?

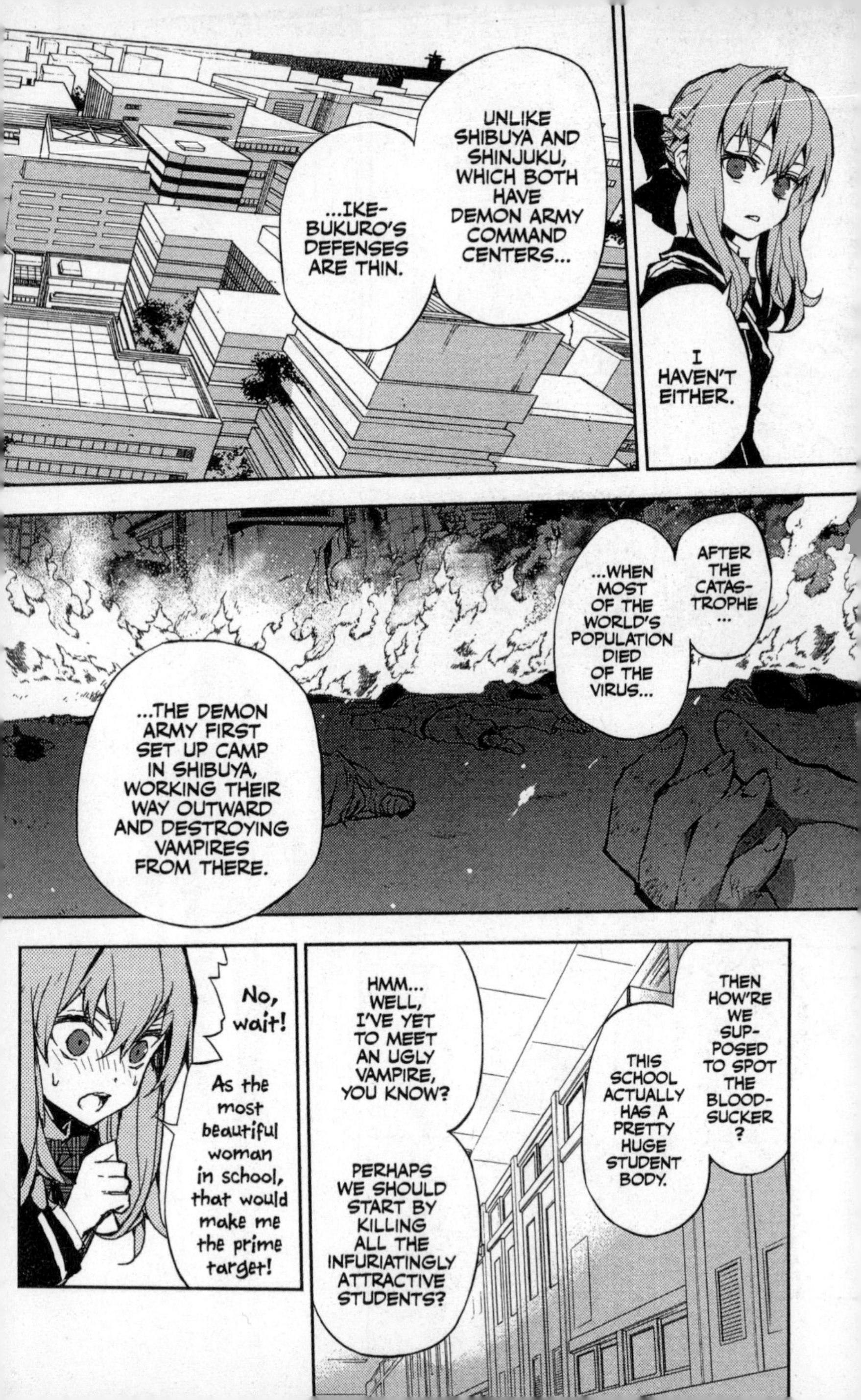
I HAVEN'T EITHER.
UNLIKE SHIBUYA AND SHINJUKU, WHICH BOTH HAVE DEMON ARMY COMMAND CENTERS...
...IKE-BUKURO'S DEFENSES ARE THIN.
AFTER THE CATAS-TROPHE...
...WHEN MOST OF THE WORLD'S POPULATION DIED OF THE VIRUS...
...THE DEMON ARMY FIRST SET UP CAMP IN SHIBUYA, WORKING THEIR WAY OUTWARD AND DESTROYING VAMPIRES FROM THERE.
THEN HOW'RE WE SUP-POSED TO SPOT THE BLOOD-SUCKER?
THIS SCHOOL ACTUALLY HAS A PRETTY HUGE STUDENT BODY.
HMM... WELL, I'VE YET TO MEET AN UGLY VAMPIRE, YOU KNOW?
PERHAPS WE SHOULD START BY KILLING ALL THE INFURIATINGLY ATTRACTIVE STUDENTS?
No, wait!
As the most beautiful woman in school, that would make me the prime target!

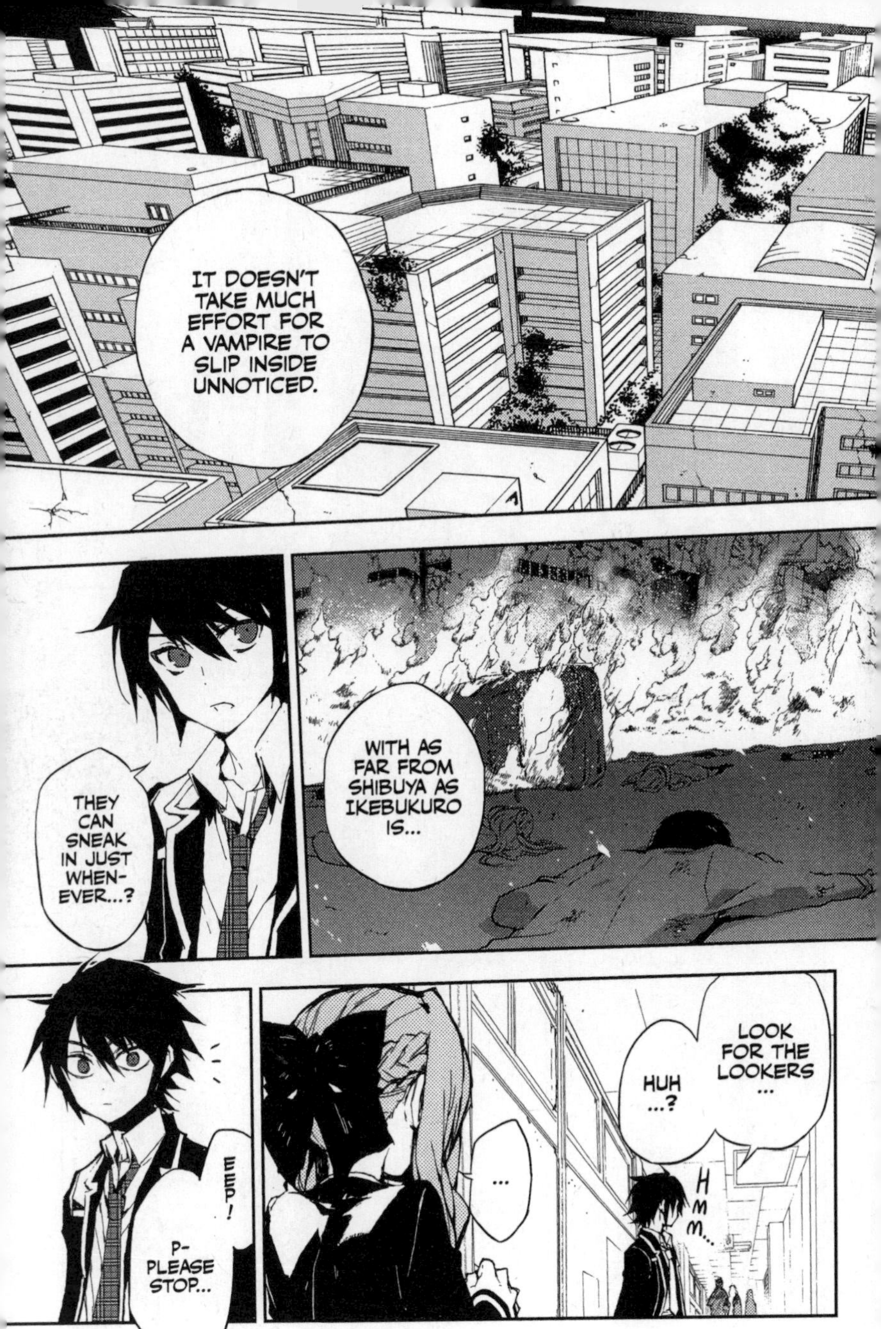
IT DOESN'T TAKE MUCH EFFORT FOR A VAMPIRE TO SLIP INSIDE UNNOTICED.
WITH AS FAR FROM SHIBUYA AS IKEBUKURO IS...
THEY CAN SNEAK IN JUST WHEN-EVER...?
LOOK FOR THE LOOKERS...
HUH...?
HMM...
...
EEP!
P-PLEASE STOP...

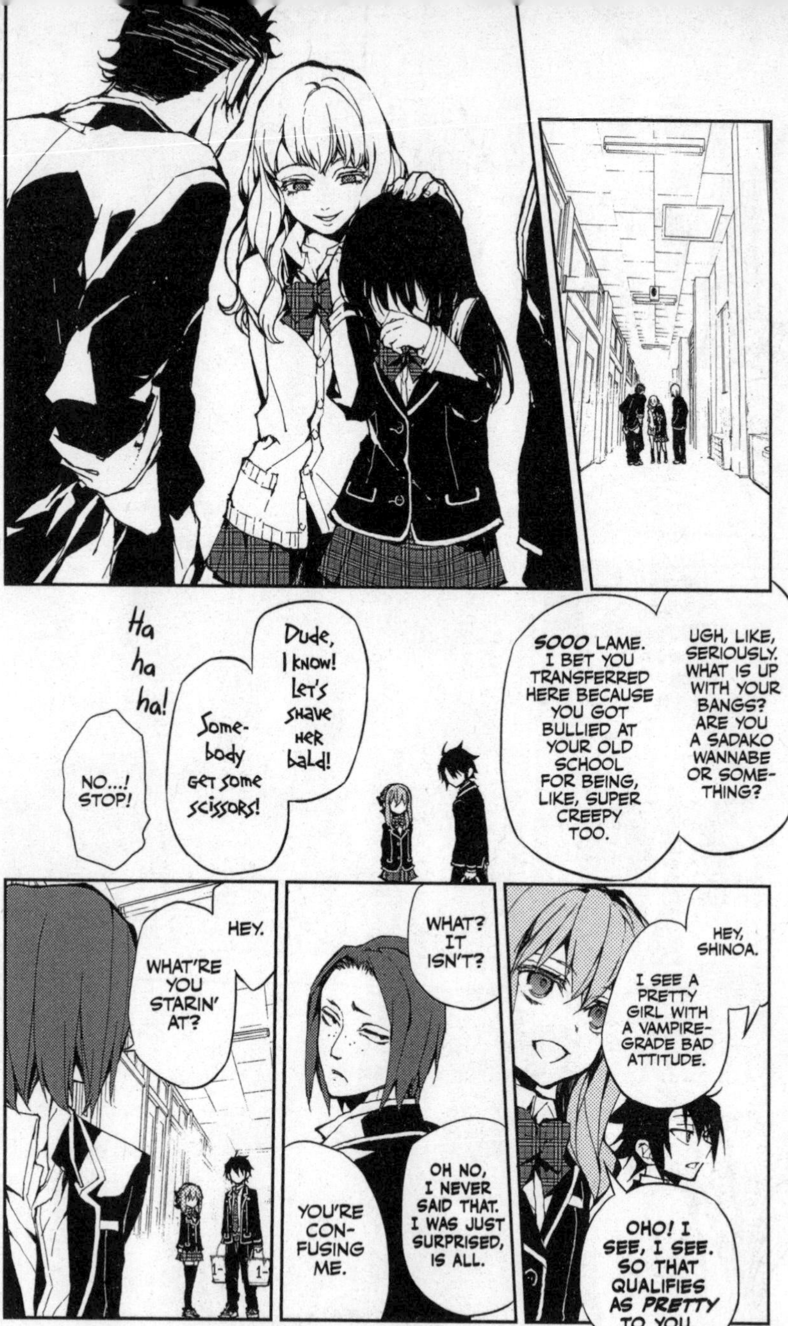
UGH, LIKE, SERIOUSLY. WHAT IS UP WITH YOUR BANGS? ARE YOU A SADAKO WANNABE OR SOME-THING?
SOOO LAME. I BET YOU TRANSFERRED HERE BECAUSE YOU GOT BULLIED AT YOUR OLD SCHOOL FOR BEING, LIKE, SUPER CREEPY TOO.
Dude, I know! Let's shave her bald!
Some-body get some scissors!
Ha ha ha!
NO...! STOP!
HEY, SHINOA.
I SEE A PRETTY GIRL WITH A VAMPIRE-GRADE BAD ATTITUDE.
OHO! I SEE, I SEE. SO THAT QUALIFIES AS PRETTY TO YOU.
WHAT? IT ISN'T?
OH NO, I NEVER SAID THAT. I WAS JUST SURPRISED, IS ALL.
YOU'RE CON-FUSING ME.
HEY.
WHAT'RE YOU STARIN' AT?

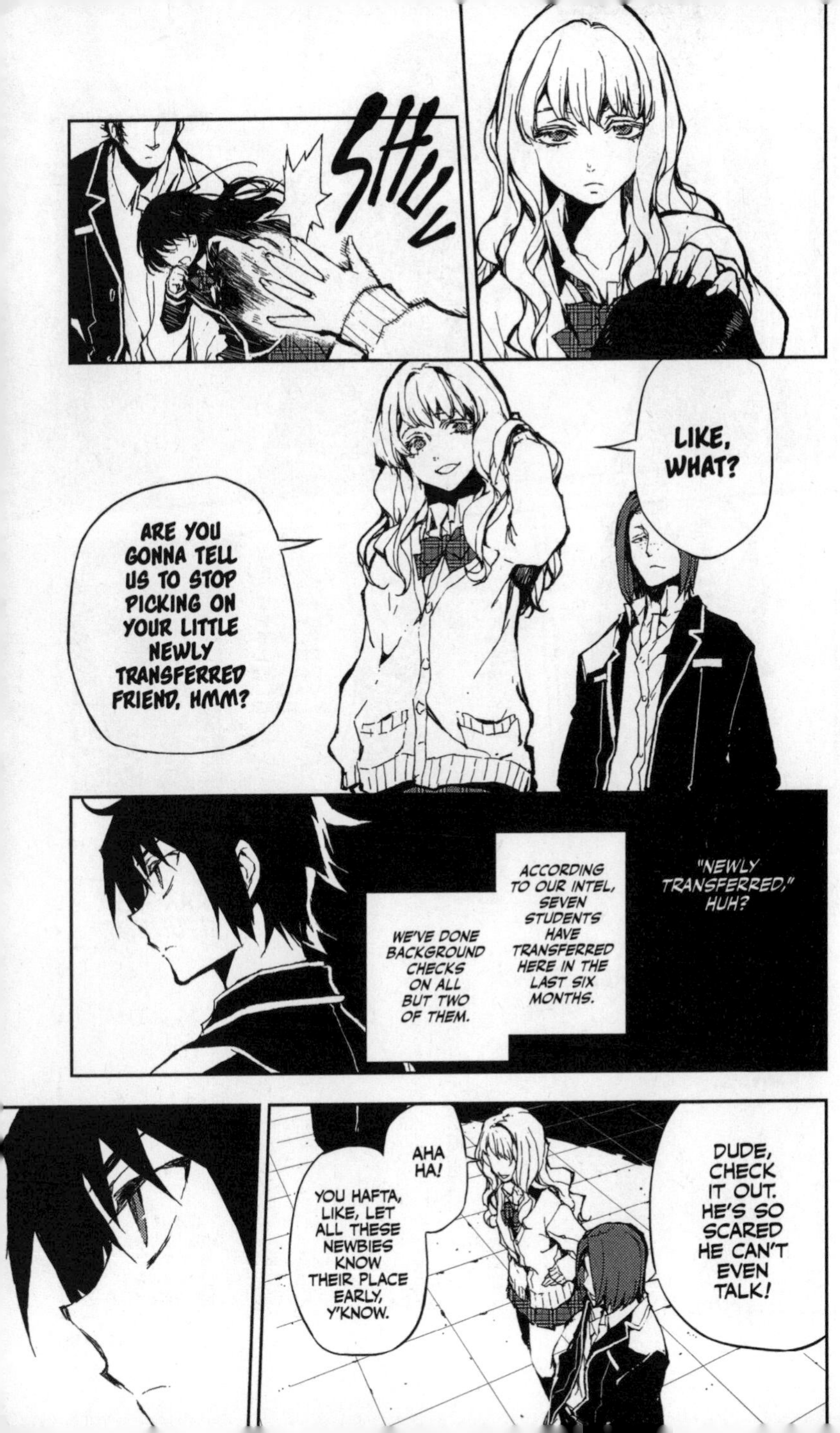
SHUV
LIKE, WHAT?
ARE YOU GONNA TELL US TO STOP PICKING ON YOUR LITTLE NEWLY TRANSFERRED FRIEND, HMM?
"NEWLY TRANSFERRED," HUH?
ACCORDING TO OUR INTEL, SEVEN STUDENTS HAVE TRANSFERRED HERE IN THE LAST SIX MONTHS.
WE'VE DONE BACKGROUND CHECKS ON ALL BUT TWO OF THEM.
DUDE, CHECK IT OUT. HE'S SO SCARED HE CAN'T EVEN TALK!
AHA HA!
YOU HAFTA, LIKE, LET ALL THESE NEWBIES KNOW THEIR PLACE EARLY, Y'KNOW.

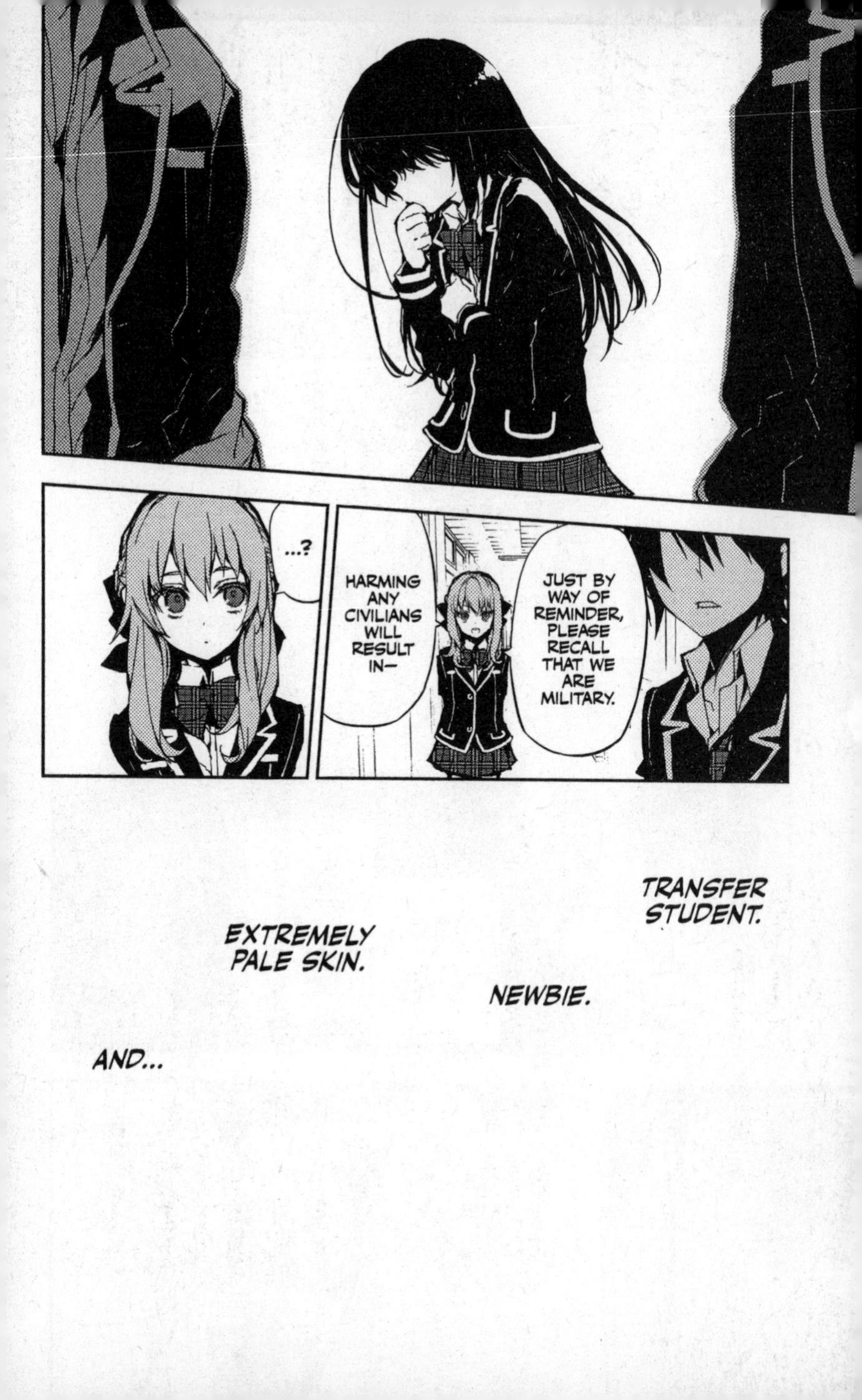
JUST BY WAY OF REMINDER, PLEASE RECALL THAT WE ARE MILITARY.
HARMING ANY CIVILIANS WILL RESULT IN—
...?
TRANSFER STUDENT.
NEWBIE.
EXTREMELY PALE SKIN.
AND...

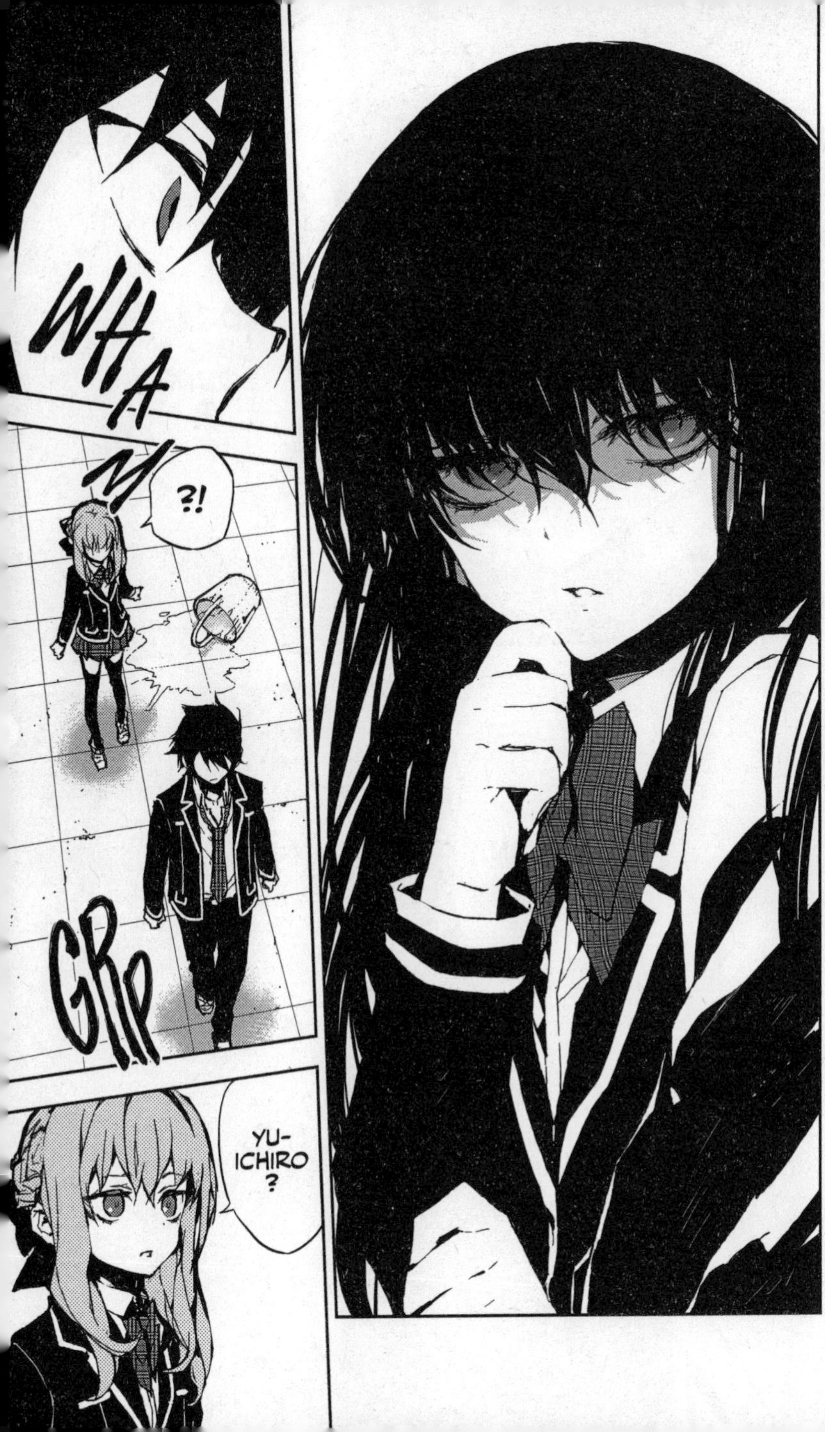
WHAM
?!
GRIP
YU-ICHIRO?

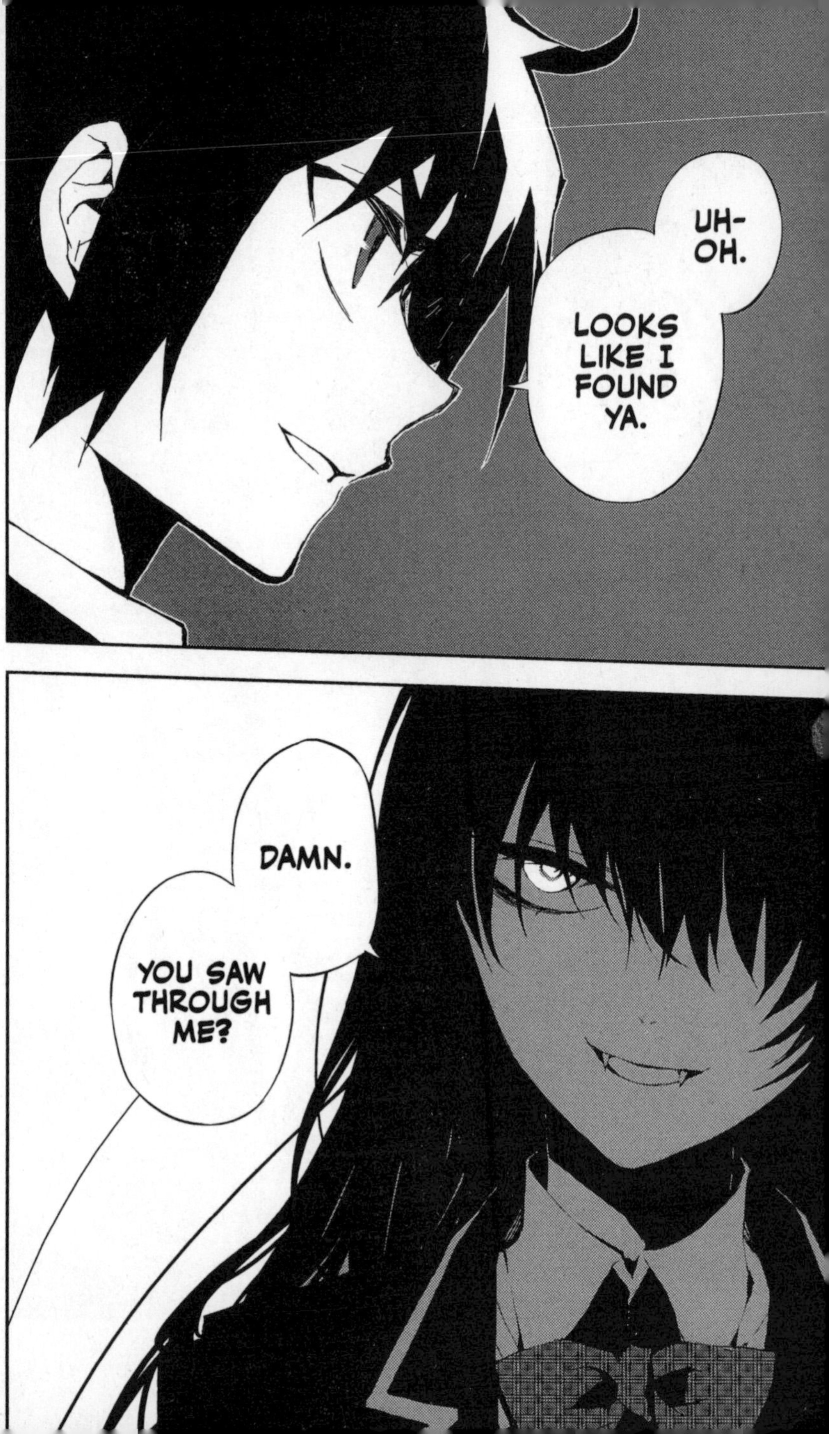
UH-OH.
LOOKS LIKE I FOUND YA.
DAMN.
YOU SAW THROUGH ME?

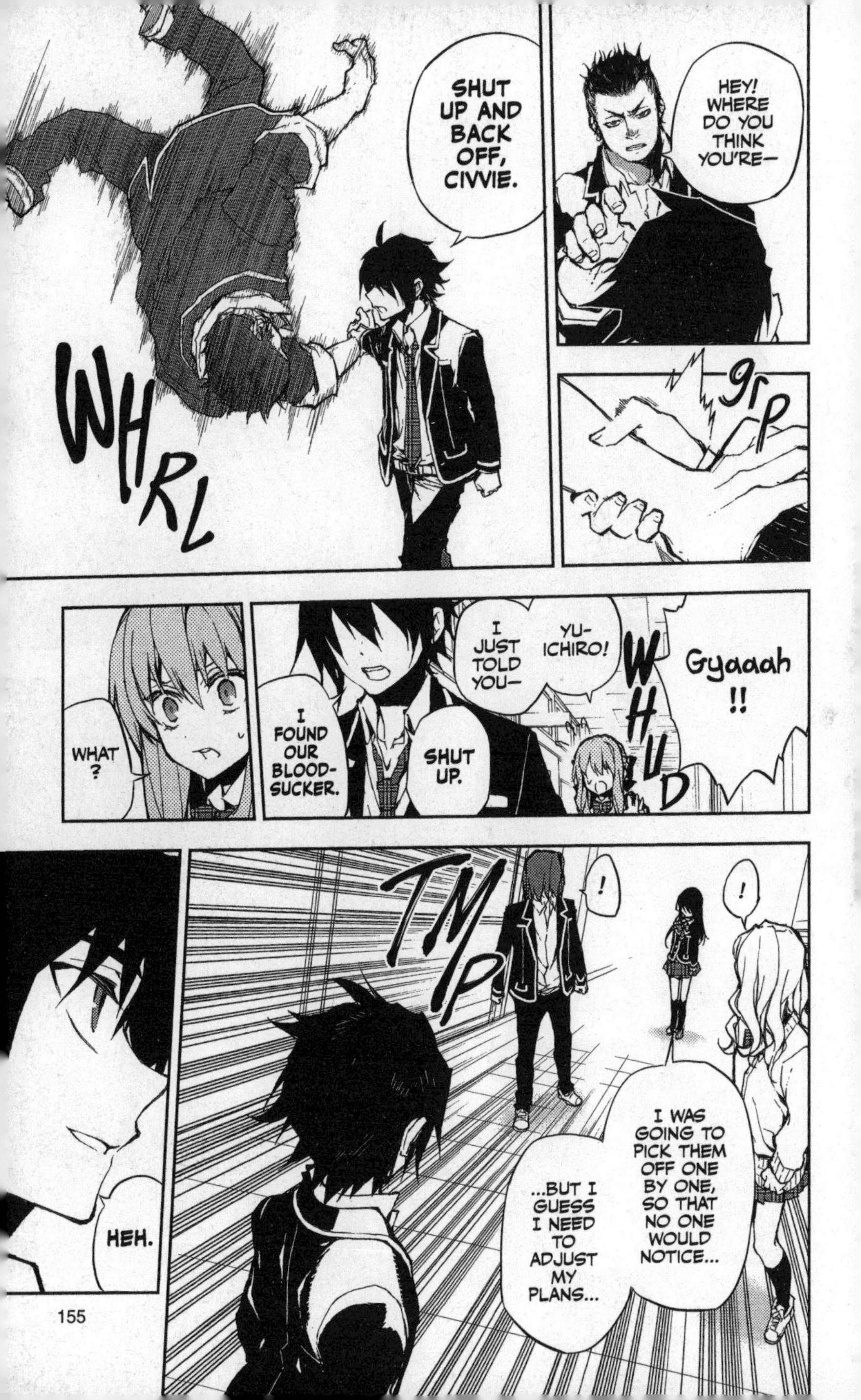
HEY! WHERE DO YOU THINK YOU'RE—
grip
SHUT UP AND BACK OFF, CIVVIE.
WHRL
Gyaaah!!
WHUD
YU-ICHIRO!
I JUST TOLD YOU—
SHUT UP.
I FOUND OUR BLOOD-SUCKER.
WHAT?
!
!
TMP
I WAS GOING TO PICK THEM OFF ONE BY ONE, SO THAT NO ONE WOULD NOTICE...
...BUT I GUESS I NEED TO ADJUST MY PLANS...
HEH.

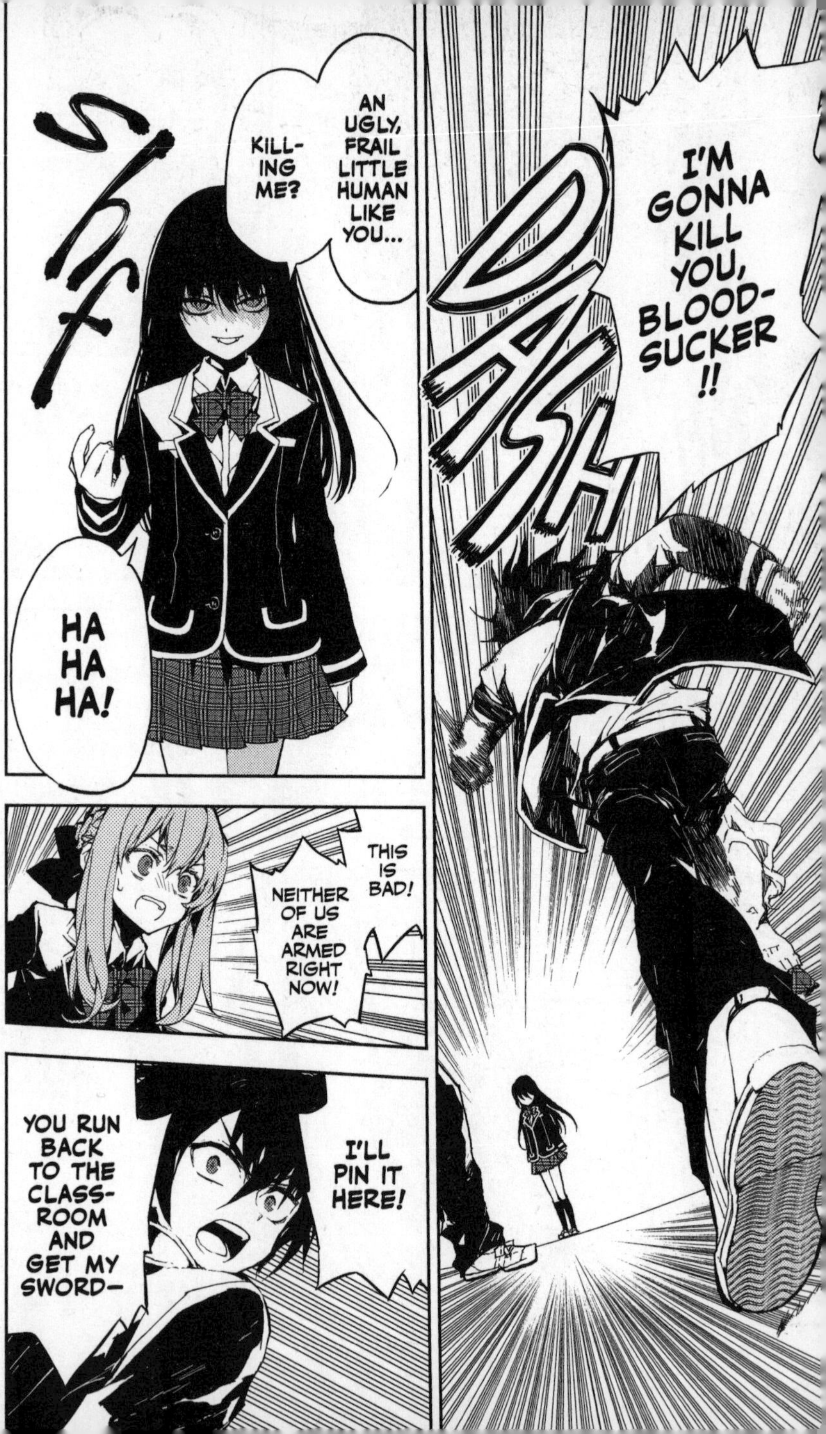
I'M GONNA KILL YOU, BLOODSUCKER!!
DASH
AN UGLY, FRAIL LITTLE HUMAN LIKE YOU...
KILLING ME?
HA HA HA!
THIS IS BAD!
NEITHER OF US ARE ARMED RIGHT NOW!
I'LL PIN IT HERE!
YOU RUN BACK TO THE CLASSROOM AND GET MY SWORD—

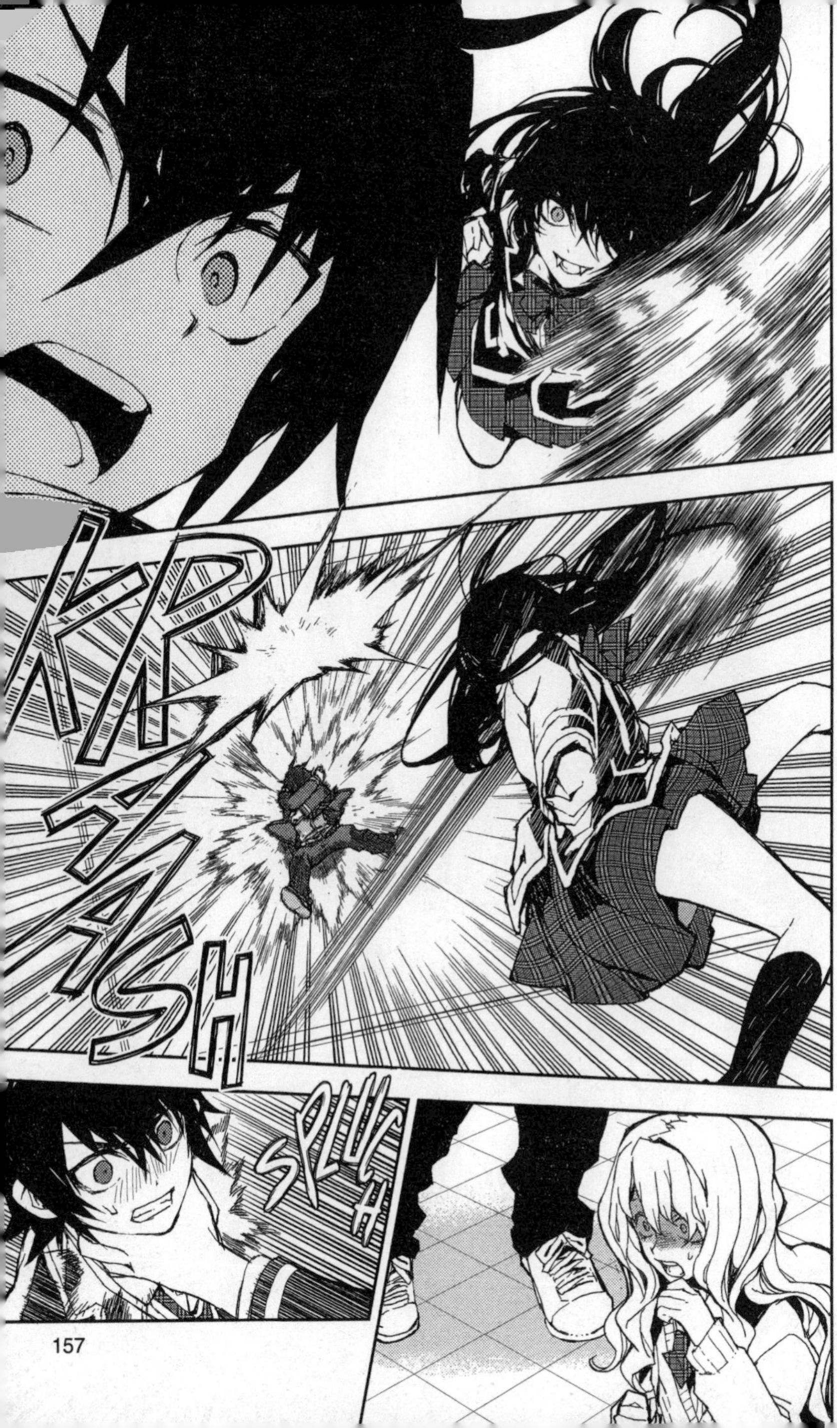
KRAAASH
SPLUCH

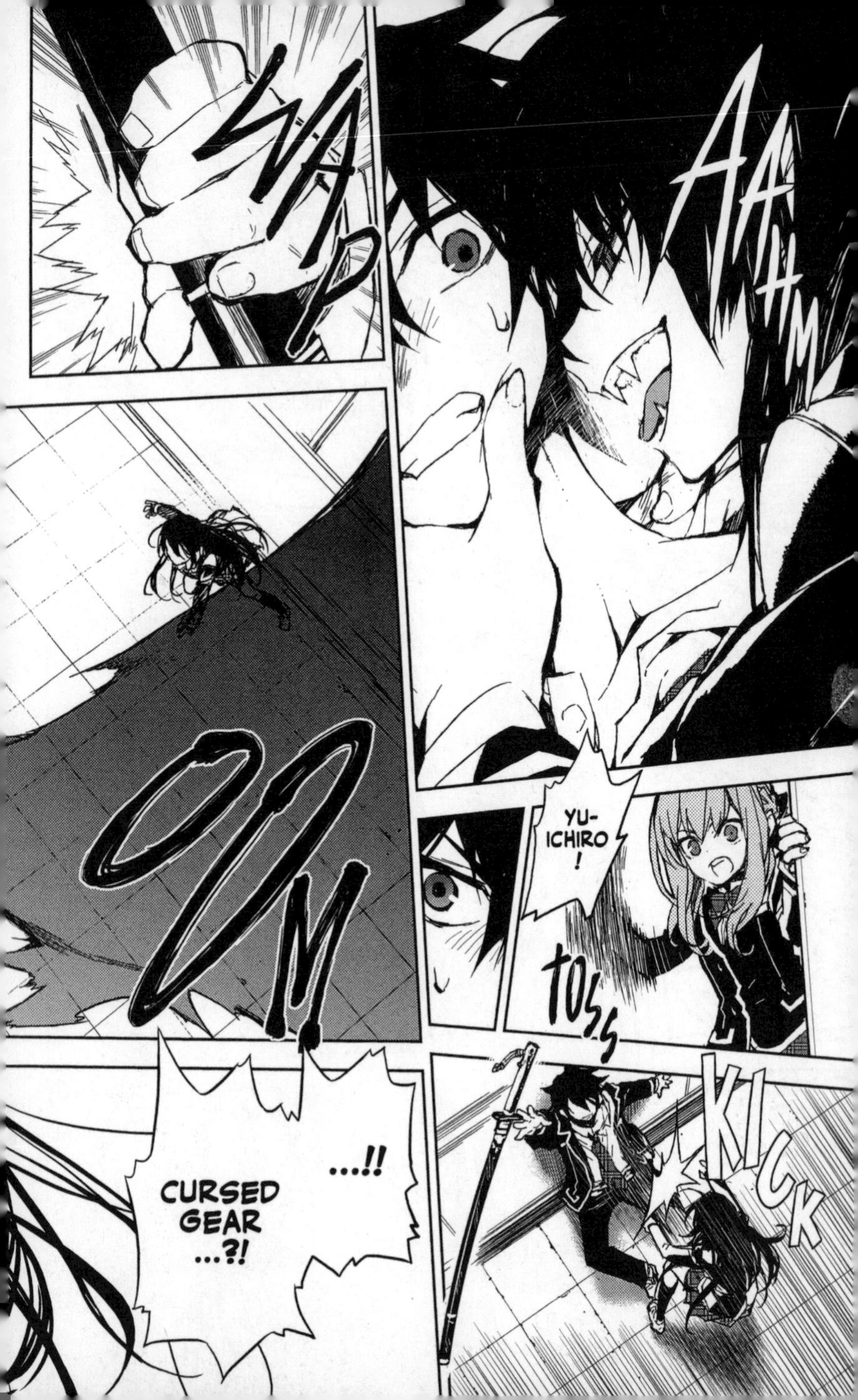
YU-ICHIRO!
TOSS
KICK
...!!
CURSED GEAR ...?!

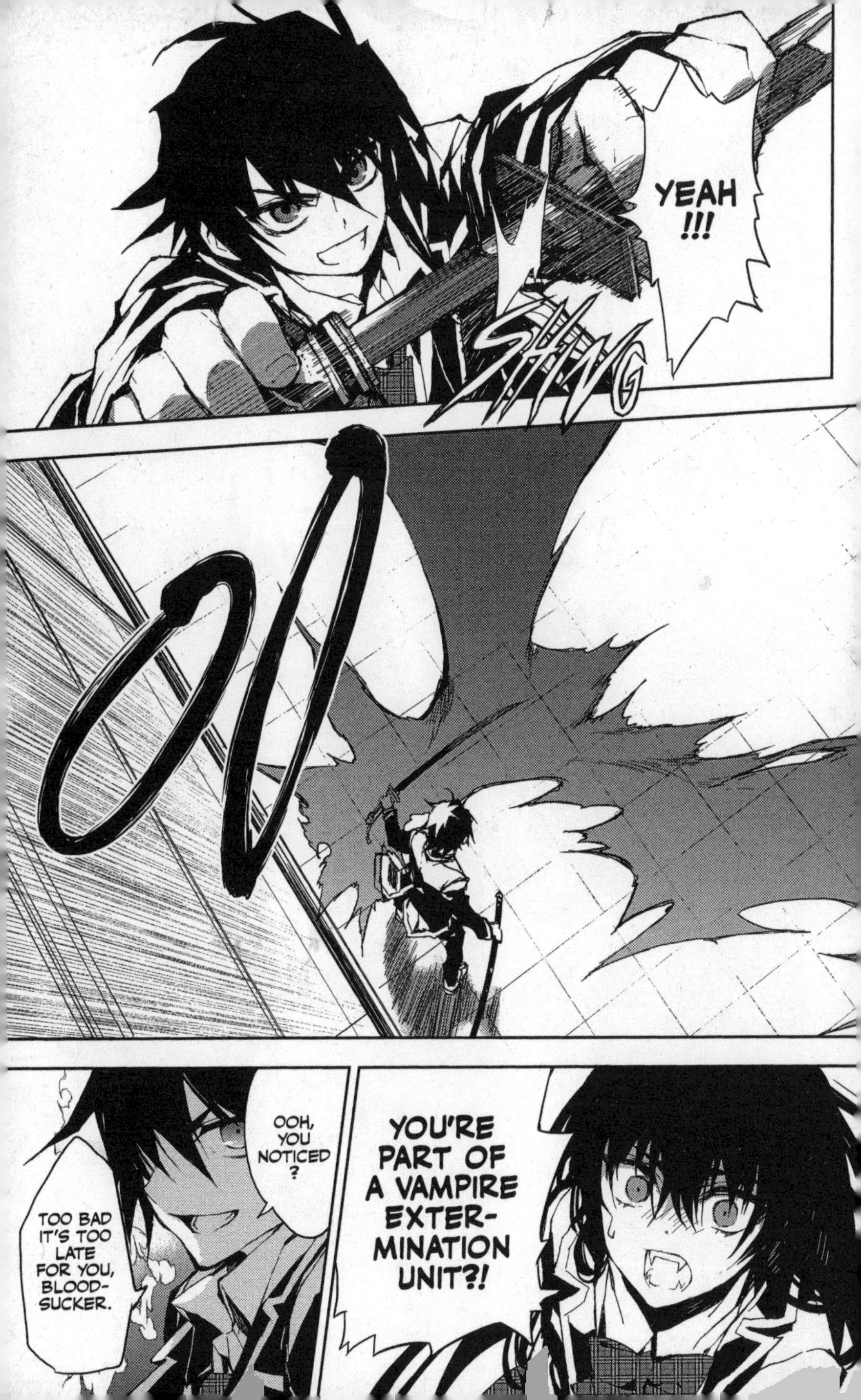
YEAH!!!
SHING
YOU'RE PART OF A VAMPIRE EXTER-MINATION UNIT?!
OOH, YOU NOTICED?
TOO BAD IT'S TOO LATE FOR YOU, BLOOD-SUCKER.

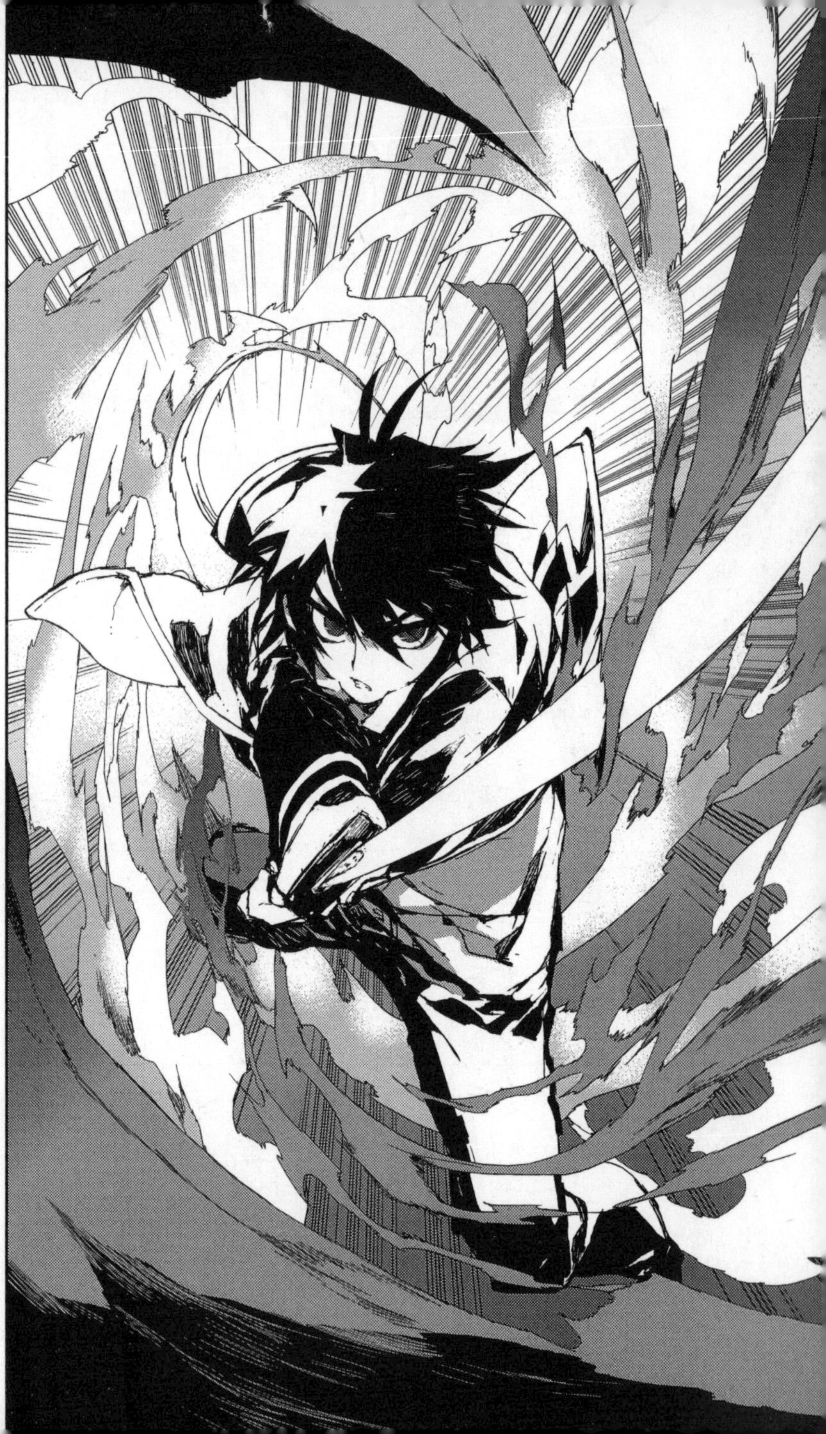

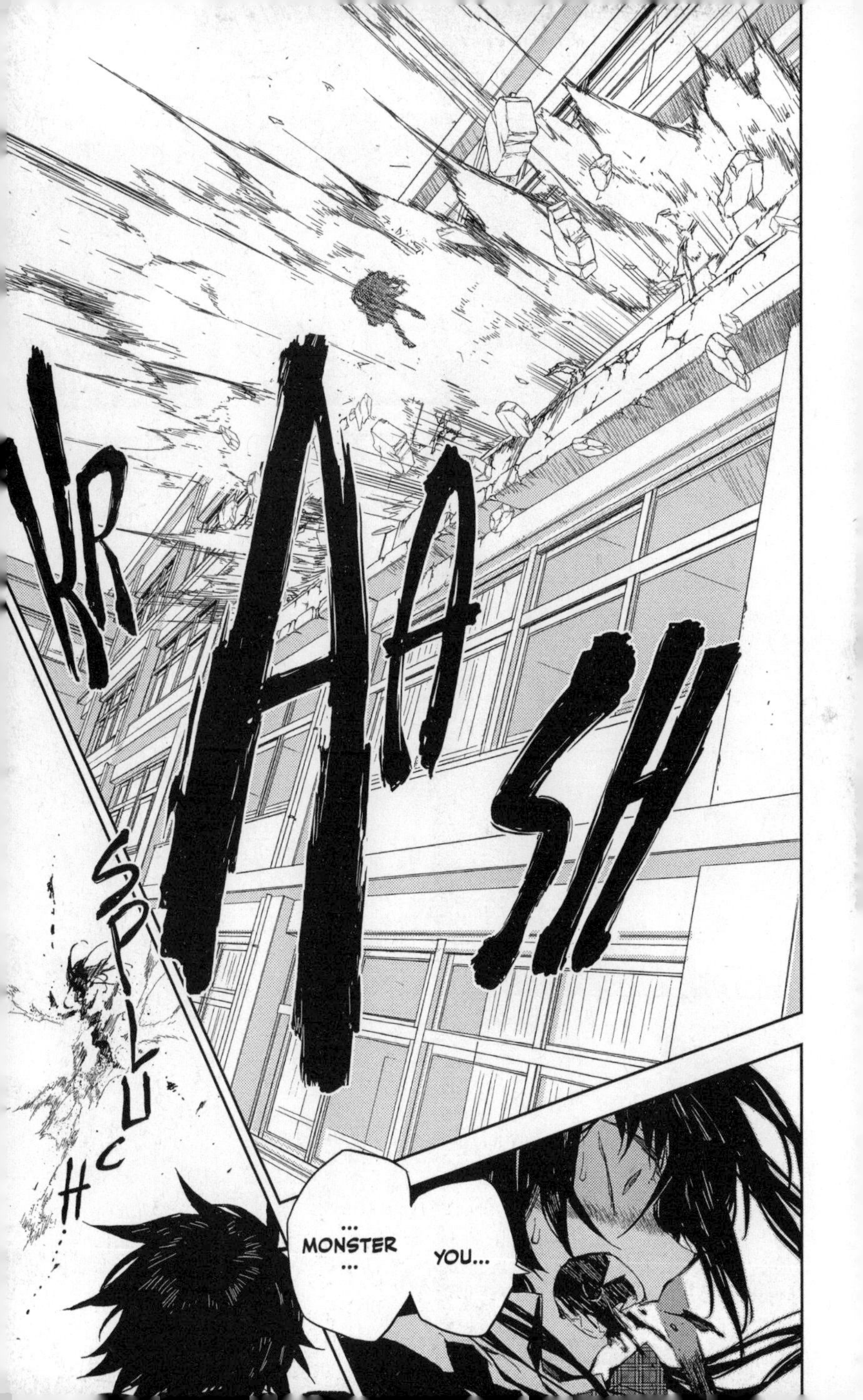
KRAASH
SPLUCH
YOU...
... MONSTER ...

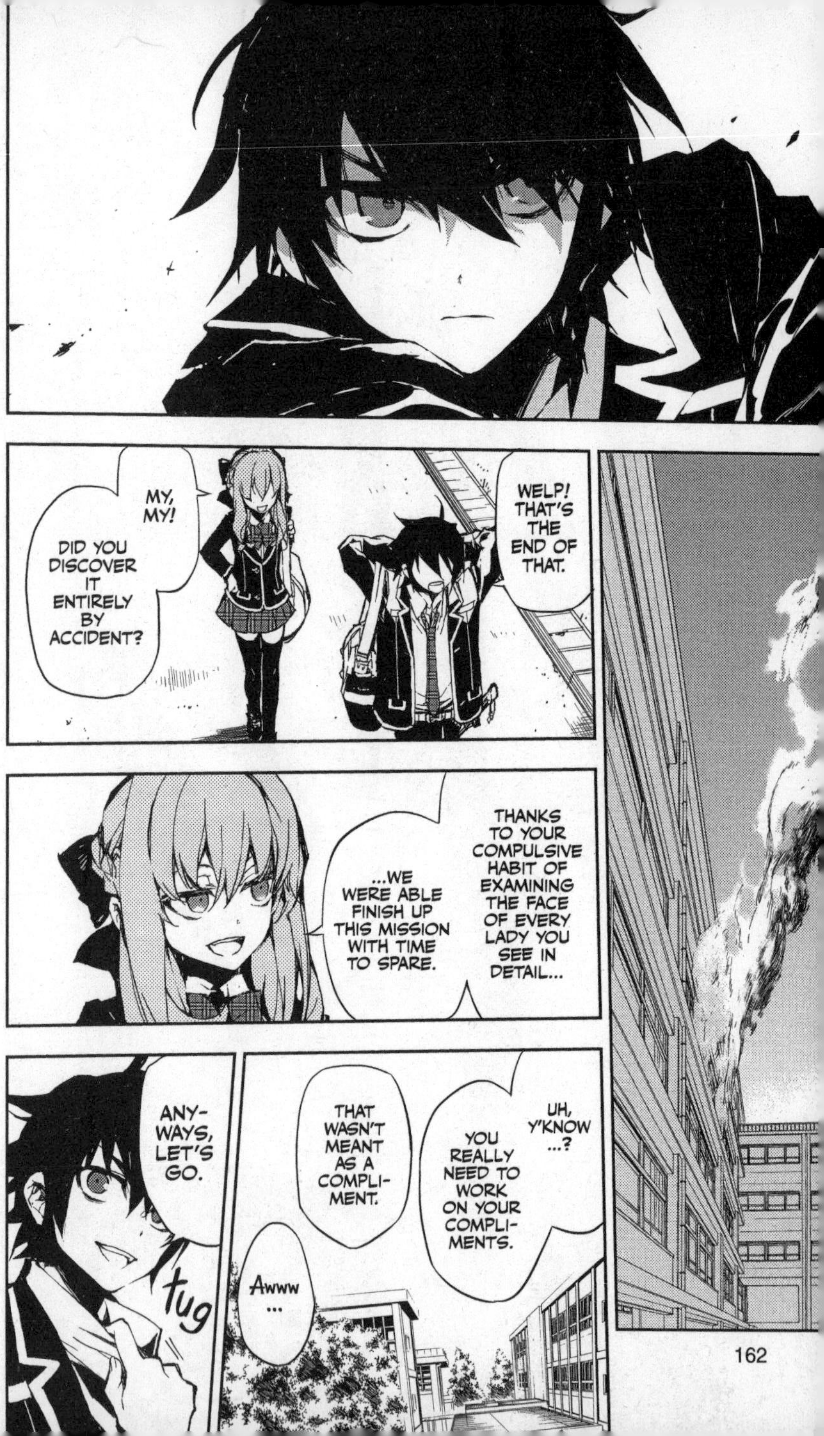
WELP! THAT'S THE END OF THAT.
MY, MY!
DID YOU DISCOVER IT ENTIRELY BY ACCIDENT?
THANKS TO YOUR COMPULSIVE HABIT OF EXAMINING THE FACE OF EVERY LADY YOU SEE IN DETAIL...
...WE WERE ABLE FINISH UP THIS MISSION WITH TIME TO SPARE.
UH, Y'KNOW ...?
YOU REALLY NEED TO WORK ON YOUR COMPLI-MENTS.
THAT WASN'T MEANT AS A COMPLI-MENT.
Awww ...
ANY-WAYS, LET'S GO.
tug

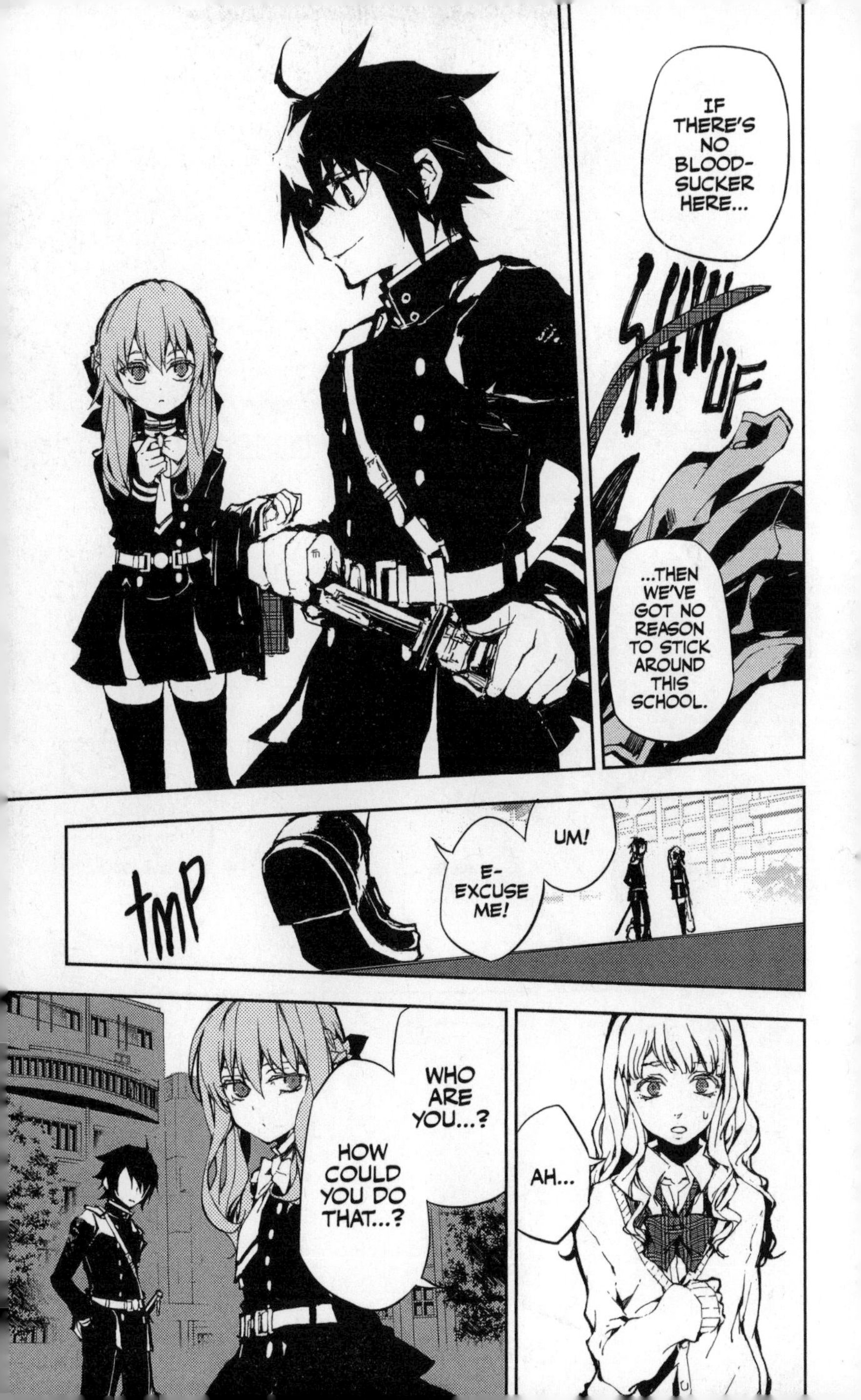
IF THERE'S NO BLOOD-SUCKER HERE...
SHWUF
...THEN WE'VE GOT NO REASON TO STICK AROUND THIS SCHOOL.
UM!
E-EXCUSE ME!
tmp
AH...
WHO ARE YOU...?
HOW COULD YOU DO THAT...?

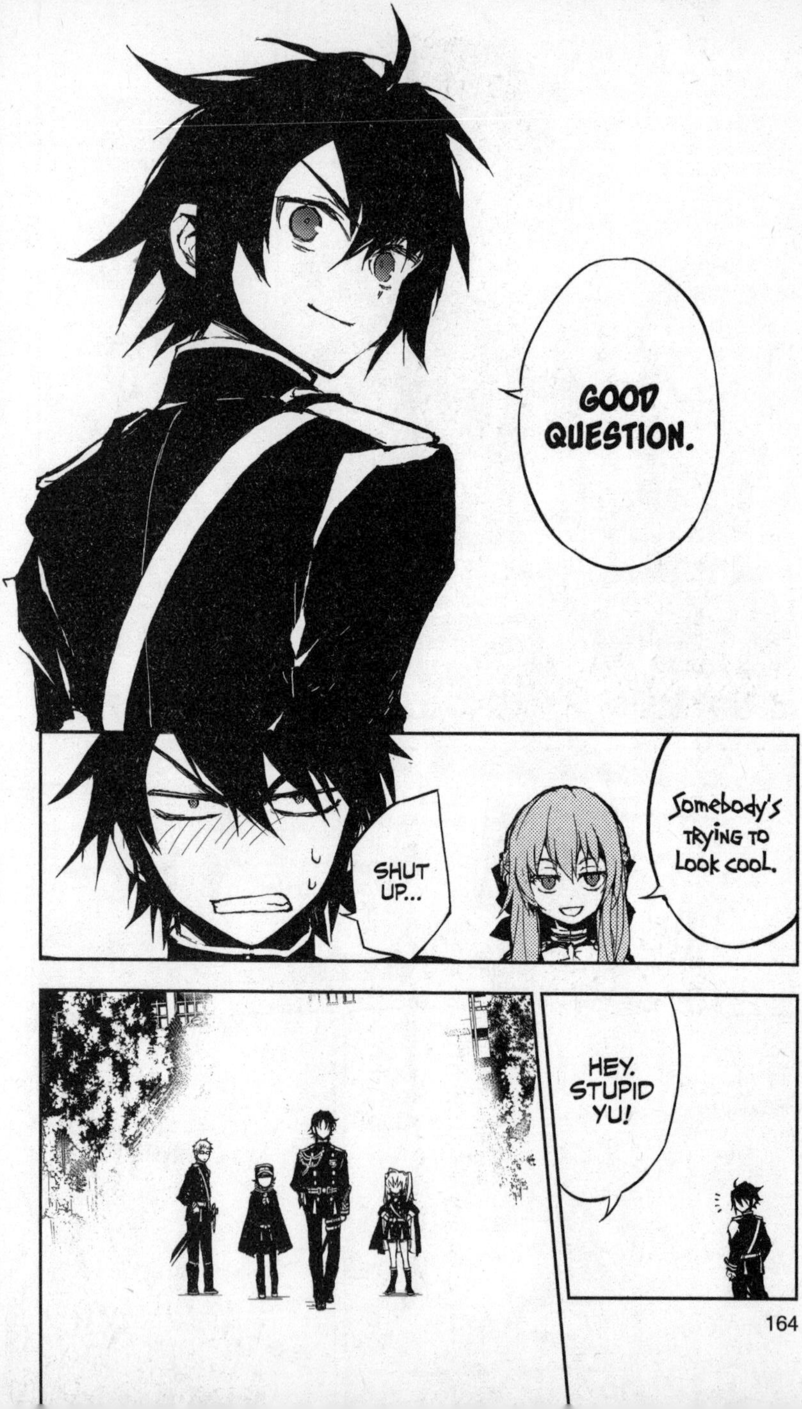
GOOD QUESTION.
Somebody's trying to look cool.
SHUT UP...
HEY. STUPID YU!

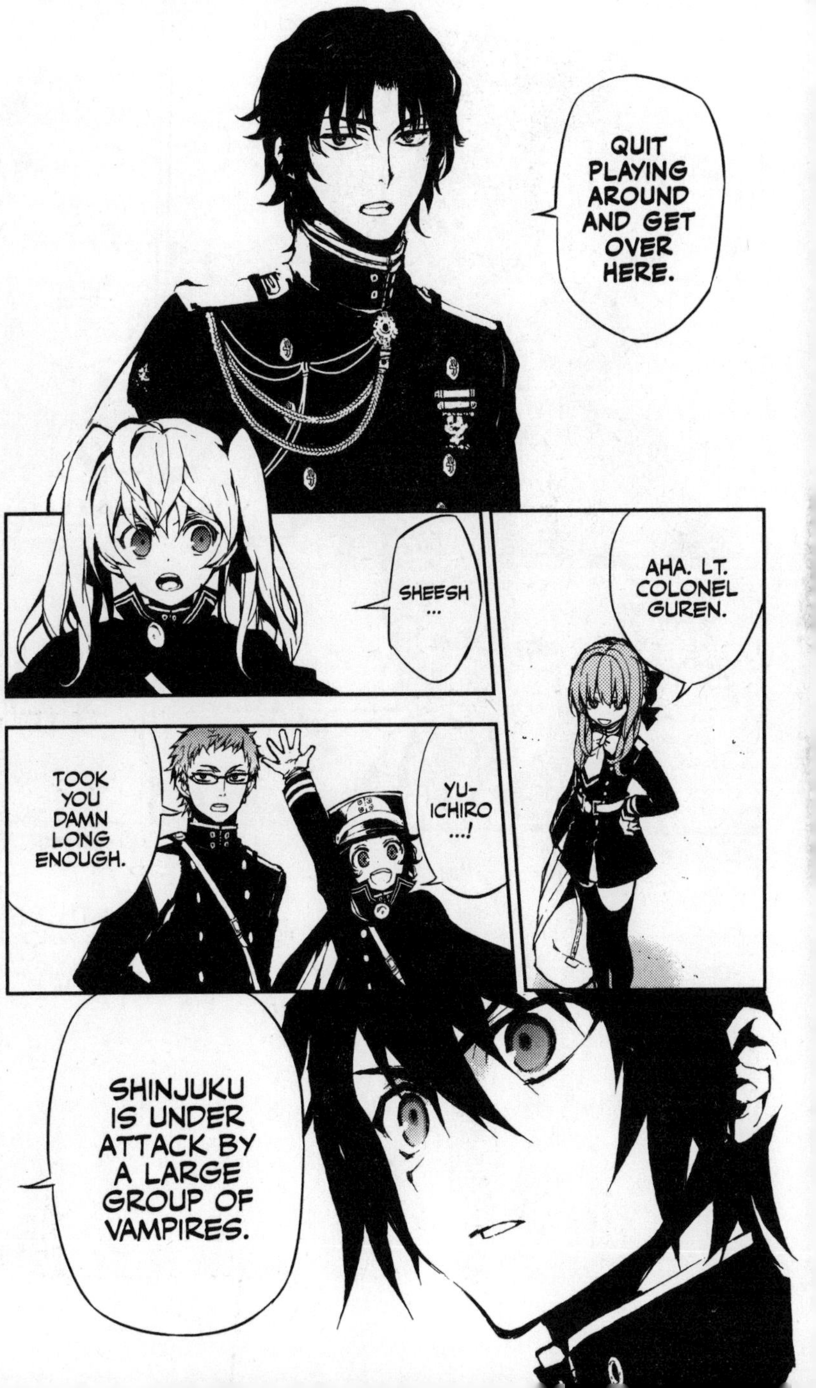
QUIT PLAYING AROUND AND GET OVER HERE.
AHA. LT. COLONEL GUREN.
SHEESH ...
YU-ICHIRO ...!
TOOK YOU DAMN LONG ENOUGH.
SHINJUKU IS UNDER ATTACK BY A LARGE GROUP OF VAMPIRES.

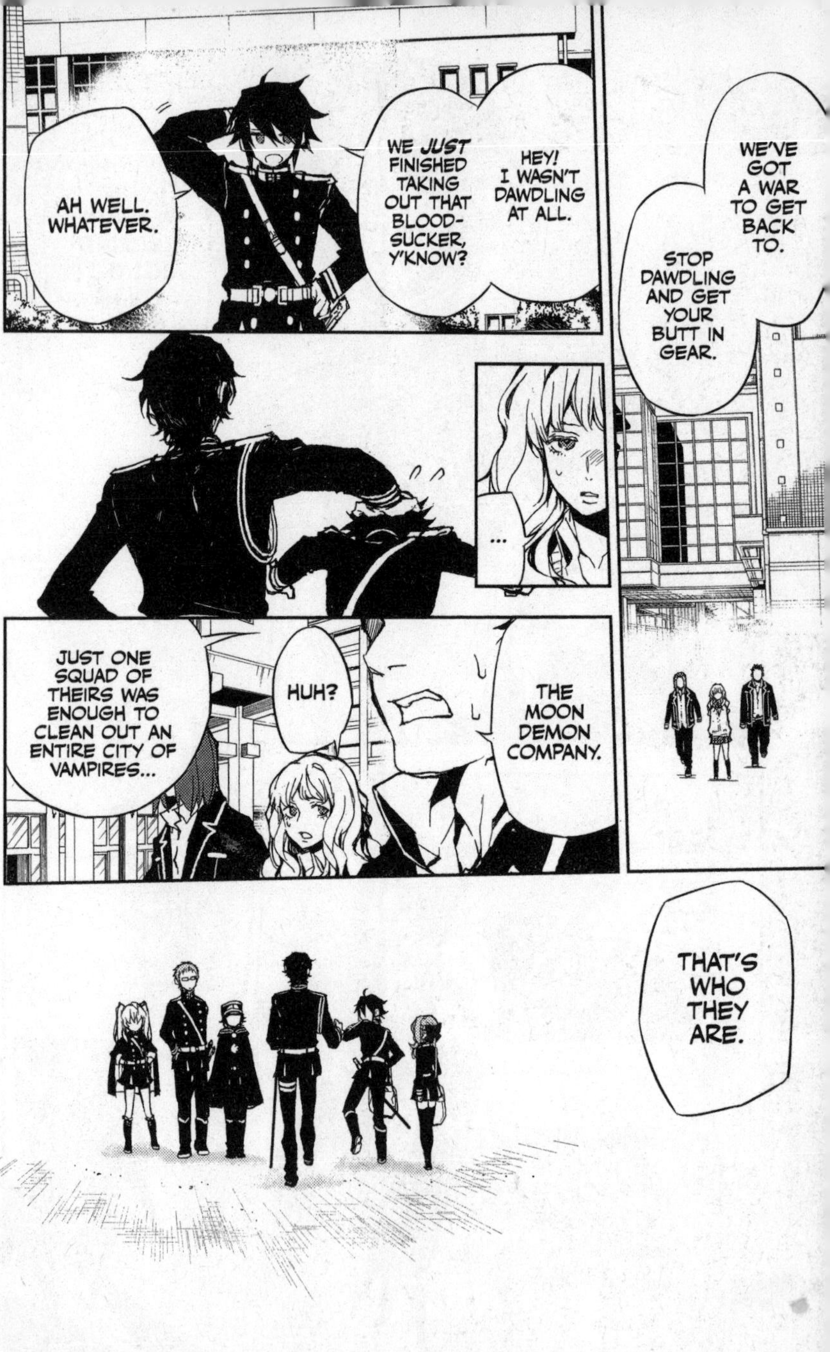
WE'VE GOT A WAR TO GET BACK TO.
STOP DAWDLING AND GET YOUR BUTT IN GEAR.
HEY! I WASN'T DAWDLING AT ALL.
WE *JUST* FINISHED TAKING OUT THAT BLOOD-SUCKER, Y'KNOW?
AH WELL. WHATEVER.
...
THE MOON DEMON COMPANY.
HUH?
JUST ONE SQUAD OF THEIRS WAS ENOUGH TO CLEAN OUT AN ENTIRE CITY OF VAMPIRES...
THAT'S WHO THEY ARE.

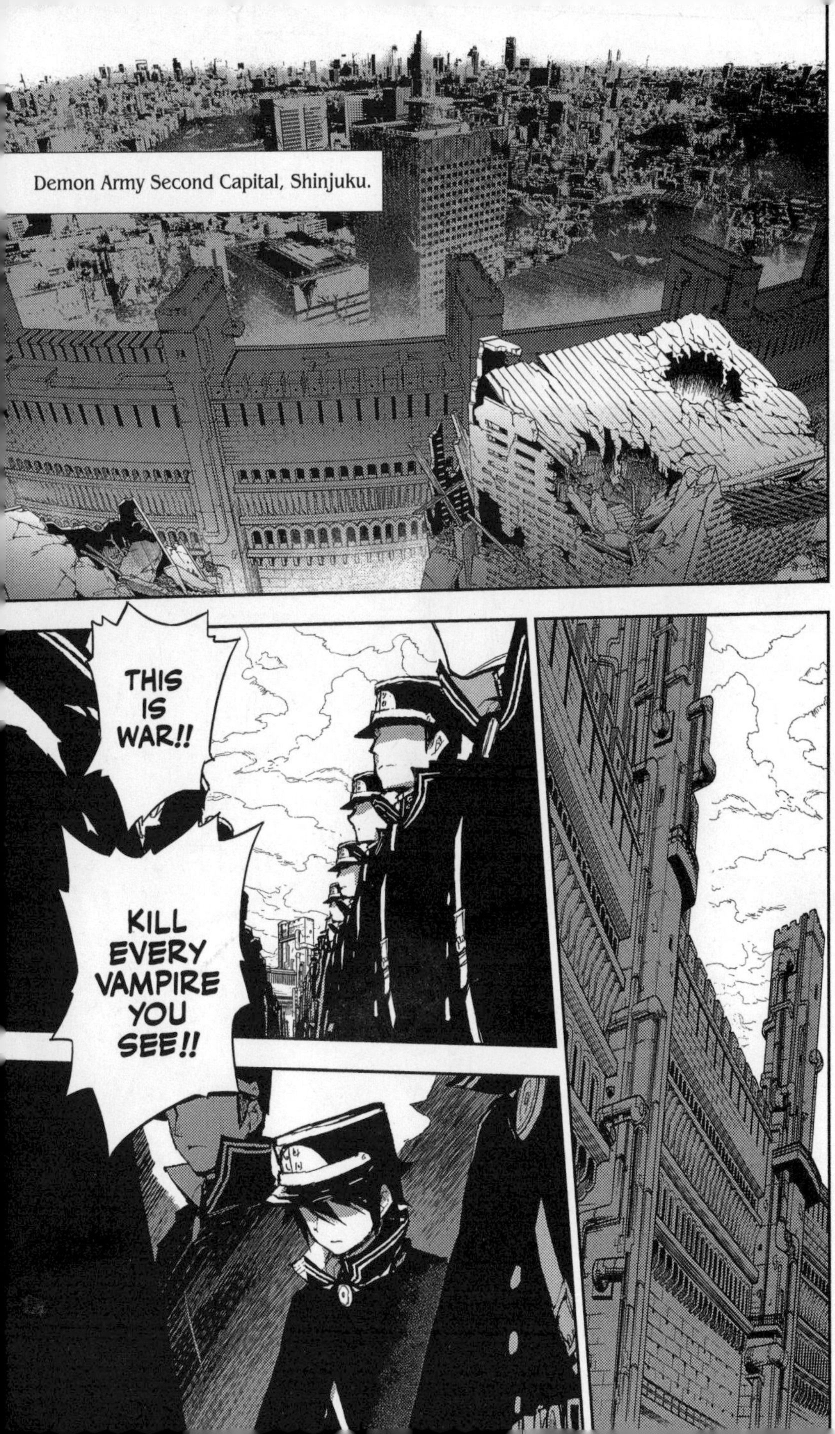
Demon Army Second Capital, Shinjuku.
THIS IS WAR!!
KILL EVERY VAMPIRE YOU SEE!!

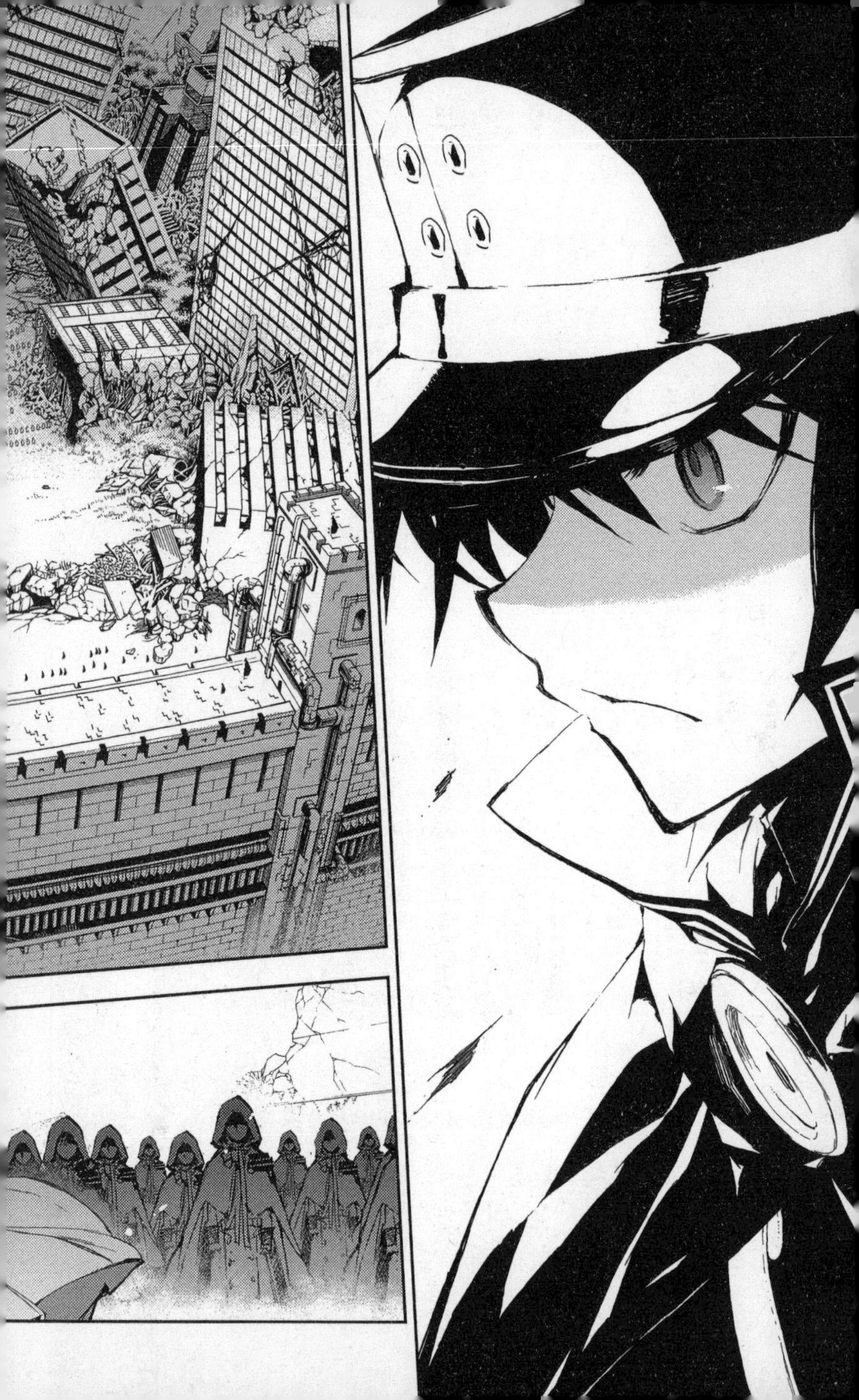

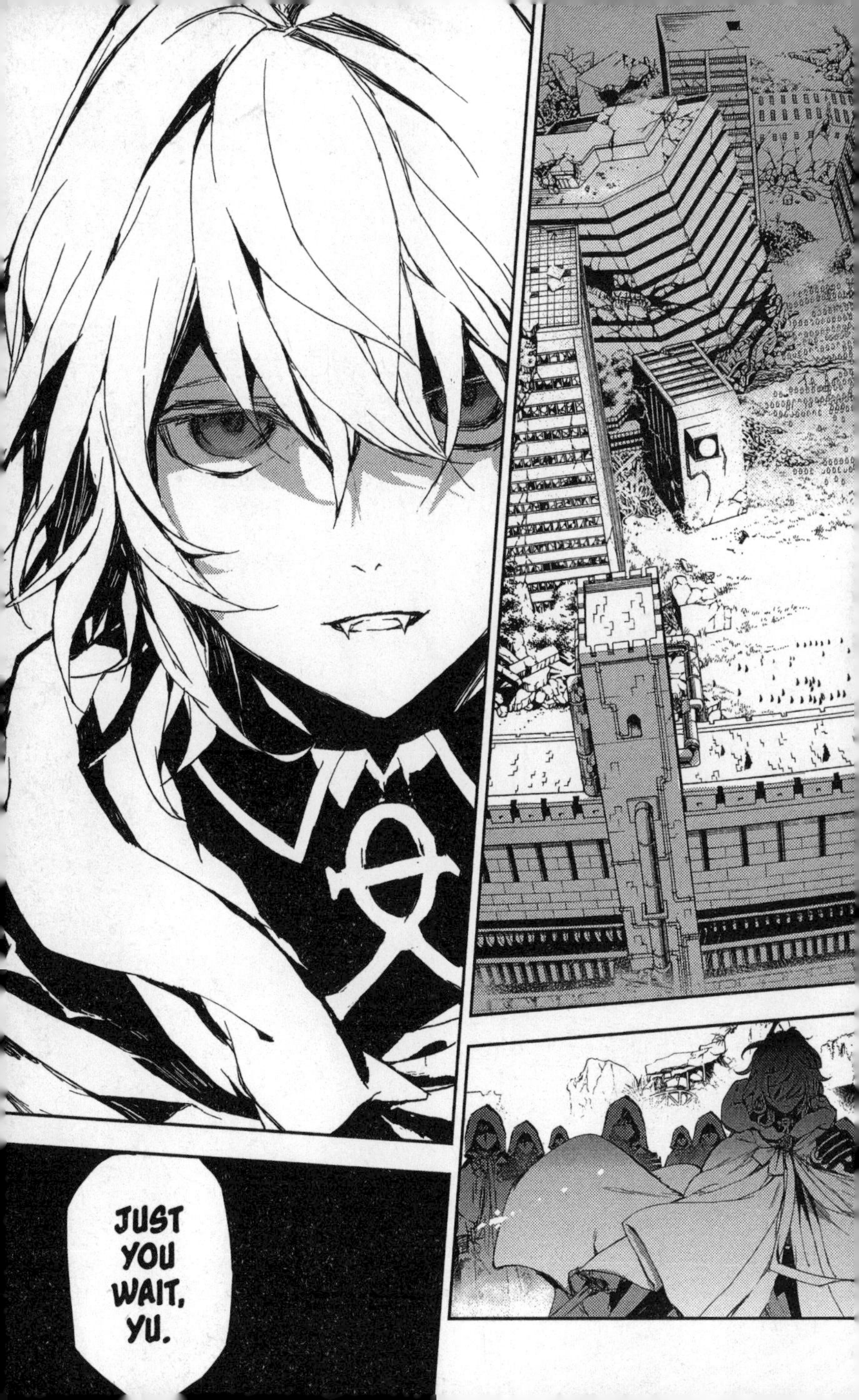
JUST YOU WAIT, YU.

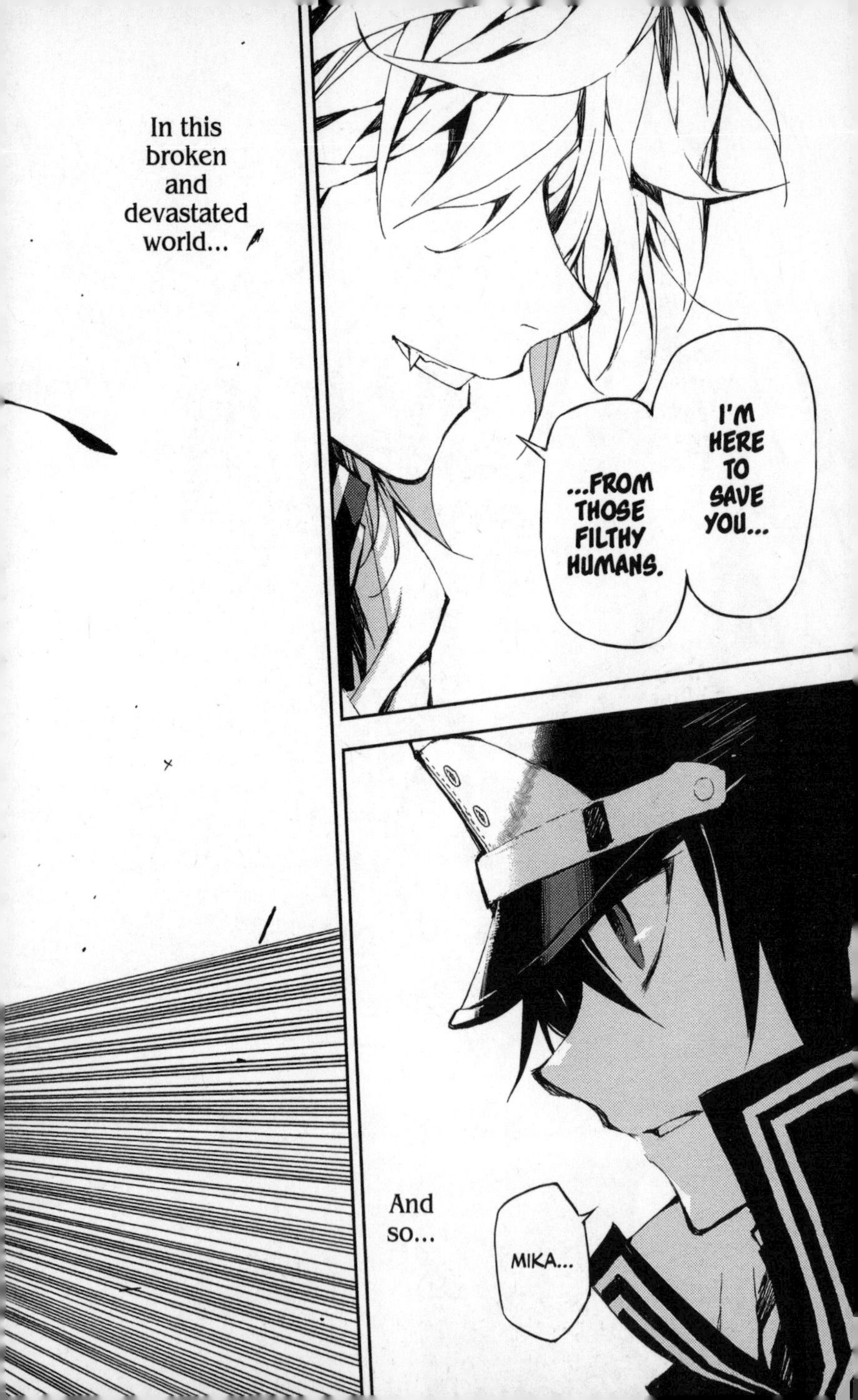
I'M HERE TO SAVE YOU...
...FROM THOSE FILTHY HUMANS.
And so...
MIKA...
In this broken and devastated world...

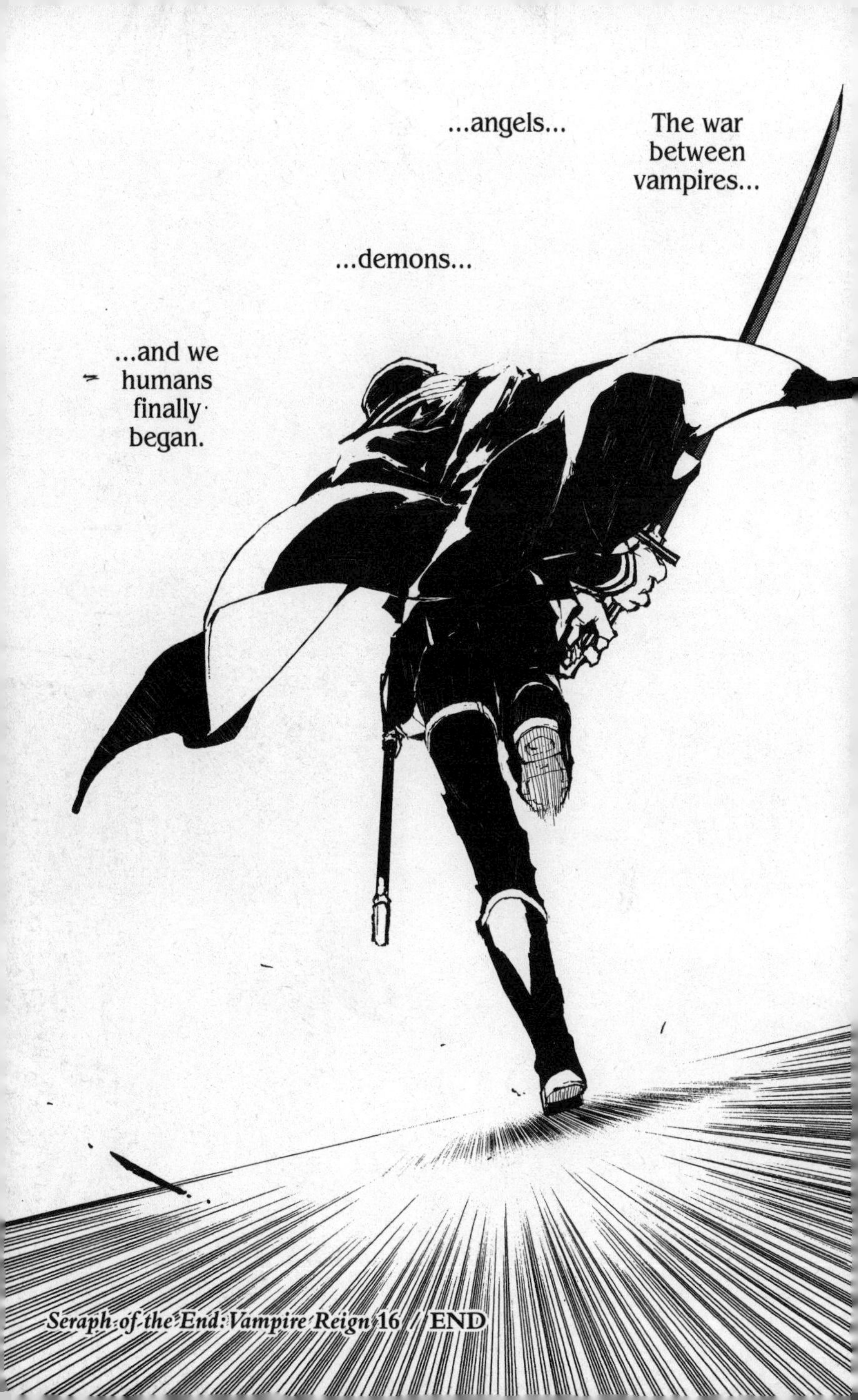
The war between vampires...
...angels...
...demons...
...and we humans finally began.
Seraph of the End: Vampire Reign 16 / END

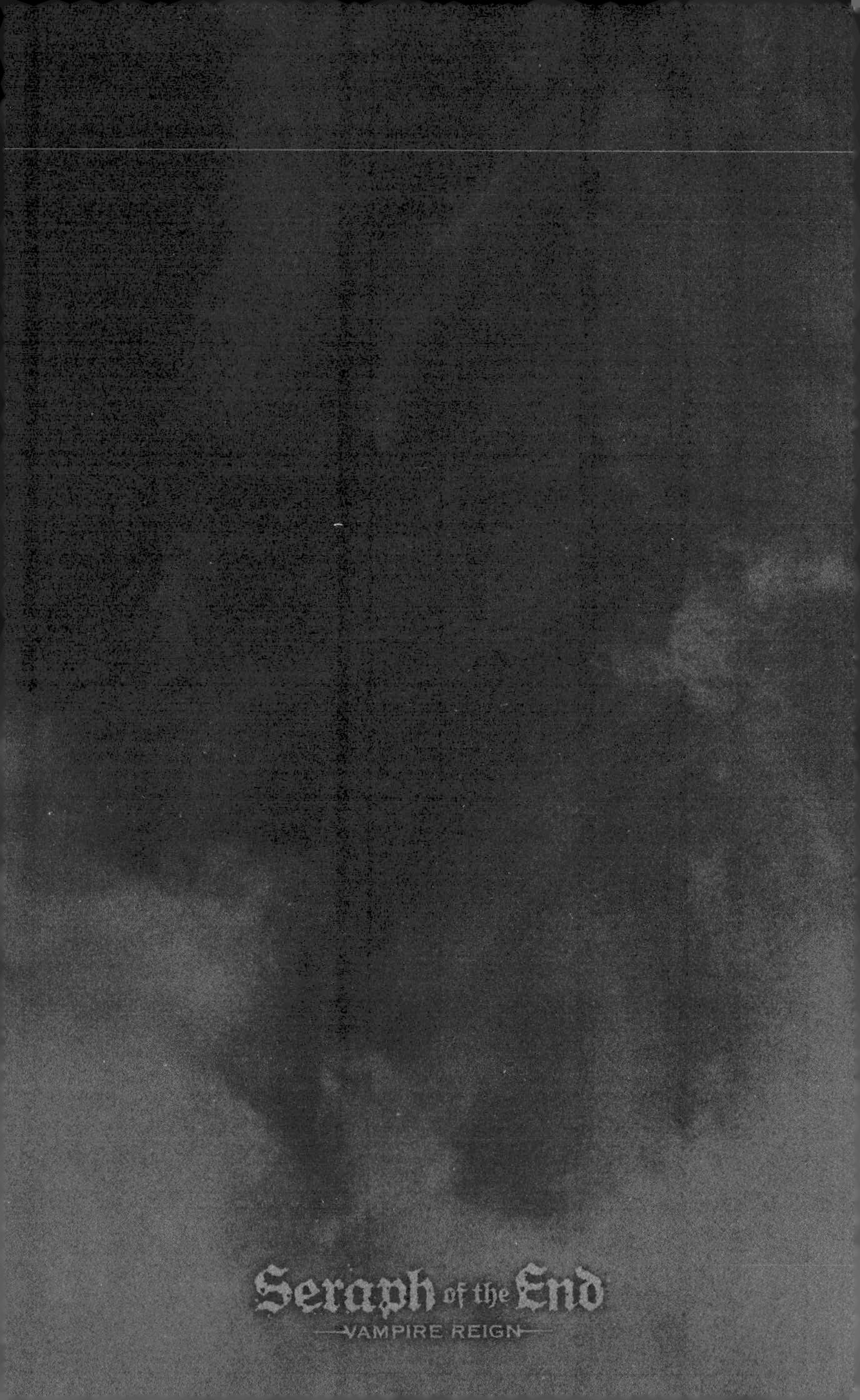
Seraph of the End
VAMPIRE REIGN

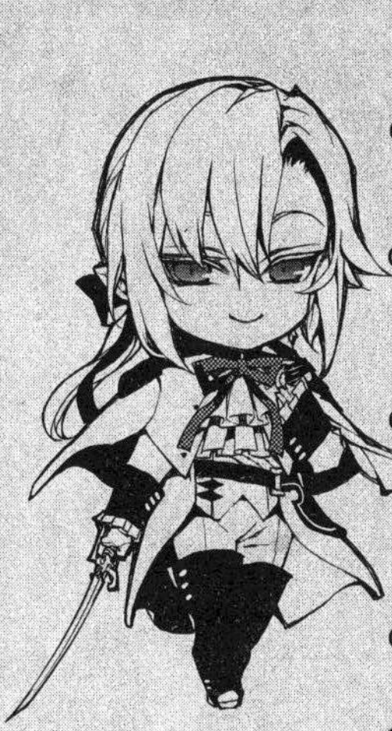

FERID: "MY, WHAT AN INTERESTING SIDE STORY! WHO KNEW ALL THAT WAS GOING ON IN IKEBUKURO BACK THEN!"

CROWLEY: "WHAT WAS GOING ON WHERE AND WHEN?"

FERID: "WHAT? YOU HAVEN'T YOU READ IT?"

CROWLEY: "NO."

FERID: "YOU'RE *KIDDING!* HOW CAN YOU NOT HAVE READ IT? EVERYBODY WHO IS ANYBODY HAS READ IT."

CROWLEY: "UMMM...IS IT REALLY SOMETHING THAT I HAVE TO READ?"

FERID: "OF COURSE. EVERYONE IN THIS WHOLE WORLD HAS READ IT. IF YOU HAVEN'T, YOU MUST BE LIVING UNDER A ROCK."

CROWLEY: "*THIS* WHOLE WORLD?"

FERID: "*THIS* WHOLE WORLD."

CROWLEY: "I KINDA DOUBT THERE'S ANY BOOK IN THIS MESSED-UP, CRUMBLING, POSTAPOCALYPTIC WORLD THAT EVERYONE HAS TO READ."

FERID: "WHAT ABOUT THE BIBLE? YOU READ THAT, DON'T YOU?"

CROWLEY: "NOT ANYMORE. I HAVEN'T PICKED IT UP EVEN ONCE SINCE I QUIT THE CRUSADES. HECK, I DON'T THINK MANY PEOPLE READ IT ANYMORE AT ALL."

FERID: "I READ IT EVERY DAY, YOU KNOW."

CROWLEY: "WHAT, YOU DO?"

FERID: "OF COURSE. AND I MAKE SURE TO SUBMIT THE READER SURVEY EVERY TIME TOO."

CROWLEY: "READER SURVEY? I DON'T THINK THE BIBLE HAD ONE OF THOSE."

FERID: "IF YOU DON'T KNOW HOW TO SEND IN THE READER SURVEY, YOU HAVE TO BE LIVING UNDER A ROCK. THERE'S A LITTLE POSTCARD TO FILL OUT AND EVERYTHING. MAKE SURE TO RANK WHICH CHAPTERS YOU THOUGHT WERE MOST INTERESTING TOO."

CROWLEY: "UM, I'M STARTING TO THINK WE AREN'T TALKING ABOUT THE SAME THING."

FERID: "AND NOW FOR SOMETHING COMPLETELY DIFFERENT."

CROWLEY: "WOW. THAT WAS A JARRING TOPIC SHIFT. WHICH MEANS NONE OF THAT WAS ACTUALLY IMPORTANT."

FERID: "WELL, IT ISN'T AS IF THERE IS ANYTHING IN THIS WORLD THAT'S VERY IMPORTANT IN THE FIRST PLACE."

CROWLEY: "I'M NOT SURE IF THAT WAS DEEPLY PHILOSOPHICAL OR INCREDIBLY SHALLOW, BUT I CAN BE SURE YOU JUST SAID IT FOR THE SAKE OF SAYING SOMETHING."

FERID: "BY THE WAY, CROWLEY."

CROWLEY: "YES?"

FERID: "DO YOU HAPPEN TO KNOW WHY WE ARE STANDING HERE WASTING PERFECTLY GOOD HOT AIR?"

CROWLEY: "HM. THAT'S A GOOD QUESTION. WHY?"

FERID: "BECAUSE SHIKAMA DOJI WAS SUPPOSED TO BE HERE TODAY, BUT HE DECIDED LAST MINUTE THAT HE COULDN'T BE BOTHERED TO SHOW UP, SO HE'LL COME NEXT VOLUME."

CROWLEY: "OH. SO THEY ASKED YOU TO REPLACE HIM?"

FERID: "NO. I THOUGHT I'D CRASH IT AND WASTE EVERYBODY'S TIME WITH A BUNCH OF MEANINGLESS NOTHINGS."

CROWLEY: "WELL THAT'S NOT VERY NICE."

FERID: "STILL, WHETHER WE ARE WASTING OUR TIME DOING NOTHING HERE, OR SPENDING IT WISELY BEING PRODUCTIVE THERE, IT'S ALL MEANINGLESS IN THE END."

CROWLEY: "AM I SUPPOSED TO TELL YOU THAT WAS DEEP?"

FERID: "IT WAS DEEP."

CROWLEY: "REALLY?"

FERID: "VERY DEEP."

CROWLEY: "WELL, IF YOU SAY SO."

FERID: "I DO INDEED SAY SO."

CROWLEY: "WE'LL GO WITH THAT THEN."

FERID: "EXCELLENT! I'M GLAD."

CROWLEY: "GOOD FOR YOU."

FERID: "THANK YOU."

CROWLEY: "I AM A LITTLE CURIOUS..."

FERID: "OH?"

CROWLEY: "DOES THE BIBLE REALLY HAVE READER SURVEYS?"

FERID: "YEP. IF IT DOESN'T PLACE WELL IN THE POPULARITY POLLS, IT WILL GET CANCELED, YOU KNOW? ALL THOSE CHAPTERS THAT KEEP GETTING STUCK AT THE BACK? I'M BETTING THOSE WILL BE WRAPPING UP SOON."

CROWLEY: "YEAH. I'M STILL NOT SO SURE ABOUT THIS."

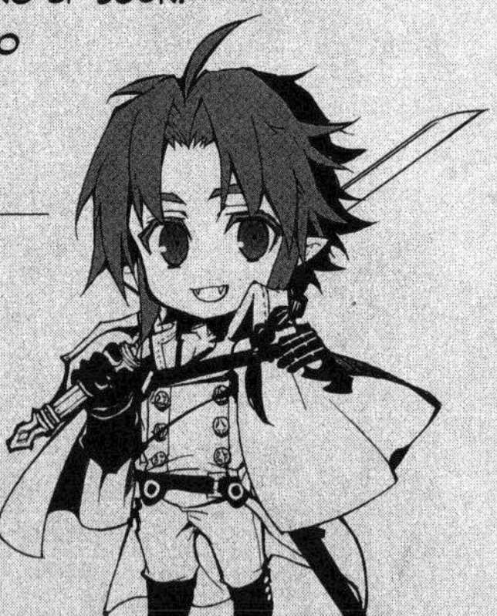

AFTERWORD

HELLO. I'M TAKAYA KAGAMI.

WE'VE REACHED VOLUME 16 ALREADY.

THE STORY IS REALLY STARTING TO PICK UP THE PACE, DELVING INTO SOME OF THE DEEPEST MYSTERIES OF THE WORLD. THINGS ARE GOING TO GET EVEN MORE EXCITING FROM HERE ON OUT, SO I HOPE YOU WILL STICK AROUND FOR THE RIDE.

NOT ONLY THAT, THE SECOND VOLUME OF KODANSHA'S MANGA ADAPTION OF *SERAPH OF THE END: GUREN ICHINOSE: CATASTROPHE AT 16* HAS GONE ON SALE IN JAPAN! BELIEVE IT OR NOT, THE COVER ILLUSTRATION FOR *MONTHLY SHONEN MAGAZINE* FOR THIS MONTH WILL ALSO BE *SERAPH OF THE END*. APRIL 2018, IS TURNING OUT TO BE *SERAPH OF THE END* MONTH! I HOPE YOU ALL WILL CONTINUE TO GIVE YOUR SUPPORT!

NOW THEN! SOME PERSONAL NEWS.

I'VE STARTED USING THE RIZAP FITNESS PROGRAM AND IN ONE MONTH I LOST OVER 15 POUNDS. THE ADS FOR IT REALLY ARE TRUE! I'M STILL SURPRISED. IF I KEEP IT UP, IN TWO MONTHS' TIME I'LL BE DOWN TO 11 PERCENT BODY FAT. SO BY THE TIME THE NEXT VOLUME COMES OUT, THAT SHOULD BE ABOUT WHERE I AM! IF I HAVEN'T COMPLETELY FALLEN OFF THE PROGRAM, THAT IS! (LAUGHS) LOOK FORWARD TO NEXT VOLUME'S AFTERWORD TO FIND OUT!

SEE YOU NEXT TIME!

—TAKAYA KAGAMI

A brilliant sketch of Yuichiro by the author!

TAKAYA KAGAMI is a prolific light novelist whose works include the action and fantasy series *The Legend of the Legendary Heroes*, which has been adapted into manga, anime and a video game. His previous series, *A Dark Rabbit Has Seven Lives*, also spawned a manga and anime series.

66 I recently bought a new computer and I had to switch out the text editing program I've been using since my professional debut 17 years ago. I went from *CoolMint* to *Hidemaru Editor*. I hope I can get 17 years of use out of this program too. 99

YAMATO YAMAMOTO, born 1983, is an artist and illustrator whose works include the *Kure-nai* manga and the light novels *Kure-nai*, *9S -Nine S-* and *Denpa Teki na Kanojo*. Both *Denpa Teki na Kanojo* and *Kure-nai* have been adapted into anime.

66 Volume 16 sees the end of the battle with Ky Luc. A certain character comes back too. I had a lot of fun drawing that scene. I hope you will continue to pay attention to that character's actions going forward. 99

DAISUKE FURUYA previously assisted Yamato Yamamoto with storyboards for *Kure-nai*.

Seraph of the End
—VAMPIRE REIGN—

VOLUME 16
SHONEN JUMP ADVANCED MANGA EDITION

STORY BY **TAKAYA KAGAMI**
ART BY **YAMATO YAMAMOTO**
STORYBOARDS BY **DAISUKE FURUYA**

TRANSLATION **Adrienne Beck**
TOUCH-UP ART & LETTERING **Sabrina Heep**
DESIGN **Shawn Carrico**
EDITOR **Marlene First**

Printed in the U.S.A.

Published by VIZ Media, LLC
P.O. Box 77010
San Francisco, CA 94107

10 9 8 7 6 5 4 3 2 1
First printing, March 2019

 **VIZ** MEDIA
viz.com

 SHONEN JUMP ADVANCED
shonenjump.com

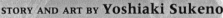

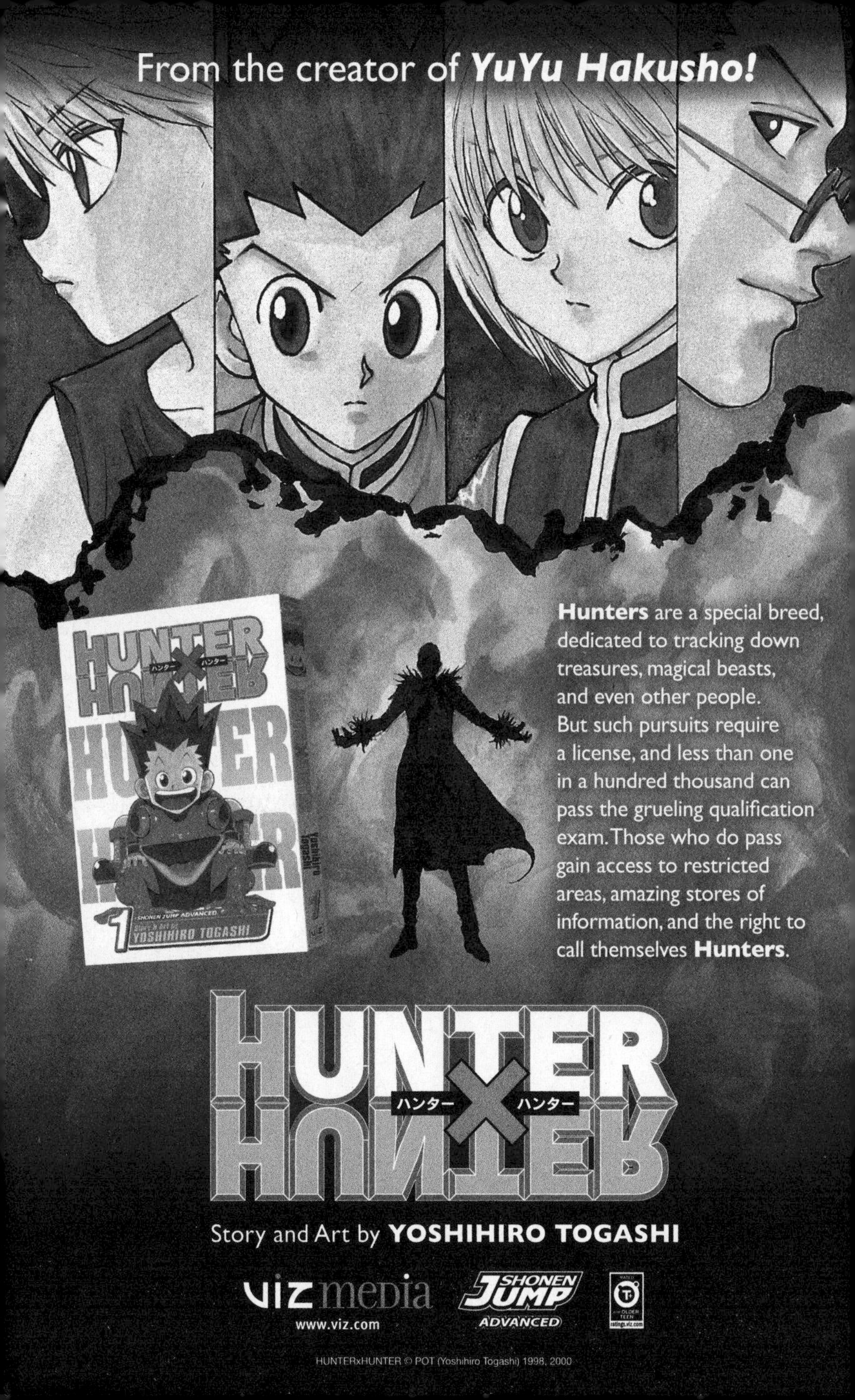
From the creator of *YuYu Hakusho!*
Hunters are a special breed, dedicated to tracking down treasures, magical beasts, and even other people. But such pursuits require a license, and less than one in a hundred thousand can pass the grueling qualification exam. Those who do pass gain access to restricted areas, amazing stores of information, and the right to call themselves **Hunters**.
HUNTER × HUNTER
ハンター ハンター
Story and Art by **YOSHIHIRO TOGASHI**
viz media
www.viz.com
SHONEN JUMP ADVANCED
HUNTERxHUNTER © POT (Yoshihiro Togashi) 1998, 2000

Black ✤ Clover

STORY & ART BY YŪKI TABATA

Asta is a young boy who dreams of becoming the greatest mage in the kingdom. Only one problem—he can't use any magic! Luckily for Asta, he receives the incredibly rare five-leaf clover grimoire that gives him the power of anti-magic. Can someone who can't use magic really become the Wizard King? One thing's for sure—Asta will never give up!

SHONEN JUMP

VIZ media
www.viz.com

YOU'RE READING THE WRONG WAY!

SERAPH OF THE END reads from right to left, starting in the upper-right corner. Japanese is read from right to left, meaning that action, sound effects, and word-balloon order are completely reversed from English order.

1
2
3
4
1
2
5
6
7
8
3
4
9
5
CALGARY PUBLIC LIBRARY
MAR 2019
142

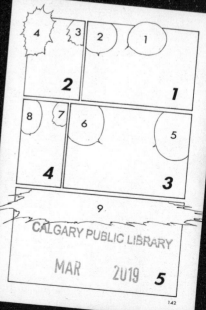